W0091382

**SAGE** was founded in 1965 by Sara Miller McCune to support the dissemination of usable knowledge by publishing innovative and high-quality research and teaching content. Today, we publish over 900 journals, including those of more than 400 learned societies, more than 800 new books per year, and a growing range of library products including archives, data, case studies, reports, and video. SAGE remains majority-owned by our founder, and after Sara's lifetime will become owned by a charitable trust that secures our continued independence.

Los Angeles | London | New Delhi | Singapore | Washington DC | Melbourne

# Analysing China's Soft Power Strategy and Comparative Indian Initiatives

# Analysing China's Soft Power Strategy and Comparative Indian Initiatives

## Parama Sinha Palit

Los Angeles | London | New Delhi
Singapore | Washington DC | Melbourne

*Copyright © Parama Sinha Palit, 2017*

All rights reserved. No part of this book may be reproduced or utilized in any form or by any means, electronic or mechanical, including photocopying, recording, or by any information storage or retrieval system, without permission in writing from the publisher.

*First published in 2017 by*

**SAGE Publications India Pvt Ltd**
B1/I-1 Mohan Cooperative Industrial Area
Mathura Road, New Delhi 110 044, India
*www.sagepub.in*

**SAGE Publications Inc**
2455 Teller Road
Thousand Oaks, California 91320, USA

**SAGE Publications Ltd**
1 Oliver's Yard, 55 City Road
London EC1Y 1SP, United Kingdom

**SAGE Publications Asia-Pacific Pte Ltd**
3 Church Street
#10-04 Samsung Hub
Singapore 049483

Published by Vivek Mehra for SAGE Publications India Pvt Ltd, typeset in 10/13 pt Berkeley Book by Fidus Design Pvt. Ltd., Chandigarh 31D, and printed at Chaman Enterprises, New Delhi.

**Library of Congress Cataloging-in-Publication Data Available**

**ISBN**: 978-93-860-6265-9 (HB)

**SAGE Team:** Supriya Das, Guneet Kaur Gulati and Ritu Chopra

*I dedicate this book to my parents, Ms Swapna and
Dr Pradip Chandra Sinha, for their endless love and support.
They have taught me the value of education and hard work—the
two fundamentals that have inspired and guided me all along.*

Thank you for choosing a SAGE product!
If you have any comment, observation or feedback,
I would like to personally hear from you.
*Please write to me at* **contactceo@sagepub.in**

**Vivek Mehra,** Managing Director and CEO, SAGE India.

## Bulk Sales

SAGE India offers special discounts
for purchase of books in bulk.
We also make available special imprints
and excerpts from our books on demand.

*For orders and enquiries, write to us at*

Marketing Department
SAGE Publications India Pvt Ltd
B1/I-1, Mohan Cooperative Industrial Area
Mathura Road, Post Bag 7
New Delhi 110044, India

*E-mail us at* **marketing@sagepub.in**

## Get to know more about SAGE

Be invited to SAGE events, get on our mailing list.
*Write today to* **marketing@sagepub.in**

This book is also available as an e-book.

# Contents

# List of Tables

# List of Abbreviations

| | |
|---|---|
| ACL | American Centre Library |
| ADB | Asian Development Bank |
| AFTA | Asia-Pacific Free Trade Agreement |
| AIIB | Asian Infrastructure Investment Bank |
| ANU | Australian National University |
| ARF | ASEAN Regional Forum |
| ASEAN | Association of Southeast Asian Nations |
| ATD | Approved Tourist Destination |
| AU | African Union |
| BCIM | Bangladesh–China–India–Myanmar |
| BDCA | Border Defence Cooperation Agreement |
| BICC | Birendra International Convention Centre |
| BNP | Bangladesh National Party |
| BPD | Barrels Per Day |
| BRICS | Brazil–Russia–India–China–South Africa |
| BSCIC | Bangladesh Small and Cottage Industries Corporation |
| CAREC | Central Asian Regional Economic Cooperation |
| CARs | Central Asian Republics |
| CASETF | China–Arab States Economic and Trade Forum |
| CASS | Chinese Academy of Social Sciences |
| CBMs | Confidence Building Measures |
| CCAFA | China–Central Asia Friendship Association |
| CCs | Confucius Classrooms |
| CD | Cultural Diplomacy |
| CDB | China Development Bank |
| CEIBS | China Europe International Business School |
| CHOGM | Commonwealth Heads of Government Meeting |
| CIC | China Investment Corporation |
| CII | Confederation of Indian Industry |
| CIs | Confucius Institutes |
| CIW | Australian Centre on China in the World |
| CLMV | Cambodia–Laos–Myanmar–Vietnam |
| CNPC | China National Petroleum Corporation |

| | |
|---|---|
| CPAFFC | Chinese People's Association for Friendship with Foreign Countries |
| CPC | Communist Party of China |
| CPEC | China–Pakistan Economic Corridor |
| CRI | China Radio International |
| CSC | China Scholarship Council |
| DFTP | Duty Free Tariff Preference |
| DWP | Defence White Paper |
| EACS | European Association for Chinese Studies |
| EAS | East Asia Summit |
| ECAN | European Union–China Academic Network |
| ECFA | Economic Cooperation Framework Agreement |
| EEU | Eurasian Economic Union |
| ESPOL | Escuela Superior Politecnica del Litoral |
| EU | European Union |
| EUNIC | European Union National Institutes for Culture |
| FDC | Fixed Dose Combination |
| FDI | Foreign Direct Investment |
| FICCI | Federation of Indian Chamber of Commerce and Industry |
| FLASCO | Latin American Faculty of Social Sciences |
| FOCAC | Forum on China–Africa Cooperation |
| FOSWAL | Foundation of SAARC Writers and Literature |
| FTA | Free Trade Agreement |
| FTZ | Free Trade Zone |
| GCC | Gulf Cooperation Council |
| GMS | Greater Mekong Subregion |
| ICBC | Industrial and Commercial Bank of China |
| ICCR | Indian Council for Cultural Relations |
| ICT | Information and Communications Technology |
| IDB | Inter-American Development Bank |
| IFCCS4 | Fourth International Forum for Contemporary Chinese Studies |
| IMF | International Monetary Fund |
| IOR | Indian Ocean Region |
| IPKF | Indian Peace Keeping Force |
| IPL | Indian Premier League |

| | |
|---|---|
| IR | International Relations |
| ITEC | Indian Technical and Economic Cooperation |
| JCPOA | Joint Comprehensive Plan of Action |
| JNU | Jawaharlal Nehru University |
| LAC | Line of Actual Control |
| LBA | Land Border Agreement |
| LDC | Least-Developed Countries |
| LEP | Look East Policy |
| LoC | Line of Credit |
| MFA | Ministry of Foreign Affairs |
| MOIA | Ministry of Overseas Indian Affairs |
| MoU | Memorandum of Understanding |
| NAM | Non-aligned Movement |
| NATRC | National Ayurveda Research and Training Centre |
| NDRC | National Development and Reform Commission |
| NOSAIC | National Online System of Access to Information on China |
| NPC | National Peoples' Congress |
| NPCIL | Nuclear Power Corporation of India |
| NSS | National Security Strategy |
| OBOR | One-Belt-One-Road |
| PC | Pacific Community |
| PD | Public Diplomacy |
| PIF | Pacific Islands Forum |
| PIOs | Persons of Indian Origin |
| PLA | People's Liberation Army |
| PNG | Papua New Guinea |
| PRC | People's Republic of China |
| PTAs | Preferential Trade Agreements |
| RFE | Russian Far East |
| RGICS | Rajiv Gandhi Institute for Contemporary Studies |
| RTAs | Regional Trading Agreements |
| SAARC | South Asian Association of Regional Cooperation |
| SACAF | Sino-American Culture and Arts Foundation |
| SAFA | Sino-American Friendship Association |
| SAU | South Asian University |
| SCO | Shanghai Cooperation Organization |

| SED | Strategic Economic Dialogue |
| SIIS | Shanghai Institute for International Studies |
| SLOC | Sea Lanes of Communication |
| SMX | Singapore Mercantile Exchange |
| TAC | Treaty of Amity and Cooperation |
| UBC | University of British Columbia |
| UNSC | UN Security Council |
| USACH | Universidad de Santiago de Chile |
| WB | World Bank |
| WDS | Western Development Strategy |

# Preface

I knew little about China except for the Sino-Indian War of 1962 that heavily influenced my perception of the neighbour since I was a toddler. I recall my mother recounting her experiences as a young National Cadet Corps (NCC) volunteer in the small town of Dibrugarh in India's northeastern state of Assam during the war and thereafter. She would narrate the sudden blackouts and deafening sirens that would send people scurrying for cover into tunnels constructed in every house for shelter. As I grew up, apart from 1962, I became increasingly familiar with Anini—a little-known town in India's northeastern state of Arunachal Pradesh bordering China, where my father served as a young doctor some years after the 1962 conflict. It was hardly surprising that Anini's geographical proximity to China made it geographically vulnerable to Chinese aggression—a fact that hung heavy over the town and its people, including my father.

During my days as a postgraduate student and a research scholar in the Jawaharlal Nehru University (JNU) at Delhi in the late 1990s, China hardly figured prominently in my academic studies with the US being my focus. It would cross my path only contextually, mostly in relation to Pakistan and the impact of the relationship on India, South Asia and the region. It was not until we (my husband Amitendu and I) shifted to Singapore in early 2008 that I began developing my research interest in the dragon's 'attraction'. The interest became intense during our travels to various parts of China and the fascinating interactions that we had (and keep having) with different scholars and experts, many of whom, over time, have become our close friends. The visits and interactions not only yielded fascinating insights into China but also revealed little-known aspects of the multifaceted engagement between China and India. One such example, gleaned from our travel to Tianjin and the Tianjin University of Finance and Economics, was the collaboration between the University and the Honeybee Network of India for patenting grass-roots innovation enabling farmers in both countries to acquire intellectual rights over frugal innovation. I also realized, rather early on during my travels to China, the importance of knowing Mandarin for comprehending the 'real' China. The motivation was strong enough to spur me on to learning the language, a decision that in hindsight proved most significant, as it has enabled me to access vast primary sources during the research for this book and engage in detailed conversations with scholars during my fieldwork.

As a regular visitor to the American Centre Library (ACL), New Delhi, from my postgraduate days, the mesmerizing 'pull' of higher education institutions in the US was my first instinctive impression of national 'soft power'. Much like China, 'soft power' was hardly a focus of my early research. The latter was influenced predominantly by the thematic foci of the research institutions I worked with in Delhi during the early years of the last decade and the key strands of the discourse in strategic policy circles in India. Soft power was as unknown and delinked from the discourse as it could be with the latter overwhelmingly dominated by realist 'hard power' notions pertaining to conflict management, military preparedness and a host of geostrategic concerns shaping India's international relations with its neighbours and other powers. While soft power has gained considerable currency in the global discussion on international and strategic relations, including in India, it continues to be treated somewhat contemptuously, particularly by hard-core realists. This was evident from the discussions that I had with scholars across the world, among whom many were sceptical about its conceptual application to the wider strategic and foreign policy discourse as well as its efficacy in securing strategic benefits.

It was, therefore, all the more surprising for me to note the traction gained by soft power in the academic and policy discourses in China, including the specific coining of *ruan shi li*, meaning soft power in Mandarin! Beijing's ceaseless efforts towards image-building for conveying positive signals on its benign intentions and responsible conduct to the international community have led to the growth of a rich and varied discourse on soft power in China. The discourse has gathered momentum from China's pursuit of cultural diplomacy—a strategy used since the ancient times—and several other soft power tools for communicating with the rest of the world. China has put a premium on culture in correcting adverse impressions produced by its remarkable strategic rise while also aiming to 'balance' the global discourse on image-building, positive perception and soft power through constructive perceptions rather than through reactive means.

I have been struck by not only the scale of efforts in China towards building its image through continuous exploration of innovative ideas and employment of soft power tools but also the vigorous debate and discussion among policymakers, government agencies, scholars and the media. Chinese government agencies and academic institutions have been working together for a clearer and pragmatic conceptual understanding of soft power and its application. In 2007, Qin Gang, the then Foreign Ministry spokesperson, outlined the eight diplomatic philosophies that were to guide China's external engagement. The pronouncement indicated China's disinterest in seeking hegemony and was similarly indicative of China's active pursuit of soft power. From the Chinese perspective, soft power has entailed more of cultural diplomacy, which has been integral to its policies of external engagement and outreach in modern times, while public diplomacy—a more developed and structured element of soft power strategy and articulation in the West—is more 'work in progress' in China. Given its newness in Chinese discourse, the Chinese leadership has been striving to gather more knowledge on public diplomacy while making its application amenable to China's specific interests and circumstances by imparting it 'Chinese characteristics'. Indeed, appreciating the importance of reciprocity and response for meaningful public diplomacy, the Chinese leadership is showing greater proclivity 'to listen' to the others, thus attempting to make it an important characteristic of its larger strategy.

Chinese soft power, in addition to exhaustive cultural diplomacy and incipient public diplomacy, is also characterized by its pronounced economic content. The Chinese leadership's use of varied economic tools in different countries underlines its tact and pragmatism in spotting and securing strategic 'windows'. This is evident from extending 'aid without strings' to countries and establishments shunned by mainstream Western aid donors and responding to needs and demands of countries suffering from chronic social and physical infrastructure deficits. By providing generous resources for overcoming infrastructure gaps, China behaves as a benign large power capable of mitigating global challenges and also succeeds in securing strategic loyalty to an extent. Recent initiatives such as One-Belt-One-Road (OBOR) and the Asian Infrastructure Investment Bank (AIIB) might be expanding the objectives further, apart from positing China as a firm alternative to the established large global powers in the ability to spend well in creating global public goods.

The other conspicuous aspect of China's soft power—a feature that is almost inescapable and has resonated variously across the chapters in this book—is its coexistence with references and emphasis on hard power (a duality inherent in Chinese diplomacy and foreign policy). Beijing's extensive employment of varied soft power tools has not refrained it from striking 'hard' postures on issues and with respect to countries with which it has outstanding contentious differences—most importantly the South China Sea and some countries of the Southeast Asian region being important examples. The reference to hard power has become more distinct and prominent under President Xi, evident from his speech at the Politburo study session in January 2013, where he emphatically underlined the importance of protecting China's core national interests.

It could well be this coexistence, apart from the Western strategic mainstream impression of China as an 'aggressor', that has led to much less study of the nuances of China's soft power, both theoretically and empirically. The lack of focused attention on modern China's extensive deployment of soft power, the distinct nuances and variations visible across countries and regions, and satisfaction of core strategic goals have been the motivation behind this book. As an Indian scholar of international relations, I have been fascinated to note the diversity of people-to-people contacts and engagements in the Sino-Indian context, which are hardly reflected and discussed.

The larger point is the substantive content of the contemporary Sino-India relationship that includes several positives. China's significance as a supplier of hardware and hand phones in facilitating India's mobile telephony expansion is hardly discussed. The suspicion over cheap Chinese goods flooding the Indian market is hardly tempered by the realization that the burgeoning diverse consumption needs of a rapidly expanding Indian economy would have been left unmet had Chinese products not been available the way they have. China has been for India, what it has been for most of the rest of the world: an inexhaustible source of cheap manufactures. On a larger collaborative plane, it is interesting that China and India have rarely found it difficult to ally on common global concerns be it trade, climate change or the international financial architecture. Such collaborations, apart from being examples of greater South–South cooperation manifesting through developing and emerging market country coalitions, can also be seen as examples of occasions where both countries are ready to overlook bilateral estrangement. Indeed, the importance of collaborating on global issues for maximizing national interests, quite a bit of which are similar for both countries, has been an important factor in influencing both countries to engage each other meaningfully. Enabling mechanisms like a hotline connection between heads of states of the two countries have been able to manage and de-escalate border tensions from time to time. At the same time, cultural and public diplomacies, in addition to business links, have become significant in promoting understanding and assimilating goodwill.

Communicating the right signal, while perceiving intentions of the 'other', underlines China's diplomatic interaction with countries far and near, including India. India has also advanced to adopt diplomatic engagement reflecting similar characteristics—a trajectory that has become increasingly visible with assumption of office by Prime Minister Narendra Modi. The Chinese President Xi Jinping and the Indian Prime Minister Narendra Modi have maintained the tradition of top leaders of both countries meeting frequently and have had several interactions on various occasions shaping conditions for facilitating further interaction and better understanding. The personal bonhomie and the larger constructive strategic engagement of each other, however, have not obliterated friction and contentious circumstances from time to time, which, needless to say, have warranted hard postures. The dichotomy remains a remarkable aspect of the current Sino-Indian relationship and is expected to become more conspicuous over time as both countries attempt to court constructive engagement while not yielding ground on sovereign concerns. While much more can be done by both on engagement, it is important to note that the constructive approach to engagement has not reversed during the last decade and a half and has quietly consolidated over time. Consolidation, no doubt, will increase further, creating greater need and scope for application of soft power on both sides. Future research on Sino-Indian relations will remain vacuous unless it pays adequate attention to the role of soft power.

While China is the context, subject and discussion for most of the book, it reflects on India too, particularly the more recent developments in India's foreign policy that focus on greater use of soft power tools. Although India's soft power efforts have been limited and less conspicuous compared to its larger eastern neighbour, Indian foreign policy is increasingly adapting exercises for expanding global soft power, such as celebrating the International Yoga Day, partly shaking off the policy inertia created by hollow beliefs that India need not be proactive on exercising soft power since the world sees it naturally benign, at least compared with China. It is only now that Indian soft power outreach is witnessing a proactive role of the state, compared with the 'hands off' policy earlier that left soft power export to non-state actors. In this respect, Indian foreign policy has arguably turned a new leaf and soft power efforts are expected to become larger and varied over time. This is consistent with New Delhi's quest for greater global strategic space and influence.

While the leadership might further hone its soft power tools to connect better with the world, India's soft power will continue to encounter formidable challenges, probably even more than what China does in some respect, given the rather dismal global perception of India in critical segments of state performance. Notwithstanding China's perception of being a more 'aggressive' state, the world appears to have much greater faith, till now, in the Chinese state's ability to deliver better qualities of lives to its citizens, compared with India. Thus, despite the emphasis on India's cultural and civilizational virtues, many remain unconvinced about India's earnestness in pursuing soft power with views ranging from dismissive to cautiously optimistic ones. More on these follow in the various chapters.

Writing the book has been an amazing and humbling journey. The most remarkable outcome of the effort has probably been the insights that I have gathered into China—a fascinating country that never ceases to surprise and endows me with new impressions each time I go back. The book is my modest effort to bring to light China's consummate efforts to change global perceptions on it in a largely unfavourable international environment, the challenges it faces and the adjustments it makes, not necessarily with best results. I also look at the Chinese context and subject to look more closely at the new trajectory of engagement in

Sino-Indian relations and the new constructivism in India's foreign policy. I can no way have the last word on these issues and can only claim to have attempted to contribute some different insights into and perspectives on the research on China's soft power and contextual assessment of Sino-Indian relations, where much more ground is left to be covered.

# Acknowledgements

It has been a fascinating journey writing this book on soft power and more so on China's evolving 'non-military strategy' (soft power) to connect with the world. The book would not have been possible without the interactions, discussions and several informal chats that I have had with many people along the way. I take this opportunity to deeply thank all of them for contributing to this book in various capacities and apologize for my inability to pen down many of them.

I express my deep gratitude to Professor Ma Jiali, deputy director, China Reform Forum, Beijing; Professors Shen Dingli and Zhang Gui Hong, Fudan University, Shanghai; Dr Yang Xiaoping, Chinese Academy of Social Sciences (CASS), Beijing; Professor Xue Tang, Shanghai University of International Business and Economics (SUIBE); Dr Zhou Xinyu, Beijing Foreign Studies University; Dr Mao Ji Kang, Academy of World Watch, Hainan; Li Yang, *China Daily*, Beijing; Professor Cai Penghong, Shanghai Academy of Social Sciences (SASS); Dr Shao Yuqun, deputy director, Center for South Asia Studies, Shanghai Institute for International Studies (SIIS); Dr Iftekar Choudhury, Institute of South Asian Studies (ISAS), National University of Singapore (NUS); and Professor Xiaohe Cheng, Renmin University, Beijing. I also sincerely thank Professor Li Mingjiang from the Rajaratnam School of International Studies (RSIS), Nanyang Technological University (NTU), Singapore, for connecting me to a lot of academics in China with whom I have had enlightening deliberations on several issues that I have discussed in the book.

I especially thank Dr Hu Yong, SUIBE for his academic inputs and prompt response to my queries. I thank Professor Rajesh Basroor, RSIS and Professor Zhao Hong, East Asia Institute (EAI), Singapore for going through parts of my manuscript and offering several useful comments. I have received several valuable suggestions from the anonymous referees of SAGE who reviewed the manuscript, and I am grateful to them for the valuable suggestions. My research on the book was considerably facilitated by my access to the wealth of resources at the library of the EAI in the NUS. I specifically thank

Mr James Tan, Manager, EAI and the staff at the library for their kind cooperation.

While researching for my book, I profited considerably from Leslie, my Chinese tutor from Xi'an in Shaanxi province, who was ever ready to help me with translation and interpretation of primary documents. My knowledge and application of the Mandarin language has benefited a lot from my various interactions with Dr Pradeep Taneja of the University of Melbourne—a good friend and academic colleague. Our dear friend, Mr Susen Dutta's anecdotes and experiences of living in China as well as his amazing hospitality will remain fond memories for their warmth and sincerity, apart from contributing variously in my understanding of perceptions.

The idea of the book came from a friend Ms Haimanti Dey, who actually coaxed me into writing this book. I also thank the entire SAGE team, New Delhi for their continuous effort and collaboration in publishing this book. I specially thank Supriya Das and Guneet Kaur Gulati at SAGE Publications for their unyielding support. I take the opportunity to thank my good friend Ms Jennifer Mitchell as well for all her support and encouraging words all through the way. Ms Mitchell and my cousin, Sohini, are the two people most excited about my book. At a personal level, I thank my in-laws Kalyani and Dibyendu Palit for their support. I also thank my aunt Saswati Sen, my brother Parijat Sinha and sister-in-law Debarati Banerjee for always being around and for their patience in hearing me out whenever I was bogged down with work. I also thank my parents for their stalwart support and encouragement at all times and also for believing in me and providing me with all the possible opportunities.

Finally there is one person I owe this book to and can never thank him enough for his relentless support all through—my husband Amitendu. It was his constant urging that helped to wash away my initial reluctance in developing the idea further and finally write the book. His patience, continuous prodding and encouraging words saw me through the long journey which we both undertook together. The book has benefitted enormously from his insights over numerous meals and weekend chats, as well as his patient edits and suggestions over the manuscript from time to time. The work would be as much his as mine, and I thank him for all his support and encouragement. All errors and shortcomings, however, are entirely mine.

# PART I

# Soft Power and China

# 1

# Soft Power: Concepts, Discussions and Debates

With military conflicts becoming resource-intensive, expensive and largely ineffective in obtaining long-term benefits, countries are focusing more on diplomatic engagement and virtuous modes like culture for achieving strategic dividends. Cultural engagement, along with other 'soft' forms of engagement, popularly christened 'soft power' (*ruan shi li*), is being increasingly deployed along with state capacity, strategic strengths and charismatic leadership for converting a state's latent capacities into 'actualized power'.[1]

While debate abounds over whether power can indeed be 'soft', the increasing prominence of 'soft power' in academic discourse underscores the 'constructivist turn in international relations (IR) theory', traditionally dominated by 'positivism'.[2] Despite significant contributions to the study and analysis of international politics for long, many argue that the relevance of the realist theory appears to be waning. As Francis Beer and Robert Hariman contend, 'Realists believe that realism is the only story of world politics....It provides neither the only plausible explanation nor the only possible world'.[3] Constructivists like Alexander Wendt argue further that contrary to realism's focus on power and its material structures, 'ideas' and 'culture' are determining relations between states.[4] The constructivist argument—'the study of international relations must

---

[1] Nayar and Paul, *India in the World Order*, 32.
[2] The positivist approach to research is based upon empirical findings founded upon the science of observable facts. Two threads of IR theory connected to the positivist side of the debate include realism and liberalism/neoliberalism.
[3] Keaney, 'The Realism of Hans Morgenthau'.
[4] Wendt, *Social Theory of International Politics*.

focus on the ideas and beliefs that inform the actors on the international scene as well as the shared understanding between them'[5]—increasingly reflects nation states' new emphasis on collaboration, cooperative social action and exchange of ideas and people.

Rooted in neoliberal and constructivist visions of power,[6] the concept of soft power is hardly recent with the British realist E.H. Carr, way back in 1939, recognizing its significance by segregating international power into three categories: military, economic and the power of opinion, with the last one implying abilities of countries to condition the opinions of others. The concept underlines power of 'attraction'[7] for nurturing and conditioning public opinion and is qualitatively equivalent to the modern notion of soft power. Other influential thinkers such as Foucault, Bourdieu, Gramsci and Habermas have also variously articulated soft power, albeit in implicit and contextual fashions. Soft power's currency in modern strategic discourse is courtesy of Joseph Nye, Jr., who expounded it in his seminal works, *Bound to Lead: The Changing Nature of American Power* (1990) and *The Paradox of American Power* (2001). Nye further provided a structured conceptual paradigm in *Soft Power: The Means to Success* (2004).

Several other scholars have also contributed to the soft power narrative from a variety of perspectives and contexts. David Leheny, for instance, traces the conceptual origins of the modern notion of soft power to debate the American decline in the late 1980s and early 1990s, in which the US's 'soft power' advantage was highlighted for offsetting anxieties about its material decline compared with a more eminent Japan. Steven Lukes argues that power need not be 'blunt' and can influence the formation of preferences in its own way. Gallarotti, on the other hand, posits the theory of 'cosmopolitan power' by employing tenets from three main paradigms of IR—realism (power), neoliberalism (cooperation) and constructivism (norms). He marks 'soft empowerment' as one of the signature processes of cosmopolitan power. Steven B. Rotham adds

[5] Jackson and Sorensen, *Introduction to International Relations*, 63.
[6] Both have been viewed largely as antithetical to the idea of power-seeking.
[7] Giulio M. Gallarotti prefers 'endearment' to 'attraction'. For details, see Gallarotti, 'Soft Power', 28.

*success* as another dimension of soft power, arguing countries emulate other cultures and systems not simply out of 'attraction' but because of 'innate attraction based on *success*.[8] He points out that failure in culture or policy procedures inhibits attraction.

Nye justifies soft power by arguing, 'when you can get others to admire your ideals and to want what you want, you do not have to spend as much on sticks and carrots to move them in your direction'. Both Nye and Kurlantzick's constructs of soft power have been expansive with economic engagement becoming a major soft power resource. Nye though, in his earlier works, was inclined to define national economic might as a coercive resource that is synonymous with hard power, given that both economic sanctions and military force are used for curbing recalcitrant states. While initially tending to identify culture, political values and national foreign policies as the core of soft power, later in the *Future of Power* (2011), Nye elaborated on economic power and its negative and positive aspects, particularly with respect to sanctions and even aid. David Baldwin discusses positive spinoffs from economic sanctions by classifying certain sanctions (e.g., tariffs, market access, aid and investment guarantees) as positive.[9] Many others include the power of economic attraction ('sticky' power) within the conceptual notion of soft power, justifying it as an influence difficult to shed once attracted to.[10] Kurlantzick opines that soft power is robust by suggesting that it 'means anything outside of the military and security realm, including not only popular culture and public diplomacy (PD) but also more coercive economic and diplomatic levers like aid and investment and participation in multilateral organizations'.[11] Both popular and contemporary academic notions of soft power are increasingly verging on this exhaustive scope.

Along with the more expansive notion of soft power, 'smart power'[12] is also being debated in IR. Combining both liberal and realist strands

---

[8] China's economic success, as discussed in various chapters later, has been a source of inspiration and occasional emulation.

[9] Baldwin, *Economic Statecraft*, 41–42.

[10] Mead, 'America's Sticky Power', 48.

[11] Kurlantzick, *Charm Offensive*, 6.

[12] In 2006, Nye espoused 'smart power' in the Boston Globe op-ed. See Nye, 'In Mideast'.

'into successful strategies in the new context of power diffusion and the "rise of the rest"'[13]—the latter primarily implying the emerging powers China, Brazil and India—the notion has become increasingly popular and relevant, given its accommodation of both soft and hard power resources. Nation states are increasingly convinced about the importance of combining economic and political capabilities with other 'soft' resources for expanding their spheres of influence and gaining international credibility. While the notion has its roots in the US President Theodore Roosevelt's idea of 'speak softly and carry a stick', China has been one of the most active employers of 'smart power' in the modern era.

## OBJECTIVES AND STRUCTURE

The primary objective of this book is to study *China's soft power strategy* from the vantage point of vigorous employment of soft power by a rising power in the modern times. The perspective is contextually extended to a comparative study of similar strategies by India. The conceptual framework employed is the exhaustive construct of soft power outlined above, including economic engagement, given the strong resonance of the notion with China's external engagement policies that include cultural diplomacy (CD), PD,[14] economic aid, education and use of the media. Different chapters in the book discuss the quantitative and qualitative aspects of employment of these tools in various parts of the world.

The motivation for the book stems from the lack of academic literature examining soft power from the perspectives of 'rising' powers. The 'rise' of China has necessitated 'de-Americanization' of the concept of soft power.[15] India's strategic elevation and greater reliance on soft power in external engagement strengthens the argument further. Indeed, the absence of literature on soft power from a non-Western and largely Asian

---

[13] Nye, *The Future of Power*, 208.
[14] In IR, PD generally means targeting people from other nations and communicating with them.
[15] Thussu, *Communicating India's Soft Power*, 14.

perspective is in marked contrast to the copious Western academic discourse on the subject.

China's rapid strategic ascent during the last three decades has focused attention on the content and goals of the Chinese foreign policy. Many Chinese scholars have highlighted institutional limitations in this regard.[16] With the foreign minister not being a part of the Standing Committee of the Communist Party of China (CPC) Politburo—the supreme decision-making body in China—many argue that the strategic link between the top party leadership and the Foreign Ministry is missing.[17]

This is an example of structural 'imperfections' in China's state apparatus that complicate the analysis of its foreign policy and soft power strategies. The fact that such imperfections have not constrained China from following a vigorous soft power strategy for international engagement points not only to the constant evolution of foreign policy-making in China, particularly policies inspired by history, cultural traits and domestic priorities, but also the 'uniqueness' of the Chinese policy-making system. The institutional role of propaganda in foreign policy-making is again a relevant example in this context. Many are unaware that China's Propaganda Department (Chinese Communist Party [CCP] Central Office of Foreign Propaganda or commonly known as the State Council Information Office) contributes to foreign policy and image-building, with the Head of the CPC Propaganda Department being a member of

---

[16] Zheng, 'Does Beijing have a Foreign Policy?' 6.

[17] However, it needs to be pointed out that Liu Qibao, Head of the CPC Propaganda Department, is a member of the Politburo. The Propaganda Department specifically controls the media and is responsible for information dissemination. The Department has assumed major significance with Xi Jinping's taking over the central leadership. In a speech at the August 2013 National Meeting on Propaganda and Thought Work, Xi stated that in response to shifting global dynamics, 'China should spread new ideas and new perspectives to emerging and developing states.' He also highlighted the need for China 'to strengthen media coverage … use innovative outreach methods … tell a good Chinese story, and promote China's views internationally', thus implying the critical role the Department plays in foreign engagement and in shaping China's soft power policy. See Brady, 'China's Foreign Propaganda Machine'.

the Politburo.[18] Further, the Chinese leadership employs the Politburo to communicate messages for global audience and major powers: 'Not only should China adhere to the peaceful development road, but other countries must also commit themselves to the peaceful development road', thus introducing 'reciprocity' as a feature of its 'peaceful development'.[19] Institutionalization of propaganda as an active instrument of external outreach policies is indeed unique to China. The institutionalization, however, has had its downsides too with China's soft power strategies, particularly CD and PD often criticized for being overtly propagandist, and not entirely honest and truly reflective of the less bright aspects of the Chinese state and society.

As Chapter 2 illustrates, soft power is integral to China's tradition of engagement for centuries and is a more natural strategic virtue for it to capitalize than perhaps the West. The mainstream (English language) literature on China's soft power is largely focused on tracking China's strategic forays into various parts of the world and their impacts on regional and global power balances from a Western perspective. There is less focus on the 'Chinese' perspective of these engagements. This work attempts to address the limitation by identifying the Chinese perspective from primary and secondary Chinese sources.

An authentic identification of modern China's non-military engagement of the world must proceed on the realization that Chinese diplomacy is not merely reactive to the West but is also driven by its struggle for resolving domestic and external challenges for consolidating national stability and economic progress. Imperatives of maintaining high economic growth for providing economic stability to a huge population, accessing critical natural resources, maintaining a stable external environment particularly in the neighbourhood and promoting balanced relations with major and rising powers are key drivers of Chinese diplomacy. The impact of all these drivers on domestic sociopolitical stability is undisputed. A 'benign' external image capable of favourably moulding international opinions is essential for China in so far as expanding and maintaining its global strategic influence are

---

[18] Ibid.
[19] Zhang, 'China's New Foreign Policy'.

concerned. It is hardly surprising therefore that the above objectives have become policy priorities as articulated in the 'China Dream' (*Zhong guo meng*) by President Xi Jinping in March 2013.[20] Many argue that China has already achieved the great power status denied to it since the First Opium War (1839–42) and has to a great extent revived and restored national confidence and self-respect eroded during a century of foreign humiliation. The history and its outcomes have led to the development of 'post-imperial ideology'[21] with implications for China's diplomatic strategies. China has never been shy to pick up from history, either it be the 'superior barbarian technique' for repelling barbarians during the Self-Strengthening Movement of the 1860s,[22] or invoking Confucian teachings and doctrines for connecting to the outside world. While 'learning' has been an important facet of Chinese strategic thinking for contemporary/historical application, 'unlearning' of history has also been equally significant for the Chinese leadership, policymakers and academics. China's participation in various regional and multilateral forums like the Association of Southeast Asian Nations (ASEAN), Shanghai Cooperation Organization (SCO) and the Brazil, Russia, India, China and South Africa (BRICS) reflects its willingness to change and work with diverse partners and associations. This is notwithstanding China's historical disinclination towards regional alliances and partnerships.[23] The strategic importance of 'socializing'

---

[20] Xi's signature narrative at the NPC symbolized these policy priorities, which later found resonance in the Third Plenary Session of the 18th CPC Central Committee. See *People's Daily Online*, 'Third Plenary Session'.

[21] A term coined by Manjari Chatterjee Miller, the concept clearly indicates a sense of grievance about the past, an insistence on entitlement in the present as restitution for the humiliation and exploitation of the past and a search for respect and status. For details, see Bajpai and Pant, 14.

[22] The peace settlement with the British and French in 1860 partly initiated the Self-Strengthening Movement which marked the beginning of industrialization and sowed the seeds of capitalism in China.

[23] Ancient China's Sino-centric worldview and its history of self-sufficiency discouraged the imperial rulers from forming any kind of interstate alliances or groupings. The attempt, instead, was to socialize foreign rulers into accepting their centrality and superiority and build a Sino-centric international order. See Kavalski, *China and the Global Politics*.

with neighbours and other countries have prioritized interaction with forums like the ASEAN for practice of 'reassurance'—considered critical since Deng Xiaoping's time[24]—for facilitating regional stability and security for enabling greater economic development, a realization resonating with Western beliefs, and whose manifestation is discussed contextually later in Chapters 4 and 8.

But while long-term objectives between the Western and Chinese perceptions of regional organizations are largely similar, they differ in strategies for region-building: while the former prioritizes compliance with norms such as 'do as I say' and 'not as I do', the latter emphasizes the practice of 'do as I do', thus underlining 'respect for the partner' and working together (cooperation).[25]

The overarching emphasis on 'peaceful development' in its contemporary external engagement, as discussed further in this book, is borne out of historical experience and contemporary demands of realpolitik, where culture emerges vital for meaningful engagement as specified in the resolution adopted at the 18th Congress of the CPC[26] (November, 2012) and repeated assertions by senior leaders on different international forums.[27] Chapter 2 attempts to study this combination of the historical and modern in shaping China's soft power strategy by specifying its evolution from ancient Chinese statecraft.

While culture is conspicuous in Beijing's external engagement, winning hearts and minds has involved adopting a more expansive strategy, where greater people-to-people communication through PD, education, media and economic assistance are equally significant. Indeed, as region-specific discussions in the later chapters reveal, culture is relatively sparsely used in some parts of the world, such as South Asia, compared with its more vigorous use elsewhere. These regional variations are interesting nuances in securing China's fundamental strategic objectives of sustained economic progress, access to natural resources and domestic stability. The significance of these objectives in understanding

---

[24] Projecting a benign image overseas and shunning Mao's revolutionary stance became Deng Xiaoping's call for the hour with economic development taking a primacy.
[25] Kavalski, *China and the Global Politics*, 11.
[26] *Xinhua* News Agency, 'Full Text of Resolution on CPC'.
[27] Pant, 'Full Text of Li Keqiang's Speech at Opening Ceremony of Boao Forum'.

contemporary China's diplomatic trajectory can hardly be overstated. These have shaped the Western Development Strategy (WDS), which, as Chapters 3 and 8 discuss with respect to the engagement of South Asia, Central Asia and the Middle East, is at the core of China's engagement of the regions. Imperatives of resources and markets drive engagement with Africa and Latin America too (Chapters 6 and 7), where cultural forays till now are less conspicuous than economic engagement. While both culture (though more cautious) and economics, along with PD, are visible in Southeast Asia (Chapter 4), culture dominates other forms of engagement in Northeast Asia (Chapter 5) and even in the US. Northeast Asia is a more potent ground for cultural connectivity, given its historical connections with the mainland and shared Buddhist legacy and the well-entrenched Chinese diaspora. Apart from the usual techniques that China has been employing for external engagement, Beijing's willingness to experiment with regional forums like the ASEAN for expanding collaborations and improving ties with neighbours is also highlighted in Chapter 4. Specific regional and multilateral imperatives such as the recognition (or non-recognition) of Taiwan and support in the United Nations (UN) also drive the engagement of the Pacific Island countries (Chapter 5) and Africa (Chapter 6).

China's deployment of soft power has not been bereft of focus on hard power. The dispute over the South China Sea is a case in point. This is understandable given the priority of safeguarding sovereignty—a vital peg in the 'China Dream'. Indeed, Beijing's deployment of soft power cannot be seen in isolation with the specific national interest (as opposed to 'enlightened' national interest), determining the combination of soft and hard for the eventual smart power.

## HOW DOES CULTURE MATTER?

Nye's emphasis on culture as the core of soft power finds increasing resonance in China's conduct of external engagement. It comprises various initiatives, policies and activities, specifically by government actors, for achieving long-term goals of national interest.[28] The distinct

---

[28] Kang, 'Reframing Cultural Diplomacy'.

use of culture in diplomacy[29] and strategic efforts vindicates the emphasis of scholars like Holden and Bound who champion the study of CD not merely as a subset of PD[30] but also as a broader context of politics: 'We should no longer think of culture as subordinate to politics. Instead, we should think of culture as providing the context for politics'.[31]

Culture has been inseparable from politics in China, highlighting the salience of the context and a prominent role by state actors in CD almost naturally. Such prominence is clearly not visible in India, where cultural communication has traditionally involved more non-state actors.[32] The difference between the two neighbours is notable in this regard. The greater prominence of culture in modern Chinese domestic and foreign policies can probably be traced to the characters of governments the two countries chose at the end of the Second World War. Culture had major roles to play in the communist state in China run by the Communist Party. The latter employed culture as a platform for uniting people under the overarching 'proletarian' banner by encouraging the growth of a homogeneous grass-roots 'mass' culture owned by the Party as opposed to the 'elitist' bourgeois culture.[33] Chapter 2 sheds light on how China has continued employing culture, often overtly, for shaping its state behaviour towards other countries in projecting a benign image while upholding long-held civilizational values. India's political history is a marked contrast in this regard. Its choice of a democratic government and efforts to accommodate various strands of socio-cultural diversities reflected the complex culture independent India inherited, which, unlike China's, was not a monolithic whole but instead a mosaic celebrating pluralism. Pluralism and diversity featured prominently in independent India's domestic and external policies with New Delhi distinctly reluctant

[29] CD comes under the purview of the Ministry of Culture in China, while education comes under the Ministry of Education.
[30] Holden, 'Cultural Diplomacy'.
[31] Bound et al., 20.
[32] CD though state agencies like the ICCR, while expanding over time, has been relatively low profile and subdued.
[33] Hong, 'Mao Zedong's Cultural Theory'.

to overemphasize and become a cultural colonizer.[34] The Nehruvian policy of external engagement focused on forging a common identity for nations based on the painful experience of colonization and imperialism, not culture. While underplaying culture, India's foreign policy since independence reflects a combination of pragmatism, realism and idealism, with scholars arguing that India's history 'offered little comfort for Nehruvian pacifism or anti-militarism or anti-war and anti-balance of power position'.[35] In more recent times, however, the Indian statecraft has begun employing culture more prominently than in the past, as discussed in Chapter 9.

In China's case, Mao Zedong highlighted the culture–politics congruence decades ago: 'There is no such thing as art for art's sake. Proletarian art and literature are.... as Lenin said, cogs and wheels in the whole revolutionary machine'.[36] He had also emphasized that the CPC would not hesitate to harness literature and art for achieving national interests. Mao's emphasis was on the creation of a New Democracy—national and anti-imperialistic—for advancing the dignity and independence of the Chinese nation, as opposed to the individual. Post-1976, Mao's vision of cultural exclusiveness made way for a more receptive outlook on cultural diversity with emphasis on coexistence and harmony, aptly reflected by the former premier Wen Jiabao: 'Cultural diversity is an objective reality in this world and only when the diversity of cultures is respected, will civilizations progress'.[37] The former president Hu Jintao, at the 17th National Congress of the CPC in October 2007, mentioned culture as a 'rejuvenating' force for China and emphasized its

---

[34] During the Bandung Conference in 1955, according to a Filipino official, Nehru's 'pronounced propensity to be dogmatic, impatient, irascible and unyielding... alienated the goodwill of many delegates', and it was argued that this aspect of Nehru typified 'the affectations of cultural superiority induced by a conscious identification with an ancient civilization' which has come to be the hallmark of Indian representatives to international conferences. For details, see Chacko, *The Indian Foreign Policy*, 61.

[35] Kapur, 'Eclipsed Moon to a Rising Star'.

[36] Tung-Tse, *Selected Works of Mao Tse-Tung*.

[37] Mission of the People's Republic of China to the European Union, 'China Sticks to Reform'.

fine traditions.[38] Xi Jinping is also keen on spreading the message of peace and harmony through culture, as is evident from his belief that the China Dream's focus on the rejuvenation of the state will not come about only through economic progress and sovereignty but cultural strength as well.

Culture is the third pillar of Chinese diplomacy after economics and politics, with the 11th Five Year Plan (2006–10) urging a greater presence of China in global cultural markets[39]—a view endorsed by the People's Liberation Army (PLA)[40] and the 18th Congress. It is hardly surprising that China has unleashed a variety of cultural initiatives for connecting with both developing countries in Africa, Asia and Latin America and developed countries and major powers such as the US, Canada, Europe, Australia and Japan. Indeed, for the latter, as later chapters discover, culture might be the key instrument for soft engagement as these countries do not offer room for strategic gains through economic aid and investments in infrastructure.

## People-to-people Communication

Soft power emphasizes nation states connecting to people in other countries for –building bridges. Looked at from this vantage point, there could be various strategies serving the purpose of PD, including cultural initiatives. China's efforts at people-to-people contact include initiatives ranging from high-level visits by senior leaders and internationalization of higher education to the use of the Chinese media. High-level visits for PD, particularly for connecting to the diaspora, are becoming key initiatives for the Modi government in India as well, as discussed in Chapter 9.

In a somewhat narrow sense, high-level visits, or face-to-face diplomacy, focus on interactions between states locked in ongoing conflict.[41] Identical initiatives by China and other nations including India have broadened the diplomatic ambit of the notion. Both Xi and

---

[38] CPC Encyclopedia, 'Full Text of Hu Jintao's Report'.
[39] Hongyi, 'China's Cultural Diplomacy', 6.
[40] Mingjiang, 'Explaining China's Proactive Engagement'.
[41] Lebovic and Saunders, 'The Diplomatic Core', 3.

Modi's use of face-to-face diplomacy highlights their intents to 'change international outcomes'.[42] This is understandable given the intricate link between altering their global/regional reputations and desire to play greater roles in international affairs. The common objective of both leaders to ensure a peaceful external environment for economic development depends squarely on their success in conveying positive and 'benign' images, an objective conspicuous in China's external engagement strategy. Face-to-face diplomacy becomes essential in ensuring an enabling external environment for greater international policy coordination, avoiding confrontations.[43]

The Chinese foreign policy and the emphasis on people-to-people contacts are becoming distinct because of the greater role being played by Chinese provinces in this regard. Although the latter do not engage directly in foreign affairs, they are active in *dui wai shi wu* (foreign exchanges)[44] pursued through the Offices of International Exchanges. Chinese provinces have the flexibility of sending or receiving less than 10 local artists overseas autonomously through local governments.[45] There are many such regular cultural exchanges between China and other countries mentioned in later chapters. The intensity and frequency of these initiatives vary between regions and countries. But exchanges related to politically sensitive regions like Taiwan, which has no diplomatic relationship with the People's Republic of China (PRC), might require the approval of the Ministry of Culture or it even might have to consider the opinions of the Ministry of Foreign Affairs.[46]

Education has emerged as a key medium for China's external interface and people-to-people communication. China aspires to establish itself as a major centre for learning and higher education—consistent with its status of a major power based on the foundations of military capabilities, remarkable economic success and constructive diplomatic engagement.

---

[42] Hall and Yarhi-Milo, 'The Personal Touch'.
[43] Lee and Hudson, 'The Old and New Significance', 343–60.
[44] The author interviewed faculty from the Shanghai University of International Business and Economics (SUIBE), Shanghai.
[45] People's Government of Guangdong Province, Foreign Affairs Office, 'Guan yu xia fang'.
[46] The author interviewed faculty from the SUIBE, Shanghai.

Internationalization of higher education by encouraging foreign students, inviting foreign education service providers and striking partnerships with global higher education institutions is critical for not only reforming China's domestic education but also for economic and social development and greater strategic influence.[47] China perceives education as a complementary initiative to culture for connecting to people and building a 'benign' image for facilitating strategic elevation. As Chapters 3–8 indicate, the number of foreign students in China is increasing rapidly with considerable inflows from neighbouring Southeast and South Asia. China's long-term objective of gaining recognition as a regional hub for higher education appears to be materializing with some of its major universities (e.g., Peking, Fudan, Tsinghua Universities) securing high positions in global rankings, and more foreign students travelling to China for studying not only Mandarin but also several technical and academic disciplines.

Confucius Institutes (CIs) are China's main arms of CD and its brand ambassadors. They are actively engaged in dealing with people in their overseas locations through a variety of tasks ranging from teaching Mandarin and offering courses on Chinese art and culture to organizing multiple cultural activities for people-to-people exchanges. Modelled after France's *Alliance Francaise*, Germany's *Goethe Institut* and the United Kingdom's British Council, the CIs, usually developed in collaboration with host institutions, mainly foreign universities, have sound financial fundamentals. They follow functional guidelines of the *Hanban*[48] affiliated with the PRC Ministry of Education. Chapters 3–8 discuss the activities of CIs in different regions within their larger ambit of engaging through education. The implicit strategic objective behind CD of CIs can be traced to the vision of China nursed by a core group of foreign affairs decision-makers in the Central Committee of the CPC striving for a globally benign image.[49] The vision models CIs on Confucius and his teachings, as brand 'Confucius' is not only benign by its emphasis on

---

[47] Litao, 'China's Higher Education', 11.
[48] *Hanban* is the Chinese National Office for teaching Chinese as a foreign language.
[49] The author interviewed Associate Professor Xufeng Zhu, Nankai University, Tianjin.

humanity, education and harmony but also capable of connecting to the ethnic Chinese around the world and 'pulling in' the unfamiliar and uninitiated towards China by its non-ideological flavour.[50] Confucian thoughts are the most representative tenets of a 'global' doctrine that the CPC is comfortable in identifying with and projecting to the world. But as the discussions in the book indicate, notwithstanding such virtuous packaging, CIs have not been able to avoid being dubbed as vehicles of state propaganda.

The role of Chinese media in engaging foreign audiences and enhancing people-to-people contact needs to be comprehended in the context of the global trend of branding territorial entities as companies and products for country branding in global markets for attracting tourists and stimulating investments. Primarily aimed to tackle the 'hegemony of discourse'[51] and its own weakness of the 'power of the word' (hua yu quan), the Chinese media has been actively brand-building China for securing the state's economic goals of business and tourism and also projecting an alternative 'Chinese' perspective on global and regional issues. Chinese media agencies such as the China Daily, CCTV, Xinhua and China Radio International (CRI) have significantly enhanced foreign presence, which is now noteworthy not only in Africa and Southeast Asia but also in the US and Europe. As noted in various chapters, there is also a noticeable increase in cooperation and exchanges with foreign media, along with a reciprocal interest reflected in a higher presence of foreign media in China.[52]

China's efforts to connect to the Chinese diaspora has also been instrumental given the latter's contributions to the mainland's domestic economic development, higher education and scientific innovations.[53]

---

[50] Ibid.
[51] It is an attempt to impose a particular discourse over all other narratives and in this case it is predominantly Western.
[52] Along with more foreign correspondents, large media delegations now cover events in China such as the Beijing Olympics, Shanghai Expo, World Economic Forum events and the CPC Party Congresses.
[53] The leadership looks at the overseas returnees as people who can deliver advanced technology, management skills, and have legal knowledge and thus be the driving force for economic growth.

The diaspora has also contributed significantly to the soft power narrative. Apart from participating in Chinese modernization and promoting unification, Beijing expects the overseas Chinese to 'actively spread Chinese civilization, and to actively promote the friendship between China and the people all over the world'.[54] In what has proved to be a pragmatic strategy for utilizing the diaspora for the national interest,[55] China has relied upon their ideas and insights for comprehending the global 'big picture' for enabling its leadership to play major roles on the world stage.[56] The role of Chinese academics like Chen Shujin and Lin Qitan has been significant in driving home the importance of making the overseas Chinese committed stakeholders in the national interest.[57] Many among the diaspora have been 'nationalists' and active in projecting alternative Chinese perspectives on various issues backed by the Chinese state.[58] The strategic appeal of the diaspora in global engagement is clearly not lost upon India as well, given their engagement for quite some time now and upped by the Modi government, as discussed in Chapter 10.

## Economic Engagement

By posing as the locomotive for regional growth and prosperity, Beijing has effectively employed economics as one of its major foreign policy instruments. This would be following its increasing adherence to neoliberal economic principles emphasizing economic interdependence

---

[54] Ren, *Haiwai Huaren Huaqiao yu Zhongguo Gaige Kaifang*, 208.

[55] The government efforts began with the 'spring light project' (*chun hui ji hua*) launched in the mid-1990s for enabling overseas Chinese to play bigger roles in Chinese development and have been backed by a major policy document prepared in 2001 urging the diaspora to 'serve the nation' (*wei guo fu wu*), even if they did not 'return to the nation' (*hui guo fu wu*). For details, see Zweig, 'Learning to Compete'.

[56] According to the Ministry of Education, China, more than half the number of students who had left to study abroad returned to China. See *China Daily*, 'Returning with a Fresh Perspective', 20.

[57] David, Fung, and Han, 'Redefining the Brain Drain'.

[58] 'Nationalists' are reportedly rewarded financially for pro-China comments posted in response to online edits perceived as critical of Beijing and assist the Chinese government in assuaging international fears about a 'rising' China. See Foreign and Commonwealth Office, 'One China?'

between nation states for promoting common interests and lessening possibilities of potential conflicts. It is in keeping with the objective of achieving economic development for all that President Xi repeatedly invokes 'community of common destiny'[59]—representing Beijing's intentions to provide a 'Chinese solution' to address the challenges faced by the Asian countries and the world to achieve stability and development[60]—to strengthen China's relationship with other countries, particularly its neighbours and Europe. The OBOR initiative attests to the 'community of common development' for strengthening ties with other countries by emphasizing economic development. At the same time, like much of China's economic assistance to infrastructure building in Asia and elsewhere, the OBOR initiative is expected to create opportunities for absorbing China's surplus capacities in various industries and provide avenues for good returns on Chinese investments compared with what they are fetching from mainland projects.

Economic tools have long been used as major diplomatic tools. As Nye argues, development assistance through grants and soft loans are important in cultivating benign images of donors in recipients.[61] In China's case, aid to capital-starved countries for building infrastructure, apart from securing benign perceptions through commitment to the development of recipients, has advanced hand in hand with providing unhindered access to strategic natural resources. Chinese aid has carved out a new niche by its characteristic of having 'no strings attached' and being far more accommodating than Western aid. As the former vice minister of commerce Fu Ziying mentioned,

---

[59] The concept of 'community of common destiny' was articulated for the first time in 2007 by the former president Hu Jintao to describe the unique relationship between the mainland and Taiwan in his report to the 17th National Party Congress. The term was again mentioned in China's 2011 White Paper on peaceful development. The concept was once again referred to by President Hu at the 18th National party Congress for developing relationships with the other countries. For details, see Zhang, 'China's New Foreign Policy'.

[60] Zhang, 'China's New Foreign Policy', 15.

[61] While economic sanctions (hard power) restricting trade and other economic exchanges are employed by economically powerful nations against recalcitrant states.

*China does not attach any political strings to its aid [emphasis added].* Our foreign aid programs are based on the principles of equality, mutual benefit and mutual development.... Many developing countries lack hospitals and roads. Our aid is concentrated on sectors where they need it most.[62]

Notwithstanding discomforts attached with the scale and ramifications of China's extensive hold over economic assets in recipient countries, as the book alludes to in specific contexts, liberal and generous economic assistance has 'garnered appreciation disproportionate to the size of its aid and thus has a large impact on recipient governments'.[63]

Over time, however, downsides of Chinese development aid have become increasingly prominent with recipient countries and agencies drawing attention to implicit 'strings' attached with financial assistance in the form of insistence on use of Chinese labour and materials in aided projects as well as dictation of operational terms. More on these have been discussed in later chapters, particularly in discussions on Chinese engagement with Africa. But the growing disenchantment of recipient countries with Chinese aid, most of whom perceived China a generous benefactor given their lack of access to other major developed countries' donors donors and institutions, underlines the grey shades of China's economic assistance and soft power efforts that, at least on certain occasions, are beginning to be perceived as more extractive than virtuous. The perception has implications for the 'honest' character of China's soft power, which, as alluded to earlier in the context of aggressive CD and PD by China, has begun getting questioned. Nonetheless criticisms about Chinese overseas projects engaging more Chinese workers than locals, or the projects using imports from the mainland, need to be viewed objectively since Chinese workers are more experienced in implementing infrastructure projects than their counterparts from the host countries.

China is also keen on consolidating its image of a major source of capital for infrastructure-deficient regions and countries of the world

---

[62] *People's Daily Online*, 'China's Foreign Aid Comes with "No Strings Attached"'.
[63] Lum, Morrison, and Vaughn, 'China's "Soft Power" in Southeast Asia', 4–5.

through initiatives like OBOR[64] and Asian Infrastructure Investment Bank (AIIB). Apart from fostering diplomacy, economic cooperation, academic research, cultural exchange and tourism through trade and investment, OBOR will also address the geographic imbalance within China by augmenting infrastructure capacities in the deficient areas of the mainland.[65] The roads provide inland border provinces—economically lagging behind the coastal provinces—with an opportunity to prosper as 'outward-looking Eurasian gateways'.[66] Through these multi-country initiatives, China also aims to secure commitments of other countries in its overall infrastructure-building efforts—a striking example of efforts at economic interdependence based on common interests mentioned earlier. From a larger strategic perspective, initiatives like the AIIB also mark China's efforts to alter the character of the global financial architecture and the balance of power within the particular architecture by counterbalancing the strategic influence of traditional financial institutions like the World Bank (WB) and Asian Development Bank (ADB).

Aid and assistance from China's soft power perspective also include humanitarian assistance extended to countries struck by natural disasters and similar catastrophes. China's economic success, surplus resources and large capacities help it to not only contribute significantly to infrastructure building but also in managing disaster distress. Indeed, as this book outlines, scale and capacity are defining attributes of China's economic engagement across the developing world and are critical determinants of the outreach of its soft power. Hu Jintao's assertion—'In the face of great natural disasters, the people of all nations should support each other, should share the same vessel when crossing a river'—reflects

---

[64] The OBOR initiative combines the Silk Road Economic Belt and the 21st century Maritime Silk Road.

[65] Arase, 'China's Two Silk Roads', 25, 31.

[66] Some of the Chinese provinces which have been designated as Eurasian gateways are Jilin facing Mongolia, Yunnan facing the Mekong River sub-region as well as the Bay of Bengal rim of the Indian Ocean (through Myanmar) and Xinjiang facing Central Asia with onward linkages to the Caspian Sea, Arabian Sea, Black Sea, Mediterranean region and Eastern and Northern Europe. For details, see Arase, 'China's Two Silk Roads', 31.

China's eagerness to refrain from being 'non-committal'[67] and assist affected countries, particularly neighbours, during crises. Engagement in the multilateral humanitarian efforts projects China as a constructive and responsible player. This image makeover is expected to facilitate its global rise. It has other dividends as well since international cooperation opens multiple avenues for obtaining advanced technology and know-how that enable China's own domestic capabilities to handle disasters. Participating in regional disaster management efforts, as well as extending humanitarian assistance to countries in the neighbourhood, has also become an important part of India's external engagement, as seen from various instances such as the tsunami in India (2004) and the earthquake in Nepal (2015).

## CHINA AND INDIA

China's strategic rise, while not matched by an equivalent exaltation on part of India, has nonetheless drawn inevitable comparisons with its largest Asian neighbour. Given that both countries are seeking strategic space in their pan-Asian neighbourhoods and also in regional and global affairs, such comparison is unavoidable. The comparison should tend to their soft power approaches as well.

India, while gradually deploying some of the 'soft' tools being used by China for strategic dividends, such as cultural initiatives, PD, education and aid, is much different in its approach, with the non-state actors playing a more pronounced role. The contemporary academic strategic discourse, either from the thematic perspective of soft power of Asian nations or as part of the changing nature of the global and regional engagement of China and India, hardly compares the soft powers of the two behemoths. Chapter 9, while briefly discussing India's foreign policy, highlights the gradual incorporation of soft power elements in the policy, which is consistent with *pragmatism* shaping such policy in recent times, especially under the Modi government. The chapter also examines different tenets of India's soft engagement strategies (e.g., development

---

[67] Binder and Conrad, 'China's Potential Role', 9.

assistance, CD, connecting to the diaspora and engaging neighbours through the religious thread of Buddhism) that might have contextual similarities with China. Notwithstanding such occasional similarities, the difference in strategic approaches of the two countries is clearly evident. For example, China's emphasis on creating long-distance nationalism by utilizing its diaspora is different from India's greater focus on assimilation. In Africa—commonly described as a contesting turf for both countries—India's approach is considered distinct from Beijing's more conspicuous commercial and resource-seeking posturing.[68] Chapter 9 reviews India's efforts to 'win hearts and minds' in keeping with its pursuit of 'enlightened national interest'[69] in the backdrop of the preceding detailed exposition of China's soft power strategies.

For both China and India, the key test of 'soft' engagement is with respect to each other. Cooperation and constructive engagement riding on the back of robust economic exchanges marks a new phase in bilateral relations. Chapter 10 discusses efforts by both countries to engage each other. With both countries realizing the significance of their bilateral relations in what is largely touted as the 'Asian century', the key roles they have begun playing in international affairs, and the expectations of the rest of the world from them in providing directions on major global issues, neither can afford to be 'irresponsible' towards the other. The search for responsible and mature attitudes necessitates the era-dication of 'trust deficit' through enhanced people-to-people contact. Both Chinese and Indian leaderships are seized of the importance of constructive engagement and have embarked on the mission in purposeful manners. Their respective visions about each other cannot be bereft of larger visions of the neighbourhood. While China's active neighbourhood policy has proceeded on creating enabling conditions for economic growth and internal stability, India's efforts to achieve similar ends has led to greater engagement of neighbours. The process,

---

[68] Venu, 'Trading a New Route'.
[69] In international diplomacy, 'enlightened' national interest is arguably the recognition that the narrow pursuit of self interest in an interdependent world can lead to inferior policy outcomes for selfish pursuit of national ambitions. Rather the objective of the government should be to pursue policies for 'common good' instead. For details, see Ganguly, *India's Foreign Policy*, 4.

accelerated by the Modi government through closer association with South Asia and initiatives like the 'Act East' policy, had gathered momentum during the earlier government itself, as is evident from the former prime minister Manmohan Singh's remark during his visit to Bangladesh in October 2011 that 'India will not be able to realize its destiny without the partnership of its South Asian neighbours'.[70] Whether, and in what manner, enlightened visions of the neighbourhood and their greater engagement by both countries will reflect on their bilateral relations will be revealed only over time.

---

[70] Tharoor, *Pax Indica*, 84.

# 2

# Chinese Soft Power: Historical Background and Contemporary Context

China is rising. China's spectacular economic success during the last three decades has awed the world. Even if countries do not view the rise favourably,[1] they can hardly ignore the phenomenon of a resurgent China. Armed with global economic clout and an expanding sphere of strategic influence, China is way ahead of other countries in being the next superpower.

China's rise is viewed with concern by nation states influenced by the realist school of thought. According to the realists, a rising power is a threat since driven by its expanding national interests the power will pursue a revisionist approach for increasing influence beyond borders. While not being an exception, China has been remarkably pragmatic in fashioning ambitions. Keen on playing a major role in global affairs without irking international displeasure, it has relied on 'soft' engagement. China's rapid strategic elevation has been accompanied by its emphasis on 'peace and development' and cooperation with neighbours ostensibly for allaying fears about an assertive China. The contemporary Chinese foreign policy, both in its global and regional dimensions, is distinct in portraying China as a peace-loving, people-based, cooperative, tolerant, confident and responsible power. Beijing appears convinced that soft power diplomacy will not only enhance its global status but also ensure peace and stability in the neighbourhood for maintaining its rapid

---

[1] Several Pew research surveys show domestic concerns like corruption and pollution and regional disputes over territories with neighbours contributing to negative perceptions about China's rise.

economic progress—crucial for cementing itself in the great power league.

Noted China scholar, Pei Minxin comments, the only thing rising faster than China 'is the hype about China'.[2] This rather uncanny truth about China has much to do with its mounting 'charm offensive'. Promulgated with typical Chinese characteristics, the charm has aroused curiosity of the world, particularly the West to probe at length China's soft power initiatives. The result has been the outpouring of a fairly large body of literature on China's soft power. Unfortunately, the literature is entirely from the Western perspective with hardly any effort to conceptualize and analyse China's soft engagement from an alternative vantage point. The limitation is mostly explained by the academic discourse on the Chinese perspective on soft power being available in Mandarin with hardly any translations in English. This Chapter attempts to provide an overview of the Chinese perspective on soft power by examining Chinese academic sources, both through secondary literature as well as the author's interviews with various scholars.

## FROM ANCIENT TO CONTEMPORARY

Use of soft power in China's foreign policy can be traced to the ancient times. This section studies the historical evolution of soft power in China's state policies.

### Soft Power: A Chinese Historical Legacy

Traditional Chinese philosophy mostly originated during the spring and the autumn era (771–476 BC), a period also known as the 'Hundred Schools of Thought', is characterized by several significant cultural and intellectual developments. The period ended with the rise of the Qin dynasty and the subsequent purge of dissent. The thoughts and ideas of this period retain their influence till date. The concept of soft power is one such example.

---

[2] Minxin, 'The Dark Side of China's Rise', 32.

The literature of the period—the 'Hundred Schools of Thought'— indicates that China's ancient strategists not only preferred diplomatic manoeuvring over military confrontation in achieving state objectives but were also averse to territorial expansion. Kong Zi or Confucius (551–479 BC) emphasized the limitation and regulation of power. As opposed to war and confrontation, Confucius' teachings focussed on education and humanity. Mencius (372–289 BC), another great thinker of the time, denounced all wars in the spring and the autumn period.[3] He believed benevolent kings had no enemies in the world and could easily win over masses. He was also against nations projecting military power. According to the Confucius–Mencius concept of government, there was never a need to possess large territories to enhance the prestige of the state. The Chou kingdom (1027–256 BC) is a pertinent example. While not being large, it was able to retain dynastic respect for 800 years—the longest span of life ever held by any dynasty.[4] Confucius–Mencius principles were espoused several centuries later in the famous treatise, *Yen t'ieh (Discourses on Salt and Iron)*, written around 81 BC.[5] The treatise argued against territorial expansion even for defensive purposes: 'If the people from afar would not submit, then it is up to the country to improve and promote its civil culture and virtue to attract. If they come, then steps must be taken to make them contended and tranquil'.[6] Wu Teh-Yao, a specialist on Confucianism, believed that the Confucius thinking was being adopted and imbibed by the Chinese leadership in the early 1970s.

In another striking articulation of constructive engagement through soft means, Mohism founded by Mo Zi, taught 'universal love' and developed at the same time as Confucianism and Taoism, advocating discussion and persuasion for solving ethical problems. Lao Zi, another ancient Chinese philosopher who wrote the main texts of Taoism along with Zhuang Zi, discounted wars, with the latter emphasizing education and humility as did Confucius. Lao Zi's classic expression 'water is the

---

[3] Ding, *The Dragon's Hidden Wings*, 24.
[4] Teh-Yao, 'Southeast Asia and China', 4.
[5] Ibid., 5.
[6] *Confucius Analects.*

softest thing, yet it can penetrate mountains and earth' underlines the philosophical sanctity behind the overarching principle of softness overpowering hardness. The expression best describes the virtuosity of soft power distinct from coercive hard power and relevant in modern times as well.

Ideas such as 'culture winning over an enemy' and 'winning a battle before it is fought' are rampant in China's ancient literature. The noted ancient military strategist Sun Zi (722–481 BC) in his *The Art of War* opined that it was better to attack the enemy's mind rather than his fortified cities. Many Chinese contemporary scholars subscribe to this school of thought. Shaohua Hu, discussing ancient China's pacifism argues, 'Imperial China seemed reluctant to initiate the use of force in its foreign relations for both moralistic and pragmatic reasons'.[7] Many Chinese scholars also argue that the imperial Chinese tributary system, which shaped China's foreign policy and trade for two centuries, was successful in integrating morality with power.[8] As a strategic instrument for serving national interests, soft power was clearly popular among the ancient Chinese and can hardly be described a product of contemporary Western thinking.[9] Unfortunately, with the turn of history, particularly after 1949, the significance of the various philosophies and ancient thoughts centralizing soft power were relegated to the background as foreign policy determinants. It is only since the beginning of the current century that Chinese foreign policy has begun reviving ancient Chinese teachings, particularly Confucius, in its contemporary application of soft power.

## Contemporary Debate and the Role of Culture

China hardly had much exposure to the contemporary global discourse on foreign relations and international affairs during its transition from the ancient to the Mao period. Mao, in his effort to enforce socialism,

---

[7] Hu, 'Revisiting Chinese Pacifism', 256–78.
[8] The Chinese tributary system, unlike other tributary systems like the West likes to understand, is unique and akin to father–son relationship where the association is 'unequal' but 'benign' like an ideal Confucian family.
[9] Palit, 'China's Cultural Diplomacy'.

sought to remove purported capitalist, traditional and cultural elements from the Chinese society. This isolated China from the international community and restrained Chinese scholars from the intellectual discussions on foreign policy and related issues. The Mao era also witnessed the downfall of Confucius doctrines. It was not until 1979 that China lifted the iron curtain and connected to the rest of the world for reviving the economy left stagnant and moribund by the Cultural Revolution. The 'opening up' also led to the beginning of the contemporary Chinese discourse on international relations and its 'initial' engagement with mainstream 'Western' International Relation theories.[10] The writings of Chen Lemin and Chen Hanwen during the period are evidence of China gradually getting exposed to the Western theories with translations becoming available. The Tiananmen Square crackdown in 1989 once again isolated China internationally. After the incident, the Chinese leadership began consciously integrating with the international community with its scholars participating more actively in the global discourse on International Relations, including soft power.

The post-Tiananmen Chinese academic literature indicates a growing interest in China's soft power. The initial interest was linked to domestic institutional reforms like downsizing of bureaucracy and increasing dialogue and communication, which were seen as neglected but crucial for China's modernization. On the other hand, the mid 1990s witnessed the growth of an active discourse on China, characterizing it as a 'destabilizing force' along with proliferation of 'China collapse' theories.[11] Such cynical portrayals of China drove it to work on its global image with Chinese experts focussing on those aspects of China they felt could be virtuous and attractive to the international community. The efforts became part of the Chinese idea of comprehensive national power born

---

[10] Zhang, 'The "English School" in China', 87–114.

[11] China collapse theories continue till date. David Shambaugh, in an article in the *Wall Street Journal* (2015), once again predicted the collapse of China. There have been such forecasts earlier as well, especially post 1990s. In 2001–02, Gordon G. Chang, in his book, looked at the rise of China from a negative perspective. Others like Segal pointed out that the rise of economic regionalism could lead to political and military regionalism in China and even its eventual break-up. See Segal, 'China and the Disintegration of the Soviet Union'.

in the late 1990s, emphasizing technological and economic capacities along with national cohesion.[12]

During the last decade and more, there has been a sharp increase in the Chinese academic discourse on soft power. Li Mingjiang refers to the wide use of the term in Chinese journals and periodicals.[13] The contemporary Chinese academic focus on soft power began with the writings of Wang Huning, earlier with the Fudan University and currently a member of the CPC Politburo. Wang is probably the first contemporary Chinese scholar to argue that culture is the main source of a state's soft power.[14] The view was subsequently expounded by other academics and scholars. Zhou Ji, He Ying and Xiang Mei suggest that the concept of soft power is relevant in analysing relationships between nations and emphasize the importance of technology, education and economy as the three key elements—as opposed to war—in defining national identity.[15] On the other hand, scholars like Xiang Shu Yong[16] and Zhao Chang Rong[17] point towards culture and language as being responsible for enhancing a nation's strength. Another noted scholar on China's international studies, Men Hong Hua from the Central Party School,[18] discusses the extent by which China's soft power diplomacy has positively enhanced its global impression.[19]

Zhao Tingyang, a contemporary Chinese scholar offers an instrumental perspective on the idea of soft power in the context of international relations and provides an alternative discourse to the Western-led theories on international relations by highlighting harmony and

---

[12] Deng, 'The New Hard Realities', 66.

[13] According to him, there were 416 papers with 'soft power' in their titles during 2005–07, compared with only 58 during 2001–04. Mingjiang, 'Soft Power in Chinese Discourse', 24.

[14] Huning, 'Culture Regarded as National Power'.

[15] Ying, Zhou and Xiang, 'Primary Analysis of a Country's "Soft Power" Theory', 5.

[16] Xiang, 'New Country Doctrine Soft Power Foreign Affairs'. (2007)

[17] Rong, 'China Needs Soft Power'.

[18] The Central Party School of the Central Committee of the CPC (*zhong gong zhong yang dang xiao*) is a higher education institution where new officials for the CPC are trained.

[19] Hua, 'China's Soft Power Evaluation Report', 37–38.

cooperation as defining elements of international relations. Zhao's theory of *Tianxia*, though utopian, illustrates the 'soft' dimensions of Chinese strategic thinking which rejects hegemony, exclusion of people, individual interests and 'internationality'.[20] The preferred political system emanating from *Tianxia* is premised on a global institution as the highest political entity caring for the entire world while ensuring universal order. The conceptual resonance of the vision with United Nations cannot be overlooked. But as rightly pointed out by Zhang Feng, the largely utopian concept is difficult to comprehend on many accounts with Zhao failing to outline a specific path that could 'lead to the creation of the world institution of the *Tianxia* system—something on which he places so much emphasis. He insists on the priority of the world institution, yet surprisingly fails to provide any description of how it might come about'.[21] Converging on central 'common interest' of all nation-states, as proposed by Zhao Tingyang is indeed significantly 'utopian' since countries fashion foreign policies on past experiences, which vary widely among nations, as does geography, thereby making national interests distinct and divergent.

Coming back again to official pronouncements of soft power, the Sixth Plenary session of the 17th Central Committee of the CPC (October 2011) further strengthened the focus on cultural development. The CPC Central Committee decided on the 'major issues pertaining to deepening reform of the cultural system and promoting the great development and flourishing of socialist culture'. The Plenary put forward China's objectives in cultural reform and development leading up to the 2020 by aiming, among other objectives, to increase the country's cultural soft power.[22] It was also notable for introducing the 'socialist cultural development' path with Chinese characteristics, which again, marks the Chinese effort to distinguish and refine the identification of its culture as much as possible in its export of the same to the rest of the world.

[20] 'Internationality' is a concept upon which Western theories on international relations are based. The attempt is to replace it by 'worldness' which is broader than 'national interests'. See Zhao, *Tian Xia System: An Introduction*.

[21] Zhang, 'The Tianxia System: World Order in a Chinese Utopia'.

[22] Li, 'Vigorously Promoting the Guiding Thought'.

The Chinese literature on soft power is ideology-driven with a pronounced presence of culture. Rong, while discussing soft power, distinguishes between Western and Chinese cultures, arguing Western culture's emphasis on hegemony in contrast to the Chinese culture's focus on Confucianism, seeking peaceful solutions to international problems.[23] Several other contemporary scholars, like Haiyan, emphasize the cultural dichotomy and argue the Western focus on materialism, science, individualism and industrialization being responsible for global conflicts and disharmony. The negative outcomes produced by the Western focus, according to these scholars, are in marked contrast to traditional Chinese approaches of 'putting people first' and 'harmony between nature and mankind',[24] which, arguably can be more effective in solving complex international problems. Chinese writings regard the country's indigenous culture based on Confucianism, Taoism, Buddhism, Mohism and other classical schools of thought like winning respect through virtues, benevolent governance, peace and harmony without suppressing differences, as embodying the soft aspects of China's national power. Scholars like Sheng Ding oppose China's branding as a 'revisionist power' by highlighting it's preference to use non-military means in conducting international relations in the present-day context:[25]

[I]n its three-decade rising process, (China) has rarely been involved in military conflicts with other countries, not mentioning launching a full-scale war to change the international order. Instead Beijing has increasingly employed its non-military power resources to increase its political, economic and cultural clout in dealing with all kinds of external issues....

Notwithstanding the emphasis on cultural dichotomy, contemporary Chinese literature on soft power reflects several strands of Nye's constructs. Studies indicate similarities between China's soft power and Nye's conceptual postulate in their emphasis on three fundamentals:

---

[23] Rong, 'China Needs Soft Power'.
[24] Haiyan, 'Promoting the Outstanding Culture of the Chinese Nation', 107–12.
[25] Ding, *The Dragon's Hidden Wings*, 10.

CD, multilateral diplomacy and overseas assistance programmes.[26] Su Chenghe's contention that national soft power depends on the ability to build international institutions, set agendas, mobilize coalitions and fulfil commitments also reflect Nye's articulation of soft power diplomacy.[27] Nye does not go unchallenged though with scholars like Yongjin Zhang questioning his conceptualization of soft power and the compartmentalization of military power as the 'only' hard power.[28]

Given its objective of constructive engagement across stakeholders and situations, effective soft power demands dynamism and regular incorporation of 'new' elements. Chinese soft power is not an exception in this regard. This is evident from the notion taking on more aspects in addition to culture and ideology. The 'Beijing Consensus' is a case in point.[29] Many Chinese scholars now consider the development model an alternative to the 'Washington Consensus'.[30] They also claim that it can be regarded a component of China's soft power, given that several developing countries, as well as many from the developed world, remain impressed by the 'Chinese' model of economic growth and development. Beijing has begun publicizing the concept as well. In November 2009, a prominent Party-run publisher produced a 630-page volume titled *China Model: A New Development Model from the Sixty Years of the People's Republic* in Chinese. The following year in January came the more modest *China Model: Experience and Predicament* by Zheng Yong Nian Zhu. Another China-model book authored by Zhao Qizheng, a former top Party propaganda official, and John Naisbitt, an American futurologist, was launched in April 2010 and debated at an expo-related forum in Shanghai.[31] The point to be noted here is clearly the expansion of the

---

[26] Lei, 'Increase of China's Soft Power Raises Attention'.

[27] Su, 'China's Soft Power: An Example in the Relationship', 27–35.

[28] Military actions do have examples of peaceful and humanitarian applications, as was evident during the tsunami in Southeast Asia in 2004.

[29] The concept was first formalized by an American economist Joshua Cooper Ramo in a paper published by the British Foreign Policy Centre.

[30] Coined in 1989, the Washington Consensus refers to a set of broadly free market economic ideas, supported by prominent economists and international organizations, such as the IMF, the World Bank, the EU and the US.

[31] *The Economist*, 'The Beijing Consensus is to Keep Quiet'.

dynamic domain of soft power for increasing national appeal through a careful combination of culture and economics, both as distinct alternative to mainstream Western notions prevailing in modern times.

## Peaceful 'Rise' to Peaceful Development

China's soft power is intricately linked to the oft-repeated pronouncement of 'peaceful rise' by the Chinese establishment. While both concepts have evolved almost together, the backgrounds against which they have are different. Soft power evolved essentially for constructing a positive image of China with the international community while 'peaceful rise' was for allaying concerns about the 'China threat'. It was perceived as a concept negating use of force and was expected to impact the international system in a positive way as argued by Meng Yangqing.[32] Indeed, the use of 'peaceful development' has been prolific and associated with symbolism too, as during President Xi's announcement of a cut in the number of personnel in the PLA during China's celebration of the 70th anniversary of the Second World War in September 2015.

The domestic discussion of China's 'rise' began in 1995 led by academics like Shi Yin Hong from the People's University, using 'peaceful rise' to define China's foreign policy for assuaging international fears. In 1998, Yan Xue Tong and three other scholars published a book—*International Environment for China's Rise*—the first analytical work on China's 'rise'.[33] The concept was further pronounced later by Zheng Bi Jian, a Professor at the Central Party School, at the Boao Forum in 2003. Central Party publications like the *Outlook* (*Liao Wang*) and *Study Times* (*Xue Xi Shi Bao*) recommended the concept as 'correct and appropriate'.[34]

Considered a continuation of Jiang Zemin's 'three represents theory' propounded in 2001, many scholars and researchers were excited about the introduction of the construct, which, however, was double-edged. On one hand it never fails to stress China's 'rise' and strategic dominance, on the other, its tries to tamper the 'hard' aspect of the 'rise' by focusing

---

[32] Hongyi, 'China's Soft Power: New Developments and Challenges', 70.
[33] 'Zhong guo he ping jue qi wenti yan jiu zong shu' (Summary of Research Problems with China's 'Peaceful Rise').
[34] Hongyi and Lu, *China's Soft Power and International Relations*, 66.

on 'peaceful' and 'love for peace and culture', in essence soft power.[35] Soft power and 'peaceful rise' were eventually combined in 2004 in *Peaceful Rise of China* by Xia Li Ping and Jiang Xi Yuan. The book used culture to justify 'peaceful rise' and proposed a new theoretical construct containing traditional Chinese values, such as unity in diversity, peace and humanity, and further proposed that China's 'peaceful rise' would facilitate establishment of a fair and reasonable international system, different from the Western international world order. Other Chinese academics soon began espousing the concept with China actively promoting 'dragon culture' (*long wen hua*) and highlighting the spread of power from morality and morality from nature. It should be noted though that China's fourth generation leaders, Hu Jintao and Wen Jiabao, officially adopted 'peaceful development' modified from 'peaceful rise' to avoid the threatening connotation associated with 'rise'.

The best formal articulation of the notion was *China's Peaceful Development*, a white paper released in September 2011 by the Information Office of the State Council, outlining China's modern notion of soft power in the context of historical tradition driving the peaceful development policy. As noted in the paper, the concept 'carries forward the Chinese historical and cultural tradition'[36] and emphasizes 'China fully respects other countries' legitimate rights to protect their interests…'.[37]

As mentioned earlier, China's current leadership under President Xi Jinping appears eager to rationalize the 'peaceful' aspects of China's rise along with emphasis on culture. At the CPC's 'collective study session' speech in early 2013, President Xi called upon 'peaceful development' as a cornerstone for China's future development. He was of the view that by better coalescing domestic development with opening up to the outside world, by aligning China's development with that of the world, converging the interests of the Chinese people with those of the rest of

---

[35] This might explain China's fourth generation leaders, Hu Jintao and Wen Jiabao, modifying 'peaceful rise' to 'peaceful development', arguably for avoiding the threatening connotation associated with 'rise'.

[36] *China.org.cn*, 'China's Path of Peaceful Development'.

[37] *China.org.cn*, 'China's Foreign Policies for Pursuing'.

the world and enhancing mutually beneficial cooperation with other countries,[38] China would strengthen its position globally. The resolution adopted earlier at the 18th Congress of the Communist Party of China in November 2012 was also emphatic about upholding China's cultural heritage and improving cultural soft power.[39] The Communiqué of the Third Plenum of the 18th Party Congress held in November 2013 had similar emphasis and stressed cultural openness while strengthening 'national cultural soft power'.[40] The role of culture in underpinning the 'peaceful' aspect of China's rise and deployment of soft power is further evident from President Xi's address at a group study session of members of the Political Bureau of the CPC Central Committee in January 2014, where he called for a solid foundation for cultural soft power by deepening reforms in the cultural system, promoting socialist core values and pushing forward the cultural industry.[41] Later in November 2014, Xi again emphasised on 'peaceful development' during a work conference on foreign policy, while calling for a better understanding of the changing international developments and linking them to China's external environment.[42]

## Official Pronouncements

The Shanghai Institute of International Studies (SIIS), having close links with the Ministry of Foreign Affairs, was established as early as in 1960 for studying diplomacy. The decision was encouraged by the belief that Shanghai had more experts in the field and was relatively more 'open' to the outside world. SIIS was preceded by the China Institute of International Studies, formerly known as the University of International Relations, established in Beijing with a similar purpose.[43] Notwithstanding these institutes, it was not until relatively recently that soft power

---

[38]  Ho and Sun, 'Beijing's Renewed Resolve', 2.
[39]  *Xinhua*, 'Full Text of Resolution on CPC'.
[40]  *China Copyright and Media*, 'Communique of the 3rd Plenum'.
[41]  *Xinhua*, 'Xi: China to Promote Cultural Soft Power'.
[42]  *Xinhua*, 'Xi Eyes More Enabling Int'l Environment for China's Peaceful Development'.
[43]  Author had interviewed a Professor from the SIIS, Shanghai.

began being employed prominently in foreign policy for international engagement. The notion was introduced officially to the state policy-making establishment at the 13th group study session of the CPC Politburo in May 2004 on the back of the leadership's eagerness to employ culture and ideology for enhancing China's soft power.[44]

## Benign Image

The imbibing of soft power as a state policy came in the backdrop of the Chinese leadership's inclination to project a benign image. The New Security Concept[45] articulated by President Jiang Zemin in 1997 offered an alternative benign narrative of China's resurgence emphasising the commitment to 'good neighbourliness' and increasing security through greater diplomatic and economic interactions. Nearly eight years later, Hu Jintao added the 'harmonious world' adage underscoring China's commitment to peace and cooperation followed later by Xi Jinping who advocated a New Model of Major Country Initiative, reaffirming Beijing's attempt to reorganise relationships with major powers beyond its neighbourhood, especially the US. The model has two important messages: The first being the desire to be acknowledged a 'major power' by the US that would confirm China's major-power status; and the second, on China's seriousness in having cordial relationships with the US notwithstanding several differences. Xi's latest initiative was in line with a series of 'benign image' initiatives undertaken since Jiang Zemin (Table 2.1) and marked the irreversibility of the priority in China's external engagement policies.

---

[44] 'Ti sheng ruan shi li' (Enhance China's Soft Power).

[45] The end of the Cold War necessitated China's policymakers and the academics to revise China's national security strategy. In 1993, the definition of security was expanded with political, economic, defense and diplomatic priorities being included within its fold. While elevating security on par with 'high politics', interrelationship between internal and external security challenges was also sought. The 'New Security Concept' which was finally articulated in 1997 thus contained all the new defining elements which was to direct its policies towards its neighbours and countries beyond its immediate neighbourhood after the end of the Cold War. For details see Thayer, *The Borderlands of Southeast Asia*, 238.

**Table 2.1**
*Official Communications of 'Benign Image'*

| 1997 | New Security Concept articulated by President Jiang Zemin rejecting the 'Old Cold War security outlook' in favour of privileging mutual trust, benefit, equality, interdependence, cooperative security and international norms. |
| --- | --- |
| Since 2003 | 'Peaceful rise' giving way to 'peaceful development' indicating disapproval of use of threat because of 'peaceful intentions', limited national capabilities, historically peaceful outlook and development trajectory. |
| 2005 | President Hu Jintao added 'harmonious world' adage emphasizing 'the right of each country to select its own social system and path of development' thus communicating to the West by example that China be left alone. |
| 2011 | President Xi Jinping's New Model of Major Country Relations for avoiding conflicts and stressing mutual respect and win-win cooperation while underlining that 'we have never thought about pushing the US out of the [Asia Pacific] region'. |

*Source:* Goh (2014, 838).

## Public Diplomacy (PD)

China's increasing global eminence, integration into the world economy and the evolution of the contemporary international order convinced the Chinese leadership that 'China cannot do without the world, and the world cannot do without China'. Cultivating a benign image is in tune with its 'peaceful' resurgence for facilitating deeper integration with the world. The teachings of Confucius have become significant in this regard. Much discredited in mid-20th century China, Confucianism has been adopted by contemporary China, whether it be through Jiang Zemin's 'rule by virtue' (*yi de zhi guo*) or Hu Jintao's 'harmonious society' (*he xie she hui*). Indeed, Confucianism has ably guided China's vision of a 'harmonious world', as opposed to the Westphalian order. The vision emphasizes greater inter-state democracy, equitable distribution of wealth among nations, tolerance of political and cultural diversity and peaceful resolution of international disputes. Many Chinese intellectuals have also advanced the traditional Chinese ideal of *tianxia*—'all under heaven'—as a universally valid model of world politics[46] in contrast to the established notions of nation state, sovereignty and the international system.

With the official endorsement of soft power in 2004, the concept has been discussed and debated extensively among policymakers. In 2008, Li Chang Chun, a member of the Standing Committee of the Politburo in charge of cultural affairs and propaganda, called for utilization of cultural resources, enhancement of soft power and expansion of the Chinese cultural industry. In March 2010, the Chinese Foreign Minister declared that PD needed to be made stronger in China's global diplomacy and encouraged Chinese diplomats to 'reach out to the public, the universities and the media' to introduce China's policies.[47] Immediately thereafter, in July 2010, the CPC Politburo held the 22nd group study session on cultural reforms. Li's proposals were formally incorporated into the Party's plan for the 12th Five Year programme in October 2010,[48] paving the way for President Hu to declare culture as a key component of China's national power.[49]

While the leadership's efforts to imbibe soft power were underway, PD had a somewhat late start. This, however, is not to suggest that there were no earlier instances of PD. Way back in 1975, Mao Zedong invited two foreigners to Shaanxi for introducing the CPC to them. These efforts, which continued for a few years, came to a halt with the Tiananmen Square incident, greatly tarnishing China's image. China revisited its PD policy after 1989 and established the State Council Information Office (SCIO) for the purpose. In addition to the SCIO, the Foreign Propaganda Office of the CPC also advices on PD plan.[50] The formal conceptual induction of PD, as a part of the national soft power strategy happened

---

[46] Zhao, *Tian Xia System: An Introduction*.

[47] *Xinhua*, 'Yang Jiechi: Public Diplomacy is Now Born Upon Demand'.

[48] Hongyi, 'China's Cultural Diplomacy', 4.

[49] 'Hu Jintao: Deepen Reform'.

[50] Hooghe, 'The Rise of China's Public Diplomacy'.

in 2007, when Zhao Qizheng, Member of the 16th CPC Central Committee, introduced the concept at the Chinese People's Political Consultative Conference (CPPCC), the top political advisory body in China. Since then, the leadership has embarked on efforts for linking PD to soft power as part of its global outreach strategy. The G20 summit at London in April 2009 was among the first such occasions, where China set up a press centre for handling news inquiries and conveying messages. Soon after, in July 2009, President Hu conveyed to Chinese diplomats the urgency of adopting PD and CD for conveying the right message internationally.[51]

More steps followed. In 2009 itself, the PD Section in the Ministry of Foreign Affairs was upgraded to the PD Office for guiding and coordinating PD efforts including managing more than two hundred websites.[52] In 2010, the Ministry set up a Consultative Committee on PD, with several high-ranking diplomats[53] for advising and participating in planning, implementation and assessment of PD efforts.[54] The *Public Diplomacy Quarterly* was launched in the same year by the Foreign Affairs Committee of the CPPCC with Zhao Qi Zheng, the former Director of the Information Office of the State Council, as the editor-in-chief.[55] These official efforts were complemented by establishment of research and teaching institutes on PD, including a research centre in the Beijing Foreign Studies University. The centre aims to become an academic exchange platform for gathering resources on China's practice of PD and establish an academic brand of the Beijing Foreign Studies University for the rest of the world.[56] In addition, the China Public Diplomacy Association was created in January 2013. Comprising former ambassadors and other strategic experts, the association is mandated to

---

[51] *People.cn.*, 'China's Public Diplomacy: Let the World Understand a Real China'.
[52] Hongyi, 'China's Soft Power: New Developments and Challenges', 6.
[53] Leaders like Zhou Wen Zhong, Chen Jian, Wu Jian Min and Liu Gui Jin are a few names to reckon with.
[54] *China News*, 'Consultative Committee of the Ministry of Foreign Affairs is Revealed'.
[55] Hongyi, 'China's Soft Power: New Developments and Challenges', 7.
[56] *People's Daily Online*, 'China's First Public Diplomacy Research Center'.

'encourage social and public sentiment for developing ties with foreign countries'.[57]

The significance of PD is also evident from the first PD report '*zhong guo gong gong wai jiao yan jue bao gao*' (China's Public Foreign Relations Research Report) published in 2012. With contributions from several Chinese researchers and reflecting varied perspectives, the report highlights China's new approach to foreign relations envisaging active participation by the people (*quan min wai jiao*) and voluntary organizations. The report also underlines *ren ben wei* ('people first' concept) signalling contemporary Chinese diplomacy's priority on building relations among people, not just between countries, thereby underpinning the salience of greater people-to-people communication in external engagement. The report draws upon ancient Chinese philosopher Meng Zi, arguably the most famous Confucian after Confucius himself, for vindicating greater engagement with people. Greater people-to-people contacts are also consistent with the 'going out' of China's culture emphasized in the 12th Five Year Plan (2011–15) resulting in extensive use of culture for engaging people—a hallmark of China's soft power strategy noticed in various parts of the world and discussed in later chapters.

There is a little doubt about PD being a relatively new concept in China compared with its much longer history of deployment by the Anglo-Saxon world. While being new, the unique aspect of Chinese PD is in its efforts to implant new concepts and impart 'Chinese' flavours to the latter. The leadership has regular discussions with academics on approaches and instruments that can best serve national interest. One of these discussions in March 2012 proposed the establishment of a PD association within the CPPCC along with instituting training programmes for its members.[58] Establishing a think tank specifically on PD is likely to be the next step.

The discussions on PD among the Chinese academia also focus on its perceived limitations, particularly with respect to certain neighbours and big powers. Even the leadership realizes this limitation with Vice Foreign Minister Fu Ying pointing to the lack of experience 'in dealing

---

[57] *China Daily*, 'China to Boost Public Diplomacy, Exchanges'.
[58] Jin 'China's Public Diplomacy at Crossroads'.

with the public and media agencies'[59] as a factor creating distorted perceptions about China's foreign policy posturing. An illustrative example is Myanmar's suspension of Myitsone dam project on Irrawaddy River being developed by the China Power Investment Corp. While the project on completion would have exported 90 per cent of its output to China, the fact that it was widely reported to have been called off due to local protests, irked China indicating to the leadership that these reactions '… acts as a reminder that the PD of China still leaves much to be desired'.[60] In yet another instance, on the occasion of the US President Obama's visit to Australia in 2011 for announcing Washington's plan to use Darwin as a new centre of operations in Asia, many scholars questioned why extra-regional actors are still being allowed greater space by a regional actor (Australia) when Chinese PD has attempted to effectively engage Canberra, and whether this reflects adversely on the quality of Chinese PD.[61]

Notwithstanding these observations, China shows no sign of diluting its focus on PD which is proceeding along with the emphasis on cultural development and soft power. The last few years under Xi have witnessed further development of a distinct 'Chinese' approach to PD. In an article based on President Xi Jinping's speech at the National Propaganda and Ideology Work Conference, Cai Mingzhao, Director of the SCIO, reflected on this new approach calling upon policymakers in China to be more attentive to the 'receiving' side of PD by taking closer look at how Chinese messages are received by audiences abroad rather than just focusing on dissemination of information on China.[62] This again demonstrates the sensitivity of the Chinese leadership to overseas people's perceptions and the willingness to change focus.

## CONCLUSION

The Chinese leadership and scholars have worked together for evolving a soft power strategy which has its roots in history, and is expected to

---

[59] Beibei, 'Public Diplomacy Gains Ground', 5.
[60] Fuller, 'Myanmar Backs Down, Suspending Dam Project'.
[61] Johnson and Calmes, 'US Making Presence Felt in Beijing's Backyard', 1.
[62] *China Copyright and Media*, 'China's Foreign Propaganda Chief Outlines'.

suit China's contemporary national interest. While projecting a benign image has driven the strategy, attaining rapid economic growth and modernization remains the top priority. The leadership will focus on reforms that will help in achieving the long-term national goal of transforming Chinese society into a 'little prosperity' (*xiaokang*) by 2020—an idea presented at the 16th CPC Congress in 2002 and later found resonance in Xi Jinping's China dream which is about its people, their well-being and economic prosperity. It is not entirely clear how good a fit the emphasis on soft power and its strategy is in this regard, given views that the strategy was not well-thought out and the leadership is probably pursuing it zealously essentially for achieving economic goals.[63] Indeed, economic goals do rationalize China's pursuit of an active soft power policy even if the leadership might not make it that explicit in official policy pronouncements. Securing peaceful external environment for economic growth necessitates employment of soft power for benign image and establishing the credibility of 'peaceful development'. Both cultural engagement and PD would remain important in this regard through combination of the 'traditional' with the 'modern'.[64]

The Chinese discourse on soft power is not uni-dimensional with the realists having differences with the Constructivists. While this Chapter has primarily reflected the latter thoughts, alternative perceptions exist, particularly on culture, with distinct segments of mainstream intellectual opinion treating culture in realist terms. These views visualize PRC locked in realist competition with the West, including the US 'not only in military and economic affairs but also in cultural affairs',[65] thus proving counterfactual to China's 'peaceful development'. Indeed, scholars like Pan Zhongqi and Huang Renwei have proposed a realist concept of 'geo-cultural strategy' emphasizing 'realist competitions amongst states operating on a geographic plane in the realm of culture'.[66]

---

[63] As noted by the author in her interviews with Chinese experts.

[64] Author interviewed Qi Huaigao, Research Assistant Professor, Institute of International Studies, Fudan University, Shanghai, in 2010.

[65] Lynch, 'Securitizing Culture in Chinese Foreign Policy Debates', 632.

[66] Pan and Huang, 'China's Geo-Cultural Strategy', 44–7.

The current discourse on China's soft power cannot, however, afford to overlook the issues involved in communication of soft power that often make it appear prosaic and formulaic. As explained briefly in Chapter 1, this might well be a result of the history of state communication in China, where the Communist Party's articulation of culture and state-building was never devoid of national interests, which, inter alia, included expanding the social and political command of the Party. The inherent characteristics of such a pattern of state communication appears to have spilled over to state actors and institutions involved in current external engagement and soft power outreach. The continuing use of propaganda in soft power cannot avoid the impression of such power being, occasionally at least, expression of the Chinese state's overt nationalistic posture, particularly when Deng Xiaoping's famous expression, 'keep a low profile and bide its time while getting something accomplished' (*tao guang yang hui, you suo zuo wei*) is gradually being replaced by greater activism on regional and global issues like the South China Sea, which concerns China's core national interest. Making soft power more effective and achieve its true potential, in line with what its exponents have repeatedly articulated at various points in history, is going to be a major challenge for China at a time when a 'confident' modern China is aware of its eminence in the global order and eager to play a leading role in global affairs. Achieving the former, however, might call for substantive rethinking within the Chinese establishment on greater nuancing of state communication and radical reform of institutions and actors involved in soft power communication. The search for a 'benign image' needs to be backed by the rethink and reform if China aims to blend soft power diplomacy with heightened activism in regional and global affairs. How China addresses the challenge is what the world would watch out for.

# PART II

# Chinese Soft Power:
# Regional Studies

China's Soft Power:
Regional Studies

# 3

# South Asia: Expanding Influence Through Economic Engagement

The southern region of the Asian continent—South Asia—includes eight countries: Afghanistan, Bangladesh, Bhutan, India, Maldives, Nepal, Pakistan and Sri Lanka. While the region has several internal complexities including territorial disputes, ethnic conflicts and religious funda-mentalism, its geographic location and proximity to China makes it an important region for engagement with Beijing. South Asia's regional dynamics is heavily influenced by India—the region's largest country and a major Asian power and a country with which China has a complex relation including unresolved territorial issues.

Beijing's engagement of South Asia is a typical example of China's leadership's effort to convert its resources into power behaviour: gener-ous employment of various soft power tools underlining China's desire to project its benignity, competence and charisma.[1] While infrastruc-ture-building, trade and investment, education and high-level visits are prominent in the larger strategic application of soft tools, cultural initiatives are relatively less. Nonetheless, economic initiatives combined with enhanced people-to-people communication are aimed at creating a 'virtuous' China brand in the region. On the other hand, the various soft power tools employed for engaging the region also highlight China's efforts to mitigate some of its major domestic challenges ranging from economic development to internal security through greater strategic linkages with South Asia.

---

[1] Nye, *The Future of Power*, 92.

China's neighbourhood policy, of which South Asia is an important part given its prominent position in China's neighbourhood, is directed towards ensuring and enabling a peaceful external environment 'conducive to its hard interests in economic development, national security and geopolitical position in its "near abroad"'.[2] This chapter reviews the main drivers of China's engagement with South Asia, which are often distinct from those identified elsewhere. China's relations with India are discussed separately in Chapter 10 with the focus of this chapter being on the rest of the region.

## CHINESE STRATEGIC PERSPECTIVE OF SOUTH ASIA

China's engagement with South Asia has been largely inspired by its vision of 'Look West'.[3] The WDS is integral to 'Look West' and aims to connect the economically backward and landlocked Western region of the mainland to new markets and economic hubs on its west. Other objectives of the WDS that make South Asia vital for China's strategic goals include getting access to energy and mineral resources and developing an integrated regional transport infrastructure comprising road and seaport facilities in different South Asian countries that would provide China's west deeper access to South and West Asia. Effective implementation of the WDS entails cooperation of the South Asian countries making it necessary for China to cultivate a benign image in the region.

Launched in 1999, the WDS—a dedicated effort for correcting regional imbalance by facilitating economic development in the West— marks efforts of successive Chinese leaderships in altering China's earlier focus on the coastal areas as the key drivers of its trade and business with the rest of the world. The latter, while leading to flourishing of the coastal provinces and cities, was an inherently 'unbalanced'

---

[2] Zhimin and Zhongqi, 'China in Its Neighbourhood'.
[3] According to Wang Jisi, a Chinese strategist who has worked with many Chinese leaders, the scripting of the new 'Look West' policy towards South Asia and beyond is a deliberate Chinese strategy at 'rebalancing'. For details see *Spotlight*, 'China's New Look West Policy to Give Primacy to India'.

strategy for economic growth and led to the hinterland and the West lagging way behind the prosperous East.

Underdevelopment in the West has been one of the several factors compounding China's challenges in managing ethnic tensions and conflicts in the region, particularly in the provinces of Xinjiang and Tibet. These are the only provinces in the mainland witnessing ethnic instability and anti-establishment protests for several years. These unrests have the potential of disrupting the development plans for the region. Lack of development has been a major factor behind the public discontent visible in the region as pointed out by the former President Hu Jintao in his speech at Xinjiang in 2009: '[T]he fundamental way to resolve the Xinjiang problem is to expedite development in Xinjiang'.[4] Economic dividends flowing from the WDS can subdue the discontent of local communities, particularly the minorities, and help China in pursuing the larger strategic goal of economic consolidation of the region with other parts of Asia.

Both Xinjiang and Tibet have contiguous geographical borders with countries from South Asia. Xinjiang shares its southwestern borders with Afghanistan, Pakistan and India, while Tibet has common borders with India, Nepal and Bhutan. These countries, therefore, become important cogs in the strategic vision of China's 'Look West' and the WDS. An economically prosperous and stable Xinjiang can be a source of substantial strategic benefits for China. It can be the mainland's gateway to the energy-rich Middle East and Africa through Afghanistan and Pakistan in South Asia. Gwadar and Karachi ports in Pakistan can link the western region deeper with global trade by facilitating the movement of commodities.[5] Afghanistan and Pakistan can be vital sources of mineral resources for China as these are part of the 'Tethyan Magmatic Arc' that extends from Mongolia to Pakistan to Turkey and is a rich reservoir of minerals such as copper, gold, zinc, lead, iron ore and

---

[4] Wei and Cuifen, 'China's New Policy in Xinjiang'.

[5] The Gwadar port in Pakistan built by China is particularly significant for Xinjiang and other Western provinces by providing them access to crude oil from the Gulf and the Middle East, as opposed to the cumbersome alternative of obtaining the same supplies from the eastern coast. For details, see Siddiqa, 'Expansion by Stealth'.

aluminium.[6] Further, Bangladesh, located at the head of Bay of Bengal, provides China access to the largest Bay in the region, which can facilitate integration of Yunnan—another major province in China's western region—with South and Southeast Asia while providing maritime access to other landlocked regions.

The security challenge becomes an integral part of the WDS in the context of Tibet. Late Dawa Norbu, an eminent scholar on Tibet, and a Tibetan himself, linked China's security to the Tibetan concern, and the importance of India in the context. He believed: '[China] feels that the Himalayas alone in this nuclear age are not enough to guarantee its national security, especially in view of Tibet's strategic location. [It], therefore, ideally wants a China of small, preferably pro-Chinese, neighbours on the cis-Himalayan region separating the two Asian giants'.[7] Beijing's engagement with Nepal, as well as Bhutan, needs to be viewed in the context of the Chinese sensitivity to the Tibetan issue. Engaging Nepal proactively is important for achieving strategic objectives with respect to Tibet, such as discouraging pro-independence Tibetan protests in the country. China's intent to stabilize its relation with Bhutan is also seen as part of the WDS: 'China is considering its relation with Bhutan as part of its "Western development strategy" that could allow Tibet to regain a central position in the Himalayan region'.[8]

While the Himalayan countries of South Asia and those in the region's west, such as Afghanistan and Pakistan, assume significance in China's 'Look West' vision, the rest of South Asia, particularly Sri Lanka, Maldives (and India) become important given the strategic vitality of the Indian Ocean, particularly the sea lanes carrying more than 80 per cent of the world's seaborne trade in oil.[9] The strategic criticality and the quest for energy security make it imperative for China to engage Sri Lanka and Maldives, and of course, India. The possibility of China–India–Sri Lanka trilateral cooperation for promoting peace, stability and

---

[6] Ibid.
[7] Norbu, 'Chinese Strategic Thinking on Tibet'.
[8] Mathew, 'China-South Asia Strategic Engagements'.
[9] Ranasinghe, 'Why the Indian Ocean Matters'.

common prosperity of the region announced by the Chinese Foreign Ministry[10] is also a strategic move for gaining deeper foothold in the Indian Ocean Region (IOR).

While the various strategic objectives discussed above encourage China's deeper engagement of the region, South Asian countries are also driven by their regional strategic and national interests in developing closer ties with China. This resonates with A.F.K. Organski's power transition theory: International politics posits a hierarchical international system that has a dominant power at the top with lesser powers following.[11] Visualized in the context of South Asia, this reflects India as the dominant power of the region and several 'middle powers' vying for greater strategic space and status. The process encourages the traditional 'middle powers' (at the regional level) to adopt a specific strategy of coalition-building and cooperation and empowering them to act as 'catalyzer' or 'facilitator'. Indeed, in this regard, 'middle powers' such as Bangladesh and Sri Lanka are valuable cooperation partners for larger pan-regional powers.[12] This complements China's strategic goals and it looks forward to engaging the 'middle powers' in South Asia.[13]

## ECONOMIC ENGAGEMENT

China's deepening economic engagement appears to have led to positive perceptions about it in both Bangladesh and Pakistan.[14] The bilateral Free Trade Agreement (FTA)[15] with Pakistan, signed in November 2006, provides preferential access to exports from both sides into each other's

---

[10] *China Daily*, 'China Urges Sri Lanka'.
[11] Nolte, 'How to Compare Regional Powers', 886.
[12] Ibid., 892.
[13] A parallel reflection of an identical function with roles reversed is that of India engaging the middle powers in northeast Asia (e.g., Korea and Mongolia).
[14] *Pew Research Centre Publications*, 'China's Image'.
[15] China's FTA strategy indicates its willingness to participate in economic globalization and regional integration, apart from pushing all-round domestic economic reforms in China. FTAs are also effective tools to influence global economic rules.

markets.[16] Both countries are also contemplating a Free Trade Zone (FTZ) for boosting trade and cross-border investments.[17] China's FTA with Bangladesh is also in the pipeline. Bangladesh is China's third largest trade partner in South Asia and both are members of the Asia-Pacific FTA (AFTA)[18] that provides duty-free access to several Bangladeshi exports in the Chinese market. Along with trade, Chinese investments have increased significantly in both Pakistan and Bangladesh over time.[19]

China's economic ties with Sri Lanka have also improved considerably with the Sri Lankan establishment viewing China as a key actor in the country's economic development given that the Chinese companies run 'at very high efficiency and at the lowest costs'.[20] China surpassed the US to become Sri Lanka's largest trade partner in 2013 after India. A Sino-Sri Lanka FTA, which was to be signed in June 2015, is at an advanced stage and would significantly deepen bilateral trade ties. Both countries have begun trading in financial services with the *Yuan* settlement service launched in Sri Lanka helping companies in the region to open and maintain Yuan accounts and transact in the currency.[21] The deepening of the economic partnership, however, has been accompanied by complications arising from the escalation in Sri Lanka's external indebtedness inflicted by high-cost Chinese loans for building domestic infrastructure, particularly ports.[22]

---

[16] 'Free Trade Agreement'. Available at: http://www.commerce.gov.pk/PCFTA. asp (accessed on 1 February 2010).

[17] A lease agreement is being processed to the China Overseas Port Holding for the establishment of the FTZ in Gwadar. The FTZ is seen as indispensable for the success of the port as they are an integral part of all modern ports and is expected to ensure optimal use of the deep seaport. For details, see *Dawn*, 'Free Trade Zone in Gwadar'.

[18] AFTA, signed in 1992, is a trade block and consists of 10 members: Brunei, Indonesia, Malaysia, Philippines, Singapore, Thailand, Vietnam Laos, Myanmar and Cambodia.

[19] Chinese investments in Pakistan span a variety of areas including telecommunication, electricity, engineering, construction and mining. Apart from infrastructure, Chinese investments in Bangladesh are increasing in textiles.

[20] *Today*, 'Made by China' Stamp'.

[21] *China Daily*, 'Silk Route Builds Bridge'.

[22] Smith, 'China's Investments in Sri Lanka'.

As discussed earlier, Nepal is a vital regional actor in the context of China's WDS. Indeed, both China and India have been proactively engaging with Nepal given their respective strategic and security interests. While an FTA is being worked out with Nepal, China has become the topmost investor in the landlocked country. A large chunk of Chinese investments into Nepal is in various infrastructure projects, more on which has been discussed in the later sections.[23]

## Infrastructure

Creating new infrastructure assets and upgrading old ones have been a key component of China's involvement in South Asia. Much of these activities are visible in Pakistan where China Mobile is engaged in developing local networks and telecom infrastructure for its *Zong* brand and is able to create job opportunities in the process.[24] Apart from telecom, rail connectivity is another important sector witnessing significant Chinese investments in Pakistan. The Chinese strategic interest in better rail connectivity is significant given the objectives of the WDS of providing faster access to China's western region to Central Asia and the Persian Gulf states, through South Asia. Beijing's Belt and Road Initiative is a step towards achieving better connectivity with a view to initiate its economic transformation. South Asian countries like Pakistan become critical in such projects, both for economic dividends, which are mutual, and for geostrategic factors.

The China–Pakistan Economic Corridor (CPEC) is an important component of the OBOR project and is being visualized by the Pakistan Government as a prospect that will not only open a long stagnant economy but unleash 'Pakistan's potential in its labor force, accessibility of goods, and role in international trade'.[25] Regional connectivity and

---

[23] Apart from its salience in the WDS, China's engagement and economic role in Nepal is likely to increase over time given Nepal's pursuit of the 'One China policy' considered critical for Beijing's inking of any diplomatic and economic relationship with any given country.

[24] 'Pakistan Welcomes more Chinese Telecom Investment'.

[25] Munter, 'Anticipating China's "One-Belt-One Road" in South Asia'.

China–Pakistan road linkages are expected to improve significantly from the CPEC. The building of the Corridor is expected to significantly alter the quality of regional transportation network.[26] The Chinese financial commitment to the project also reaffirms the strategic priority it attaches to relations with Pakistan. While the Corridor would arguably signify China's largest infrastructure involvement in the South Asian region, Pakistan has been a major beneficiary of Chinese support in the development of energy, infrastructure and mining projects under the Pakistan–China Joint Five Year Economic and Trade Cooperation Plan.[27] These include the Three Gorges Corporation's commitment to assist Pakistan in developing several energy projects.[28] The Chinese-built Gwadar port is another key Chinese infrastructure investment in Pakistan aimed at increasing its access to Asia's maritime routes.

The Chinese involvement in regional infrastructure for expanding its linkages with South Asia and further on to West Asia is evident from its infrastructure-building efforts in Afghanistan (e.g., rail link from Tajikistan to Afghanistan to Pakistan's Gwadar port and the Karakorum highway) as a part of its role in the country's reconstruction. China has written off all matured debts that Afghanistan owed to China.[29] On the basis of the bilateral Agreement on Trade and Economic Cooperation signed in 2006, China is helping Afghanistan in education, agriculture and administrative capacity-building.[30]

[26] During his visit to Pakistan in April 2015, Xi Jinping announced, '[T]he building of the China–Pakistan corridor concerns, and has bearing on, the national strategy [and livelihoods] of the two countries and their long-term development'. The CPEC is expected to improve infrastructure along this corridor helping the transit of goods and services from the Arabian Sea and the Indian Ocean to China. For details, see *The Wall Street Journal*, 'China's Xi Jinping Launches Investment Deal in Pakistan'.

[27] *Embassy of the People's Republic of China in the Islamic Republic of Pakistan*, 'PM Gilani Concludes Successful Visit to China'.

[28] *China Daily*, 'Shopping for Power'.

[29] *Ministry of Foreign Affairs of the People's Republic of China*, 'Remarks of Chinese Vice Foreign Minister Song Tao'.

[30] *Official Website of SCO Summit*, 'China to Provide 150 mln Yuan'.

Given the rich reservoir of untapped mineral resources in Afghanistan, China's commercial interest in Afghanistan is hardly surprising. Many Chinese companies are also active in Pakistan in the provinces of Khyber Pakhtunkhwa (mining), Sindh (mainly oil, gas and mining) and Balochistan (mining and road construction). Indeed, greater economic presence in the Pakistan–Afghanistan region, as opposed to military presence, is a visible aspect of Chinese diplomacy in the region, as pointed out by Ayesha Siddiqa, a noted strategic scholar and an expert on Pakistan. She specifically refers to China's infrastructure-building efforts in both countries as reflective of Beijing's strategic agendas. She argues: '[I]nstead of providing general economic assistance or military support, China is bringing direct investments into the two countries, focusing particularly in areas that are most beneficial to Chinese interests'.[31] She further points out: '[T]hese projects are meant to be mutually beneficial. However, the extent of the relative benefits for the recipient states is an issue worth evaluating'.[32]

Apart from Pakistan and Afghanistan, other countries in South Asia are also benefitting from Chinese infrastructure projects. Indeed, South Asia's deficient infrastructure, particularly poor physical connectivity, has been a major hindrance to growth of intra-regional trade and commerce. Lack of good roads, ports, advanced telecommunication networks and adequate electricity is conspicuous across the region. The infrastructure deficit has allowed China the opportunity of creating strategic space and goodwill in the region by assisting individual countries in creating new infrastructure capacities. China's growing strategic influence in the region flowing from its role in addressing the regional infrastructure deficit is visible from the regional dynamics that now has considerable support for China becoming a member of the South Asian Association of Regional Cooperation (SAARC).[33] A bigger role by China in augmenting regional infrastructure through initiatives

---

[31] Ibid.
[32] Ibid.
[33] Sri Lanka, Pakistan and Maldives are supporting Beijing in joining SAARC.

such as the OBOR[34] and the AIIB[35] is likely to influence the dynamic more favourably.

Both Sri Lanka and Bangladesh are benefitting from China's support in infrastructure development through a variety of projects. Major projects in Sri Lanka include the much-discussed Hambantota seaport[36] and upgrading the container terminal at Colombo port. Sri Lanka's strategic geographic location on the maritime route connecting Asia and Europe makes it an important country for engagement with China from the perspective of greater access to commercial oil routes in the IOR. China is also contributing to the development of other components of domestic infrastructure within Sri Lanka (e.g., the Matara–Beliatta section of the Matara-Kataragama railway extension project,[37] the Norochcholai thermal power plant and the Lotus telecommunication tower in Colombo) including its support to post-war reconstruction in Sri Lanka since 2009. Infrastructure capacities are also being expanded by Chinese businesses like the Huawei Technologies engaged in augmenting telecommunication services.

---

[34] The OBOR [*yidai-yilu*] initiative comprises the Silk Road Economic Belt—a programme to build land transportation corridors that connect China to Europe and all other major Eurasian subregions including South Asia—and the 21st century Maritime Silk Road—a port development initiative to broaden Chinese trade channels targeting the maritime regions of Southeast Asia, South Asia, the Middle East, East Africa and the Mediterranean.

[35] The AIIB was proposed by China in 2013 and launched in 2014 in Beijing to support infrastructure construction in the Asia-Pacific region.

[36] The Hambantota port, along with the Gwadar port in Pakistan, is often cited as examples of China's efforts to strategically encircle India by building facilities at different coastal locations in South Asia. Hambantota was originally offered to India for development. India, however, refrained from doing so on both diplomatic and economic grounds. The Indian Peace Keeping Force's (IPKF's) involvement in the ethnic conflict in Sri Lanka had contributed to an adverse perception of India, which the latter did not wish to aggravate by building a 'military facility' in Hambantota. For details, see *MarineBuzz.com*, 'China Funds Sri Lanka Hambantota Port Development Project' (2007). India's reluctance eventually led Sri Lankan authorities to approach China enabling it to participate actively in a major infrastructure project in the island state and expanding its soft power outreach.

[37] *People's Daily Online*, 'China Grants 200 mln USD'.

Infrastructure-building in Sri Lanka, apart from reflecting pursuit of China's core strategic interests in South Asia, has brought to light the downsides of Chinese economic assistance for some of the recipient countries. Sri Lanka is probably the first such example in South Asia where China's political and economic support to the Mahinda Rajapaksa Government—particularly the latter extended at a time when similar support was hardly forthcoming from other major donors—is beginning to extract a heavy cost. Not only has Sri Lanka experienced a sharp increase in its external debt due to costly Chinese loans—whose conditions it was not in a positon to negotiate due to political gratitude— but debt servicing obligations also have shrunk the macroeconomic space for other development expenditure by the current Sirisena Government. The indebtedness of Sri Lanka is of such a magnitude that its strategic support to the OBOR is confirmed making Sri Lanka a certain, if reluctant, 'ally' in the OBOR. Doubts have also begun to be raised over the usefulness of Chinese-funded infrastructure in Sri Lanka. While the Colombo port has indeed benefitted and reached new levels of operational efficiency, the Hambantota seaport and international airport hardly have traffic for generating revenue to pay off the large debts they are saddled with.[38]

Telecommunication, energy, health and physical infrastructure are the areas in which Chinese presence has become conspicuous in Bangladesh. China has contributed to building several 'friendship' bridges[39] for improving domestic connectivity within Bangladesh.[40] Bangladesh's location near the Bay of Bengal makes it an important gateway in the larger strategic vision of China's WDS for providing the landlocked western region access to the sea. This explains China's proposed technical and financial support for a deep seaport at Sonadia in Chittagong. Chinese support is also visible in a large number of projects covering various significant industries in Bangladesh. These include, inter alia, the Shahjalal Fertilizer Factory in Sylhet being built by the China National

---

[38] Shepard, 'The Story Behind the World's Emptiest International Airport'.

[39] For instance, the Angaria bridge on the Kirtirasa river and the Kazirtek bridge on the Dhaka–Barisal Highway.

[40] *China Daily*, 'Silk Route Builds Bridge'.

Complete Plant Import and Export Corporation, which is one of the largest foreign investments by China and is expected to help Bangladesh in significantly reducing its dependence on urea imports.[41]

China's infrastructure development efforts in Maldives and Nepal—two relatively smaller countries in South Asia—are also significant and driven by strategic motives of gaining greater access to new markets and resources. Like Sri Lanka, Maldives's strategic geography of being located in the Indian Ocean, and midway between the Middle East and Southeast Asia, makes it an important country to engage with.[42] Nepal, as mentioned earlier, is also critical from the perspective of the WDS. Land connectivity projects have been the main areas of Chinese involvement in Nepal,[43] apart from hydel power (Three Gorges Corporation's Seti hydel power) projects.[44]

## Humanitarian Assistance

China has been proactive in supporting South Asian countries during their periods of hardship inflicted by natural calamities. The Tsunami in the Indian Ocean in 2004 was one of the early instances of China's humanitarian assistance to the region through medical assistance and food supplies provided to Sri Lanka.[45] China extended a further helping hand by attending to difficulties faced by internally displaced civilians during the ethnic conflict of 2009 in Sri Lanka. Bangladesh, which is heavily vulnerable to the catastrophic effects of cyclones, has found

---

[41] Other major Chinese industrial investments include the Barapukuria power project of the China National Machinery Import and Export Corporation and the collaborative venture with Bangladesh Small and Cottage Industries Corporation (BSCIC) for developing a leather park for leather exports.

[42] China has built the new Ministry of Foreign Affairs building and the national museum in Male and provided concessional loans for housing projects. China has built the Ministry of Foreign Affairs building in Maldives as well as the national museum. It has also provided concessional loans for building the 1,000 Housing Units Project.

[43] It includes upgrading the 115 km Araniko highway linking Nepal with China, constructing four cross-country north–south highways, rail link connecting the Tibetan capital of Lhasa to Khasa on the Sino-Nepal border and so on.

[44] *China Daily*, 'Shopping for Power', 1.

[45] *World Food Programme*, 'WFP Lauds Landmark Chinese Aid Shipment'.

China a prompt partner in relief and rehabilitation on various occasions [e.g., cyclones Sidr (2007) and Alia (2009)]. Similarly, Pakistan, received generous humanitarian aid support during the calamitous floods ravaging its southern regions in 2011. The latest occasion witnessing China's intervention on humanitarian grounds in South Asia was during the devastating Nepal earthquake of April 2014. Apart from sending medical and rescue teams, China also dispatched a large military personnel and members of armed forces—the largest such group it has sent to foreign soil for humanitarian aid missions since 1949.[46]

China's economic engagement of the South Asian region reveals a mix of commercial engagement through trade and strategic initiatives in addressing the institutional and natural downsides of the region—the infrastructure deficit and vulnerability to disasters. Both the latter have enabled China to deepen its strategic foothold in the region during the last decade while trying to improve its image in South Asia as well. Some quantitative reflections of the 'impact' of China's soft power efforts in the region come out through a Pew Research Centre study conducted in July 2014 that found it having a favourable perception rating in Bangladesh and Pakistan. However, the perception could well be country specific and is not backed by large enough evidence to be taken as a regional perception. From a Chinese vantage point, the greater geostrategic objective of maintaining 'all weather' friendships, like that with Pakistan, and winning new allies—Bangladesh, Nepal and Sri Lanka—appear to have been achieved to a reasonably satisfactory extent. While popular impressions in a country like Sri Lanka might not necessarily be rosy about China, the latter has been able to convert the region's weakness—lack of external funds for public goods, primarily infrastructure—into an opportunity and has successfully 'tied' most of the region into obligatory reciprocation, flowing from gratitude.

## Regional Connectivity Initiatives

Infrastructure and regional connectivity would undoubtedly remain major planks of China's economic engagement with its neighbours,

---

[46] *Xinhua*, 'China Focus: China Continues to Help Quake-stricken Nepal'.

including South Asia. This is evident from the OBOR initiative announced by President Xi in September 2013. The plan proposes to bring together China, Central Asia, Russia and Europe (the Baltic), thus linking China with the Persian Gulf and the Mediterranean Sea through Central Asia and the IOR. China's access to new markets and resources from the project will indeed be phenomenal and would add new expansive dimensions to the scope of the WDS. China has attempted to gain greater solidarity and consensus on the project by emphasizing a 'common destiny' for Asia that focuses on shared development and intertwines China's prosperity and growth with its neighbours. The strategy is expected to connect neighbours, including South Asia, to the 'China Dream'[47] and conjure the dream for all based on *cheng* (earnestness), *hui* (benefit) *qin* (closeness) and *rong* (inclusiveness).

In addition to the OBOR, another regional initiative like the development of the Bangladesh–China–India–Myanmar (BCIM) Economic Corridor is also expected to provide a fillip to infrastructure capacities in South Asia. The BCIM can produce substantive economic gains for the region through cross-country collaborations in energy: Substantial opportunities exist given the untapped resources in the members (e.g., natural gas reserves in Myanmar, hydrocarbons in Bangladesh, hydroelectric and mineral resources in Northeast India and coal reserves in East Indian states such as Odisha, Chhattisgarh and Jharkhand and China's Yunnan province).[48] As the largest actor in economic initiatives, China would, undoubtedly, benefit from the economic gains produced

---

[47] Addressing the First Session of the 12th National People's Congress, 17 March, 2013, President Xi Jinping articulated:

> [T]he Chinese Dream of the rejuvenation of the Chinese nation means that we will make China prosperous and strong, rejuvenate the nation, and bring happiness to the Chinese people. They both embody the ideals of the Chinese people today and represent our forefather's glorious tradition of untiring pursuit of progress.

The dream aims to build a moderately prosperous society, drive change and improve China's image externally by undertaking reforms.

[48] Sahoo and Bhunia, 'BCIM Corridor a Game Changer for South Asian Trade'.

by the sub-regional cooperation, particularly by gaining access to new supplies of energy.

Infrastructure initiatives such as the OBOR and the BCIM are being further complemented by the AIIB—the latest regional financial institution coming up under China's leadership with a strong focus on infrastructure development and regional connectivity in Asia. South Asian countries have already become founding members of the AIIB that will provide them an alternative source of institutional finance for building infrastructure in addition to the International Monetary Fund (IMF), the WB and the ADB. Obtaining a wide range of founding members for the AIIB, including NATO members,[49] which heeded China's call notwithstanding the US objections, marked a strategic victory for China in its effort to establish itself as a credible leader in providing resources for infrastructure development to Asia, and the willingness of other countries to support it.

## PEOPLE-TO-PEOPLE COMMUNICATION

Apart from the substantive economic engagement, China's strategic interface with South Asia has also been marked by efforts to increase people-to-people contact. Cultural communication and exchanges through education have been significant in this regard as have been diplomatic interfaces through high-level state visits.

### Cultural Initiatives

Compared with their application elsewhere in Asia, or the West, the deployment of cultural tools in South Asia has been scant. The relatively low cultural engagement might be due to the absence of a sizeable Chinese diaspora in the region (except for a small community in Kolkata in the eastern part of India,[50] which might well be more 'Indian' than

---

[49] NATO members such as Germany, France, the United Kingdom and Turkey have decided to join the AIIB.

[50] A project called 'Cha' (meaning tea in both Bengali and Chinese) is underway to revive one of the world's oldest Chinese settlements outside mainland China

'Chinese') in contrast to a much larger diaspora in other parts of Asia which has been particularly useful in harnessing China's cultural initiatives. Another important factor could be the overarching and deep-rooted influence of the Indian cultural influence in the region. The Indian culture is indeed as 'formidable' as its Chinese counterpart, in terms of long history, rich tradition and variety, and with both being distinct in their attributes from the Western culture. The similarity between the Chinese and Indian cultures in their emphasis on common core values of sympathy, accommodation, respect and tolerance makes it unproductive for China to re-emphasize these in a region already familiar with their nuances. Buddhism, for example, while stitching Bhutan, Nepal, Sri Lanka and China in a common thread, acts identically in linking India and parts of Southeast Asia (as also China as discussed later), thereby reducing its exclusivity as a cultural tool for China in connecting to South Asia.

Nonetheless, cultural exchanges between China and South Asia—heavy on signification and with the communicative goal in mind—are gradually increasing. This is evident from the several agreements on cultural exchanges taken up by Beijing with specific South Asian countries. Cultural exchanges feature in the various partnerships China has in the region, such as with Pakistan, Bangladesh, Sri Lanka and Afghanistan.[51] Cultural interface with Bhutan and Maldives, however, is negligible. It is limited with respect to Afghanistan as well notwithstanding the bilateral Treaty of Friendship, Cooperation and Good-neighbourly Relations (2006), subsequently updated in 2008, facilitating cultural and educational interfaces. These exchanges are likely to increase in the days to come given Afghanistan's strategic importance to China and uplifting of the relationship to a 'new strategic level' on the sidelines of a meeting of the Shanghai Cooperation Organization (SCO) in Beijing in 2012.

---

in Tiretta Bazar and Tangra in Kolkata. An initiative by the Singaporean conglomerate, it has a large number of Kolkata-born Singaporeans on board, many of whom are of Chinese origin from Tangra. See Pandey, 'Chinatown Revival at Tiretta Bazar, Tangra'.

[51] Zhimin and Zhongqi, 'China in Its Neighbourhood...' (2011).

Bangladesh finds mention in ancient Chinese documents as the geographic region Pundravardhana—a kingdom on the banks of the river Brahmaputra corresponding to present-day Bangladesh. Friendly ties between the two countries can be traced back to the Ming dynasty. The relationship has changed over the years with the pronounced military dimension of the 1970s getting balanced by adding on other dimensions like cultural communication. A senior Awami League leader—Obaidul Quader, a member of the party's Presidium—believes in the possibility of Sino-Bangladesh relations getting characterized by 'a proactive and *balanced* (a key expression, as it has ramifications for India) diplomacy', similar to that between Washington and New Delhi,[52] with the view being endorsed by other experts suggesting Dhaka's perception of relations with China as an important alliance in terms of linking a South Asian state to a major global power. Cultural cooperation could well become an important driver of the relations following periodic review and upgradation of the bilateral Agreement of Cooperation signed in November 1979 for strengthening cultural exchanges and initiatives for enhancing greater people-to-people contact.

Given Nepal's strategic importance, Beijing's efforts to engage Kathmandu more closely through cultural ties is only natural. Sino-Nepal cultural exchanges are on an upswing, made easier by the common thread of Buddhism,[53] notwithstanding Nepal being predominantly a Hindu state. Both countries announced 2012 as the Year of Friendly Exchanges and organizations like the China Kulun Group are actively promoting bilateral cultural exchanges and tourism.[54] Bilateral people-to-people communication is being accelerated through proactive roles of Chinese media agencies as well with the CRI launching a local FM radio station in Nepal with a bureau in Kathmandu. This was probably necessitated by the importance of offering a Chinese perspective to local

---

[52] *Thaindian News*, 'Indo-US Ties'.
[53] The Buddhist Philosophy Promotion and Monastery Development Committee of the Ministry of Local Development in Nepal has close contacts and exchanges with China and discusses the development of Buddhism in Nepal and other bilateral exchanges. The Committee is supportive of the 'One China Policy'.
[54] *Global Times*, 'More Cultural Exchanges'.

Nepalese following the fall of the monarchy in Nepal and 'anti-China' demonstrations by Tibetan refugees in Kathmandu in March 2008.[55]

Christened 'China's Israel' in Chinese domestic policy circles,[56] China enjoys considerable goodwill in Pakistan, its 'all weather' partner. The imperatives of the WDS and the geostrategic dynamics of the South, West and Central Asian regions ensure continued engagement with Pakistan. Economics, as mentioned earlier, has been the prominent aspect of Sino-Pakistan engagement, though cultural exchanges are not entirely insignificant. An agreement signed in 1965 has been the basis for these exchanges with nine plans having been signed subsequently.[57] The year 2011 was celebrated as the bilateral Year of Friendship and to commemorate the occasion, the Pakistan–China Friendship Centre was built in Islamabad with state-of-art facilities.

Like Bangladesh, Sri Lanka is also mentioned in ancient Chinese records dating back to the 4th century. Despite the historical connection, the Sri Lankan perception of China has essentially been that of a 'huge, powerful and distant Asian power'.[58] Geographical proximity and issues concerning ethnic Tamils make India feature more prominently in Sri Lanka's strategic vision. As mentioned earlier, China is keen on altering its prevailing perception in Sri Lanka and has stepped up its interface with the island State. Bilateral cultural exchanges are being facilitated through an agreement signed in August 1979,[59] supplemented in 2008, by provisions encouraging regular movements of artistes between the two countries and a further agreement signed during the erstwhile Sri Lankan President Rajapaksa's state visit to China in 2007 for celebrating 50 years of diplomatic ties between the two countries[60] with Chinese Film Festivals being organized in Colombo and Kandy.

---

[55] *Media Network*, 'CRI Expands Its FM'.
[56] *Daily Star*, 'Analysis: Pakistan Is Our Israel'.
[57] *Ministry of Foreign Affairs of the People's Republic of China*, 'China and Pakistan'.
[58] Jayantha and Gooneratne, *A Resurgent China: South Asian Perspectives*, 237.
[59] A cultural agreement was signed between the Government of the People's Republic of China and the Government of the Democratic Socialist Republic of Sri Lanka.
[60] The agreement was signed by the Ministry of Cultural Affairs and National Heritage of Sri Lanka and the Ministry of Culture of China.

As noted for Nepal earlier, the common thread of Buddhism is enabling greater Sino-Sri Lankan engagement as well. This is evident from the visit of the Chinese Buddhist Association to Sri Lanka during the *Esala Perahera*[61] in August 2007 which witnessed the honouring of the leaders of the Association. The cultural interface through Buddhism continued to strengthen given the later visit by another delegation in 2009 led by the Vice President of the Buddhist Association of China (also the Chief Abbot of the Ling Guang Temple in Beijing) for strengthening cultural relations.

## Education

China's soft power strategy involves the use of education as a significant tool for achieving strategic dividends including global positioning of the 'China' brand. Internationalizing higher education and developing the country as an education 'hub' have been a key priority for China. This is consistent with its ambition of achieving the status of a global power given that the latter are recognized for their advanced higher education capabilities and scientific and innovative acumen. The US, the UK, France, Germany and Japan are leading entities in global education, known as quality providers of best higher education, an image that positively influences their global perceptions. Students from various parts of the world aspire to study in higher education institutions of these countries reflecting their 'soft power' and 'global strategic' influence flowing from their capacities in education.

The Chinese effort in 'opening up' the country's higher education is also significant given its role 'in serving China's education reform and development, serving China's economic and social development, serving China's overall diplomacy'.[62] The strategy, in this regard, envisages adopting innovative measures for internationalizing Chinese higher education, including making English the medium of instruction in Chinese universities and developing specialized education institutes for attracting more foreign students and scholars.[63] Importing quality

---

[61] It is a Buddhist festival of the Tooth Relic in Sri Lanka.
[62] Litao, 'China's Higher Education as Soft Power'.
[63] Palit, 'Soft Power Through Education'.

textbooks, enhancing the number of foreign faculty in local universities, building partnerships with leading foreign institutions and granting more scholarships and financial assistance to overseas students are all part of the larger objective to attract more international students, including those from South Asia. There are also ongoing exchanges of scholars with almost all South Asian countries for facilitating better understanding of each other. Over time, education cooperation between China and South Asia is expected to extend to mutual recognition of academic credentials and qualifications and joint awards of academic degrees.

China's sustained efforts to project itself as a credible education hub in the Asian region combined with various enabling conditions and initiatives such as grant of scholarships, geographical proximity of China to South Asia and cheaper costs of higher education in China has led to large increases in the number of South Asian students studying in the mainland. Generous scholarships for studying Mandarin (*Putonghua*) and other subjects and research have significantly contributed to the increase. During Xi Jinping's visit to India in 2014, he announced plans to offer 10,000 scholarships to South Asia along with training opportunities for South Asian students and faculty. These opportunities will be complemented by the China-South Asia Expo and the China-South Asia Partnership Initiative for Science and Technology.[64]

China has been able to reach out to South Asian students through aggressive marketing of its education facilities through exhibitions and similar events, as it has in Southeast Asia and other countries. Professional education in China has become an attractive option for South Asian students as is evident from the large number of Bangladeshi and Sri Lankan students studying medicine in China, helped by enabling conditions provided by professional institutions.

CIs in South Asia (Annexure II) are aiming to increase people-to-people contact by expanding the outreach and appeal of Chinese culture through educative means. The CIs in South Asia have expansive roles including teaching Mandarin, espousing Chinese culture and facilitating study tours. The CIs are important vehicles for promoting greater

---

[64] Liu, 'China Threat in South Asia'.

understanding of China in the region, often with the larger strategic objective of highlighting China's increasing role in regional development[65] that is found yielding positive results.[66] The CIs are combining their initiatives with the China-funded China Study Centres that are active in facilitating bilateral business links[67] as well as organizing academic seminars and taking youth delegations to China.

The initiatives of CIs are beginning to provide results as far as arousing local interest in Chinese culture is concerned. This is evident from more and more students learning Mandarin at the CI in the North South University in Dhaka (the first CI in South Asia), with the University of Kelaniya in Sri Lanka (the University hosts a CI) enlisting study of Chinese culture on its credit award system and the Sindh Provincial Government in Pakistan making *Putonghua* compulsory for students at Grade six and above.[68] Strife-torn Afghanistan has also allowed a foothold to CIs by setting up one at Kabul University for meeting the demand of the Dari speakers[69] to learn Chinese. Deeper spread and penetration of the Chinese language in South Asia should follow given the on-air CIs teaching Mandarin through radio in Pakistan, Bangladesh,

[65] The CI at Kathmandu University took its Chinese teachers and Nepalese students for surveying five projects [Birendra International Convention Centre (BICC), Civil Service Hospital of Nepal, National Ayurveda Research and Training Centre (NATRC), Dashrath Stadium, the Shooting range for the 8th South Asian Games and the National Swimming Complex] being developed with Chinese assistance. Following the visit, a young Nepalese student, born in India and educated at the Bangalore University, wrote: 'Today, we felt so good to see the things provided by Chinese govt. As we say, seeing is believing. This trip means a lot to us. We could see the generosity of Chinese government, the quality management of Confucius Institute...'.
[66] *Xinhua* News Agency, 'Confucius Institute Builds Bridge Between Bangladesh and China'.
[67] The China Study Centre at Jhapa in Nepal has been playing a major role in this regard.
[68] *China.org.cn*, 'Top 30 Confucius Institutes in 2011'.
[69] In Afghanistan, Dari refers to a modern dialect form of Persian that is the standard language used in administration, radio, television and print media in Afghanistan, as well as in parts of Iran and Tajikistan.

Nepal and Sri Lanka,[70] and the establishment of Confucius Classrooms (CCs) in these countries.[71]

## State Visits

High-level state visits (Annexure III) have been important in China's diplomatic engagement of South Asia and regarded as a priority by successive leaderships. Apart from communicating positive intents on mutual understanding and collaboration, these visits are significant in various other respects. As pointed out by Hall and Yarhi-Milo, face-to-face diplomacy helps in assessing other states' intentions[72] and future situations based on behavioural patterns of the senior leaders and functionaries in host countries. It also enables deeper communication with the overseas public, thus generating familiarity and positive impressions. All these objectives are crucial for China given its sensitivity to global perception and efforts to cultivate a benign image. China's Ministry of Foreign Affairs has listed public engagement as one of its official 'main responsibilities' planning specific activities during high-level visits of its leaders, media work and interaction with the public.[73] President Xi has kept up the momentum on high-level visits. Globetrotting, ever since he took over the central leadership, President Xi has been trying to weave a sound diplomatic network with major countries including those in the neighbourhood. According to Ruan Zongze, the effort is to foster 'good neighbours', 'good brothers', making 'good partners' and making 'new friends'.[74] By gaining support of its neighbours China aspires to ink 'new type of international relations' founded on mutual coexistence and development.[75] South Asia is an important part of this agenda and Xi Jinping's three-nation (Maldives, Sri Lanka and India) tour to South Asia in September 2014 was in

---

[70] 'Confucius Institute at CRI'.
[71] CCs function as language learning hubs at the primary and middle school levels. They are approved and funded by the *Hanban* and coordinated by the CIs.
[72] Hall and Yarhi-Milo, 'The Personal Touch'.
[73] Hooghe, *China's Public Diplomacy*.
[74] Zongze, 'Winning the Next Decade'.
[75] *China.org.cn*, 'Xi Seeks New Outlook on Foreign Affairs'.

line with its overall objective in the region. While highlighting regional development and harmony through accelerating connectivity, the objective of the Chinese President seemed to be to 'reassure' the neighbours of its 'benign' intentions.

While high-level visits are setting new parameters of partnership, official announcements during these visits are also being employed to strengthen ties with many South Asian neighbours. Bhutan is a case in point. While China has resolved its border problems with almost all countries except India and Bhutan, the announcement in 2012 to resolve the border issue with Bhutan is in keeping with its 'good neighbourly' policy. China's Vice Foreign Minister Fu Ying, during her visit to Bhutan in August 2012, announced China's intent to seek 'a reasonable and fair solution acceptable to both through bilateral negotiation, and make the border a bridge between the two peoples',[76] also indicating Beijing's willingness to settle disputes through dialogue. Apart from communicating messages and intent, the visits are also undertaken for achieving economic agendas and image building. Xi's visit to Pakistan in 2015, for example, indicated the economic undertone of the relationship. The CPEC project was the main focus of the visit, given its criticality to the more ambitious OBOR initiative. The Beijing leadership did not shy away from demonstrating its constructive image at the SCO in Ufa, Russia, where it initiated the procedures of granting Pakistan (and India) full membership of the organization while taking in Nepal as the new dialogue partner.[77]

## CONCLUSION

As discussed in this chapter, the WDS outlines China's strategic priority of the South Asian region. Given China's quest for untapped resources and new markets for generating economic momentum in its landlocked western region, connecting to the South Asian neighbourhood is an imperative the Chinese leadership cannot afford to ignore.

---

[76] *Sina English*, '28 Years On: China, Bhutan Gain'.
[77] Nepal became the new dialogue partner along with Azerbaijan, Armenia and Cambodia.

Beijing has been employing a variety of resources for deepening its engagement with the South Asian countries. The most visible among these are its efforts in building infrastructure and regional connectivity. The latter are strategically important for both the region and China: while new infrastructure helps South Asian countries augment movement of goods and people, linking such infrastructure to China provides the latter the connectivity it aspires through the WDS. Furthermore, China's financial support in building these projects makes it a strategic stakeholder in regional connectivity that is expected to enlarge through multi-country initiatives such as the OBOR and the AIIB. As a result, initiatives like these also generate widespread criticism. Many analysts view the Belt and Road project as a major step towards Chinese projection of power outside its borders, thus putting to rest Beijing's old policy of hesitance and conservatism and a 'new manifestation of its global role'.[78] It can be argued that these often-projected mutually beneficial enterprises, in combination with cultural engagement and education exchanges, are designed for establishing long-term Chinese strategic clout in the region.

However, it also needs to be considered that in its effort to win over South Asian neighbours, Beijing has been sensitive to the regional dynamics. It has been cautious in determining the pace of its engagement with the rest of South Asia keeping in mind the overarching presence of India in the region. The historical reality of South Asia being a homogeneous entity and a unified whole has led to extensive cultural and traditional commonalities across the region, among countries which are no longer territorially together but are part of the greater Indian subcontinent. These geopolitical/cultural factors have motivated China to be pragmatic in South Asia. Not wanting to jeopardize its economic development by creating further tension in an already volatile South Asia, China has been primarily relying on specific soft power tools such as economic assistance, education and high-level visits to engage the region.

---

[78] Munter, 'Anticipating China's "One-Belt-One Road" in South Asia'.

# 4

# Southeast Asia: Cultural Diplomacy, Economics and Regional Cooperation

Southeast Asia—brought together as the Association of Southeast Asian Nations (ASEAN) in 1967—comprises 10 countries: Brunei, Cambodia, Indonesia, Laos, Malaysia, Myanmar, Singapore, Philippines, Thailand and Vietnam.[1] China has been active in building a benign-constructive image in the region given its importance as a neighbour, its economic significance and geostrategic criticality pertaining to the South China Sea.

Despite the Southeast Asian states being more ethnically integrated with China with no tight military alliances,[2] the issue of national sovereignty connected to the South China Sea has made partnerships with the states difficult. With several Southeast Asian countries bordering the disputed Sea (Brunei, Indonesia, Malaysia, Vietnam and Philippines), creating an enabling external environment in the region has been challenging for China. Matters have been further complicated by the strong interest of the US in the region as an extra-regional actor.

Notwithstanding tensions over territorial rights, Beijing has been pragmatic in engaging the region given its strategic attributes of geographic location, availability of energy resources and the importance of South China Sea as essential Sea Lanes of Communication (SLOC). The dexterity in managing occasionally difficult relations with different Southeast Asian countries holds the key to cultivating a stable and

---

[1] The new nation of East Timor, formerly part of Indonesia, has become the 11th Southeast Asian country.
[2] In contrast, Japan and South Korea in Northeast Asia have tight military alliances with the US.

peaceful neighbourhood. The latter, in turn, is essential for producing benign impressions of China that can facilitate its leadership in Asia and make Southeast Asian countries reluctant to become 'complicit in any attempt by the US to constrain China'.[1] Deploying soft power for meaningfully engaging the region becomes critical in this regard.

China's 'good neighbour' diplomacy flows out of its conviction of 'befriending and maintaining good relationships with neighbours' as against projecting military power—a belief ingrained in ancient Chinese thinking on statecraft. The ideals of Confucius and Mencius, discussed in Chapter 2 earlier, resonate in China's contemporary foreign policy, particularly with its neighbours. The policy is guided by the ideal of 'be harmonious, pacify and enrich thy neighbours' and has 'peace, security, cooperation, prosperity' as its goals. The tactic is applied in pursuing regional cooperation and partnership with Southeast Asia and other regions of Asia as well.

Some scholars working on the interface between Southeast Asia and China point to the successful use of forums such as the ASEAN by China 'as a demonstration precinct for its socialization with Southeast Asia's reciprocal responses to Chinese participation and proposals such as ACFTA, a defence minister's dialogue, and a regional bond market' boosting China's claims of 'peaceful development'.[2] Others have also drawn on China's participation in the ASEAN to develop 'constructivist theories' of socialization with Chinese characteristics, emphasizing 'power as relationships' and the importance of 'process for the sake of processes'.[3] These views must reconcile with the reality that Beijing's push for cooperation does not entail compromising on national sovereignty. The latter is a fundamental priority for the Chinese leadership evident from Beijing's hard 'posturing' on security and sovereignty-related issues pertaining to the region.

China's attention on Southeast Asia goes back to several centuries in history. The exploits of Zheng He, who commanded seven voyages of trade and discovery in Southeast and South Asian waters (1405–33)

---

[1] Goh, 'The Modes of China's Influence,' 847.
[2] Ibid., 839.
[3] Ibid.

during the Ming dynasty, is repeatedly referred to by the Chinese leaders as a symbol of China's 'benign' naval presence in the region. Beijing's contemporary application of soft power policies in Southeast Asia must be looked at in this historical context. However, the role of extra-regional powers, primarily the US, influences power politics in the region as well.

Washington's presence in Asia has had bearings on China's strategic position in the region from time to time. The emergence of the US as the dominant global power post-Cold War saw a perceptive de-scaling of American engagement efforts in Asia. But the US still had its allies in the region with implications for regional power dynamics. However, Washington's shifting focus after the 9/11 and identification of certain parts of Asia as hubs of terrorism, primarily West and South Asia, left enough room for China to engage the region through various 'soft' means. But the Obama administration's renewed focus on the region as a part of its 'pivot to Asia' strategy has altered the regional strategic dynamics.

China's escalating strategic influence in Southeast Asia has been a subject of profuse debate amongst academics and experts with the scale and scope of the debate being large enough to accommodate diverse impressions. While David Shambaugh argues that China's rise is construed as positive by the region—'[M]ost nations in the region now see China as a good neighbour, a constructive partner, a careful listener, and a nonthreatening regional power'[4]—Nicholas Khoo and Michael Smith argue the contrary: '[A] strong case can be made that many Southeast Asian states are economic competitors with China. And that some are hedging against its rise by consolidating their long-standing relations with the United States'.[5] China, on its part, notwithstanding the conflicting opinions on outcomes of its engagement, continues to engage its neighbours.

## CULTURAL INITIATIVES

Cultural initiatives have been a conspicuous part of Chinese engagement with Southeast Asia, compared with South Asia discussed earlier in

---

[4] Shambaugh, 'China Engages Asia,' 64.
[5] Khoo et al., 'Correspondence,' 196–97.

Chapter 3. This could be due to more enabling factors facilitating the exercise of cultural diplomacy (CD) including the presence of a large Chinese diaspora,[6] greater prevalence of Chinese traditions and customs and the absence of an equally formidable or 'competitive', cultural presence like that of the Indian culture in South Asia. While the latter factors may be true when it comes to China's cultural advances in Southeast Asia, a closer study of China's cultural engagement in the region reveals Beijing's cautiousness in not pushing cultural initiatives too hard in the region—a strand in some respect identical to India's restraint in exporting culture to the neighbourhood—which could be due to the common apprehension of being branded 'cultural colonizers' by smaller neighbours in the region. Indeed, factors that otherwise appear enabling for strong cultural engagement, such as the presence of a sizeable Chinese diaspora in the region, might, on the contrary, present challenges for CD, given the indigenous cultural growth of the diaspora distinct from mainstream mainland culture and the unfavourable perception of the overseas Chinese by the locals of the host country.[7] The role of the CIs becomes somewhat different in a milieu dominated by the diaspora as pointed out by Chinh with respect to CIs in the Mekong region, specifically Thailand and Cambodia, that aim at 'connecting

---

[6] The Chinese living outside Greater China (mainland China, Taiwan and Hong Kong) comprise two major groups: *hua qiao* and the *hua ren*. The former are immigrants who are temporarily overseas and residing abroad, while the latter are ethnic Chinese settled overseas, no longer Chinese citizens. While both groups are loosely referred to as Chinese diaspora in the text, many scholars opine that diaspora is used to refer to Jews exiled from Israel in early history and might not be apt for describing the overseas Chinese. See Liu, 'The Chinese Diaspora,' 150.

[7] In both Malaysia and Indonesia, the locals are envious of the wealthier Chinese diaspora. This has led the locals in Malaysia to unite under the idea of 'ketuanan Melayu' (Malay pre-eminence), against the Chinese domination of their commerce and economy. In Indonesia, on the other hand, quite a few instances of violence against the ethnic Chinese including the anti-China riots in 1998 have further contributed to the general hostility towards each other. The massacre of a large number of ethnic Chinese during the era of the former Indonesian president and military strongman Suharto continue to cast a shadow on China–Indonesia ties.

China's mainland and overseas Chinese communities in the region'[8] rather than expanding mainland cultural influence. Chinh argues that China's cultural advances in the region are aimed at expanding its 'soft borders' without using military force.[9] Cultural engagement of Southeast Asia has indeed been more subtle and low-key than similar engagement in other parts of the world as this chapter and others would reveal. Along with CD, education has been a powerful tool for deepening engagement with the region complemented by deeper cultivation of civilizational links created by Buddhism and high-level visits for fostering greater people-to-people communication.

## Cultural Diplomacy

It is perhaps only natural that culture be used as a strategic tool by China for deeper engagement with a region where vignettes of Chinese culture already exist, along with a sizeable Chinese diaspora. Xi Jinping and senior Chinese officials have repeatedly stressed the importance of overseas Chinese as a 'bridge' for strengthening the relationship between China and the 'host' countries.[10] While being, arguably, in a position to facilitate CD and expansion of CIs in their native turfs, cultural engagement of Southeast Asia by Beijing also needs to take note of the occasional adverse perceptions existing against the resident Chinese among the local population and the resultant 'effectiveness' of utilizing the diaspora for advancing Chinese culture as discussed earlier. Nonetheless, Beijing's cultural advances, while nuanced and cautious, particularly with respect to countries in the region where recent history has been complex and unfavourable for aggressive cultural advancement,[11] have

---

[8]  Chinh, 'Confucius Institutes in the Mekong Region'.

[9]  Ibid.

[10] *Ministry of Foreign Affairs of the People's Republic of China*, 'Xi Jinping Attends Welcome Luncheon Hosted by Overseas Chinese in Malaysia'.

[11] In a country like Vietnam (China ruled it for 1,000 years), establishing CIs has a political undertone and, therefore, has not been easy for the Chinese Government. Chinese language not only conveys Chinese culture and ways of thinking but is a reminder of the hapless historical parts of the relationship to the Vietnamese society. The politics of the South China Sea also influences the relationship. In 1979, during the border skirmish, Chinese language teaching in

made incremental progress for creating a benign image through the 'neighbourhood policy' and turning disapproval into approval to an extent.

The framework for China's cultural engagement with the region is the 'convention on protection of cultural and artistic diversity' of 2004 that was issued through the 'Shanghai Declaration' during the seventh annual ministerial meeting of the International Network on Cultural Policy.[12] Ever since, various bilateral initiatives with Southeast Asian countries have followed [e.g., China–Thailand Cultural Agreement (2012), Philippine-China Year of Friendly Exchanges (2012), China-Cambodian Friendly Year (2013), opening the Sino-Laos Youth Friendly Exchange Centre and cultural centres in Thailand, Singapore and Myanmar[13]]. Most of these initiatives, aiming to increase cultural exchanges through cultural performances, arts exhibitions and showcasing visual and performing artists abroad, are China's attempt at 'arts diplomacy'.

The ASEAN, as a forum, also is being utilized for deeper cultural exchanges with China[14] for greater cultural interface with Brunei, Indonesia, Laos and Vietnam.[15] As mentioned in Chapter 1, Chinese provinces are specifically playing a leading role in cultural interface with Southeast Asian neighbours being a major example as is evident from initiatives of the Yunnan province.[16] The scale of the engagement, as can be seen from the variety of bilateral initiatives with individual Southeast Asian countries, is larger than that observed for South Asia.

---

Vietnam was abandoned. For details, see Chinh, 'Confucius Institutes in the Mekong Region'.

[12] Lawrence, 'China's "Soft Power" Strategy Threatened by Obama'.

[13] *ChinaCulture.Org.*, 'Chinese Cultural Centre in Bangkok'.

[14] For instance, the China-ASEAN Journey of Friendship—a cultural and art exhibition tour—was launched in April 2012.

[15] *Borneo Bulletin*, 'Brunei, China Extend Cultural Ties'.

[16] Jiangheng district (Yunnan province) hosted the traditional 'con' throwing festival in 2011and 2012, respectively, for participants from Vietnam and Laos. The 'con' festival is an annual event hosted to develop and promote tourism in the region. Kunming hosted the Second Asia Cultural Forum in 2013 where Southeast Asian countries (e.g., Cambodia and Thailand) participated along with South Asian countries.

The Chinese media has been particularly active in expanding people-to-people communication in Southeast Asia through the 24 hour broadcasts by the CRI (*zhong guo guo ji guang bo*). The CRI Southeast Asia Broadcasting Centre has been actively engaging its counterparts in the region through 'cooperation tours'. Apart from the CRI, China's leading news agency *Xinhua* has launched NewChineseNet.com, a Chinese news portal, with Malaysia's leading Chinese-language media group (Media Chinese International Limited).[17] Notwithstanding major differences with Vietnam on the South China Sea, there are collaborations that the *Xinhua* undertakes in Vietnam[18] with the objective of facilitating greater mutual awareness among the youth in both countries.

As noted for bilateral cultural exchanges earlier, Chinese provinces like Yunnan are connecting to Southeast Asia through their media agencies as well.[19] The state media is expected to further ramp up its efforts to increase, outreach and expand China's sphere of influence in Southeast Asia at the grass-roots level.[20] These efforts, along with the state-led CD initiatives are complemented by initiatives like youth delegations that regularly travel to various Southeast Asian countries[21] and the Chinese version of the Peace Corps, run by the Chinese Young Volunteers Association that despatches young Chinese on long-term volunteer service projects to relatively backward countries of Southeast Asia (e.g., Laos and Myanmar).

[17] *China Daily*, 'Xinhua, MCIL Jointly Launch News Portal in Malaysia'.

[18] *Xinhua* organized a photo exhibition in 2010 for marking the 60th anniversary of Sino-Vietnam diplomatic relations. *Embassy of the People's Republic of China in Australia*, 'Chinese, Vietnamese New Agencies Hold Photo Exhibition to Mark 60 Years of Diplomatic Relations'.

[19] The Yunnan TV had a Memorandum of Understanding (MOU) with Myanmar's Shwe Than Lwin Media Group for producing a television series—'The Dancing Girl from the Pyu Kingdom'. The production re-lived the historical cultural communication between China and Myanmar by focusing on the Chorus of Pyu kingdom (ancient city state of Myanmar) sent by the King of Pyu to visit the Tang Dynasty in 802 AD.

[20] Hsiao and Yang, 'Ins and Outs of China Courtship'.

[21] *The Voice of Vietnam*, 'Chinese Youths Join Cultural Exchanges in Vietnam'.

## Education

As discussed earlier in Chapter 3, internationalization of higher education has emerged as an important instrument of Chinese external engagement policies, particularly with respect to the neighbourhood. A key aspect of this strategy is encouraging greater inflow of foreign students, for which the Ministry of Education has boosted financial aid and relaxed visa requirements.[22]

Greater inflow of students from Southeast Asia to China reflect the increasing positive perception of China as a major regional education hub. Southeast Asian students are a significant proportion of Asian students studying in China, who comprise almost 70 per cent of China's foreign students. Vietnam, Thailand and Indonesia are the major sources of foreign students for China in the region. Along with attracting foreign students from the neighbourhood, China is also attempting to export its education facilities to the region by encouraging its universities to open foreign campuses [e.g., The Malaysia campus of the Xiamen University (also called the Xia Da)[23]—the first Chinese university to go overseas].[24] Regular education exhibitions organized in Southeast Asia have been useful in showcasing Chinese higher education in the region and attracting students. The China Scholarship Council (CSC)[25] has been holding these educational fairs in collaboration with prominent Chinese higher education institutions (e.g., Fudan University, Shanghai Jiaotong University and Beijing Normal University) for effective regional branding of Chinese higher education. Foreign student inflows have also been facilitated by bilateral education agreements (e.g., China–Malaysia agreement on mutual recognition of academic degrees and diplomas) and specific collaborations between universities.[26]

---

[22] Kurlantzick, 'China's Charm: Implications of Chinese Soft Power'.

[23] Xiamen is ranked as one of the top universities (501–50) by the QS World University Rankings 2013.

[24] *China Daily*, 'Schools in for First Overseas Campus,' 1, 6.

[25] The CSC is an organization under the Ministry of Education which funds Chinese and overseas students to study abroad or in China, respectively.

[26] The Department of International Cooperation and Exchanges at the Ministry of Education lists 31 Southeast Asian universities having 135 cooperation

China's ability to attract foreign students, particularly from the neighbourhood, has been influenced by the generous scholarships it has been offering. The Ministry of Education fixes the number and quantity of these scholarship schemes annually and entrusts the responsibility of administering them on the CSC.[27] Several scholarships are targeted specifically towards students from Southeast Asia and include long-term postgraduate and doctoral degree studies. As part of the action plan for implementing the Joint Declaration on the China–ASEAN Strategic Partnership for Peace and Prosperity announced in 2011, China decided to grant scholarships to students from Southeast Asia. The Plan also focused on extensive collaborations between educational institutions. Several Chinese universities are also engaged in running training programmes for Southeast Asian government agencies (e.g., Chengdu University of Traditional Chinese Medicine's programme for the Ministry of Public Health in Thailand)[28] with such collaborations to deepen over time.

The emphasis on education has provided China the opportunity of engaging neighbours by exposing them to the Chinese culture and way of life through teaching Mandarin. Active promotion of instruction in Mandarin and awareness about the Chinese culture at primary schools in many Southeast Asian countries have been enabled through bilateral institutional agreements with the latter for including Mandarin in public school curriculum and helping students in low-income countries like Cambodia to attend private local Chinese-language primary schools.[29] The CIs have also been significant in teaching Mandarin and spreading the knowledge and the awareness of Chinese culture in the region in 'an effort to downplay the image of China as a fire breathing dragon, and promote that of China as a cute, cuddly panda'.[30] Their numbers in Southeast Asia though are still small compared to some other parts of

agreements with 47 Chinese universities. *The Global Times Ticker*, 'China and Southeast Asian Nations Expand Study-Abroad Ties'.

[27] *Study in China*, 'Chinese Government Scholarship Programmes for International Students'.

[28] Yongkun, 'A History of Socio-cultural Cooperation with Southeast Asia'.

[29] Kurlantzick, 'China's Charm Offensive in Southeast Asia'.

[30] Randall, 'The Fire Breathing Dragon and the Cute, Cuddly Panda,' 17.

the world.[31] China might be reluctant to proliferate the region with these ambassador institutes as that could be assumed propagandist and spoil the larger strategic objective of securing a benign national image.

The CIs in the region have also occasionally encountered popular discontent and resistance presumably on account of their presence and agenda being suspected to be associated with 'Fifth Column' intentions.[32] This reflects the strategic downsides of CIs. As Sheng Ding points out,

> [Many Chinese observers believe that] despite their neutral scholarly appearance, the new network of Confucius Institutes does have a political agenda.... The Institutes will teach Beijing's preferred version of Chinese, characters that are (not) used in Taiwan. This would help advance Beijing's goal of marginalizing Taiwan in the battle for global influence.[33]

Other opinions suggest CIs 'have been effective at expanding China's network of relationships, but in terms of cultivating cultural soft power, they are yet to substantiate the nominal use of Confucius as a representative of Chinese culture'.[34] Further, China's efforts to locate the CIs within host country universities have also had its fair share of problems. Countries like Vietnam are not particularly pleased with the idea as such location impedes the functioning of national university education by adding 'foreign' teaching content and study materials that are independently used by the CIs.[35]

## Religion and Buddhism

Buddhism is a common thread connecting both China and India with Southeast Asia, as much as it connects them to South Asia. Notwithstanding

---

[31] Out of 295 CIs across the world (Annexure II), 27 are located in Southeast Asia. Twelve of these are in Thailand followed by Indonesia (7), Malaysia (2), Philippines (3), Cambodia (1), Laos (1) and Singapore (1).
[32] Fifth columns have often been orchestrated by countries in host countries for seizing power.
[33] Ding, *The Dragon's Hidden Wings*.
[34] Benavides, 'When Soft Power is too Soft'.
[35] Chinh, 'Confucius Institutes in the Mekong Region'.

modern socialist China discouraging the official practice of religion, Chinese history underlines the practice of multiple religions. The Cultural Revolution[36] radically altered China's attitude towards religious practices. Subsequently, however, China has made efforts to revive and implement freedom of personal religious beliefs.[37] At the same time, the significance of religion, particularly Buddhism, as a force for facilitating greater neighbourhood engagement has been recognized by China. The Chinese leadership acknowledges Buddhism as a common socio-cultural and religious thread running through the region. This has encouraged China to project a Buddhist-friendly image and engage the region by drawing attention to a shared Buddhist heritage through initiatives like the World Buddhist Forum in April 2006 organized to 'showcase its CD and its willingness to use traditional beliefs to ease social tension'.[38]

Religion (Buddhism, in this particular context) is important in conditioning public opinion. According to Holmes Welch, '[W]here there was a need to influence public opinion abroad, [Buddhism] helped to have developed friendly relations—through the exchange of visits—with politicians, students, businessmen and other social circles, all of whom could be called upon to cooperate in agitation and propaganda'.[39] In Southeast Asia, Buddhism was critical in fostering Sino-Singapore relations in the period prior to the official establishment of diplomatic missions for deepening commercial and bilateral engagement in October 1990.[40] There were several bilateral exchange visits facilitated by Buddhist institutions like the Singapore Buddhist Federation that provided a 'source of legitimacy for accommodation and collaboration

---

[36] Launched by Mao Zedong, then Chairman of the Communist Party of China, between 1966and 1976, the Cultural Revolution (also called the Great proletarian Cultural Revolution) seeked to purge the 'impure' elements of capitalism from the Chinese society thereby reviving the revolutionary spirit, especially amongst the Chinese youth.

[37] Article 36 of the Constitution of the People's Republic of China (PRC) provides for freedom of religious belief as a basic right for its citizens. See Information Office of the State Council of the People's Republic of China, 'Freedom of Religious Freedom in China'.

[38] Mingjiang, 'Soft Power in Chinese Discourse'.

[39] Welch, *Buddhism under Mao*, 202.

[40] Tat and Chia, 'Buddhism in Singapore–China Relations,' 1.

between nations' and were important influences on the 'linkage between domestic and international politics'.[41]

The exchanges also had distinct strategic and economic goals as is evident from the Chinese leader Ulanfa's statement during one of the visits of the Venerable Hong Choon, the then President of the Singapore Buddhist Federation: 'Singapore is an economically developed country. We sincerely welcome Singaporean business persons to make investments in China…'.[42] Singapore, though, is not the only Southeast Asian country that has been engaged with China through Buddhism. Myanmar is another example where Buddhist cultural exchanges have been instrumental in enhancing people-to-people contact. These exchanges have involved the transfer of ancient relics (Chinese Buddha sacred tooth relics have been conveyed to Myanmar on several occasions)[43] and the establishment of closer relations between religious institutions on both sides.[44]

Buddhism and shared religious beliefs have been implicit facilitators in China's greater engagement of its diaspora in the region. The overseas Chinese in Southeast Asia are a large and growing community, many among whom retain family, cultural and linguistic ties with China. The financial wealth of the overseas Chinese proved the 'locomotive' for Deng Xiaoping's vision of China as a global player.[45] The overseas Chinese in Southeast Asia have lived up to Deng's vision by being a major source of inward investment into China since the late 1970s.[46] On the other hand,

---

[41] Fox and Sandler, *Bringing Religion into International into International Relations*, 4.

[42] Fa, 'Wu Langfu Fuzhuxi huijiao Xinjiapo Fojiao Chaoshan Gunagguan Tuan,' 42.

[43] The Chinese Buddha sacred tooth relic had been conveyed to Myanmar three times earlier in 1955–56, 1994 and 1996–97, respectively. For details, see *Xinhua*, 'Chinese Buddha Sacred'.

[44] There is an MoU between the Lingguang Si Temple in Beijing and the Shwedagon Pagoda of Yangon. See *English.chinamil.com.cn*, 'China–Myanmar Religious Exchange Enters New Phase of Friendly Cooperation'.

[45] Schmetzer, *The Chinese Juggernaut*, 11.

[46] However, Beijing's economic reasons for cultivating the Chinese diaspora in countries specifically like Malaysia hold little traction now given China's economic rise and the large Chinese investments in states like Penang. Chinese

China has provided the diaspora new opportunities for investing in its huge untapped markets. For instance, the Indonesian investment in China is driven by the ethnic Chinese from Indonesia who control almost all of Indonesia's major businesses, and who get to become the major financial actors in the mainland economy.[47] The strategic combination has been quite successful in Cambodia as well and has assisted the overseas Chinese community in both Indonesia and Cambodia to act as a bridge for business opportunities in China and facilitate China's economic involvement and cultural outreach in these countries.[48]

## High-level Visits

Bilateral diplomatic exchanges manifesting through high-level state visits (Annexure III) have not only been important in increasing the interface between China and Southeast Asia but have also succeeded in creating greater synergies and communication between China and the region's leaderships, and are, therefore, considered useful in improving perceptions of China. Meaningful communication is an imperative for Beijing in a region where countries such as Vietnam and Philippines are agitated with Beijing on the South China Sea and are vocal critics of its maritime actions. High-level diplomacy has been found particularly useful in dissipating tensions surrounding the South China Sea as is evident from President Xi's visit to Malaysia in October 2013 for assuaging misunderstandings with specific countries in the region with an eye on regional stability.

However, despite the rising incidence of high-level state visits, apprehension and mistrust regarding China has not been eliminated from all segments of Southeast Asian leaderships, as Hall and Yarhi-Milo argue: '[L]eaders may profess benign intentions to lure their target into a

---

financial investments are also substantive in infrastructure development in Indonesia.

[47] Harding, 'The Role of the Chinese Diaspora in Sino-Indonesian Relations'.

[48] There are reportedly 75 schools in Cambodia teaching Chinese to around 40,000 students, many of whom are ethnic Chinese. See Sambath, 'Cambodia–China Relation'.

false sense of security'.[49] China has been a prominent source of political divisiveness within Southeast Asia[50] and might continue to remain so till greater strategic convergence is achieved between countries on South China Sea.

## The Regionalization Strategy

Southeast Asia provides an interesting example of China's efforts to be a part of regional frameworks for building closer strategic relationships. While building a benign image was probably not the top priority for the Chinese leadership way back in the 1950s, its efforts to stay engaged with the region were visible from as early as the Bandung Conference in 1955. Two major policy initiatives emanating from the occasion indicated its desire to project friendly and benevolent impressions: the Five Principles of Peaceful Coexistence and a promise to negotiate dual nationality with Southeast Asia for the overseas Chinese. The advent of the Cold War and political developments within China influenced its interaction with the region in the subsequent decades.

While Southeast Asia began organizing itself since 1967, China's interactions with the ASEAN kicked off much later, only from the 1990s, driven by its economic rise and increasing economic integration with the ASEAN. China's economic growth encouraged Southeast Asia to invite China to become a full-dialogue partner of the ASEAN, notwithstanding strategic discomfort of some ASEAN members for specific reasons.[51] For

---

[49] Hall and Yarhi-Milo, 'The Personal Touch,' 561.

[50] ASEAN remains perturbed and divided over China's rapid rise as is evident from its failure to issue a joint communique in the ASEAN Summit at Phnom Penh in July 2012—the first such occurrence in 45 years. While China has succeeded in making allies like Cambodia in the region, its soft engagement is clearly yet to persuade the rest of the region. The differences arose during the ASEAN summit over member country perceptions on China's role in the South China Sea with the countries failing to arrive at a common view—divided between relatively critical (e.g., Vietnam and Philippines) and accommodating (e.g., Cambodia) views. For details, see Grant et al., 'South China Sea Issue Divides ASEAN'.

[51] ASEAN's expansion in the 1990s was partly prompted by fear of China's increasing influence both at the regional as well as the global level.

China, a closer association with ASEAN (it became a Dialogue Partner in 1995) provided the opportunity of improving relations with neighbours and beginning the end of international isolation thrust on it by the West post-Tiananmen. Attempting confidence-building, as argued by Wu Yongnian, was probably the most fundamental motivation for China in engaging the ASEAN.[52] Indeed, Beijing's decision was amply reflective of its urge to engage:[53]

> Engagement with ASEAN reflects an increased appreciation by China of the importance of norms and 'soft power' in foreign policy. Chinese print media, television, music, food and popular culture are disseminating across Asia at an unprecedented level. China's growing appreciation of soft power is also evident in its efforts to popularize Chinese culture throughout the region. At the same time, China also makes an effort to train future generations of intellectuals, technicians and political elites around the world in its universities and technical schools. China increasingly sees higher education as an instrument of foreign policy.

Engagement with ASEAN marked the beginning of China's similar engagement with bigger regional forums like the East Asia Summit (EAS)[54] with the Chinese leadership realizing the relevance of regional platforms for communicating China's resolve to actively participate, demonstrate restraint, offer reassurance, open markets, foster inter-dependence, create common interests and reduce conflict (*jiji canyu, biaoshi kezhi, tigong baozheng, kaifang shichang, cujin xianghu yicun, chuangzao gongtong liyi, and jiangdi chongtu*).[55] These forums not only helped Beijing to 'guarantee China's status, exclude Taiwan's political inroads and reassure neighbours',[56] but also helped in countering 'the

---

[52] The author interviewed Professor Wu Yongnian, from the Shanghai International Studies University, in Shanghai on18 November 2015.
[53] Shambaugh, 'China Engages Asia'.
[54] The EAS members are China, Japan, South Korea, India, Australia and New Zealand.
[55] Yunling and Shiping, 'China's Regional Strategy,' 50–51.
[56] Palitiel, 'China's Regionalization Policies,' 49.

attempts by the regional actors to stem its re-emergence through demands for "westernization" and "transformation".[57] However, closer ties with ASEAN have not prevented China's relations with some Southeast Asian countries becoming more contentious over time. Territorial differences over segments of the South China Sea have been the main factors behind such contention. ASEAN is experiencing the turbulence of these contentions with China insisting on omission of references to South China Sea issue at the ASEAN forums and the lack of unanimity within ASEAN on the matter. Indeed, the engagement with ASEAN and China's effort at regionalization is perceived by some analysts as 'soft' counter-hegemony—aligning with secondary powers[58]—for limiting the US geostrategic influence in the region. That undoubtedly is a far more geo-strategic national interest focused objective than the more virtuous notion of peaceful regional development usually articulated by China in its regional engagement exercises.

## ECONOMIC INITIATIVES

China's significance in the Asian economy has grown sharply since the Asian financial crisis of 1997 and the global financial crisis of 2008. China was able to withstand both crises and remain a major source of economic momentum for Asia. Southeast Asian economies have particularly benefitted from the ability of China to remain the major 'engine' of growth in the region. While their trade and investment links with China have strengthened over time, some of the countries have also benefitted from China's extension of generous development assistance, particularly in infrastructure.

The perception of China in the region began undergoing changes in the aftermath of the Asian financial crisis of 1997.[59] China's territorial

---

[57] Wang, 'Preservation, Prosperity and Power,' 669–94.

[58] The main objective of the Southeast Asian countries is to keep all the major powers—including foreign ministers of India, Japan, Russia, the US and the EU—involved in the region in an attempt to limit China's growing influence to an extent possible and benefit from their presence. See Kavalski (2009: 48).

[59] Kurlantzick, 'China's Charm: Implications of Chinese Soft Power'.

claims on parts of the South China Sea made the ASEAN countries increasingly wary of an 'aggressive' and 'rising' China. Since 1997, a year that many scholars mark as a turning point in China–Southeast Asia relations, the wary perceptions begun to be slowly matched by more positive perceptions of China emanating from the latter's enthusiasm for bilateral trade agreements and active participation in regional multilateral frameworks like the ASEAN.[60] China's refusal to devalue its currency following the Asian financial crisis signalled 'its decision as standing up for Asia'[61] and improved further after extension of economic packages and low interest loans to Southeast Asian countries. As noted by Shambaugh, this posture 'punctured the prevailing image of China in the region as either aloof or hegemonic and began to replace it with an image of China as a responsible power'.[62] Subsequent initiatives, including China's role as a responsible actor in the regional architecture and emphasis on the retention of ASEAN centrality in various regional arrangements (e.g., ASEAN+3 and ASEAN+6) has gone down well in the region.

China has not spared efforts to convey its intention to 'work' with Southeast Asia in maintaining regional stability. These efforts include signing Southeast Asia's Treaty of Amity and Cooperation (TAC) in 2003, renouncing force and calling for greater economic and political cooperation[63] and signing the China–ASEAN Joint Declaration on Strategic Partnership for Peace and Prosperity.[64] China was quick to conclude a bilateral FTA with the ASEAN and implement the Early Harvest Programme in 2004 with some ASEAN states involving lifting of trade barriers on several commodities signalling China's eagerness to develop closer economic ties with the region by giving them more access

[60] China has been deliberately pursuing regionalism for projecting its responsible and constructive image.
[61] Kurlantzick, 'China's Charm'.
[62] Shambaugh, 'China Engages Asia,' 68.
[63] 'China Joins Treaty of Amity, Cooperation in Southeast Asia'. Available at: http://english.peopledaily.com.cn/200310/08/eng20031008_125556.shtml (accessed on 7 May 2009).
[64] 'Joint Declaration of the Heads of State/Government of the Association of Southeast Asian Nations and the People's Republic of China, Bali'. Available at: http://www.aseansec.org/15265.htm (accessed on 21 June 2010).

to its market amounting to the impression that Beijing 'gave more and took less'.[65] China also committed itself to a code of conduct on the South China Sea[66] in addition to its policy of 'non-interference in domestic affairs'.[67]

China's OBOR initiative, while being an instrument for facilitating the next stage of Chinese economic expansion by linking its underdeveloped western region to major economic hubs in Asia and Europe, is also, from the official Chinese vantage point, an upholder of the Five Principles of Peaceful Coexistence resonating China's efforts at regional integration and cooperation. Southeast Asia, given its geographic proximity to China with continental states closest to Chinese land borders and linked to their big neighbour politically and demographically, is a vital partner in the project. The region's ability to be the connective link between sea and land makes ASEAN an important stakeholder in the initiative. The Belt and Road project also underlines the Chinese leadership's deftness at employing certain parts of history for communicating benign intentions. The most recent effort has been to project the initiative as symbolizing *communication* and *cooperation* not only within the region but between the East and the West capturing the 'ancient' Silk Road Spirit of 'peace and cooperation, openness and inclusiveness, mutual learning and mutual benefit'. Chinese scholar Valerie Hansen notes China's Silk Road as a soft power initiative by its imperial rulers: 'It is one of the few terms that people remember from history classes that does not involve hard power..... And it's precisely those positive associations that the Chinese want to emphasize'.[68]

### Development Assistance and Regional Cooperation

Chinese development assistance or economic aid has been filling an important vacuum in the development space of Southeast Asia by build-ing new infrastructure. For China, extending such assistance serves the

---

[65] Goh, 'The Modes of China's Influence,' 840.

[66] Kurlantzick, 'China's Charm Offensive in Southeast Asia,' 2.

[67] Notwithstanding such commitment, the South China Sea remains a heavily contentious zone.

[68] Clover and Hornby, 'China's Great Game,' 16.

critical objectives of enhancing its soft power in the recipient countries that are deficient in stocks of physical infrastructure and financial resources. Providing economic aid also helps China in securing strategic economic objectives such as improving cross-border connectivity and accessing essential resources, much like it does in South Asia mentioned in Chapter 3.

The CLMV (Cambodia–Laos–Myanmar–Vietnam) countries in Southeast Asia have been among the major recipients of Chinese development assistance. This includes Cambodia, one of the least developed and low-income countries in the region, that has been a major beneficiary of extensive Chinese aid in infrastructure.[69] China's support of the repressive Khmer Rouge regime in the 1970s had seriously dented its image with the local people in Cambodia. It has been able to recover some of the lost ground through its significant role in the country's economic development so much so that its willingness to accommodate China was clearly visible during the ASEAN summit in 2012, when the member countries were deliberating over their perceptions on China's role in the South China Sea, leading to a deadlock. China is now the highest donor for Cambodia, surpassing the EU and Japan. Chinese aid has been a huge support for Cambodia given the reluctance of Western multi-lateral donors and agencies to disburse resources to the country on various grounds including human rights issues.[70] The major Chinese infrastructure projects in Cambodia include electricity provision (hydroelectric project being constructed by Sinohydro) with a few Cambodian households having access to reliable electricity and road connectivity (the road between Preah Vihar and Kampong Thom provinces, the Cambodia–China Prek Kdam Friendship Bridge in Kandal province and so on)—crucial for improving the daily lives of an average Cambodian, apart from enabling more easy trade and travel.

The use of development assistance in extracting strategic capital is particularly visible in China's engagement with Myanmar. As a gateway to Southeast Asia and a reservoir of untapped energy resources, Myanmar

---

[69] *Congressional Research Service (CRS) Library of Congress*, 'China's Foreign Policy and "Soft Power"'.

[70] Sambath, 'Cambodia–China Relation'.

is a foreign policy priority for China (and India).[71] China has been active in the construction of multiple infrastructure assets (e.g., roads, railways, airfields and seaports) in Myanmar. A particularly significant project is between the China National Petroleum Corporation (CNPC) and Myanmar's Ministry of Energy for building a crude oil and a natural gas pipeline. The project has considerable economic benefits for both China and Myanmar by creating new infrastructure in the form of highway and railway envisaged along the pipelines for connecting Kunming in China with the new deep-seaport and the industrial zone being constructed at Kyaukpyu. The mutually agreed terms on the project entitle Myanmar to two million tons of the transported crude oil for domestic consumption. The project is also expected to increase Myanmar's foreign exchange earnings and provide an alternative export market for its natural gas and other commercial goods.

China's other major infrastructure projects in Myanmar include the deep underwater crude oil unloading port and oil storage facility at Maday Island (Arakan Coast) poised to serve as terminus for tankers coming in from West Asia and Africa and developing a major port at Sittwe, the capital of Rakhine province. Furthermore, Ruili at Myanmar border has been a focus of Beijing as a potential hub for cross-border trade between Southwest China and Southeast Asia leading to major investments in infrastructure in what some refer to as 'the new Shenzhen'.[72] But while infrastructure-building efforts have no doubt increased China's strategic eminence for Myanmar, there have been certain downsides in the form of local discontent over Chinese projects, particularly forced acquisition of land and dispossession of livelihoods, leading to protests against some upcoming pipeline projects.[73] These resonate similar discontent noticed in parts of Africa as well, mentioned later in this book.

---

[71] India also has plans to build a 1,200 MW hydroelectric power station on the Chindwin River, across from India's Northeastern region, including other major road construction projects. India's engagement of Myanmar will be discussed in detail in a separate chapter.

[72] Boehler, 'China's Gateway to Burma Booming'.

[73] Shivananda, 'China's Pipelines in Myanmar'.

Beijing has been striving hard to improve ties with Vietnam through economic engagement as well. Apart from a robust bilateral trade and Sino-Vietnam collaborative ventures in export-oriented manufacturing, China is financing railway construction, hydro power development and ship-building facilities in Vietnam.[74] China and Vietnam are working on developing bilateral tourist flows through the 'Two corridors, One circle' programme.[75] Compared with Cambodia and Myanmar, however, China's foothold in strategic economic asset-building in Vietnam has been much less till now, given the shadow hanging over bilateral relations due to territorial squabbles in the South China Sea. Nonetheless, it is interesting to note the perseverance in China's efforts in engaging Vietnam economically, which has focused more on facilitating bilateral trade and investment, as opposed to greater economic aid to Cambodia and Myanmar. Vietnam's relatively larger, dynamic and more globally integrated economy, compared with Cambodia, Myanmar and Laos, has no doubt encouraged Chinese businesses to seek greater gains from deeper economic links with Vietnam.

As far as development assistance for Laos is concerned, China's presence in the country, again, is yet to assume significant proportions. It is providing the country grants and low-interest loans for development projects, along with technical assistance, mostly for developing transportation infrastructure and hydroelectric power projects. However, with Xi's Belt and Road initiative gaining traction, the relevance of Laos for China is increasing. Seeking to transform the economy of Laos, the initiative is looked at with major interest by the government. The rail connection between Kunming and Vientiane, an infrastructure megaproject, is seen by Laos as having huge economic benefits for the country. Though many fear that the project will put Laos at an unreasonable level of debt, the government is ready to overlook it for achieving bigger advantages that will accompany the project in the long term.[76] In the meantime,

---

[74] Lum et al., 'China's Foreign Aid Activities'.

[75] The Two Corridors refer to the transport links between Hanoi and Kunming, and between Hanoi and Nanning, while the One Circle refers to the Beibu Gulf economic area.

[76] Experts from the ADB and the WB feel that the loans will amount to almost 90 per cent of the country's annual GDP, transforming Laos into one of the world's

China, keen on securing the cooperation of Laos in the OBOR, has been pushing cooperation in strategic industries such as energy, green tourism and infrastructure development.

China's development assistance in Southeast Asia has not been confined to only the low-income CLMV countries but has also extended to larger middle-income economies of the region like Thailand. A significant infrastructure project in Thailand involving Chinese financial support and technical expertise is the canal to be constructed across the Kra Isthmus for allowing ships to bypass the Strait of Malacca by creating a port, warehouses and other infrastructure facilities.[77] The project is a typical example of Chinese development assistance aiming to secure multiple objectives. As a key stakeholder in the project, China gains access to important SLOC and is also able to cast a positive impression on the neighbourhood by responding to regional development needs. China and Thailand are also working together for constructing high-speed rail links and in producing clean energy.[78] Thailand has approved a negotiating framework for Thailand–China cooperation in high-speed rail between Kunming to Thailand, through Laos and Vietnam.[79]

The first instance of Chinese financial support to Indonesia was during the financial crisis of 1997, when China was inclined to provide line of credit (LoCs)[80] to the region and offered stand-by loans as part of an IMF rescue package to Indonesia along with export credit facilities.[81] Subsequently, China has been proactively extending financial support to Indonesia including investment credit and 'soft' loans for infrastructure development. Developing strategic stakes in infrastructure development

---

most indebted countries. See Corben, 'Laos Looks to Balance China's Growing Economic Influence'.

[77] *Infolanka.Asia*, 'China's Silicon Sea Route'.

[78] *People's Daily Online*, 'China, Thailand to Cement Cooperation on High-speed Railway Construction'.

[79] Srivalo, 'Thailand-China High-speed Rail Talks to Get Cabinet Go-ahead'.

[80] Governments of various countries have been extending LOC to the governments of friendly developing foreign countries: first, to promote the export of major goods of their manufacture to these countries, and second, to achieve the political objective, that is, goodwill of beneficiary countries.

[81] Sukma, 'Indonesia-China Relations'.

in Indonesia is important for China given Indonesia's geopolitical importance in the archipelago. China and Indonesia have various MoUs focusing on creating new assets in several segments of infrastructure (e.g., electricity, mining, telecommunication, gas transmission, housing and health care).[82] Several Chinese firms are actively participating in infrastructure development in Indonesia making the latter an important destination for Chinese commercial investment in the region.[83]

Philippines and China have been engaged in acrimonious exchanges over their territorial claims in South China for several years. The territorial dispute and Philippines's close ties with the US continue to influence Sino-Philippines relations. Notwithstanding the difficult geopolitical relations, Beijing has emerged as a major financier and investor in infrastructure development, including energy and mining in Philippines. Railways are noted as the sector having major Chinese involvement[84] with both countries having signed multiple collaborative agreements on railways development.[85] Mining is also another industry in Philippines where leading Chinese firms are displaying considerable interest.

Malaysia, one of the major economies in the region and a leading provider of infrastructure services, is not deficient in infrastructure capacities as many other countries in the region. Nonetheless, the easy availability of Chinese capital, and the eagerness of Chinese investors to expand overseas, has found Chinese business presence expanding in Malaysia, particularly in creating new infrastructure capacities, or upgrading old facilities. The major projects involving Chinese funding in

---

[82] Bank of Indonesia, 'Trade and Investment News'.
[83] China Building Civil Constructions Co. Ltd, Changjiang Waterway Engineering Bureau and the China Foundation for Desertification Control are interested in investing in ports, roads and railway development in Java. The Aluminium Corp of China Ltd (CHALCO) has an MoU with the PT Aneka Tambang, the leading Indonesian mining and minerals processing company on a smelter grade alumina project.
[84] The North Rail line, the rail link connecting Metro Manila to the Luzon region in Northern Philippines, upgrading railway connectivity between the Manila metropolis and its southern provinces are some of the examples.
[85] Lum et al., 'Comparing Global Influence', 86.

Malaysia include the rail double-tracking project from Gemas to Johor Bahru[86] and the Penang Bridge.[87]

The dynamics of China's engagement with Singapore needs to be viewed separately from the rest of the region given Singapore's high-income mature economy, expertise in providing specialized sophisticated economic services and dense integration with the global economy. Indeed, Singapore is attributed a role in China's economic 'going out' strategy. Deng Xiaoping visited Singapore in 1978, shortly before the Third Plenary Session of the 11th Party Central Committee, and was impressed by the development of Singapore and its outward-oriented economic strategy, particularly measures for attracting foreign investment.[88] China's subsequent economic strategies have drawn inspiration from the Singaporean experience.[89] Deng Xiaoping considered Singapore a classic example of economic and social reforms for China to emulate. Consequently, bilateral economic engagement has flourished since China's opening up.

The Chinese proposal to develop the multi-country Nanning–Singapore Economic Corridor, which began in 2010, shows Beijing's earnestness in involving Singapore in its own growth and development. The Corridor is a significant initiative in expanding China's connectivity with the region through 'high speed rail diplomacy' and augmenting regional connectivity as a whole. Proposed by the Guangxi Academy of Social Sciences in 2004,[90] the Corridor will begin from Nanning in the Guangxi province and span Hanoi (Vietnam), Vien Chang (Laos), Phnom Penh (Cambodia), Bangkok (Thailand) Kuala Lumpur (Malaysia) and Singapore through railways, expressways, waterways and air routes. This is in keeping with the concept of ASEAN connectivity[91] and facilitating

---

[86] Seng, 'Renewing 35 Years of Malaysia-China Relations,' 6.

[87] The bridge is expected to be the longest bridge in Southeast Asia stretching 24km. See Pak, 'Will China's Rise Shape Malaysian Chinese Community'.

[88] *Suzhou Industrial Park*, 'New Mode of International Cooperation'.

[89] Ibid.

[90] Wong et al., 'The Nanning-Singapore Economic Corridor,' i.

[91] The concept of ASEAN Connectivity was mooted by the ASEAN state leaders at the 15th ASEAN Summit in Thailand in October 2009 to narrow the development gap that exists within the ASEAN.

greater interaction and communication between China and its Southeast Asian neighbours. Apart from the Corridor, the Singapore Suzhou Industrial Park in 1994 and the Sino-Singapore Tianjin Ecocity in 2007 have been two other major projects successfully undertaken by the two countries. Another joint venture, the Sino-Singapore industrial park in Guangzhou, the capital of Guangdong, is also being planned to develop the port city into a knowledge city.

In addition to the joint ventures, China's regional connectivity initiatives are also spanning around countries from the Greater Mekong Subregion (GMS) sharing the Mekong River [Cambodia, Chinese mainland (Yunnan province and Guangxi Zhuang autonomous region in the country's South), Laos, Myanmar, Thailand and Vietnam]. Indeed, China's role in expanding regional connectivity has been facilitated by its active participation in various regional and multilateral groupings involving Southeast Asia such as ASEAN + 3 (ASEAN, China, Japan and South Korea), ASEAN + 1 (ASEAN and China), the ASEAN Regional Forum (ARF) and the ASEAN Vision Group. China and the ASEAN countries have agreed to establish a fund on investment cooperation for supporting infrastructural development in the region.[92] Further, China has proposed establishing an ASEAN–China fund for providing soft loans to ASEAN countries for developing their trade mechanisms.[93] All these initiatives would be complemented by China's latest initiative—the AIIB—having the Southeast Asian countries among its founding members. China's commitment to infrastructure-building in the region is also facilitated through collaboration with 'sister/friendly cities'. These cities reflect bilateral cooperation between Chinese and the non-Chinese city authorities in urban infrastructure and civic facilities.[94]

As discussed earlier for South Asia, China's humanitarian assistance to Southeast Asia has also been noteworthy. Thailand and Laos suffered from large-scale floods and tropical storms in 2011, during which China

[92] *China Daily*, 'China, ASEAN Sign Agreement on Investment'.
[93] Singh, 'China to Set Up Two ASEAN Funds'.
[94] Nanning in Guangxi province, for example, is a 'friendly/sister city' with Khon Kaen in Thailand and Bandar Seri Begawan in Brunei. Several other cities in China have similar relations with cities in Philippines, Vietnam, Indonesia and Cambodia.

extended financial aid, flood relief equipment and other relief packages to both countries.[95] Myanmar, a country as much vulnerable to cyclones as Bangladesh in South Asia, was extended generous aid support during the *Nargis* cyclone in 2008.[96] Chinese humanitarian assistance in Myanmar, however, has not been limited to managing natural disasters alone and has manifested through initiatives aiming to provide better health facilities like free eye surgical treatment to people in Yangon.[97]

## CONCLUSION

Southeast Asia has witnessed interesting application of economic and cultural tools by China in exerting soft power. Cultural engagement has been more pronounced for the region than in South Asia with the Chinese media and provinces playing active roles in enhancing people-to-people contacts. At the same time, China has been cautious in show-casing culture. CD has had enabling conditions in the region through shared religious heritage and practice of Buddhism while the diaspora's role in transmitting Chinese culture appears problematic.

Economic engagement, on the other hand, has been employed through trade, investment, and substantive development assistance in infrastructure projects aiming to extract commercial and strategic benefits of greater linkages from the vibrant economies in the region. These initiatives seems to have generated some strategic goodwill for China. A Pew survey conducted in September 2015 shows favourable perception of China in Indonesia and Malaysia, perhaps a reflection of China's meaningful economic engagement of these countries and greater communication through ASEAN, as opposed to the adverse impression on the Chinese diaspora shared earlier in this chapter. However, country opinions get divided on specific issues, like the OBOR, where, while showing an overall favourable opinion, countries like Indonesia might not be an enthusiastic partner along with Vietnam and Philippines as

---

[95] *English.xinhuanet.com*. 'Chinese Premier Expresses Sympathy with Thai Flood'.
[96] *USA Today*, 'China: Aid to Burma Should Not Be Politicized'.
[97] *People's Daily Online*, 'Chinese Medical Team Renews Free Eye Surgery in Myanmar'.

they are unlikely to relish the prospect of influx of greater Chinese workers or more Chinese loans,[98] which is probably an unavoidable implication of OBOR.

Many scholars have argued that in forging closer relationship with Southeast Asia, China has 'chosen to limit its own sovereign interest for the sake of engagement in multilateral frameworks and pursuit of greater regional interdependence'.[99] Its expanded engagement with Southeast Asia through regional forums like the ASEAN reflects the emergence of a power ready to march an extra mile for erasing memories of its difficult past with its neighbours. While there is considerable contemporary evidence in support of this view, assessed in terms of the degree and quality of China's soft power targeted at the region, there is no distinct indication, as yet, of China's reluctance to marginalize its national interests in the region. China's aggressive posturing on territorial claims in the South China Sea, its rising military expenditures[100] and reforms have been in contrast to its efforts to engage the region through diplomatic endeavours.[101]

The contrast in China's strategies towards Southeast Asia has been particularly marked in terms of the dichotomy between uncompromising postures on the South China Sea on the one hand, and intensive cultural, economic engagement and active role in regional forums on the other. China's involvement in all ASEAN forums including the EAS and the 10-member ASEAN reflects mutual willingness to act together on regional issues. Indeed, a 'more Asia-oriented grouping' is garnering

---

[98] Dollar, 'China's Rise as a Regional and a Global Power'.

[99] Shambaugh, 'China Engages Asia,' 76.

[100] While China announced a 10.1 per cent increase in its national defence budget in 2015, making it the second largest military spender after the US, the government also highlighted that it was the lowest since 2010. For details see *Xinhua*, 'China Focus: China 2015 Defense Budget To Grow 10.1 pct, Lowest in 5 Years'.

[101] In March 2010, China claimed that the South China Sea was within its 'core interests' of sovereignty, on par with Taiwan and Tibet, and it 'would brook no foreign interference in its territorial issues in the South China Sea'. Later Beijing's decision in 2014 to station a giant oil-drilling rig into disputed waters off the Vietnamese coast led to riots and violence against Chinese businesses and was seen as the most serious confrontation between the two neighbours since 1979.

increased regional support for China[102] reflecting the intention on part of some regional states for a more Asia-centred focus to the regional architecture, as opposed to a more trans-Pacific group led by Washington. Many argue that China's role as a regional leader in this regard is becoming larger with its willingness to mediate disputes in Southeast Asia that resonates with its evolving soft power strategy.[103] Nevertheless, ASEAN remains perturbed and divided not only over China's rapid rise but also over its position on the South China Sea.

Both China and the ASEAN are conscious of the evolving regional order and their respective importance in influencing the strategic dynamics of the Asia-Pacific. China's desire to remain embedded as a 'great power' in the region is critically dependent upon the perception it enjoys in the neighbourhood. Contradictory posturing will leave the region confused and suspicious of China's motives. This might create more space for extra-regional presence—primarily the US—given that several Southeast Asian countries are US allies. Washington's renewed strategic focus on the Asia-Pacific and its new commitment to enhance military presence in Asia[104] might lead to larger roles of extra-regional entities in the South China Sea, thereby complicating the regional strategic dynamic.

India is another country being looked at by many of the Southeast Asian nations as having the ability to limit Beijing's growing influence. India's presence in the region is increasing as it becomes a deeper part of an Asia experiencing dense economic integration between its northeastern and southeastern parts. India's influence on Southeast Asia is evident in multiple respects: religion, language and civilization, which are products of close economic and cultural interactions over centuries. The somewhat tepid engagement between India and Southeast Asia during the Cold War years has given way to a more robust association through the Look East Policy (LEP) that is now upgraded to the 'Act East' strategy. Much as India is wary about China's expanding

---

[102] *Congressional Research Service (CRS) Library of Congress*, 'China's Foreign Policy and "Soft Power"'.

[103] Kurlantzick, 'China's Charm Offensive in Southeast Asia'.

[104] Perlez, 'Drawing Spheres of Influence, Without the US,' 3.

strategic influence in South Asia, China might also, over time, become similarly apprehensive about India's influence on Southeast Asia. India's soft power might indeed be more effective in this regard than China's.

# 5

# Northeast Asia, Oceania and South Pacific: From Periphery to Greater Periphery

Beyond Southeast Asia, the Asian region bordering the Pacific—comprising Northeast Asia (Japan, South Korea, North Korea and Taiwan), Oceania (Australia and New Zealand) and the South Pacific Islands—occupies strong significance in China's foreign policy matrix. The region is part of China's extended neighbourhood and critical for the effective realization of the 'China dream' along with the provision of sustained impetus to China's economic development. China's engagement of the countries in the region and the application of soft power tools, as discussed in the chapter, have varied in accordance with its assessment of maximizing strategic values and national interests.

## NORTHEAST ASIA: COMPLEXITIES COMPLICATE COOPERATION

China itself is the largest country in Northeast Asia that also includes Taiwan, Japan and the North and South Koreas in the Korean peninsula. China has had complex relations with all these countries compounded by long histories of civilizational and cultural interfaces and geopolitical developments in the modern times. Countries in the region have profound cultural similarities with China reflected particularly in the Chinese writing system adopted by many of these countries since historical times through the borrowing of complete Chinese alphabetical characters, invention of new 'Chinese-like' characters and rendering native scripts using Chinese characters.[1]

---

[1] Flyingzone, 'Chinese Letters in Japan, Korea and Vietnam'.

Cultural affinities, however, have not been able to contain difficulties from permeating China's relationships with its Northeast Asian neighbours, which continue to be characterized by major irritants manifesting in regional tensions. Cross-straits relations between China and Taiwan are a case in point. These dynamic relations change periodically with changes in national leaderships. Relations during former President Hu reflected Beijing's inclination to adopt a relatively 'non-confrontationist' policy towards Taiwan for facilitating its own rise. The then Chinese leadership had accommodated Taiwan within its overall strategy of 'peaceful development' with a 'newly changing' Beijing appearing keen on being seen benign to Taiwan and a 'responsible stakeholder' in the international community.[2] From the latter perspective, the 'Taiwan' test has been critical for China for demonstrating to the rest of the world its commitment to global stability by not stoking regional tensions. The Hu-Wen regime was equally keen on signalling its Taiwan policy having shifted from the narrow confines of cross-straits relations for ensuring regional stability, as he himself submitted: '[W]e fully understand and respect the Taiwan compatriot's love for their own home and their wish to be masters of their own house...',[3] and the empathy with Taiwan highlighted.[4]

The 'soft' perspective, however, seems to have given way to a tougher stance under President Xi. While committing to trust and peace with Taipei, Xi reiterates the more forceful 'One China' posture: '[T]hough the mainland and Taiwan are yet to be reunified, they belong to one China and are inseparable parts of the country'.[5] The 'One China' policy has ramifications for Taiwan in Beijing-led initiatives, such as the AIIB, where, while welcoming Taiwan, China has insisted on its entry being conditional on the acceptance of the 'One China' principle.

Sino-Japan relations are among the most dichotomous ties in the modern era. While history has conditioned the relationship, the ties also

---

[2] Huang and Li, *Inseparable Separation: The Making of China's Taiwan Policy*, 3.
[3] Ibid, 309.
[4] Binhua and Yong, 'Hu Jinatao he Lian Zhan zai Beijing Juxing Jengshi Huitan' [Hu Jintao and Lien Zhan Hold Formal Meeting in Beijing].
[5] *Global Times*, 'Xi Meets with'.

witnesses coexistence of intense territorial spats with economic robustness. The Japanese Archipelago was first mentioned in the Chinese historic text—the *Book of the Later Han* (*Hou Han shu*)—compiled in the 5th century that noted Han Emperor's gift of a golden seal to Wa (Japan),[6] discovered in northern Kyushu (third largest island in Japan) in the 18th century. Since then, Japan has been repeatedly mentioned in Chinese historical texts with references increasing with Japan's evolution as a prominent regional power. Japan's political subjugation of China during World War II and the wartime atrocities committed on ordinary Chinese continue to rankle modern China. At the same time, the align-ment of political forces in Japan critical of China have kept the anti-China tirade high, particularly over the disputed Senkaku/Diaoyu islands, and other contentious matters like rare earth export quotas.[7] The US–Japan security alliance has contributed to further political and strategic mistrust though some analysts argue China's perception of Japan as a 'junior partner' of the US might encourage it to work pragmatically with Tokyo.[8] On the whole, however, political tensions have been prevented from assuming conflictual proportions by robust and variegated economic ties.

Sino-South Korea ties have strengthened since formalization of diplo-matic relations in 1992. South Korea, a US ally, has been searching for a new role in Asia that has influenced its engagement with China. As Charles Armstrong points out, '[T]here is a real fascination with China in South Korea, and the flow of investment, exports, students, tourists, and businessmen going to China from South Korea have exploded in the last several years'.[9] Two strands of strategic opinion exist in South Korea on

---

[6] 'People's Republic of China–Japan Relations'. Available at: http://en.wikipedia.org/wiki/People's_Republic_of_China%E2%80%93Japan_relations (accessed on 25 January 2012).

[7] In March 2012, Japan, the US and the EU jointly filed a WTO dispute settlement case against China over its limits on rare earth exports, but failed to restore Chinese rare earth supply to a satisfying level. See Ka-ho YU, 'Japan Challenging China's Rare Earth Hegemony'.

[8] Cheng and Brown, *China under Hu Jintao: Opportunities, Dangers, and Dilemmas*, 402.

[9] Pan, 'South-Korea's Ties with China, Japan and the US'.

China: The first suggests the Koguryo (or Goguryeo) dispute[10] has adversely affected the perception of China encouraging closer ties with the US,[11] while the other points to China's success in winning hearts and minds of the elite and the common Koreans alike.[12] The view draws support from public opinion surveys pointing to limited success of China's engagement efforts.[13] The second view, on the other hand, is largely shared by those who are confident of China playing an even greater global role than the US in the future.[14] The leadership does seem inspired to seek greater engagement with China as is evident from the signing of the bilateral FTA and President Park Geun-hye being one of the few heads of state, along with President Putin, to attend the gala ceremony commemorating the 70th anniversary of World War II in Beijing in September 2015. The bonhomie, however, does not signal the end of South Korea's discomfort with China on several security issues pertaining to the Korean peninsula (e.g., aggressive posturing in the region, tensions with Taiwan and Japan, and disputes in the South China Sea). Indeed, the graduation of ties to a 'strategic cooperative partnership'[15]

---

[10] The Koguryo kingdom (37 BC to 668 AD) responsible for spreading Buddhism throughout the region, straddled between what is now North Korea and part of South Korea and the Northeastern Chinese region of Manchuria, is a 'war of history' between the two countries. Wei Cuncheng, a professor at Jilin University, China, in 2004, declared that 'Koguryo was a regime established by ethnic groups in northern China some 2,000 years ago, representing an important part of Chinese culture'. Subsequently, South Koreans discovered that China's Ministry of Foreign Affairs (MFA) had deleted Koguryo from a summary of Korean history on its website. For details see Gries, 'The Koguryo Controversy', 3.

[11] Klingner, 'China Shock for South Korea'.

[12] Ho, 'The "Rise" of China and Its Impact on South Korea'. 2.

[13] Moon, 'South Korean Public Opinion Trends and Effects on the ROK–US Alliance'.

[14] Lee, 'The ROK's Perception of China's Role', 24.

[15] The Lee Myung-bak administration committed to the establishment of a 'strategic cooperative partnership' with China during Lee's inaugural visit to Beijing as the new president of South Korea in 2008, thus reflecting growth in bilateral economic interdependence. However, as far as political relations are concerned between the two countries, the partnership remains an aspiration.

has not prevented clashes over China's North Korea policy and the South Korea–US alliance.[16]

North Korea fits well in China's 'peaceful development' strategy given that a friendly neighbour in the Northeast can be a buffer between China and the democratic South Korea, which has US military presence. A bulwark on the Northeastern flank also eases military deployment enabling greater focus on Taiwan and domestic issues. The special relationship does not entirely exclude conflicts with Beijing's penchant to be a 'constructive' player in the region resulting in the adjustment of its North Korean policies in the last few years reflected in a lack of opposition to stricter international sanctions after Pyongyang's second nuclear test in May 2009 and greater cozying up to South Korea. The latter, according to some scholars, has been at the expense of its traditional ally North Korea with Beijing choosing to marginalize political and military alliances with Pyongyang for greater economic benefits from deeper engagement with South Korea.[17]

Remarkably, the multiple tensions in Beijing's political ties with Tokyo, Seoul, Pyongyang and Taipei have not constrained its economic relations. Indeed, the dichotomy symbolizes *zheng leng jing re* (cold in politics, warm in economy) with China's major politico-diplomatic issues with Northeast Asian neighbours not manifesting in major political crises due to high economic stakes. Robust economic relations have also provided the foundation for greater diplomatic engagement, particularly cultural initiatives.

### Economic Initiatives

China's economic engagement with North Korea is distinct from those with other countries in the region in its 'development' characteristic. Development assistance is limited to North Korea given its irrelevance for the rest. Supporting North Korea's infrastructure growth safeguards China's strategic interests by securing access to mineral and energy resources for helping its relatively economically backward northeastern provinces. Better economic exchanges between these provinces and

---

[16]  Byun, 'Sino-South Korea Ties Warming?'
[17]  Klingner, 'China Shock for South Korea'.

North Korea also stabilize Chinese borders by reducing incentives for North Koreans to migrate to China. China has reportedly invested billions in building seaports, roads, railways and tourist infrastructure in North Korea and its economic assistance has extended to the supply of food, energy and consumer goods.[18] The significance of China's infrastructure investments was highlighted by Jang Songthaek, the Director of the Central Administrative Department of the Worker's Party of Korea, and also the Chairman of the National Defence Commission—during their visit to Beijing in August 2012. A press release issued on the occasion revealed that both leaderships were keen on exploring cooperation in developing economic zones[19] and agreeing on the joint development of two such zones in North Korea.[20]

Chinese business presence is significant in North Korea through companies such as the Tonghua Iron and Steel Group that has invested in the Musan mine—the largest open-cut iron mine in Asia with verified iron-ore reserves—and the Tangshan Iron and Steel Company and the China Iron and Steel Group that have also invested in mining. Chinese investment has also flown into transport infrastructure, such as in the road linking Rason to China's border with North Korea,[21] a project with significant economic benefits for China in reducing transportation time for products from the Liaoning province to the Yellow Sea by giving the inland Jilin province access to the Sea of Japan.[22] The Jilin province is partnering with North Korea in different mining projects, which include one aiming to transmit electricity from Jilin's Changbai County to North Korea in exchange for gold, copper and other ores.

China is now a bigger trade partner for South Korea than the US. It is also one of the main recipients of foreign direct investment (FDI) from

---

[18] Since early 1990s, China has provided 70 per cent of all food aid, almost 90 per cent of energy imports and 80 per cent of North Korea's consumer goods.
[19] Li, 'Neighbours Explore Cooperation', 1.
[20] At the east coast port of Rason near Northeast China's Jilin province, and on the west at Hwanggumpyong and Wihwa islands near Dandong in Liaoning province. For details, see *Global Times*, 'China Gets Sea of Japan Trade Access'.
[21] *Asahi Shimbun*, 'China, Russia Developing Infrastructure in N. Korean Port City'.
[22] Ibid.

South Korea with the latter keen on more FDI from China. China's insatiable appetite for energy has benefitted major South Korean companies, particularly the LS Group conglomerate which has large investments in China.[23] China too, on the other hand, plans to invest in South Korea's energy sector for acquiring electricity generated abroad.[24] Greater trade, investment and movement of people will clearly be facilitated by the recently concluded bilateral FTA.

China's push for greater economic engagement with Taiwan is driven by the objective of its eventual unification with the mainland. Business interaction over several years has led to increasing synchronization of the Chinese and the Taiwanese markets and investor sentiments[25] with the China–Taiwan Economic Cooperation Framework Agreement (ECFA) playing an enabling role. Greater access in the Chinese market has benefitted Taiwanese farmers and fishermen[26] with an increase in direct flights and sea links between the major cities. Positive economic sentiments have been augmented by Beijing's encouraging policies, such as providing cheap air tickets to roughly 400,000 of the one million Taiwanese living in China for returning home to vote in Taiwan's presidential election in January 2012.

Scholars point to the structures of the Chinese and Japanese economies being largely complimentary. Apart from a growing trade, 'the relationship with Japan has been important for China's "catching up" to the frontier of industrial technology'.[27] It has also helped its transition from a lower to a higher income country through the access to industrial technology and investment provided by Japan.[28] Therefore, once again, good economics has positively impacted the relationship and highlights its importance even when bilateral ties are uneasy. In China's case (and even with respect to Japan) the leadership has decided to overlook the

---

[23] *Energy Daily*, 'China Investing in South Korean Power Grid'.
[24] Ibid.
[25] When Shanghai stocks fell by about 20 per cent in 2011, Taiwanese stocks fell by a similar amount almost simultaneously.
[26] Koike, 'China's Softly, Softly Approach', 1.
[27] Armstrong, 'The Politics of Japan–China Trade and the Role of the World Trade System', 2.
[28] Ibid.

complexities in the relationship for economic benefits which is evident from being both major trade partners and investors of each other. However, good economics can hardly erase the decades of historical discomfort that both countries continue to be saddled with, which continue to prevail in their engagement in recent times, including spats over territories as well the fact that both continue to be sensitive to each other's rise and spheres of geostrategic influence. Indeed, 'kind' words as about each other are seldom spoken officially and much of the responses continue to be dominated by emotional throwbacks at history and mistrust of current postures. For China, the relationship with Japan is perhaps one of the sternest challenges for its soft power given the high emotional content of the ties, which often prevent objective and rational outlooks on part of people and actors on both sides.

A positive aspect of the strategic and economic engagement of Japan has been the assistance extended during natural disasters, particularly after the 2011 Tohoku earthquake and the Tsunami. Chinese provinces have also been active in this regard [e.g., the northeastern Chinese city Changchun, a sister-city of Sendai (Japan), dispatched drinking water to its people]. The Chinese media has also repeatedly highlighted the resilience and lawfulness of the Japanese people despite extreme power, food and water shortages and personal grief.[29] China also contributed significantly after the Fukushima crisis by providing emergency relief, material and search and rescue support with the Sany Heavy Industry Co. along with a team of engineers and consultants, helping quell overheating and radiation in the crippled nuclear plant.

## Cultural Initiatives

China's long influence on Japanese culture dates back to 200 AD. Japan's accommodation of Chinese cultural influences has been dependent on the receptivity of the latter at particular historical junctures. Whether language, religion, urban planning or governance, the Chinese influence on Japan has been pronounced. While the introduction of the Chinese script in the 4th century AD was instrumental in Japan's cultural

---

[29] Hongmei, 'China, Japan Endeavor to Seek Win-win Relationship'.

development, the Buddhist ethics, and the Confucius legal codes increased the legitimacy of the Japanese rulers and the Chinese-style bureaucracy, thus creating the first genuine state in Japanese history.[30] Given such cultural legacy, the relatively low people-to-people contact in modern times is surprising.

A survey conducted in 2011 by *China Daily* and the Japanese Genron NPO revealed that majorities in both countries have hardly visited each other and rely on news reports for mutual learning.[31] Low people-to-people contact is also reflected in the low direct exchange.[32] Notwithstanding a bilateral Cultural Exchange Agreement in place since 1979, which could have encouraged both countries to impart more vigour to people-to-people contacts in culture, education, sports and academics, the various official exchanges under its rubric have done little in bringing people closer. However, high-level initiatives have been significant in this regard. The Beijing-Tokyo Forum cofounded in 2005 by *China Daily* and the Genron NPO is a major bilateral public diplomatic communication platform focusing on cooperation in politics, business, culture and media. The Chinese leadership's push for deeper cultural exchange is primarily tactical given Japan's strategic relevance and pivotal presence in Northeast Asia, though some scholars are sceptical about such significance.[33] Further, with China's rise raising questions about the continuation of American supremacy, Japan's decisions have probably become relatively more critical from a regional stability perspective.

Keen to play the 'cultural independence' card,[34] Taiwan has been eager to advance its own soft power through overseas cultural centres, similar to Chinese CIs, opened first in the US, and then in Europe and Asia.[35] Taiwan's efforts to establish a distinct cultural identity is in contrast to China's pursuit of deeper bilateral cultural engagement as evident from

---

[30] Stearns, 'The Spread of Chinese Civilization to Japan'.

[31] Wenting, 'Accurate Information and Calm Analysis Media's Duty'.

[32] *China Daily*, 'Former Ambassador Shares His Views on Sino-Japan Relations'.

[33] Ness, 'Japan, the Indispensable Power in Northeast Asia'.

[34] The Democratic Progressive Party in Taiwan attempts to break the cultural bond shared by the mainland and Taiwan and seek 'cultural independence' which further complicates the cross-straits relationship.

[35] Poon, 'Soft Power Smackdown! Confucius Institute vs Taiwan Academy'.

China's Minister of Culture's emphasis on greater cross-straits cultural exchanges and cooperation between schools, troupes, museums and libraries.[36] Companies from Mainland China are being encouraged to hold cultural fairs on the island and welcome Taiwanese companies for similar events in the mainland.[37] Indeed, banners on Taipei boulevards, which earlier promoted Western or Japanese performances, now advertise the Shanghai Symphony Orchestra or the *Kunqu* opera troupe, underscoring the quiet penetration of cultural exports from the mainland.

With the enormous challenge of cross-straits relations and the effect it could have on regional stability, both China and Taiwan have also employed personal diplomacy for assessing each other's intentions, considered essential building blocks for future cooperation. The criticality of face-to-face diplomacy for effective communication in interstate relations emerged an effective tool once again during the Xi-Ma Summit meeting in Singapore in November 2015. The historic meeting, held for the first time since the Chinese civil war in 1949, signalled the leadership's (more for Beijing) preference for engagement and was perhaps aimed at conveying an implicit signal towards the regional and extra-regional actors to that effect. It carried a specific message: To help manage conflict and gain 'wide support from all walks of life across the Strait and the international community'.[38] Apart from the 'support' China wanted to achieve through this meet, it was partly a strategy for 'reassuring' the neighbours and extra-regional powers about China's commitment to ensuring regional peace and stability.

Cross-straits CD has been flourishing through cooperation between museums, provinces and temples. In October 2009, the Palace Museums of Beijing and Taipei held their first-ever joint exhibition in Taipei, displaying exhibits from a long-splintered imperial collection. Museums are also collaborating in coordinating catalogues, web sites and restoring artefacts.[39] Old ties and cultural connects are encouraging mainland provinces to add fillip to cross-straits ties led by Henan and Guizhou

[36] Shu-ling, 'Officials Propose Taiwan, China Cultural Exchanges'.
[37] *China Daily*, 'Mainland, Taiwan Cultural Exchanges Promoted'.
[38] *Asiaone*, 'Taiwan, China Leaders to Hold Surprise Meeting in Singapore'.
[39] Ibid.

provinces.[40] Cultural engagement through temples is also contributing to greater people-to-people contacts through the Matsu[41] culture and exchange of statues as gifts between sister temples.[42] The Mainland's decision to lift entry-permit requirement for Taiwan residents[43] in 2015 is another development to increase people-to-people communication.

The CIs have been active vehicles of cultural and public diplomacy in Northeast Asia. Their propagation began in 2004 from South Korea, which was ideal for launching brand 'Confucius' given the Korean peninsula's long history of following the Confucian system of thought, society and governance. South Korea's significance as an economic partner for China and the importance of not allowing territorial tensions to spoil economic ties was also responsible for upping cultural communication through CIs. Furthermore, Korea being a major US ally and a conduit for facilitating extra-regional presence in the region made it and the geography perfect for communicating China's 'arrival' on the world stage[44] through dedicated cultural engagement and the clear message: China was back into the 'first-world club after a century of semi-colonial status and 50 years of third world membership'.[45] The efforts appear to be paying off with the Chinese Government's effort to promote Chinese language overseas, indicating 'Chinese is as popular in Korea today as English is in China'.[46] The strong revival of the language after years of ban has primary school children learning about 2,000 Chinese characters following the reintroduction of Mandarin in the school curriculum.[47]

---

[40] Ibid.

[41] Matsu (or Mazu) is the goddess of the sea protecting sailors and fishermen and is invoked as the patron-deity of all Southern Chinese and East Asians.

[42] *Xinhua*, 'Cross-strait Cultural Exchange Continues with Chinese Mainland Statue Donated to Taiwan'.

[43] Currently, Taiwan residents must apply for a visa-like entry permit in order to visit the mainland.

[44] Palit, 'China's Cultural Diplomacy'.

[45] Starr, 'Chinese Language Education in Europe', 65–80.

[46] French, 'Another Chinese Export is all the Rage',

[47] *China.org.cn*, 'South Korea–China Cultural Exchange'.

Chinese language education appears to have made deep inroads in North Korea as well, which is interesting given North Korea's banning of the language in the 1950s, as part of its overall strategy towards foreign languages. While it continues to shun European languages and cultural missions including the German Goethe Institute and the French Alliance Francoise,[48] Mandarin is becoming increasingly popular along with greater interface among the youth of both countries. The CIs in Japan (Annexure II) too have been active and successful in upping interest in Mandarin by organizing language classes on varied subjects (e.g., legal translation, business Chinese and Chinese for children) with the CI at Ritsumeikan University earning the distinction of being the 'school, window and bridge' for bilateral friendship.[49]

The Shanghai Action Plan (2012) has been attempting to increase trilateral cooperation between Japan, China and South Korea for protecting cultural heritage and increasing exchanges between cultural industries.[50] In this regard, it is important to note the key role played by education in promoting cultural exchanges and people-to-people communication with more and more Japanese and Korean students coming to study in China.[51] Already popular for its cosmopolitan education systems, Asian students comprise around 70 per cent of foreign students in China. Korea and Japan have emerged as top sources of foreign students for China with Korea leading the pack at 62,442, followed by US (23,292) and Japan (17,961).[52] Education can emerge as vital a strategic conduit as economics in maintaining and deepening bilateral engagement between China and its Northeast Asian neighbours notwithstanding their 'cold politics'.

The interplay of the cultural dynamics in Northeast Asia can hardly overlook the cardinal aspect of culture being an implicit unifying force

[48] 'Lux Sinica: China's Civilizing Influence in North Korea'. Available at: http://adamcathcart.wordpress.com/2011/06/17/lux-sinica/ (accessed on 31 January 2012).
[49] Confucius Institute at Ritsumeikan, Japan.
[50] *People's Daily Online*, 'China, Japan, ROK Agree to Enhance Cultural Cooperation'.
[51] Introduction Export Education.
[52] *Study in China*, 'Statistics of International Students in China in 2011'.

in the region. Notwithstanding strategic interpersonal differences, which are often gigantic in proportion, culture provides an enabling platform for interface and exchange. It is, therefore, hardly surprising that notwithstanding difficulties, China, Japan and Korea continue to work towards a trilateral partnership, which, while gaining credence and conviction from economic grounds, would nonetheless be a step towards cultural consolidation. Such consolidation is noticeable in the slow but distinct efforts between China and Taiwan as well. Perhaps it is still too early to reflect on the possibility of culture drawing the countries of the region to a strategic convergence at some distant point of time in future. But the potential of the idea will definitely continue to provide opportunities for greater bilateral exchange among countries, particularly at the people-to-people level. The role of CD will remain vital in the region, and China, particularly, is expected to up the ante more in this regard in future.

## OCEANIA (AUSTRALIA AND NEW ZEALAND): EDGING CLOSER

Oceania is part of China's 'greater periphery' (*da zhou bian*).[53] The vision is consistent with the contemporary concept of 'greater periphery diplomacy' (*da zhou bian wai jiao*) as opposed to the earlier 'periphery diplomacy' (*zhou bian wai jiao*) that focused only on the immediate neighbourhood (e.g., Southeast Asia).[54] As Ruan Zong Ze points out: '[G]reater peripheral environment is not just a geographical concept. It is more a three-dimensional concept (*li ti gai nian*). This concept includes the countries literally neighbouring China and the countries or forces which do not neighbour China but are important to China's critical interest'.[55]

---

[53] In addition to former President Deng Xiaoping's focus on great power relations, particularly with the US, Xi Jinping's government is witnessing a reprioritization of periphery relations, with the neighbourhood diplomacy gaining renewed traction.

[54] Yang, *The Pacific Islands in China's Grand Strategy*, 136.

[55] Zongze, 'Winning the Next Decade'.

China's interactions with Australia and New Zealand represent fairly wholesome two-way engagements, particularly in trade and culture. Economic engagement is almost completely bereft of development assistance and infrastructure-building given both Australia and New Zealand are developed economies with negligible deficits in their socio-economic development indicators. Bilateral economic engagement, therefore, has focused on trade and investment. China's economic 'rise' and high demand for primary commodity exports make it a top priority country for Australia and New Zealand. Their geographic proximity to China also fuels mutual interest and the imperative for PD manifesting in high-level visits characterizing China's major-nation initiative launched after President Xi's assumption of office (Annexure III).

China's earlier 'negative' public opinion in Australia produced by the excesses committed during the Cultural Revolution and the May Fourth Movement is, very gradually, giving way to a more-positive perception, particularly since the Beijing Olympic Games that showcased China as a 'more sophisticated, modern, evolving nation and culture'.[56] The Australian Defence White Paper (DWP; 2013) noted: 'Australia does not approach China as an adversary'.[57] This was at least a partial correction of the concern of neighbours expressed in the DWP of 2009 over the pace and scope of China's force modernization. Discomforts continue to remain as revealed by the Lowy Institute's study in 2013 with 41 per cent respondents expecting China to be a 'military threat' to Australia in the next 20 years and 57 per cent believing that Australia was allowing 'too much investment from China'.[58] But there are other surveys reflecting the positive impact of China's economic growth on Australia[59] as well as underlining the coexistence of contradictory perceptions.

The realization that China needs to continue working on its image in even the region compels greater engagement: such engagement with Australia and New Zealand, apart from strategic access to high-income markets and mining resources (e.g., copper and gold), is also driven by

---

[56] Dover, 'The Image of China in Australia'.
[57] Raska, 'Australia's Evolving "Smart Power" Strategy'.
[58] Ho, 'Australia "Biting the Hand" of China'.
[59] Hanson, 'Chinese Aid in Fiji'.

the desire to connect deeper with the English-speaking, developed, OECD world in the Asia-Pacific. This is facilitated by the keen interest in 'learning' about each other, particularly in the Australia academic community,[60] which is consistent with the emphasis on Australia's White Paper (October 2012) on mapping out its Asia 'pivot' and deeper Canberra–Beijing engagement with similar emphasis on India as well.[61] Other drivers are also pushing deeper engagement from the Chinese perspective with the South Pacific region considered Australia's 'patch'[62] or New Zealand's 'neighbourhood', given their overarching presences. China recognizes Australia's strategic influence on Southeast Asia[63] and the South Pacific,[64] more so given Taiwan's shadow on the region. China's strategy towards Australia and New Zealand is influenced by the additional expectation of their discouraging others in the region, particularly South Pacific Island countries, from diplomatically recognizing Taiwan.[65]

Economics will continue to remain the major driver of China's bilateral ties in the region given Beijing's effective economic pull. China is not only Australia's largest trading partner but a major investor in its mining industry as well. The China–Australia bilateral FTA concluded in 2014 lays the foundation for deepening the economic relationship with China. The robust economic ties should continue notwithstanding Australia being a formal US ally and its reservations over China's human rights record. New Zealand, on the other hand, was the first developed country to recognize China's market economy status and conclude talks on China's entry into the WTO. China is New Zealand's second largest

---

[60] The author's discussions with several Australian academics and media experts revealed the importance being attached to knowing China with generous government funding flowing into China study centres and research programmes.

[61] *China Daily*, 'Australia Maps Out Its Asia "Pivot"', 12.

[62] A paper entitled 'Big enough for both of us' by the Lowy Institute in Sydney in 2013 pointed out that Australia remains the biggest aid donor in the region, and while China is playing a bigger part in the region's trade, it is still a small player. See *ABC Radio Australia*, 'China an Example to Others',

[63] Lyon, 'The Southeast Asian Emphasis in DWP2013'.

[64] Brown, 'Australian Influence in the South Pacific'.

[65] Yang, *The Pacific Islands in China's Grand Strategy*.

trading partner and a major source of migrants, students and tourists. New Zealand was also the first developed country to sign a bilateral FTA with China in April 2008—a move that clearly had economic and geo-strategic motivations.[66] Notwithstanding such support and despite classifying China as one of the six 'bedrock' relationships by the Ministry of Foreign Affairs and Trade in 2004, there are concerns in New Zealand over China's role in the region, particularly increasing overtures in the South Pacific and the diplomatic rivalry with Taiwan.

## Cultural Initiatives

China's cultural engagement of Australia and New Zealand is a relatively recent but pragmatic move. Australian efforts to showcase China to local audiences have been underway for much longer. Film Australia's series, 'The Human Face of China', completed in 1979, was the first documentary on the Chinese society since the Cultural Revolution.[67] While China's efforts are far more recent, they come with the confidence backed by its economic rise and aimed at building a benign image. Efforts like the Year of Chinese Culture in Australia (2011–12) are useful in this regard with their focus on milestone Chinese art performances.[68] Cross-cultural collaborations like the *Cho Cho*[69] are also being attempted though these initiatives are yet to become successes given the 'cross-cultural conflict' that continues to crop up. Nonetheless, Chinese art and culture is making

---

[66] The evidence on determinants of FTAs and regional trading agreements (RTAs) points to maintaining stable relations as a major driver of such agreements. See Palit, *China-India Economics*, 97.

[67] Chey, 'From Rosny to the Great Wall', 168.

[68] Performances include the 'Legend of Shangri-la'—a song and dance blockbuster directed and starred by the famous Chinese artist Yang Liping of the *Bai* (The Bai people, also mean the 'white' people, is an ethnic minority and is one of the 56 ethnic groups recognized by the PRC. Essentially Buddhist, they also worship nature god and mostly live in certain areas of Yunnan, Guizhou and Hunam, speaking Bai language), solo recitals by Pianist Lang Lang and the famous ballet 'The Last Emperor'. See *China.org.cn*, 'Experience China to Promote Mutual Understanding'.

[69] The Cho Cho collaboration between Chinese and Australian producers and actors are efforts to explore common themes of love and freedom.

inroads in Australia evident from the acclaim received by several performances.[70] The Nanjing Acrobatic Troupe's training of the Australian Flying Fruit Fly Circus is an example of emerging cultural partnerships. The discovery of the 'New English Calligraphy' for teaching an invented language based on English phonetics and Chinese pictographs also indicates mutual interest and appreciation.

It is interesting to note the conspicuous Chinese cultural influence in several aspects of Australian daily lives—the most notable being Chinese food and probably the most popular non-British cuisine in Australia. Educationalist Elizabeth Chon feels Chinese food has become integral to Australian eating habits.[71] Australians are comfortable with chopsticks and the Chinese New Year is celebrated with gusto in 'Chinatowns' all over Australia. Chinese movies are equally popular with the Sydney China Film festival and the Golden Koala Chinese Film Festival screening many.[72] Australians are also travelling to China in large numbers with the numbers likely to increase with the signing of the FTA and the introduction of direct flights to new cities such as Chongqing, Hangzhou, Nanjing and Tianjin. The emphasis on 'people-to-people' contacts and greater exposure to China has not been left to CD alone with 'panda' diplomacy playing a prominent role.[73] A practice revived during the Mao era, the gifting of pandas is part of China's traditional diplomacy in engaging friends with its roots going back to around 700 AD when Empress Wu Zetian had sent a pair of pandas to Japan.

China's heightened regional profile is evident in New Zealand as well. There appears to be urgency on part of the latter to be noticed by China: 'China will loom so large in world affairs by mid-century that a failure to seize the moment now to build the relationship will mean opportunities

---

[70] Like the Shanghai Quartet, exhibitions of Cai Guoqiang, Shanghai Symphony Orchestra and so on.

[71] *International Market News*, 'Australian Food Goes Asian'.

[72] The Sydney China Film Festival is Australia's largest Asian Film festival and a platform for promoting Chinese films (e.g., 'Cheng Du I Love You', 'Cow' and 'Ocean Flame').

[73] Several countries have received these cuddly giants as China's national gift with Australia receiving them in 2010.

lost'.[74] New Zealand is keen on prominence in China's priorities and has introduced Chinese history, culture, geography and language in the primary and secondary school curricula. China, on its part, is pushing ahead on 'arts diplomacy' through art exhibitions, film shows and performing art presentations with active support of the diaspora and Chinese provinces.[75] Bilateral cultural interfaces are facilitated by people-to-people communication generated by the long history of scientific and technological cooperation between the two countries.

The Chinese media has also not shied away from contributing to PD in Australia and New Zealand by expanding on-ground presence and meaningful collaborations with local counterparts (e.g., CCTV and Sky News Australia,[76] ABC's agreement with Chongqing Television and Radio Group,[77] *Chinese Herald* and the AM936 Chinese Radio's operations in New Zealand). Finally, CIs, China's active cultural ambassadors, have come up all over Australia and New Zealand (Annexure II) and are primarily focusing on teaching Mandarin and celebrating Chinese Culture Days.

Like in several other countries, education also contribute to greater people-to-people contacts between China and the Oceania. Interesting initiatives like the Chinese telecom giant Huawei's sponsoring of Australian students annually to study in China[78] are expected to enlarge over time. While these would steadily increase the inflows of Australian students to China, Chinese studies are gaining rapid popularity in Australian and New Zealand universities with focus on collaborative learning and research between Chinese and Australian universities.[79] Major examples include the La Trobe University in Melbourne's

---

[74] Kember and Clark, *China and New Zealand*, 116.

[75] There are examples of provinces like Gansu continuing to play its ancient role of being the communications link during the Chinese empire by sending its acrobatic and shadow puppet performers to the New Zealand.

[76] Bullbeck, 'Sky News Australia, China's CCTV Ink Live News Agreement'.

[77] Ibid.

[78] In 2013, the company sent 11 Australian ICT undergraduate students to China for a three-week education programme.

[79] 'Centre for China Studies'. Available at: http://www.latrobe.edu.au/china-centre/about (accessed on 21 January 2012).

collaboration with the Peking University and the Beijing Foreign Studies University on a China Studies Programme for facilitating research collaborations among scholars from all over the world. More than 400 researchers in Australia are working in China with the Australian Centre on China in the World (CIW) at the Australian National University (ANU) examining bilateral issues for building on both sides a *zheng you*—'an empathetic and engaged friend who can disagree, a trusted interlocutor, a principled partner in understanding'.[80] The CIW, announced in 2010, is also active in partnering with influential Chinese think tanks (e.g., the China Institute of Contemporary International Relations). The New Zealand Contemporary China Research Centre has also engaged in organizing symposiums involving senior Chinese academics, offering fellowships, apart from the National Online System of Access to Information on China (NOSAIC)[81]—an effort to close information gap aiming to boost cooperation based on mutual understanding.

## SOUTH PACIFIC ISLAND COUNTRIES: THE CHINA–TAIWAN TURF

Given their strategic geography and natural resources, the South Pacific Islands are natural locations for China's involvement. China's maritime ambitions are linked to the Pacific Islands and the latter also serves its economic objectives given their abundant natural resources.[82]

China's interest and interaction with the Pacific Islands dates back to the early 1980s, when it sent diplomats to Hawaii for studying the history, politics and culture of the South Pacific.[83] The engagement with

---

[80] Ibid.

[81] 'New Zealand Contemporary China Research Centre System of Access to Information on China (NOSAIC)'. Available at: http://www.victoria.ac.nz/china researchcentre/China%20Studies/NOSAIC.aspx (accessed on 22 January 2012).

[82] For example, timber in the Solomon Islands, fish in Solomon Islands and Fiji, natural gas and minerals in Papua New Guinea make the region important and essential to engage.

[83] Smith-Wesley and Porter, *China in Oceania*, 1.

the region became deep and substantive from the late 1990s. The Pacific Community (PC) and the Pacific Islands Forum (PIF)[84] are two crucial regional organizations involving the Pacific Islands with China's interactions more with the PIF. The expanding engagement with the region, apart from larger strategic goals, might have been influenced by the Taiwan factor:[85] '[F]ostering friendship and cooperation with the Pacific Island countries is not a diplomatic expediency. Rather, it is a strategic decision'.[86]

Beijing's economic engagement with the South Pacific comprises development assistance, investment and infrastructure-building. With the exception of North Korea, none of the countries in Northeast Asia, and Oceania discussed till now, have been keen on Chinese aid primarily due to their lack of need for such assistance. South Pacific Islands, however, are different. Though Australia remains the largest donor for the region, China's significance has become as much as those of other traditional players such as New Zealand and Japan.[87] Fiji, Papua New Guinea (PNG), Samoa and Vanuatu were among the largest beneficiaries of Chinese aid between 2006 and 2013, which was spent on 167 projects across the region.[88] The character of the Chinese aid, though, is changing from grants and interest-free loans that were eventually forgiven and funded smaller programmes to compete with Taiwan for regional recognition, to greater number of 'soft' concessional loans that might not be written off.

Fiji has been a major beneficiary of Chinese aid flowing into infrastructure development.[89] Notwithstanding more aid, experts point

---

[84] The 16 PIF countries are Australia, Cook Islands, Fiji, Kiribati, Marshall Islands, Micronesia, Nauru, New Zealand, Niue, Palau, Papua New Guinea, Samoa, Solomon Islands, Tonga, Tuvalu and Vanuatu.
[85] Currently 6 of the 16 members of the PIF, that is, Palau, Marshall Islands, Kiribati, the Solomon Islands, Nauru and Tuvalu, formally recognize Taiwan. The remaining members, including New Zealand and Australia recognize China.
[86] Wen, 'Win-win Cooperation for Common Development'.
[87] Brant, 'The Geopolitics of Chinese Aid'.
[88] *Loop*, 'China Boosting Aid to Pacific'.
[89] Few examples in this regard are the Fiji–China e-Government Programme, squatter settlement, China–Fiji Friendship Bridge and the Nadarivatu Hydro Power Project.

to the tardy progress of these projects as an indication of Beijing 'having second thoughts about being the military regime's saviour'.[90] China might well be overhauling its aid policy towards 'pariah' states for gaining more credence in the international community, while being firm on 'non-interference' in other country's domestic issues, both evident from its uninterrupted economic engagement with Fiji's military regime. Strategically, Fiji's vast untapped land, minerals and fisheries make it impossible to be ignored. Any possible overhaul of the aid policy will not restrict China from occupying the vacuum created by the Western donor's apathy towards the military regime.

Taiwan is a key factor conditioning China's relationship with the Pacific Islands. Samoa is a pertinent example. The Samoan Prime Minister Tofilau Eti was the first foreign leader to visit China after the Tiananmen Square incident in 1989 and was rewarded with an economic support for a new government building as a mark of friendship.[91] Samoa has ever since received more Chinese soft loans for various projects[92] than Fiji, which could be because of its steady support to China over Taiwan.[93] China's appeal as a donor has enhanced due to its occasional write-off of past debts.[94] But despite large aid and generous write-offs, China's image in the region is not all virtuous. The Ramu Nico Project in Medang, PNG, launched in 1999 and China's biggest investment in the South Pacific involving the PNG Government and the local landowners have stoked anti-China sentiments particularly for damaging marine life and threatening livelihoods of the local fishermen.[95]

The South Pacific Islands are notable as the turf for China–Taiwan strategic rivalry. Consequently, chequebook diplomacy by both countries in return for political recognition and the occasional playing off of one against the other by the Island countries are notable. Both PNG and Fiji,

---

[90] Hanson', Chinese Aid in Fiji'.

[91] Smith-Wesley and Porter, *China in Oceania*, 154.

[92] Projects include the Parliament Office, Ministry of Justice and Courts Administration court house, multipurpose Conference Centre, and the National Medical Centre. See Yang, *The Pacific Islands in China's Grand Strategy*, 77.

[93] *China.org.cn*, 'Samoa Re-affirms One China Policy'.

[94] Smith-Wesley and Porter, *China in Oceania: Shaping the Pacific?* 159.

[95] *Pacific Media Centre*, 'PNGs Ramu NiCo Mine'.

for example, trade with Taiwan, but recognize China, which might partly explain the generous Chinese aid support to both. Solomon Islands and Palau recognize Taiwan and also trade with China with the former receiving development assistance from Taiwan. While Tonga pursues a 'friendship to all' policy, China has emerged as a major donor for Tonga and was keen on funding its budget deficit too.[96] It would be interesting to note if greater China–Taiwan engagement, as discussed earlier in this chapter, might have any effect on their aid rivalry in the region.

## Cultural Initiatives

Cultural interaction between China and the region is quite low-key. The CIs (Annexure II), while promoting cultural cooperation, appear to have relatively limited functions. There are, however, exceptions like the CI at Laucala in Fiji that engage in research and facilitate student and staff exchange programmes. *Hanban* has also sent teachers to Samoa, Tonga, Vanuatu and Micronesia for exposing Chinese culture to the region.[97] In an effort to increase people-to-people contact, China is not only providing full scholarships to students from the South Pacific Island countries under the PIF scholarship scheme for studying in China[98] but also facilitating intergovernmental exchanges and interactions. In 2013, a delegation of the Pacific Island countries comprising of parliamentarians and media personnel visited China to learn about the Chinese system of government and what the CCP has achieved since the founding of the PRC in 1949.[99] Such exchanges between China and the South Pacific Island countries have picked up in recent years.

Public Diplomacy, through high-level visits (Annexure III), is also becoming more frequent and occasions for declaring major Chinese policy initiatives.[100] Xi Jinping's visit to Fiji and his subsequent bilateral

---

[96] Ibid., 172.

[97] Smith-Wesley and Porter, *China in Oceania: Shaping the Pacific?*

[98] At0086, 'Twelve Kinds of Chinese Scholarships Available to International Students'.

[99] *Matangi Tonga Online*, 'Pacific Islands Parliamentarians Visit China'.

[100] In April 2006, Wen Jiabao, during his visit to Fiji, had announced preferential loans to the Pacific Island countries. During his visit, he also met leaders from the

meetings with leaders from Samoa, Vanuatu, Niue, Tonga, PNG and the Federated States of Micronesia in 2014 highlight China's focus on 'greater periphery diplomacy' while signalling its prominent role in the region. It also vindicated the current leadership's continuing efforts for deepening trust and cooperation with the Pacific Island countries. These might help in consolidating certain positive impressions of China contributed by prominent local luminaries such as Terry Tavita, editor of Samoa's *Savali* newspaper, Fijian Commodore Josaia Voreqe (Frank) Bainimarama and Palauan Senator Alan Seid. While Terry Tavita's accounts of China were positive,[101] Frank and Palauan Senator Alan Seid's admiration of China's urban planning and rapid economic development after they attended the Beijing Olympics[102] helped improve China's image in these countries and the region.

## CONCLUSION

Northeast Asia, Oceania and South Pacific Islands comprise strategic priorities for China that extends from those that apply to its immediate neighbourhood, and further to the extended neighbourhood. In this sense, the regions represent the panning of China's 'periphery diplomacy' to 'greater periphery diplomacy', which, as explained earlier, is an evolving aspect of China's contemporary foreign policy. While the former will continue to be dominated by China's historical ties (or baggage) and individual country-specific issues, Oceania and South Pacific would continue to experience a qualitatively different 'greater periphery' engagement. In several respects, the countries and the regions discussed in this chapter represent the gamut of challenges China faces in building a benign image and applying soft power. The latter needs to accommodate fragile ties with difficult neighbours bound by multiple elements of common culture (Northeast Asia); large developed countries with different cultures and strong economic synergy, but strategic distance

---

Pacific Island (countries which recognize China)—Fiji, Samoa, PNG, Vanuatu and Tonga. For details see Smith-Wesley and Porter, *China in Oceania*, 123.

[101] Smith-Wesley and Porter, *China in Oceania*, 155.

[102] Ibid., 189.

(Australia and New Zealand) and small island economies whose political support is essential for cementing regional leadership and initiatives. In all three spheres, China's active efforts have enlarged its presence in the scope of strategic thinking of the countries but, at the same time, have probably created more challenges for China as far as the effectiveness of its engagement policies is concerned.

Among the regions discussed in this chapter, Northeast Asia presents numerous strategic challenges for constructive engagement and deployment of soft power by Beijing. These include Japan and South Korea's close alliances with the 'extra-regional' power the US and the complicated regional counter-balancing alliances that are produced as a result. Democratic Taiwan continues to pose as another fundamental challenge. China's difficulty in handling Taiwan, as discussed, is reflected in its changing policy postures from time to time. The Chinese leadership under Hu was noted for displaying a more flexible approach. The 2012 presidential election was the best example when military intimidation was entirely missing during the election though Ma (a candidate of the KMT—the National Party of China who was re-elected) and Tsai Ing-wen ran a tight race.[103] The flexibility appears to have eroded under President Xi, notwithstanding greater cultural engagement. During the run up to the 2016 election, and thereafter, the relations with China have been labelled 'turbulent' by the *People's Daily*. China's continuous attempt to prevail upon Taiwan to accept the '1992 Consensus' and thereby acknowledge the 'One China' policy may see some major challenges with the new Democratic Progressive Party leader Tsai Ing-wen preferring *status quo* of cross-straits ties and remaining non-committal to the consensus giving rise to doubt and anxiety over the final unification that Beijing seeks. The eventual China–Taiwan interface would have significant implications for all countries in the region, as well as Australia, New Zealand and South Pacific countries, given that they are all in the strategic backyards of China and Taiwan.

---

[103] Koike, 'China's Softly, Softly Approach'.

# 6

# Africa and Europe: Warmer Relations, New Partnerships

Africa and Europe, while not being neighbours to China, are continents with considerable strategic value for China and occasionally pose as contrasting examples of China's varied deployment of soft power. Africa is critical to China for strategic outreach and influence. The continent's untapped natural and energy resources and presence in multilateral forums and global groupings of the South makes it a strategic priority for all major powers. African support is crucial for China in pushing its agenda in forums traditionally dominated by the West. By counterbalancing Western influence, strategic alliance with Africa helps China in contributing to international rules formulation, negotiations and international processes.[1] On the other hand, engaging Europe is also critical to China's strategic outreach given its aspiration to connect closer to the First World. While senior leaders like Zhao Ziyang held the West in high esteem,[2] Europe and China have remained distant on socio-cultural and geopolitical issues reflecting limited mutual understanding. Compared with the US, Chinese academic opinions, such as those of influential scholars like Xinning Song, have been sceptical about the EU's strategic capacity to influence international opinion.[3]

---

[1] Ahrari, *The Great Powers versus Hegemon*, 59.

[2] Zhao Ziyang, the third Premier of the PRC (1980–87) was a firm believer in Western parliamentary democracy and held that it could help China in overcoming corruption and the rich–poor divide. *The Prisoner of the State: The Secret Journal of Premier Zhao Ziyang* crafted over four years from tapes recorded in secret by Zhao, who lived under tightly monitored house arrest for 15 years before dying in 2005, reveals China's admiration of the West by the leadership.

[3] European Union Committee, 'Stars and Dragons'.

Interestingly, however, the apparent distance between China and the EU has also contributed to less acrimony with both sides appreciating the limitations conditioning the relationship. Indeed, Europe's absence from strategic alliances in the Asia-Pacific region, in contrast to the US, has rubbed off positively on China.[4] The China-led AIIB has deepened engagement between China and Europe with several European countries becoming founding members of the institution.

## CHINA–AFRICA RELATIONS: ECONOMICS DOMINATES ENGAGEMENT

China's relations with Africa can be traced to the 14th century and the visit of the Moroccan scholar and traveller Ibn Battuta to China. Admiral Zheng He's voyage rounding the coast of Somalia and further down to the Mozambique Channel during the Ming dynasty illustrates another historical contact. Subsequently, Chinese involvement in Africa was driven by its revolutionary and anti-colonial ideology with the post-Cold War years witnessing expanding relations with Africa as 'the most important dynamic in the foreign relations and politics of the continent'.[5] Deng Xiaoping's address at the UN in April 1974 marked a watershed in bilateral ties. Deng divided the world into three groups: the first comprising the US and the former Soviet Union, the second developing countries from Africa, Asia and Latin America, and the third all other developed nations. This categorization elevated the status of developing countries within the comity of nations and also cast China as the voice of the developing world. Since then, China has emphasized its status of a 'developing country' for connecting to the rest of the developing world, particularly Africa, with which it has also repeatedly recalled colonization as a point of convergence. President Xi was also emphatic in

---

[4] A Chinese policy paper on Europe emphasized: '[N]o fundamental conflict of interest between China and the EU and neither side poses a threat to the other'. See 'China's EU Policy Paper'.

[5] Ahrari, *The Great Powers Versus Hegemon*, 55.

highlighting China as a developing country during his early days.[6] Over time, however, the reference has become less and less conspicuous in his addresses though China strongly continues to empathize with the developing world. References to 'peace' and 'common development' have now increased in official pronouncements for projecting a China that 'has upheld justice, stood alongside developing countries and led by example in maintaining world peace and promoting common development'.[7]

Africa symbolizes China's strategic dividends through soft power along with certain downsides of the latter. Adverse local perceptions on greater Chinese presence and economic activity in the continent are becoming noticeable. Both in Cameroon and South Africa people appear 'disturbed by the Chinese influx',[8] whereas Kenya and Nigeria are perturbed over rapid disappearance of elephants from their habitats, arguably due to greater poaching of ivory facilitated by Chinese workers in local road projects for catering to the thriving unregulated market for ivory chopsticks, bookmarks, combs and rings in China.[9] While China has denounced smuggling of ivory,[10] the perceptions probably remain, casting shadows on the brighter impressions of China emanating from its commitment to the continent's economic development and leaving many confused in defining China as an opportunity or a threat.[11] China, however, appears determined to engage Africa notwithstanding occasional negative impressions and is increasing its cultural and economic presence in Africa. PD through high-level visits (Annexure III) are now facilitating engagement, with the leadership keen on conveying 'China's embrace of big and small states alike, and prov[ing] Beijing's sincerity in consolidating long-term friendship with Africa as a whole'.[12]

---

[6] Xi had mentioned China's 'developing status' (*fa zhan zhong guo jia*) in 2012, in one of his first meetings with foreign guests, while co-opting 'peaceful development' and 'opening up' in his conversation. For details see *Xinhua*, 'China's Xi Pledges Peace'.

[7] *Xinhua*, 'China Celebrates 65th Anniversary'.

[8] Rebol, 'Public Perceptions and Reactions'.

[9] Gettleman, 'As ivory fuels African wars', 5.

[10] *People's Daily Online*, 'China Reiterates Opposition'.

[11] *Africa practice Report*, 'The Impact of the Chinese Presence in Africa', 17.

[12] Hong, 'Sino-African Relations', 1–2.

The bilateral engagement is expected to be further pushed by China given Africa's historical reciprocation of Chinese overtures. Indeed, in 1971, among the 76 countries voting in favour of the resumption of China's legal seat in the UN, as many as 26 were from Africa, prompting Chairman Mao to point out: 'It was the African people who carried China in the UN'.[13] Africa stood firmly with China even after the Tiananmen Square incident in 1989 that sparked widespread international protests. The Sino-Africa partnership is expected to widen and deepen over the years to come with both providing each other strategic support on various issues. This is exemplified through bilateral institutional initiatives like the inter-ministerial triennial Forum on China-Africa Cooperation (FOCAC) Summits[14] held alternately in China and Africa and including all aspects of bilateral interactions ranging from economic exchanges, cultural interfaces to humanitarian assistance that have underscored 'China's arrival in Africa'[15] and 'institutionalised Sino-African relations at a time of intensified interactions and following a period of exponential growth in such linkages'.[16]

## Economic Initiatives

As mentioned earlier, Africa provides China access to large unutilized reserves of mineral and energy resources. The urge to exploit untapped resources in a continent grappling with poverty, malnourishment and critical deficits in physical and social infrastructure affecting delivery of public services has given China ample investment opportunities. At the same time, it has also emerged for many African countries as the only major source of development assistance given the reluctance of Western donors to disburse aid to the former on account of their poor performances on human rights, conflict management and democratic development. This is similar to the circumstances encountered by Cambodia as mentioned in Chapter 4 (also Myanmar till some years ago) enabling

---

[13] Xiaomin and Jianbo, 'China's African Policy and Its Soft Power'.
[14] The FOCAC was established in 2000 but it was not until 2006 that the engagement further escalated through the body.
[15] Ahrari, *The Great Powers versus Hegemon*, 56.
[16] Taylor, 'China Views India's Rise'.

China to commit to extensive national economic developments (e.g., investment, trade, development assistance, health care facilities and humanitarian assistance) for substantive strategic returns, including access to resources and international support on issues of significant importance to China, like the 'One China' policy.[17]

Chinese investments and businesses are visible in almost all walks of life in Africa. From selling doughnuts in Congo-Brazzaville, second-hand garments in Nigeria to loincloths in Tonga, Chinese traders are catering to all local markets across the continent and integrating deeper into its economy. The integration continues despite occasional complaints of shoddy wares and concerns of indigenous industry.[18] Loss of livelihoods for locals following expansion of Chinese businesses is emerging a major concern.[19] China is aware of the concerns and is attempting to counter them by focusing on greater local employment in Chinese projects. Whether the Malawi International Conference Centre project, projects in Uganda or the port and telecom projects in Tanzania and South Africa announced by President Xi during his maiden visit to Africa,[20] they all attempt at creating jobs for the locals, thus trying to assuage local concerns to an extent possible.

Apart from generating greater employment, China's image in Africa can benefit from its successful execution of projects delivering basic services (e.g., low-cost housing, drinking water, sewage treatment and radio, television and telecommunications networks).[21] China's role in

---

[17] Only three out of 53 African countries recognize Taiwan. With its growing economic clout, China has been able to wean away several African countries (e.g., South Africa, Senegal, Liberia, Gambia and Malawi) from recognizing Taiwan.

[18] The textile factories in Nigeria were closed due to competition from cheap Chinese imports. See *The Economist*, 'Trying to Pull Together'.

[19] In Angola, the movement of Chinese workers in different China-funded projects has led to almost 100,000 Chinese residents settling in the country casting serious doubts over whether the projects are generating employment for locals. Such concerns have the state-owned Angolan company, Sonangol, to impose restrictions on the number of Chinese workers.

[20] *The Diplomat* 'China Set to Expand Influence in Africa'.

[21] Chinese funded low-cost housing projects are coming up in Seychelles, Mozambique, Angola and Ethiopia, while drinking water projects are being

infrastructure-building in Africa has been significant in the creation of primary education capacities in various countries (e.g., Kenya and Nigeria). Apart from the fact that these projects are expanding Chinese footprints in countries that are rich in mineral resources, China's commitment to infrastructure-building is also earning accolades from the African leadership.[22] On the whole, higher per capita incomes and living standards in Africa, as and when they manifest, can be at least partly attributable to rising Chinese investments.[23]

Telecommunications and renewable energy are two 'strategic resource-seeking' sectors attracting Chinese investments in Africa. While Chinese mobile phones are being sold all over Africa and Chinese telecom companies ZTE and Huawei are having large operations in Congo[24] (the Democratic Republic of the Congo is also one of the largest sources of 'coltan'—an essential mineral used in various electronic products ranging from iPhones to PlayStations), Zambia has benefitted from Chinese loans for improving its telecommunications network.[25] The information and communications technology (ICT) sector has been a key focus in Ethiopia too (e.g., the Ethiopia Millennium Project for creating a fibre-optic transmission backbone across the country and rolling out the GSM network).[26] Kenya, on the other hand, is a major beneficiary of Chinese initiatives in developing renewable energy for addressing local power deficits.[27] Moreover, for improving the capacities of African countries to adapt to climate change, China has launched 100 clean energy projects in Africa including solar power, biogas and small hydropower projects.

---

implemented in Nigeria, Senegal, Equatorial Guinea, Tanzania and Niger. Television network is being expanded in Equatorial Guinea. See *Xinhua*, 'Full Text: China–Africa Economic and Trade Cooperation'.

[22] Ethiopian Prime Minister Meles Zenawi hailed China's 'fundamental and transformative' involvement in the continent's infrastructure-building. See Liena and Sihao, 'Interview: "China's involvement in Africa's infrastructure"'.

[23] Moyo, *Winner Take All*, 4.

[24] Cheru and Obi, *The Rise of China and India in Africa*, 113.

[25] Weston et al., 'China's Foreign Assistance in Review'.

[26] Ibid.

[27] Cheru and Obi, *The Rise of China and India in Africa*, 116.

China's role in building infrastructure in Africa is long and extensive. There are various countries where China is helping to build physical infrastructure through cross-continental railways (e.g., the Atlantic–Indian Ocean rail link connecting the Angolan port city of Benguela to Dar es Salaam in Tanzania and Nacala in Mozambique, and in Nigeria and Sudan). Some of the Chinese infrastructure-building is also targeted at urban infrastructure needs of specific countries (e.g., conference facilities in Lilongwe, Malawi and Addis Ababa, Ethiopia, and a sports stadium in Guinea), while some more is focused on electricity generation (e.g., the 2,600 MW Mambilla hydropower project in Nigeria and the Merowe hydropower scheme in Sudan). It is interesting to note the active Chinese infrastructure building in African countries rich in oil and mineral resources—Angola, Nigeria, Ethiopia, Mozambique and Sudan. It is surely not coincidental that these countries are among China's largest sources of crude oil. China's infrastructure investments in some of these countries are in projects that fetch oil in exchange for resources being invested (e.g., Angola and Sudan).[28]

Chinese initiatives in infrastructure building in Africa, while noticeable for their presence in resource-intensive countries, draw attention to Chinese aid and development assistance strategy for the continent. During the 5th FOCAC Ministerial in July 2012 in Beijing, former President Hu reiterated China's commitment to Africa by emphasizing that Beijing will 'continue to expand aid to Africa, so that the benefits of development can be realized by the African people'.[29] The commitment was consistent with China's international aid strategy outlined in *China's African Policy* and *China's Foreign Aid*, released in 2006 and 2011, respectively,[30] both of which reflect the effort to develop a long-term and permanent institutionalized platform for aid to Africa.[31] Chinese aid, or development assistance in Africa, has been institutionalized through the FOCAC by not only significantly enlarging the volume of aid but also

---

[28] Palit, 'China Crucial to India's Mobile Revolution', 52.
[29] Li, 'Hu Vows More Aid for Africa', 9.
[30] China's foreign aid strategy has some distinct characteristics as mentioned in the Aid document. For details, see *Xinhua*, 'Full Text: China's Foreign Aid'.
[31] Forum on China–Africa Cooperation, 'China's Aid to Africa: Enters Institutionalized New Stage'.

the cancellation of interest-free loans for poor African countries. In order to shield African countries from the ramifications of the financial crisis in 2010, China established a funding facility with local African Banks for lending to small and medium businesses and wrote off outstanding debts of 35 African countries.[32] This was in addition to China's commitment at the Fifth FOCAC Ministerial in Beijing in 2012 to expand LoCs to African countries for supporting infrastructure, agriculture, manufacturing and the development of small and medium businesses.

In continuation of Premier Zhou Enlai's *Eight Principles for Economic Aid and Technical Cooperation to Other Countries*, China's aid policy operates under specific rules such as non-interference in internal affairs of recipient countries, interest-free or low-interest loans, fostering self-reliance of the recipients and so on.[33] The aid is usually disbursed as concessional loans or export credits provided through the Ministry of Commerce and the Exim Bank. Unlike the Western donor and investor countries, China is not fussy about human rights records and its development assistance (Annexure I) and has 'no strings attached'. This has enhanced the virtuous appeal of China's aid in Africa compared with that from the West.

But while generous aid support has earned China plaudits from the region, the strategic objectives of such aid have often been distinct and criticized for being 'driven by its objective of securing access to oil and minerals for its growing economy'.[34] China has occasionally tweaked the conditions of aid for specific countries for obtaining mutually beneficial outcomes—financial relief for the recipient and assurance of access to resources for China, such as waiving off interest payments on a loan granted to mineral-rich Uganda and replacing it with a grant.[35] The strategic goals have not only been limited to access to energy and mineral resources (e.g., Chad, Gabon, Angola, Sudan, Uganda and Sierra Leone)[36]

---

[32] *Xinhua*, 'Full Text: China–Africa Economic and Trade Cooperation'.

[33] Lengauer, 'China's Foreign Aid Policy', 38.

[34] Ibid.

[35] Cheng and Yanrong, 'China to Strengthen Ties with Uganda'.

[36] It is interesting to note Sierra Leone's President Koroma's comments on his country's 'special relation' with China: 'Sierra Leone has always maintained the

but have also emphasized adherence to the 'One China' policy.[37] The Chinese counter argument has been that its aid is not conditioned by any political or economic agenda and is aimed at the promotion and development of African countries and at consolidating the Sino-African cooperation.[38] Indeed, China conspicuously avoids the use of phrases such as 'donor', 'aid receiver', 'poverty' and 'backwardness' with respect to Africa and emphasizes 'solidarity, mutual help, equality, mutual benefit and common development'[39] instead. Nonetheless, Chinese aid in Africa and its role in infrastructure building will continue to remain a controversial aspect of China's engagement of Africa.

China's commitment to Africa's development and its involvement in the process has manifested in its playing a large role in expanding Africa's health care capacities. This 'social' infrastructure building is much less noticed in China's engagement of South and Southeast Asia, where the emphasis is almost entirely on physical infrastructure such as road and rail links. Expanding the access of poor Africans to quality and affordable health care is another effort by the Chinese leadership to build a benign image in the region. The strategy appears to be working with Chinese medicines and medical practices (including

---

assistant friendship and special relation with China on the basis of mutual benefit'. *People's Daily Online*, 'China Grants 30 mln USD to Sierra Leone'.

[37] Only four African countries (Burkina Faso, Gambia, Sao Tome and Swaziland) recognize Taiwan officially. See *Xinhua*, 'Full Text: China's Foreign Aid'.

[38] Xiaomin and Jianbo, 'China's African Policy and Its Soft Power'.

[39] In January 2006, the Chinese Government issued Documents of China's Africa Policy which stressed that one of China's overall objectives of China's Africa policy was:

mutual benefit and common prosperity. To achieve that goal, the Chinese government pledged 'to support African countries to develop their economy and build their own nations, to carry out various forms of cooperation in the field of economy, trade and social development and to promote the common development.

See Xiaomin and Jianbo, 'China's African Policy and Its Soft Power'.

*qigong*)[40] and *taichi*[41] becoming increasingly popular with the African urban middle class.[42] China has been steadily expanding support to the management of critical medical issues such as the HIV epidemic, malaria and growing blindness among the local population.[43] According to China's Ministry of Health statistics, till 2010, there were 17,000 Chinese medical workers in 48 African countries treating 200 million patients.[44] Public health is an area where China's commitment is evident from the significant long-term institutional initiatives it has taken on, such as the research collaboration between Peking University, Foreign Ministry and the International Poverty Reduction Centre in China for improving medical cooperation with the African nations.[45] Chinese armed forces are also contributing to greater Chinese provision of health services in Africa, again in geo-strategically important countries in the Indian Ocean (Djibouti and Seychelles, for example) and mineral-rich locations (such as Kenya and Tanzania).[46]

Chinese commitment is also visible in its support to the creation of medical infrastructure, particularly hospitals (Liberia, Uganda, Ethiopia and Zambia). Combined with extensive humanitarian assistance on a variety of occasions (food supplies to drought victims in Zimbabwe and

---

[40] A practice of aligning breath, movement and awareness for exercise, healing and meditation, with roots in martial arts and Chinese philosophy.

[41] Another form of martial art invented by a Taoist monk while dreaming of a fight between a snake and a crane in the Wu-dang mountains according to a legend.

[42] Forum on China–Africa Cooperation, 'Chinese Medicine in East Africa'.

[43] Chinese medical expertise is trying to help Malawi where 10 per cent of the local population is threatened by HIV. China has also been supplying anti-malaria drugs to several African countries and dispatching ophthalmologists to countries such as Sudan and Mozambique for addressing eye ailments of local people.

[44] Forum on China–Africa Cooperation, 'China's Medical Aid Benefits 48 African Countries'.

[45] Forum on China–Africa Cooperation 'China Forms Research Alliance to Upgrade China–Africa Medical Cooperation'.

[46] The 'Peace Ark' naval hospital—the first international medical mission by the Chinese armed forces—visited Seychelles, Djibouti, Tanzania and Kenya on a multination service mission in October 2012. Apart from treating patients, the mission exchanged medical ideas and visited African schools. See *People's Daily Online*, 'China's "Peace Ark" Hospital Ship'.

Ethiopia—the largest grain donation by China since 1949,[47] and emergency relief supplies to Algeria, Burundi, Sudan, Madagascar, Tanzania, Somalia and Lesotho at different points in time), China's role in creation of medical infrastructure in Africa appears to have effectively complemented its contribution to physical infrastructure. Indeed, as the WB points out 'China's role has been critical in bridging a variety of infrastructure deficits in Africa' in a report. [48]

China's humanitarian role became evident during the Ebola crisis that hit West African states in 2014–15. Apart from dispatching disease control experts to fight the virus, China provided financial, technical, material and human resources assistance to the three most affected countries—Guinea, Sierra Leone and Liberia—and to 10 other countries of the sub-region. In fact, it is interesting to note the important role played by the Chinese news media in communicating Beijing's actions targeting its own people and the global audience. *China Daily* carried out many stories including the one titled 'Timeline of China's Anti-Ebola Aid in Africa' during the time highlighting the generous and timely intervention of the Chinese Government in Nairobi and other places.

China's significant economic role in Africa has helped in consolidating the already impressive views held by several African countries about China's remarkable economic success. These views are regularly reflected in local media, particularly on China's achievements in tackling poverty and underdevelopment over a relatively short period of time of around three decades.[49] In what could be assumed a rather definitive strategic dividend, China's calibrated approach to economic reforms, along with

---

[47] Chenxi and Jianhua, 'China–Africa Friendship Enhanced'.

[48] Foster et al., 'Building Bridges'.

[49] Ethiopia's *Addis Fortune* reported: 'Beijing is almost becoming the Mecca for Ethiopian officials. It seems that they are in search of inspiration for a miracle akin to that which the Chinese achieved during the last 25 years of economic reform...'. Rwanda's *New Times* reflects similar sentiment:

> From a weak and not so developed country, China has managed to surpass every other developing country to become one of the leading economies, its high population notwithstanding.... So the Africans feel they can do the same, after all their populations are also high.

See Taylor, 'China Views India's Rise', 96.

effective management of economic stability, posits an alternate development model for Africa as against the approaches advocated by Western
experts and institutions with the latter appearing particularly frail
after the global financial crisis. One of the best examples of the conviction is articulated by Thabo Mbeki, the former President of South
Africa, who had effusive praise for China's 'great achievements in
development' and its practical significance for Africa.[50] On its part,
China's non-interference in domestic affairs of African countries, repeated
emphasis on 'co-development' has resonated well in Africa as has its
greater facilitation of exports from many African countries in its domestic
market by allowing zero-tariff treatment to least-developed countries
(LDC) exports.[51]

It is ironical that effusive views of segments of the African leadership
on China's economic support and engagement with the continent exist
with impressions that are on the contrary. The downsides of Chinese aid
are probably most visible in African countries, where the 'hidden'
conditions attached with Chinese development assistance—insistence
on procurement of materials and products only from Chinese companies,
use of Chinese labour and control over operational functions of the
funded-infrastructure projects—are increasingly becoming points of
concern.[52] Anxieties over China using its financial clout for extracting
strategic-commercial advantages—such as dictating terms and conditions
for running infrastructure projects in Sierra Leone where the national
leadership is in no position to disagree even on relatively minor
conditions due to the gratitude for Chinese support in crises like Ebola—
are beginning to distance the common people from country leaderships
in perceptions on China. Greater percolation of these concerns might
end up damaging China's efforts to secure the coveted benign image.
While countries badly in need of financial support will probably have no

---

[50] Mbeki, 'President Thabo Mbeki'.
[51] The LDCs—33 from Africa, 14 from Asia plus Haiti—are defined by the UN
as those with a per capita income of less than 745 dollars a year.
[52] It must be noted that the insistence of Chinese contractors on procuring
material from China and engaging Chinese labour might be influenced by lack of
availability of required raw materials in investment locations and greater
experience of Chinese workers in implementing infrastructure projects.

choice other than turning to China, they, over time, might have to overcome rising domestic opposition to availing such support.

## Cultural Initiatives

Africa shows a pattern of strategic engagement by China where economic involvement, particularly through development assistance in physical and social infrastructure projects, is more conspicuous than CD. Nonetheless, efforts to increase people-to-people communication through cultural initiatives, education and PD manifesting through high-level state visits and initiatives by the Chinese media are visible and gradually increasing over time. The strategic goal in this regard is to complement the benign impressions obtained from economic support and commitment to African development by projecting China's 'charm' as a civilized Oriental power with a rich history emphasizing 'soft' engagement.

China has bilateral cultural agreements with 36 African countries.[53] The FOCAC Beijing Summit of 2006 prepared a blueprint for future bilateral cultural cooperation[54] leading to the organization of the 'African Culture Focus' in Shenzhen in 2008 followed by the 'Chinese Culture Focus' in 2009 that reached more than 20 African countries showcasing various aspects of Chinese tradition and culture.[55] The CIs—22 in 16 African countries—are also contributing to the cultural showcasing (Annexure II). Other regular initiatives such as bilateral cultural weeks (held between China and Congo, Kenya, South Africa, Nigeria, Ghana and Zambia) and documentary films produced on bilateral cooperation (in Congo and China) are also accelerating people-to-people contacts. The local response to China's cultural showcasing has been positive paving the ground for greater cultural exports.[56]

---

[53] *People's Daily Online*, 'Cultural Exchange Plays Important Role'.
[54] Ministry of Foreign Affairs of the People's Republic of China, 'Declaration of the Beijing Summit'.
[55] *People's Daily Online*, 'Cultural Exchange Plays Important Role'.
[56] The Gansu Art troupe enthralled viewers in Nairobi with a spectator commenting: 'those who have not tasted the Chinese culture do not know what they are missing... It is so addictive that once you embrace it, you can never let

China's efforts to brand itself as a global education hub and an important destination for foreign students are visible with respect to Africa as much as it is in other parts of Asia. Scholarships have been important tools for expanding people-to-people contacts. These scholarships are offered to African students for higher studies in a wide-range of subjects (such as agriculture, forestry, fisheries, medicine, linguistics, economy and management) including doctoral degrees.[57] Apart from scholarships, people-to-people contacts are also expanding through the African Visiting Scholars Programme, running since 2006, and accommodating officials, experts and artists from various African countries. These visits are also aimed to expand capacity, particularly in science and technology, and have found further resonance in institutional partnerships like the China–Africa Science and Technology Partnership Programme launched in November 2009.[58] Training and human re-source developments are strong imperatives for most African countries and China has responded positively to bridge the supply gaps through a variety of diverse efforts engaging researchers, civil servants and the youth from various African countries (like research study trips for surveying the vegetation in the water-fluctuation belt of the Three Gorges Reservoir; the China–Africa Inter-governmental Human Resources Development for middle- and high-ranking African economic and management officials;[59] and the Africa–China Young Leaders Forum for discussing various subjects of mutual concern[60]).

---

go of it'. See Forum on China–Africa Cooperation, 'Chinese Cultural Group Thrills Audience in Nairobi'.

[57] *People's Daily Online*, 'Cultural Exchange Plays Important Role'.

[58] Various joint projects under the programme focus on equipment donation, technique training courses and workshops, and popularization of technology and research. Country-specific projects include Chinese experts working with local farmers in Nigeria in fisheries, animal husbandry, crop production and processing and establishing a high-tech agricultural experimental study and demonstration centre at Harare, Zimbabwe. See Chenxi and Jianhua, 'China–Africa Friendship Enhanced'.

[59] *Africa practice Report*, 'The Impact of the Chinese Presence in Africa', 7.

[60] Forum on China–Africa Cooperation, 'First Africa–China Young Leaders Forum Concluded'.

Chinese media has been particularly active in increasing the 'China' presence in Africa with steady increase in the number of news bureaus, correspondents and offices. *Xinhua* has more than 20 bureaus in Africa, including 18 in Sub-Saharan Africa.[61] Its growth in Africa has been unabated despite occasional criticisms of the lack of objectivity and the endorsement of the official line.[62] The Chinese media is spearheading efforts to project China as the voice of the developing world and spread the impression deep and wide within Africa as was evident during the Durban Climate Change Conference in 2011.[63] Media is also active in projecting China as an 'open' country, unhesitant in reporting domestic developments for countering the prevalent sanitized and censured image of the Chinese state agencies and the state-controlled media. These include efforts to disseminate greater knowledge about domestic institutions and processes in China.[64] The *Xinhua* (English version) and *China Daily* (English version) also strive for much-needed political support from Africa in a world order that is still unwilling to yield enough strategic space to emerging market economies, particularly the Brazil–Russia–India–China–South Africa (BRICS).[65]

Africa has witnessed sustained efforts by China to project an alternative perspective by countering the views and opinions about China and the developing world emanating from dominant segments of the Western

---

[61] Gagliardone et al., 'China in Africa a New Approach'.

[62] Ibid.

[63] *China Daily* had reported that the onus for addressing climate change concerns was on developed nations since they had industrialized earlier.

[64] In March 2011, the Chinese Embassy in Morocco sent a press release to more than 20 major media organizations, including Moroccan Ministry of Foreign Affairs and Cooperation, National TV Station, Moroccan Maghrebe Arab Press, *The Morning*, *The Opinion*, *The Economist* and *The Journal Weekly* for disseminating information on the Fourth Session of the 11th NPC in an effort to apprise local audiences of domestic developments in China. See Forum on China–Africa Cooperation, 'Chinese Embassy in Morocco Briefing Media'.

[65] These were views expressed by some participants discussing external outreach of the Chinese media at the 4th International Forum for Contemporary Chinese Studies (IFCCS4) on 'China: Prospects and Challenges to 2020' held in September 2011, at the University of Nottingham, the UK.

media and opinion makers.[66] These views are perceived by the Chinese leadership as 'distorted impressions' necessitating efforts for overcoming weakness of the 'power of the word', mentioned in Chapter 1. The CCTV's plans to launch English and Swahili service for Africa are pertinent examples. The convergence of opinions between Chinese and African perceptions on striking an alternative posture is clearly discernible. Repeated references in the Western media to China as 'neo-colonialist' and Africa as a 'failed continent' have actually succeeded in drawing both closer, as noted by the Chinese Foreign Minister Wang Yi during President Xi's visit to Africa in 2013,[67] as having shared values like prioritizing the community over the individual.[68] Such shared commitment is manifesting in more media partnerships (like *Xinhua's* training of African journalists, launching of the *Xinhua* mobile newspaper and agreements with Botswana's *Daily News* and Botswana Press Agency). Kabareng Solomon, Director of Botswana's Information Services Department, points out: '[W]e know it is not good to accept a one-sided perspective',[69] underlining Africa's willingness to accept Chinese perspectives by stepping beyond Western news feeds.

Indeed, efforts to carry Africa along with itself in projecting an alternative perspective are not limited to initiatives by the state media and extend to China's overall diplomatic esteem and regard for Africa by treating the latter at par with other major powers, disregarding other issues of international concern. African political elites, irrespective of their background (like Omar al-Bashir, the controversial President of Sudan), receive the highest hospitality in China. Beijing does not spare efforts to make African people and its leaders feel important. Indeed, it is

---

[66] An article published in *Qiushi* (Seeking Truth) in 2009, a periodical of the CPC Central Committee, asserted the Western media was playing 'a dominant role in global information flow and in setting news agendas, thus shaping public opinion on a wide variety of issues'. See Forum on China–Africa Cooperation, 'China–Africa Media Cooperation'.

[67] Wang Yi commented on the occasion African leaders dismissed fears of 'Chinese neo-colonialism' in Africa. See *The Diplomat*, 'China Set to Expand Influence in Africa'.

[68] Gagliardone et al., 'China in Africa a New Approach'.

[69] Ibid.

hardly a coincidence that President Xi's first official overseas visit included Africa signalling its high priority for the Chinese leadership.

## CHINA–EUROPE: FROM 'DISTANT PARTNERS' TO 'HAO PENG YOU' ('GOOD FRIENDS')

Despite years of lukewarm ties produced by the Cold War, China and Europe are keen on leaving behind decades of benign indifference and striking a new strategic chord. Economic compulsions are driving these intentions. China is keen on connecting closer to Europe through the OBOR initiative. Apart from providing deeper access to European markets, the initiative is also important for China from security perspectives: for obtaining firm foothold in the Central Asian region bordering Europe, as well as forging closer ties with a country like Turkey, located at the crossroads of Europe and Asia.[70] On the other hand, Europe is motivated to deeper cooperation with China, largely on account of China's unshakable grasp on the world economy making it imperative for Europe to respond positively to the changes in the global financial order and participate in China-led regional financial initiatives like the AIIB.[71] China's sustained high economic growth rates have continued to surprise many, including Europe.[72] The latter now wants to exploit the consumption propensity of China's burgeoning middle class by targeting it for its exports.

Notwithstanding the establishment of diplomatic relations as early as 1975, China and Europe decided to carve out a 'comprehensive strategic partnership' only in 2001. Over the years, however, what has

---

[70] A strategic partnership between the two countries was inked in 2010 seeking Ankara's assistance for quelling insurgency in Xinjiang, apart from promising mutual economic benefits.

[71] Six European nations—Britain, France, Germany, Luxembourg, Switzerland and Austria—are set to join the China-led AIIB despite warnings from Washington over the AIIB's governance and environmental standards. The French President Françoise Hollande's resolve to strengthen China–France relationship exemplifies Europe's interest in developing closer ties with China appreciating the latter's growing influence.

[72] Shambaugh, 'China Eyes Europe in the World', 134.

evolved is more a 'collaborative partnership' with both sides keen on upgrading it to 'strategic partnership'. China's *EU Policy Paper* (2003) illustrated Beijing's EU policy and outlined the areas and plans for cooperation to be undertaken till 2008 for enhancing bilateral collaboration and stable relations.[73] Various issues discussed in the paper included the importance of conveying the Chinese perspective to the EU on Tibet and mentioning the 'One-China' policy as a 'cornerstone underpinning China–EU relations'. While highlighting economic ties, the paper also called for expanding cultural and people-to-people exchanges. While intentions clearly remain positive on both sides, clarity in mutual perceptions still appears missing given the prevalence of impressions that the Chinese knowledge of Europe is 'relatively shallow and ill-informed'[74] with matters being hardly different on the other side as well.

### Cultural Initiatives

Both China and Europe have been utilizing the bilateral summits for augmenting bilateral dialogues and people-to-people contact.[75] To that extent, these summits have been performing as important strategic mechanisms for bridging cultural distance.[76] The 12th EU–China Summit in Nanjing in November 2009 established the EU–China High Level Cultural Forum for enhancing people-to-people communication. Since then 'Getting to know China' has driven most bilateral cultural initiatives such as the Europe–China Cultural Compass project of 2011 [a collaboration between the European Union National Institutes for Culture (EUNIC), China; Goethe-Institute, Germany; British Council,

---

[73] Ministry of Foreign Affairs of the People's Republic of China, 'China's EU Policy Paper'.

[74] European Union Committee, 'Stars and Dragons', 10.

[75] Ministry of Foreign Affairs of the People's Republic of China, 'Wen Jiabao Attends the 13th EU–China Summit'.

[76] The erstwhile European Commission President Jose Manuel Barroso had commented Europe and China must 'invest more in the great potential of our people-to-people relations' to fully benefit from their strategic partnership. See *EU-China News*, 'European Culture in Constant Evolution'.

the UK; and Danish Cultural Institute, Denmark] for promoting dialogue and understanding of bilateral cultural cooperation.

Cultural familiarity has clearly increased in recent years with Chinese cultural exports, such as art exhibitions, and displays by Chinese museums across Europe becoming more frequent.[77] Many European countries, Britain in particular, have been actively promoting ties with Chinese museums and organizing visits for cultural leaders and curators. Chinese cultural exports also include greater staging of Chinese films such as in the China Image Film Festival—the largest Chinese film festival in Europe established in 2009—for European audiences. Chinese

**Table 6.1**
*China–Europe Cultural Activities*

| Year | Initiative/Event/Programme |
|---|---|
| 2007–10 | Project: 'Germany and China—moving ahead together' |
| 2009–10 | China the Guest of Honour at the Europalia arts festival |
| 2010 | (a) Launch of the First EU–China high-level Cultural Forum in Brussels (b) Switzerland's 'Culturescapes' festival with China as the Guest of Honour country |
| 2010–12 | Chinese Culture Year in Italy |
| 2011 | (a) EU–China Year of Youth (b) Chinese Language Year in Spain and China–Spain Cultural Dialogue |
| 2012 | (a) EU–China Year of Inter-cultural Dialogue and launch of bilateral high-level people-to-people dialogue (b) Chinese Culture Year in Turkey, Germany |
| 2013 | (a) EU–China Year of Inter-cultural Dialogue in Xi'an |
| 2014 | (a) EU–China Year of Inter-cultural Dialogue in Bucharest |
| 2015 | (a) Year of UK–China Year of Cultural Exchange |

*Source:* Compiled from various sources like the Europe–China Cultural Activities, *People's Daily Online*, Ministry of Foreign Affairs of the PRC.

[77] The Dazu rock carvings of the Song dynasty were exhibited for the first time outside China in the National Museum of Wales in 2011. Another significant exhibition of Chinese traditional paintings ('Mountain Echo, Chinese Painting') was held opened at the Museum of Young Art in Vienna in 2012.

movies and actors enjoy considerable following in Europe as is evident from actor Chen Jianbin winning the most popular actor award at the Fourth China Image Film Festival in London in 2012 and *People Mountain People Sea* winning the Silver Lion at the Venice Film Festival in 2011. A variety of cultural initiatives are being partnered by China and various European countries, some of which are documented in Table 6.1. Some of these, such as the China Culture Year in Italy, have generated an enthusiastic local response evident from the participation of more than 20 Italian municipalities and provinces from 12 regions. Certain bilateral links have proved particularly strong in facilitating cultural engagement like Sino-Irish cultural ties that are prospering through voluntary associations such as the Chinese–Irish Cultural Academy and the Ireland–China Association. China has also been pursuing 'Panda diplomacy' with several European countries (e.g., Britain, France and Belgium) similar to countries such as Japan and Australia discussed in Chapter 11.

Like in other parts of the world, education figures high in China's soft power outreach with Europe. In order to achieve the larger strategic goal of emerging as a global education hub, it is imperative for China to ensure its higher education systems and institutions gain reputation in the West. Connecting with Europe through education is, therefore, an important objective for China. An important step in this regard is opening overseas campuses of Chinese universities, as exemplified through efforts of the Zhejiang University in London for marking a presence in Europe.[78] Chinese university campuses in the UK (and Europe) are complementary to Chinese campuses opened by major European Universities, such as the University of Nottingham at Ningbo in Jiangsu province. These efforts pave the way for extensive people-to-people contacts, particularly among the youth, as does efforts like the China–Cyprus Higher Education Cooperation Agreement. China is becoming a popular destination for European students with the latter being the second largest group of foreign students in China comprising

---

[78] *China Daily*, 'School's in for First Overseas Campus'.

around 15 per cent of the total.[79] Public interface is also being significantly enhanced by the large number of CIs (Annexure II) and CCs in the UK and other EU member states. More than 100 CIs in Europe (Annexure II) are teaching Mandarin and offering training programmes on China.

The fragmented European scholarship on China remains a problem in the continent's deeper understanding of contemporary China. The limitation is compounded by the lack of sufficient centres studying China across European higher education institutions and the research on China being confined to a handful of scholars in specific disciplines.[80] Nonetheless, a thematic transition in China Studies in Europe with greater focus on contemporary issues is gradually becoming noticeable with several major universities (e.g., Cambridge, Copenhagen, Nottingham, Heidelberg and London) embarking on such studies along with research institutes working specifically on China [e.g., Brussels Institute of Contemporary China Studies, Belgium; Europe–China Institute at the Nyenrode Business Universiteit, the Netherlands; European Association for Chinese Studies (EACS) in Paris, France; and the Sino-European Forum *Pang Diwo* (Friends of Chinese Culture) in the Institute of Humanities at the Universidad Rey Juan Carlos, Spain].[81] These efforts follow the footsteps of the EU–China Academic Network (ECAN)—a brainchild of noted strategic scholar David Shambaugh— created in 1996 as one of the earliest initiatives for encouraging contemporary China Studies in Europe. Institutions created jointly by academic expertise from both sides [e.g., China Europe International Business School (CEIBS) with campuses in Shanghai and Beijing] not only enhance people-to-people contact but contribute to the growth of shared academic output and research. At the same time, high-level state visits (Annexure III) have also been instrumental in facilitating dialogue and communication between China and Europe. As Professor Chen Yugang points out: '[I]mproving links between the two sides has become mutually beneficial, if not necessary. The recent visits by Chinese leaders

---

[79]  Ministry of Education of the People's Republic of China, 'International Student Enrolments Exceeded 230,000 in 2009'.

[80]  Brodsgaard, 'China Studies in Europe', 35.

[81]  Sino-African Forum *Pang Diwo*.

can lead to various cooperative projects and foster a substantiate Sino-European relationship'.[82]

Image remains China's formidable challenge in Europe. A Pew Research Centre study conducted on global attitudes and trends in July 2014 reveals Europeans (Italy, Germany, Spain and France) having an unfavourable rating for China with the exception of the UK where impressions are more favourable. In fact, European perception of President Xi Jinping is also unfavourable in several parts of the continent. It is only China's growing economic power that reveals a mixed bag.[83] People in the UK believe that China's economic success is good for them, but Italians, Polish and French believe that China's economic rise hurts their economies. These negative perceptions about China could partly be due to ignorance. Nonetheless, negative perceptions are creating challenges for China in expanding the effectiveness of its soft power. According to Joshua Cooper Ramo, a former senior editor and foreign editor of *Time*, 'China's greatest strategic threat today is its national image'.[84] As Bernard Cohen further suggests in the context of China, '[The press] may not be successful much of the time in telling people what to think, but it is stunningly successful in telling its readers what to think about. The world will look different to different people'.[85] The strategic imperative of an image 'makeover' has encouraged China to pursue a dedicated media policy in Europe given the critical role of media in communicating its 'correct' image to the continent. The objective resonates similar efforts by China mentioned earlier in Africa as well, though the contexts are different.

While in Africa, Chinese media is more focused on presenting an 'alternative' perspective, similar attempts in Europe are more nuanced. The latter efforts are directed towards appealing to Europe's traditional principles of objectivity and credibility, particularly with respect to national media, and in the process securing greater legitimacy among

---

[82] *Want China Times*, 'With Europe Visits, Chinese Leaders Signal Region's Importance'.

[83] Pew Research Centre Publications, 'China's Image'.

[84] Ramo, 'Brand China'.

[85] *Wikinews.org*, 'Agenda-setting Theory'.

sceptical European constituencies. They also attempt to bridge the knowledge 'gap' that continues to remain substantive in several areas between China and Europe. As a result, *China Daily*'s presence in Europe has become noticeable[86] with *Xinhua* opening more bureaus in Europe and the *Caixin* (Financial News) Media Company Limited—a Chinese media group providing perspectives on global and national business— also having its journalists stationed in Europe. Bilateral efforts like the Europe–China Media Exchange workshops that have European journalists working with their Chinese counterparts might also pave the way for deeper mutual insights into various issues. It is still early to judge though whether the Chinese media's efforts to convey objective and credible perceptions are bearing fruit in Europe, unlike Africa, where, as discussed earlier, they appear to be more successful.

## Economic Initiatives

China's economic engagement of Europe, needless to say, is not tailored to respond to national capacity deficits that significantly characterize its economic interfaces with South and Southeast Asia, or Africa. Infrastructure gaps do not exist in the First World Europe the way they do elsewhere in the Third World.[87] Nonetheless, trade and investment have been important arms of China's linkages with the European continent. While Europe is China's largest trade partner and one of its key export markets, China's rapid economic growth and rising per capita income has encouraged several European companies to invest in China. Such investments should increase further given the sluggish domestic demand

---

[86] At the launch of the European edition of the *China Daily* in 2010, Renzhong Zhi, General Manager of *China Daily*, the UK, said,

> [W]e identified a gap to provide a useful source of news and analysis to European businesses seeking to better understand and engage with China. As more partnerships develop between China and the West, it is crucial that there exists a regular source of insight on changing trends.

> See *The Guardian*, 'China Daily Launches Europe Issue'.

[87] China's leading sovereign wealth fund—the China Investment Corporation (CIC)—has been participating as equity investor in the EU's infrastructure sector PPPs. See Jiwei, 'China Can help West Build Economic Growth'.

in Europe and the opportunity of earning higher returns from China. China's ability to support the debt-ridden EU is well known to the region. Former Chinese Premier Wen Jiabao had assured the visiting German Chancellor Angela Merkel in Beijing in 2012: 'China is considering greater involvement in resolving Europe's debt crisis by participating in the European Financial Stability Fund and the European Stability Mechanism'.[88] It's only natural for Europe, therefore, to send positive strategic signals to China.

On the other hand, by constructively engaging the EU, China plans to dig an indispensable niche for itself in Europe's external economic relations. China's need for European capital, advanced technology (e.g., in clean energy and safe environmental practices)[89] and corporate management practices makes it vital to engage the EU. Europe's domestic market has been a key motivator for Chinese producers, particularly automakers (e.g., Great Wall Motor,[90] Chery Automobile and the Geely–Volvo merger). Chinese firms are also acquiring infrastructure assets in Europe such as in ports and railways. Japan and China lead the pack of Asian firms aggressively taking over corporate enterprises in Europe.[91]

Infrastructure might eventually become a fundamental part of economic engagement between China and Europe given the ambitious connectivity plans taken up by the former. These include the 2000-mile high-speed rail cross-continental railway network between Asia and Europe with trains capable of travelling at more than 200mph.[92] The plan might eventually be subsumed within the OBOR programme given that the latter is increasingly emerging as the overarching architecture guiding Chinese ambitions of regional and cross-continental connectivity.

---

[88] *Asian Correspondent.com*, 'Wen Says China Might Contribute to Europe Fund'.
[89] *People's Daily Online*, 'China Eyes Urbanisation, Energy Cooperation with Europe'.
[90] *Channelnewsasia.com*, 'Chinese Firms Buy into Europe'.
[91] *People's Daily Online*, 'Chinese Firms Look More and More to Europe'.
[92] The different components of the programme involve trains travelling to Singapore, India and Pakistan, followed by connections with Germany via Russia, and a third link extending south from China to Vietnam, Thailand, Burma and Malaysia. See Jones, 'London to Beijing....by rail?'

Europe has also enthusiastically responded to OBOR, which is not surprising given the economic opportunities the European nations sense from the envisaged increase in connectivity capacities in the project at a time when Europe is searching hard for new markets and sources of economic growth. Apart from the land component of the OBOR that will give Europe road access to Central Asia, South Asia and China, the new maritime silk road route connecting Europe to Far East promises significant upsurge in commercial traffic through European ports after the creation of new infrastructure along the way given that the maritime route between Europe and Northeast Asia is one of the busiest in the world. Notwithstanding the specific form and taxonomy of the OBOR, it is evident that China and Europe are likely to become parts of a modern and integrated road and sea transport infrastructure that would enable more efficient economic exchanges apart from facilitating strategic proximity and serving mutual security objectives.

## CONCLUSION

Africa and Europe have distinct strategic connotations for China. Africa is home to the largest number of developing countries and Europe comprises the maximum developed nations. As quintessential representatives of the Third World and the First World, respectively, strategic support of both is critical for China in global and regional fora. By vigorously engaging both continents, apart from securing bilateral strategic interests, China is also perhaps seeking to announce to the world its emergence as a major global player.

It is interesting to note the re-evaluation of China's policy towards Africa after the Tiananmen crisis in 1989. Prior to the incident, China's interest in Africa had waned leading African students to demonstrate in Beijing in 1986 against the neglect of the continent by holding aloft banners 'Remember the United Nations in 1971'—a reminder of Africa's support facilitating China's entry into the UN. Africa's support to China after the Tiananmen incident reaffirmed the vital importance of Africa as a strategic ally to the leadership: '[I]t was still those Third World countries and old friends which gave China the necessary sympathy and support. Therefore from now on China [would] put more efforts in resuming and developing relation with those [countries]'.[93]

Mutual strategic benefits, as discussed in this chapter, constitute the basis of the Sino-African partnership making it a pragmatic and rewarding relationship. China's strong ties with Africa are consistent with its larger policy of evolving friendly ties with poorer nations of the world and improving its image among developing countries. China's focused engagement, particularly economic commitment, has provided Africa an important ally, most essentially a stable source of development funds without 'strings attached'.[94] As noted for South Asia earlier, China has been able to obtain strategic benefits by responding to critical deficiencies of Africa in physical and social infrastructures. Indeed, China has largely been responsible for Africa's emergence from its 'lost decades' of the 1980s and the 1990s. The relationship has certainly blossomed causing some anxiety among Western strategic experts. Du Xudong, a commentator for *People's Daily*, points out that the Western media's misunderstanding of the proximity between China and Africa is partly due to the fact that they 'just saw the flower but did not realize how deep the roots have extended'.[95]

Economics has been the driving force behind the China–EU relationship for more than three decades. In more recent times, regional connectivity has become the key aspect of Sino-Europe engagement. Connectivity is expected to remain a key driver of bilateral relations in the years to come given Europe's critical importance in the OBOR scheme and its willing participation in regional-infrastructure-financing efforts in the AIIB. At the same time, Sino-Europe cultural engagement is also increasing rapidly, which is essential for deeper understanding on both sides. This is vital given the weak political foundation of the partnership. While both share visions of a multilateral world order, they differ on

---

[93] Taylor, 'China Views India's Rise', 4.

[94] China has reportedly committed around USD 75billion on aid and development projects in Africa in the past decade. *Global Development*, 'China Commits Billions in Aid'.

[95] Li, 'Hu Vows More Aid for Africa', 9.

the underlying ideation. The difference can cause some concerns with China's rising power status in international affairs, as is evident from the disagreements over Libya and Syria. Further, domestic developments in China, such as those involving the blind social activist Chen Guangcheng[96] continue to create adverse perceptions about China in the West. And finally, notwithstanding the escalating economic engagement and the potential of such engagement enhancing further through cross-continental connectivity schemes like the OBOR, the European legislature's recent vote against granting China 'market economy' status reflects the concerns that European lawmakers and businesses have in so far as the quality of China's economic systems, practices and institutions are concerned.[97]

[96] Chen Guangcheng is a Chinese civil rights activist who received international attention in 2005 after he had organized a class-action law suit against Chinese authorities for the excessive enforcement of one-child policy. He was subsequently arrested and in 2012 escaped his house arrest and fled to the US Embassy.
[97] Vincenti, 'EU Lawmakers Reject Granting China the Market Economy Status'.

# 7

## US, Canada, Latin America: Bridging Distance for New Alignments

Mao Zedong and Zhou Enlai were quick to realize that improved relations with the US can help China counterbalance the erstwhile Soviet Union. This was an imperative after the Sino-Soviet border clashes in 1969. The urgency to engage was strong on both sides. On the American side, this urgency was motivated by several academics, particularly those in the realist tradition—John K. Fairbank and A. Doak Barnett—who argued for a more pragmatic US treatment of China. The National Committee on the US–China Relations[1] created the ground for better future relations, and the efforts were reinforced by President Nixon's belief that successful courting of China might improve his prospects in the 1972 presidential re-election.[2] There was consequently an upswing in bilateral ties during the late 1960s and early 1970s. But since the Cold War, Sino-US relations have been a complex blend of escalating power rivalry, dense economic ties and heightened anxieties over each other's actions and motives in a world showing distinct signs of greater multi-polarity.

The economic interaction between the world's two largest economies is a heavily pronounced aspect of Sino-US bilateral ties. China is the second largest trading partner of the US after Canada, and also a major buyer of US treasury bonds providing the US much needed liquidity in

---

[1] The National Committee on US–China Relations, founded in 1966 and based in New York, encourages constructive engagement between the US and China. It relies on constructive dialogue, face-to-face interaction and the forthrightly exchange of ideas while educating Americans and Chinese about each other.

[2] Sino-American relations, see http://en.wikipedia.org/wiki/Sino-American_relations (accessed on 19 July 2012).

the aftermath of the financial crisis of 2008.[3] Apart from economics, culture and communication are also becoming conspicuous in bilateral engagement, as was evident from the former Chinese President Hu Jintao's emphasis on high-level strategic communication, bilateral visits, telephone conversations and culture in his four-point proposal for a new China–US model for the 21st century.[4]

Chinese strategic interests in the rest of the Americas are obviously far less significant compared with those in the US. Canada was a noted partner after its recognition of the PRC as the sole legal government of China in 1970, indeed much before the US in 1979, and remained important in Chinese foreign policy space due to geographical proximity to the US and independent foreign policy. Chinese Premier Zhu Rongji referred to Canada as China's 'best friend in the world' notwithstanding Canada not being the yardstick of a major global power against which China can measure its own emergence.[5] Canadian scholars examining the dynamics of the China–Canada relationship rightly argue that while the US represents power and modernity, the Chinese 'check-in with Canada to work out how to make progress towards that goal'.[6]

The Chinese interest in Latin America[7] has become prominent, given the desire for new markets, commodities and natural resources. Way back in 1988, Deng Xiaoping had asserted that the 21st century would not only be the 'Pacific era' but also the 'Latin American era'. To that extent, both China and Latin American countries have been allies in South–South cooperation as well as in major regional forums like the Asia-Pacific Economic Cooperation (APEC). Notwithstanding economic and multilateral motivations, deeper Chinese engagement of Latin America has also been attributed to the larger goal of isolating Taiwan.[8]

---

[3] China.org.cn, 'China–US Economic Relations'.
[4] China.org.cn, 'Hu, Obama Meet on Sidelines of G20 Summit'.
[5] Potter and Adams, 'Issues in Canada–China Relations'.
[6] Ibid.
[7] Latin America includes all the countries in the Caribbean, Central America and South America, depending on the country China engages with.
[8] Shambaugh, 'China eyes Europe in the World'.

## CHINA–US: PRAGMATISM DRIVES ENGAGEMENT

China's ambition of being accepted as a 'great' power can be partly fulfilled if it is recognized as such in its neighbourhood, and, as a result of the recognition, the neighbours hesitate from drifting naturally towards the US—an extra-regional power in the region. President Xi's articulation of 'New Type of Great Power Relations' in early 2012 during his visit to Washington was arguably motivated by these sentiments. The 'post-imperial ideology'[9] in China produced by years of 'victimization' by the West appears to have influenced the motivation. The 'New Type of Great Power Relations' seeks recognition of China's primacy in Asia by the US.[10] Thus, it is quite obvious that Asia looms large in Beijing–Washington relations and to a great extent drives the current engagement.

The contemporary complexities in the Sino-US relations have much to do with Washington's refocus on the region through its 'pivot to Asia'. The interest was spelt out in the former US Secretary of State, Hillary Clinton's articulation of America's foreign policy direction in July 2012 in an article published in *Foreign Policy*, indicating that Washington planned 'to lock in a substantially increased investment—diplomatic, economic, strategic, and otherwise—in the Asia-Pacific region' in the foreseeable future.[11] This 'pivot to Asia' was reaffirmed by the incumbent US Secretary of State, John Kerry, during his visit to the Southeast Asia (Brunei) in 2013. Subsequently, China and Xi Jinping's 'Asia-Pacific dream' has often been interpreted by the West as an ambition to dominate Asia-Pacific, which could surpass 'even what Imperial China managed to achieve at the height of its powers in the 18th century'.[12]

The National Security Strategy of 2015 reiterated Washington's intention to promote 'rebalancing' in the region while keeping a watch

---

[9] Miller, 'Re-collecting Empire', 14.

[10] An alternative school of thought, however, rationalizes the concept as a pacifist means for avoiding conflict with the US suggesting the Chinese leadership 'never thought about pushing the US out of the [Asia Pacific] region'. See Wang Yi, 'Toward a New Model'.

[11] Clinton, 'America's Pacific Century'.

[12] Browne, 'A Kinder, Gentler Regional Hegemon?'

on China's 'expanding existence'.[13] The US refocus on Asia has complicated the strategic dynamics of the Asia-Pacific with significant implications for China as well as India. As Kalevi Holsti points out, absence of a peaceful mechanism for rising powers such as China and India for being accepted in the international hierarchy is a major weakness of the present international system.[14] The weakness is being particularly manifested in the Asia-Pacific, where the China–US dichotomy is forcing China to blend both soft and hard powers for making its presence felt in the region.

China's perception of the US and the West is saddled with contrast. The conviction that the West never ceases to create hurdles for its global ambitions[15] coexists with the eagerness to connect more closely with the West, particularly the US, as also Europe discussed earlier. Multiple tensions exist in Sino-US relations ranging from US arms sales and Taiwan to its sympathetic overtures towards the Dalai Lama and Tibet. But China appears to have accepted the irreconcilability of perspectives on several issues with the US, as much as the US also possibly has. The realization of the importance of 'working together', particularly for preserving the significant economic relationship, has encouraged mature perspectives and 'friendly competition'.[16] The major milestones in the relationship with respect to institutional efforts towards engagement including high-level state visits since President Nixon's visit to China in 1971 are documented in Table 7.1.

## Cultural Engagement and Public Diplomacy

In line with the dichotomy characterizing the Sino-US relations, concerns and collaborations are evident in China's 'engagement' of the US. Cultural exports through CIs (Annexure II) are keeping pace with trenchant criticism of US policies in official documents (the National Defence

---

[13] Su, 'What Changes Does the US See'.
[14] Holsti, *Peace and War*, 339.
[15] Rong, 'China needs soft power', 1.
[16] The White House, 'Press Conference with President Obama'.

**Table 7.1**
*Major Landmarks in Sino-US Relationship*

| Year | Event |
| --- | --- |
| April 1971 | China's Ping-Pong team invites the US team to China in the first public sign of warming relations. |
| February 1972 | Shanghai Communique prepares the ground for better Sino-US ties by allowing discussion on difficult issues like Taiwan. |
| January 1979 | President Carter grants China full diplomatic recognition. |
| September 1993 | President Bill Clinton launches the policy of 'constructive engagement' with China. |
| October 2000 | President Clinton signs the US–China Relations Act of 2000, granting Beijing permanent normal trade relations with the US and paving the way for China's entry in the World Trade Organization in 2001. |
| September 2005 | US Deputy Secretary of State Robert B. Zoellick's speech initiates strategic dialogue with China, recognizing it as an emerging power and urging it to serve as a 'responsible stakeholder'. |
| April 2009 | Strategic and Economic Dialogue agreement between US and China. |
| May 2010 | Three agreements were signed:<br>i. MoU establishing high-level consultation on people-to-people exchange.<br>ii. Renewal of the Implementing Accord for Cultural Exchange.<br>iii. Renewal of the Agreement for Cooperation in educational exchanges. |
| January 2011 | During Hu's visit to Washington, President Obama welcomed the 'rise of China'. |
| February 2012 | Xi Jinping visit the US. |
| June 2013 | Xi Jinping visits the US with his wife. Obama once again welcomed the rise of a peaceful China while urging 'to chart the future of China–US relations and draw a blueprint for this relationship'. |

*Source:* 'Timeline: US Relations with China', available at: http://www.cfr.org/china/us-relations-china-1949---present/p17698 (accessed on 18 July 2012); 'Barack Obama on China', available at: http://www.thepoliticalguide.com/Profiles/President/US/Barack_Obama/Views/China/ (accessed on 21 March 2013); 'Chinese leader Xi Jinping joins Obama for Summit', available at: http://www.bbc.co.uk/news/world-asia-china-22798572 (accessed on 11 July 2013).

White Paper, 2011).[17] The US, too, is keen to tango. The bonhomie is visible in joint performance of military bands,[18] while formal mechanisms for bilateral cultural exchanges (e.g., the China–US Cultural Forum) have been active for several years. The Sino-American Culture and Arts Foundation (SACAF) is a particularly notable mechanism that aims to 'establish a bridge to increase friendship between the two cultures and promote cultural activities and educational workshops'.[19] The SACAF has been facilitating Sino-US student exchanges with emphasis on greater exposure to language and culture.[20]

The 'Chinese Culture Club', another SACAF initiative, has been active in raising American students' interest in Chinese culture through promotion of arts and bringing Chinese artists to the US for teaching traditional art forms. The SACAF's efforts are complemented by the Sino-American Friendship Association (SAFA) that hosts 'Chinese Culture Weeks' and helps US schools to run Chinese cultural clubs. The SACAF has succeeded in making celebration of Chinese culture an annual event in the US, with such events showcasing Chinese traditional and contemporary music, jujitsu (a method of self-defence without weapons developed in China and Japan), ribbon dances and acrobatics. People-to-people contact among the youth is also prospering through sister schools.[21]

---

[17] Bristow, 'China white paper highlights'.

[18] The two military bands played together for the first time in the US and China in October 2012 since the establishment of diplomatic relations in 1979. See *China Daily*, 'Band of Brothers Sets Tone', 1.

[19] SACAF, see http://www.sacaf.org/index.html

[20] It organizes several programmes including the 'US–China Student Hand-in-hand, East Meets West Educational and Cultural Exchange', targeting the school students.

[21] Sister school programmes are part of the international exchange programmes in which schools in China and the US collaborate to enhance their understanding of each other. Sister school programmes can take place at the basic level (pen pal arrangements whereby students of the same grade write to each other), moderate level (individual teachers and classes can choose to communicate with one another via video) and exchange programmes (administrative staff, teachers and students are given the opportunity to travel abroad and learn about another culture and work together for the greater good of their school and community,

As noticed in Europe in Chapter 6, museums and movies are active vehicles in promoting China's cultural engagement of the US as well. Collaborations between museums are rising fast with reputed US museums like the Berkeley Art Museum and Stanford Cantor Arts Centre showcasing exotic Chinese art collections, while movies are carrying forward the 'charm offensive'. The Dalian Wanda Group acquired America's second largest theatre chain, the AMC Entertainment, in 2012, increasing the flow of Chinese movies in American entertainment space.[22] Chinese movies are gaining rapid popularity with the American audience with the *Amazon* giving regular listing of top Chinese movies.[23] The popularity has sparked off collaborative ventures between Chinese, American, Hong Kong and Taiwanese film companies.[24] Chinese actors have also become lead casts in Hollywood productions (Bai Ling, Jackie Chan and Joan Chen). At the same time, Hollywood movies have also become heavily popular with Chinese audiences, particularly the young,[25] with Hollywood stars like Donald Sutherland and Christian Bale featuring in Chinese movies.

The state-owned Chinese media has been active in projecting the 'alternative' perception in the US as well. While it is hard to discern whether the efforts have borne fruit, Chinese media has become more conspicuous in the American public life, which is evident from the sparkling *Xinhua's* logos in the buzzing Times Square of New York. The *China Daily* has also been spreading its wings deep in the US through aggressive marketing techniques, including supplements circulated with daily editions of the *New York Times* and the *Washington Post*. The CCTV

---

implemented on a goodwill basis). See Chinese Culture and Education Centre, http://www.ccecbridge.org/school.html

[22] *Los Angeles Times*, 'Wanda of China Set to Buy'.

[23] Ang Lee's period *Wuxia* (martial arts) film *Crouching Tiger and Hidden Dragon* made in 2000 set off a successful journey of Chinese movies in the US. Other remarkably popular Chinese film productions include *Hero* that made Chinese actors Jet Li, Zhang Ziyi, Maggie Cheung and Tony Leung hugely popular with American audiences.

[24] Successful movies include *The Warlords* (2007), *Bodyguards and Assassins* (2009), *Red Cliff* (2008–09) and *Iron Man 3* (2013).

[25] CRIEnglish.com, 'Chinese Audiences Has A Favour'.

America cable network is also producing from its new centre in Washington. The challenge of projecting the 'alternative' is substantial for Chinese media in the US, where the mainstream media narrative is usually harsh on China. The Chinese media as an 'alternative' mouthpiece has played its role well, particularly on China's domestic matters. For instance, the Chinese media resorted to an aggressive rebuttal of Chen being 'packaged' by the American and the Western media to 'discredit China' and pointed out 'how eager American politicians are to unhesitatingly try whatever they can to make trouble for Chinese society'.[26] Developments over the CIA whistle-blower Edward Snowden was another example where the *China Daily* argued that the 'Snowden evidence' established that it was China that was the victim of cyberattacks and not otherwise as alleged by the US on several occasions.[27] The projection of the 'alternative' and counterfactual has not hindered bilateral efforts to boost people-to-people communication with both the Chinese and the US leaderships stepping up engagement through visits and institutional platforms (high-level consultation on people-to-people exchange and the Governors Forum). With more than three million people travelling across the Pacific annually on both sides,[28] these efforts are yielding results. The Chinese leadership is unlikely to spare PD efforts for increasing people-to-people contact, as is evident from Foreign Minister Yang Jiechi's remarks at the Conference on China–US Relations in Washington, for marking the 40th anniversary of President Nixon's visit to China:[29]

> Over the past 40 years, and particularly the past few years, our leaders have maintained close contacts through mutual visits, meetings at multilateral occasions, telephone conversations, and letters. These high-level contacts have played an irreplaceable part in steering the growth of Sino-US bilateral ties. There are now over 60 bilateral dialogue and consultation mechanisms, including...

---

[26] *Beijing Daily*, 'Chen Guangcheng: A Tool Used by American Politicians'.
[27] Mengzi, 'Fallout of Snowden Expose'.
[28] *China Daily*, 'Advance Sino-US Partnership'.
[29] Ibid.

the High-Level Consultation on People-to-People Exchange. These mechanisms cover political, economic, security, cultural and many other fields.

Indeed, effective PD through charismas and style statements of iconic leaders has been a tested ply of Chinese leaders for engaging the American audience. Beginning from the popularity gained by Deng Xiaoping's cowboy hat in Texas and Jiang Zemin's English utterances and jiving to Broadway tunes, Xi Jinping made it a point to emphasize 'informality' in his first visit to the US as President in June 2013. The image makeover was probably a conscious attempt to infuse fresh energy and optimism in a relationship that had become noticeably acrid in the years just before the fifth generation of the Chinese leadership assumed office: Xi's 'natural and relaxed' demeanour was in sharp contrast to his predecessor Hu Jintao's stiff and formal appearance and was arguably meant to signal new beginnings.[30] Apart from style and looks, high-level state visits by Chinese leaders, particularly those of Xi Jinping's, are also notable for imparting 'personal' touches, facilitating deeper bonding with foreign audiences. Xi's visit to the US in 2012 as vice-president made headlines for his visit to Iowa and reminiscence of the days he spent there as a young member of the CPC in the 1980s. As several experts argued, 'It sends a signal that the new leader is not a stranger to the US and that he has experience and familiarity with America by reaching right into the heartland'.[31]

Education has also emerged as an effective medium for expanding people-to-people contacts. Chinese students have been travelling to the West, particularly the US, for more than a century now. This, according to Joseph Nye, has had a 'reverse' soft power impact by transforming Chinese perception of the US: 'Most of China's leaders have a son or daughter educated in the States who can portray a realistic view of the US that is often at odds with the caricatures in official Chinese propaganda'.[32] The shifting global balance of power following China's

---

[30] Ming'ai, 'VP's Visit Warms US Impressions of China'.
[31] *Mail Online*, 'China's Vice President Revisits Youth'.
[32] Matthews (2012).

rise makes it natural for China to be keen on further reversing the perceptions in its favour by attracting more and more American students to the mainland. Two-way student flows are being enabled through the bilateral Agreement for Cooperation in Educational Exchanges, signed in 2006[33] and renewed in 2010. The number of American students in China has increased significantly due to President Obama's '100,000 Strong' initiative announced in 2009.[34] Robust bilateral business inter-actions are encouraging agencies like the Bank of China to sponsor American students in China.[35] China is also offering several scholar-ships to American students backed by the commitment to expand taught courses in English. The efforts are producing results with major universities reporting sharp increase in the number of American students.[36] However, the number of American students in China in 2012 was still far lesser than the Chinese students in the US.[37]

The CIs, as elsewhere in the world, are responding to the heavy demand for learning Mandarin in the US with more than 80 CIs operating in North America alone (Annexure II). CIs would remain active and expansive given Mandarin is the second largest foreign language in the US after Spanish with strong interest among students even at schools.[38] Some of the CIs have stepped beyond language teaching and assumed advanced academic roles, such as research (CI at the Stanford University focuses on research and literature of the Tang dynasty, while those at the Chicago and Columbia Universities declare themselves 'research

---

[33] China-US Focus, 'Agreement between US and China'.

[34] President Obama had announced the '100,000 Strong' Initiative in November 2009 as a national effort designed to increase dramatically the number and diver-sify the composition of American students studying in China. The Secretary of State Hillary Clinton officially launched the initiative in Beijing the following year.

[35] Ryan and Wei, 'China's "look West" Policy'.

[36] The number of on-campus US students in Fudan University, for example, increased from 720 in 2008 to 989 in 2011.

[37] Embassy of the People's Republic of China in the US, 'China–US Relations'.

[38] As of 2011, there were at least 50 Chinese-language immersion programmes at schools in grades 12 and below. See Dobuzinskis, 'More U.S. students learning Chinese'.

oriented').[39] However, CIs have also run into problems of adverse perception with some closing down due to 'lack of transparency and academic freedom'.[40]

China's efforts to augment 'people-to-people' contacts in the US also include those aimed at engaging the overseas Chinese. While the engagement began as early as in 1978, the strategy of 'brain circulation' as opposed to 'brain drain' is relatively new 'to overcome the loss of talented people' and is particularly relevant to the Chinese in North America.[41] The Chinese government has taken initiatives to support 'brain circulation' by encouraging overseas Chinese in the US to contribute to the home country. These include efforts to disseminate information among the overseas Chinese about business and academic opportunities in the mainland, and incentivizing efforts by local academics and experts to collaborate with their overseas counterparts.[42]

Emphasis on engaging the US through a variety of soft power means has not, however, eroded the intensity of competitiveness in China–US bilateral relations, perhaps the most significant bilateral ties of the modern times. China's global ambitions and the determined efforts to achieve it irk the US with none, other than China, displaying the likelihood of matching the US in some of the latter's established capacities for expanding geo-strategic influence, including soft power. While the Chinese communication of 'soft' intentions and soft power application in the US is substantive, Beijing has also not hesitated from being aggressive, particularly in its 'home' turf of the South China Sea, leaving little scope of doubt for the US on China's firm resolve to resist all anti-China

[39] Palit, 'China's Cultural Diplomacy'.
[40] Two Universities in the US—University of Chicago and Pennsylvania State University—decided to terminate their CI partnerships in 2014.
[41] Zweig, Fung and Han, 'Redefining the Brain Drain'.
[42] The Economic and Technology Division of the Shanghai Government's Overseas Chinese Office is strengthening university alumni associations in the US for disseminating information on various opportunities to mainlanders in the US. Furthermore, A Chinese geography professor at the University of California, Berkeley, is setting up a research centre at Nanjing University for introducing students and faculty to Western methods of research. Such projects are being incentivized by grants to local researchers for collaborating with their overseas counterparts. See Zweig, Fung and Han, 'Redefining the Brain Drain', 16.

territorial posturing in the region. China's global economic initiatives like the AIIB and the OBOR have also not been overlooked by the US and its allies as projects for curbing the US and the Western hegemonies over global development finance. Consequently, Washington is showing concerns with 'the largest shift in the global distribution of power since the rise of the US in the late 19th and early 20th centuries',[43] and might even 'find it extremely difficult to treat the Chinese as an equal partner… because force of habit and attitude has ingrained in them a sense of superiority and ascendancy when dealing with others…'.[44]

Has Chinese soft power then failed to achieve what it could have from a global perspective—constructive and balanced relations between the world's two largest powers—which, undoubtedly, could have improved chances of finding easier solutions to several global problems? Till now, the success of soft power appears to have been limited in this respect. Regardless of soft power applications by both, ample conditions exist for sustaining bilateral friction, the most important among which is probably uneasiness over replacement of the US hegemony by the Chinese—a possibility not necessarily considered best by many in even Asia and the developing world, making other countries and agencies important stakeholders in maintaining the US–China distance. Both country leaderships, however, recognize the importance of avoiding military confrontations in respective national interests. For China, hard confrontation will be inimical to the prospects of sustained economic development and expansion of geostrategic influence. While avoiding such possibilities, Beijing is likely to focus on mutually beneficial win-win outcomes by resorting to more vigorous application of soft power tools in the bilateral space. Notwithstanding such application, China is not expected to stop asserting its national interests and power ambitions at all available opportunities, making the task for soft power that much more challenging.

Regional dynamics do complicate issues for soft power far more from the US–China perspective. While 'softly' engaging other Asian countries, China would simultaneously exercise hard power, sending mixed signals

[43] Johnson et al, 'Decoding China's Emerging'.
[44] Jacques, *When China Rules the World*.

and implying a comeback for realism. Defensive realists might describe this as regional security competition at the risk of oversimplification. Beijing's continued emphasis on harmony and mutual development through connectivity designs like the OBOR, accompanied by aggressive posturing on territorial issues and strengthening of military capacities will continue to remain a source of considerable uneasiness for the region and a key extra-regional stakeholder like the US. As alluded earlier in Chapter 3, middle powers vying for greater strategic space and status are likely to choose their alignment between the US and China, depending on specific national interests. This was evident from several US allies flocking to join the AIIB, notwithstanding the US declaring its un-happiness over the choice. The world order does look indeterminate in face of China's grand designs and Washington's 'hedging' strategy for containing China. So far, pragmatism has succeeded in restraining escalation of friction and conflict. Whether such pragmatism has in any way been contributed by soft power is debatable. Nonetheless, the hope that soft power will indeed produce more restrain and objectivity should see its greater exercise in more spheres of the US–China ties.

## CHINA–CANADA: TOWARDS 'DISTINCT' RELATIONS

Taiwan has been a major factor in the China–Canada relationship, though Canada has been careful in avoiding confrontations on the issue. It has honoured 'One China' policy in principle while maintaining relations with Taiwan.[45] Canada, as mentioned earlier, while not being among the topmost strategic priorities for China, does nonetheless figure prominently in its strategic calculations and order of engagement. Former Foreign Minister Yang Jiechi, while reviewing China's foreign relations over the last 30 years in September 2008, listed 'the stable development of relations with the major powers'—Russia, the US, the EU and Japan—as China's first priority, followed by relations with neighbouring Asian countries, the developing world, multilateral

---

[45] Potter and Adams, 'Issues in Canada–China Relations'.

relations with the UN and finally the G-8[46]+5 (Brazil, China, India, Mexico and South Africa); which was the closest Canada came to be mentioned without being named.[47] Sino-Canada ties have gained momentum from growing business links with the bilateral agreement on promotion and protection of investments and the possibility of an FTA in foreseeable future. The decision to increase the use of renminbi in bilateral trade, commerce and investment[48] underlines China's gradual acceptability and recognition in North America as a major economic intermediary and significant economic actor.

## People-to-People Engagement

During his visit to Ottawa in 2012, Li Changchun, a senior CPC official expressed the desire to work together with Canada for strengthening cultural exchanges and turning a new leaf in bilateral relations.[49] Chinese art and culture has begun making its presence felt in Canada through performances like those of the Wuxi Song and Dance Troupe that received prominent coverage in local media. Nonetheless, the space for greater cultural engagement continues to remain large making agencies, like the Canada–China Cultural Exchange Association, particularly relevant. Establishment of 12 CIs (Annexure II) and 16 CCs in Canada underlines the emphasis awarded to these institutes for deepening cultural contacts, which, as it is, is increasing due to high Chinese migration to Canada as revealed by the 2012 census figures, indicating the number of Mandarin-speaking Canadians to have increased by 50 per cent between 2007 and 2011.[50]

As with most other partners in different parts of the world, interactions between national leaderships through high-level visits are stepping up

---

[46] The G-8countries are Canada, France, Germany, Italy, Japan, Russia, UK and the US.

[47] Ibid.

[48] Prime Minister of Canada, 'PM Wraps-up Third Official Visit to Canada'.

[49] A new beginning can indeed be noticed from Canada issuing dragon stamps in 2012 for commemorating the Chinese Year of the Dragon and the Chinese Film festival held in Montreal the same year.

[50] CRIEnglish.com, 'Mandarin-speaking Canadians Population'.

between China and Canada as well. The Canadian PM Stephen Harper has travelled to China thrice within five years, beginning from 2009. Former President Hu Jintao's visit to Canada in 2010 was reciprocated by the governor general of Canada, Michaelle Jean's 'friendship visit' the same year. The frequent high-level exchanges have enhanced the role of the strategic working group, a bilateral mechanism established in 2005, for the purpose. Apart from PD, the high-level exchanges have also focused on 'common good' targets like health care and environment.[51] Interestingly, Canada has had lessons to offer to China in PD, given the latter's young vintage in Chinese strategic exercise as is evident from Minister Zhao Qizheng's (in charge of the subcommittee of foreign affairs of the CPPCC) several meetings with the Canadian Consul of Public Diplomacy.[52]

Education and mobility of students are also expanding people-to-people contacts in a manner similar to that witnessed between China and the US. While the number of Canadian students in China was at a much lower level, the presence of the former is growing steadily. Cooperation between schools is rising with several principals of Canadian middle and primary schools visiting China along with students attending summer camps.[53] The role of provinces in expanding people-to-people contact is also visible through 'twinning' relationships between Chinese and

---

[51] The Canadian Health Minister Leona Aglukkaq hosted his Chinese counterpart Chen Zhu in Ottawa in 2009 for discussing various health issues, including reforming health care systems, primary health care and food safety leading to signing of a bilateral Action Plan for cooperation on health. See, Potter and Adams, 'Issues in Canada–China Relations'.

[52] Potter and Adams, 'Issues in Canada–China Relations'.

[53] These exchanges are expected to flourish given the institutional mechanisms like the China–Canada Strategic Working Group and collaborations between China's Ministry of Education and Canadian provinces on mutual recognition of academic degrees, apart from the commitment to bilateral cooperation in education affirmed by senior Ministers. The Canadian Foreign Minister John Baird and the Chinese Education Minister Yuan Guiren reiterated the significance they attached to education collaboration during the former's visit to China in 2010. See Embassy of India, 'Embrace A Better Tomorrow'.

Canadian cities.[54] Such arrangements, needless to say, boost tourist flows, which are already picking up fast with China declaring Canada a 'new state-approved tourist destination' (ATD) for the Chinese in 2009.

Unlike in Europe and the US, where Chinese studies are growing at a fast clip, they are yet to expand as much in Canada, at least, in contrast with other areas study programmes (e.g., Africa, Korea, South Asia and Central Asia). China is still studied mostly as part of a greater Asia (e.g., as in the University of Toronto's Central and Inner Asia Studies programme, or the Department of East Asian Studies in McGill University). Specific foci on China are noticed in some university programmes (e.g., Certificate in Chinese Studies in the Asia, Canada Programme of the Simon Fraser University, and similar initiatives in the Universities of Winnipeg, Waterloo and Victoria) though. The Chinese Language Program in the Department of Asian Studies in the University of British Columbia (UBC) has had the distinction of becoming North America's largest programme in Chinese Language.

## CHINA–LATIN AMERICA: NEW BEGINNING

China's links with South America (or Latin America) can be traced to the Ming dynasty (1368–1644) when it traded in silk, porcelain and cotton with Mexico and Peru. Later the Qing dynasty (1644–1911) forged diplomatic relations with Peru, Brazil, Mexico, Cuba and Panama between 1870 and 1900.[55] In modern times, notwithstanding the geographic distance, China has stepped up engagement with Latin America largely with the strategic goal of tapping its abundant energy and mineral resources (Table 7.2 lists a few of them). This is in line with China's 'Policy Paper on Latin America and the Caribbean' issued in 2008 that emphasized the importance of viewing China's relations with these

---

[54] There are many Canada–China twinning relationships: between Barrier, Ontario and Taizhou, Jiangsu (an example of city twinning) and Ontario and Jiangsu (an example of provincial twinning).

[55] Zhiqun, *China's New Diplomacy*, 79.

**Table 7.2**
*Energy and Mineral Resources in Latin America*

| Energy and Mineral Resources | Countries |
| --- | --- |
| Oil & gas | Brazil, Colombia, Cuba, Ecuador, Mexico, Venezuela |
| Bauxite | Jamaica, Venezuela |
| Coal | Colombia |
| Copper | Chile, Colombia, Mexico, Peru |
| Iron ore | Brazil, Bolivia, Chile, Venezuela |
| Uranium | Argentina, Brazil |
| Zinc | Argentina, Mexico, Peru |
| Lead, Manganese | Argentina |
| Molybdenum | Chile |
| Nickel | Cuba |
| Gypsum, limestone | Jamaica |
| Silicon | Peru |

*Source:* Compiled from Ellis (2011).

regions from a strategic perspective and developing a comprehensive and cooperative partnership.[56]

The imperative for engagement emanating from access to resources can make the region as strategically valuable for China as Africa. Furthermore, the 'One China' policy is also a major driver of Chinese engagement of Latin America given 12 out of 33 countries in the region, including Central, South and the Caribbean, have diplomatic relations with Taiwan. The tide has begun changing in China's favour with Costa Rica, ending a 63-year old relationship with Taiwan in June 2007, and recognizing China, though St Lucia in Caribbean continues to vacillate.[57] China's engagement of the region through institutional mechanisms like

---

[56] *Xinhua News Agency*, 'China's Policy paper on Latin America'.
[57] St Lucia had relations with Taiwan from 1984 to 1997, with China from 1997 to 2006 and again with Taiwan since 2006.

the three-way foreign ministers' dialogue—China and the Community of Latin American and Caribbean States (CELAC)[58]—and the China–Latin America cooperation forums are expected to consolidate its strategic bonding with the region, particularly economic, with China already the largest investor in Latin America after the US and the Netherlands, and the largest source of inward FDI in Brazil, and also having signed FTAs with Chile, Peru and Costa Rica.

## Economic Initiatives

Apart from trade and investments, China's economic engagement with Latin America includes means that have been noted in its strategic involvement in other parts of the world as well—development assistance, commitment to infrastructure and humanitarian aid. As noted earlier, Chinese aid and development assistance have flown into infrastructure development of recipient countries in a manner that has made traditional donor, particularly from the West, distinctly uncomfortable about the impact of Chinese aid on the global aid dynamics. Indeed, Sergio Gabrielli, the President of the Brazilian national oil company Petrobras, makes it evident that China's ability to negotiate large deals and integrating government and private sector activities is remarkable.[59] The sentiment echoes across much of Latin America, where China's 'no strings attached' development assistance has won friends and partners, like in Bolivia, Ecuador and Venezuela (Annexure I). Bolivia has benefitted from the China Development Bank's (CDB) loan for developing the world's largest iron ore deposit, including connecting rail and port infrastructure.[60] Cash-strapped Ecuador was financially aided by China after it defaulted on its global repayments[61] and has been helped by China in building transport infrastructure for new mines as well as medical facilities.[62] Venezuela, on the other hand, has been a part of

---

[58] Gov.cn, 'China, Latin American and Caribbean States'.
[59] Ellis, 'Chinese Soft Power in Latin America'.
[60] The CDB has extended a LoC for creating infrastructure in the region, including road and rail networks, ports, electricity and telecommunications.
[61] *Bloomberg*, 'Ecuador Seeking up to $1.4 Billion'.
[62] *People's Daily Online*, 'China Donates Mobile Hospital to Ecuador'.

China's 'loan-for-oil' deals,[63] similar to some in Africa. Chinese companies are active in the mature oilfields of Maracaibo and Anzoátegui, a vital current revenue stream for the Chavez regime. Furthermore, a bilateral agreement signed in May 2010 makes Chinese companies key players in extracting iron, gold, bauxite and coal from Venezuela. Some of the major Chinese-supported infrastructure initiatives in Latin American countries, both through development assistance and investment, are mentioned in Table 7.3. Apart from development assistance in infrastructure, health care diplomacy, again a strategic initiative witnessed in Africa, is visible in the Caribbean region.[64]

**Table 7.3**
*Major Chinese-supported Infrastructure Projects in Latin America*

| Country | Projects |
| --- | --- |
| Venezuela | US$ 16.3 billion loan for the Junin-4 oil block in Orinoco oil belt. |
| Argentina | US$10 billion for modernizing railways system; US$ 3.1 billion for purchasing the petroleum company Bridas. |
| Ecuador | US$ 1 billion advance payment for petroleum; US$ 1.7 billion for a hydroelectric project with negotiations under way for US$ 3–5 billion additional investments. |
| Peru | US$ 4.4 billion for developing mines (Toromocho, Rio Blanco, Galleno, and Marcona). |
| Brazil | US$ 5 billion for a steel plant in Açu Port; US$ 3.1 billion for buying a stake in offshore oil blocks from the Norwegian company Statoil; US$ 10 billion loan to Petrobras for developing offshore oil reserves; US$ 1.7 billion for purchasing seven power companies. |

*Source:* Compiled from Ellis (2011).

[63] Weston, Campbell and Koleski, China's Foreign Assistance in Review', 9.
[64] CCTV.com, 'China Helps Build First Children's Hospital'.

Unlike in Africa, where Chinese involvement through resources and technology in the host country infrastructures is almost a one-way process, Latin America displays a more balanced engagement. For example, China is benefitting from application of Brazilian and Argentinian technologies in its own infrastructure and scientific development. Brazilian technical expertise in deep-water exploration and oil drilling technology has been attempted to be used in the Three Gorges Dam hydroelectric project.[65] China and Brazil are collaborating in space technology, a field which is also witnessing China's collaboration with Argentina.[66] As noticed in Africa earlier, Chinese business presence in Latin American telecom space is increasing given the prominence of Huawei and ZTE, while China Shipping, China Overseas Shipping and Hutchison Whampoa are playing major roles in Latin America's foreign trade. Again, a downside of Chinese economic involvement noticed in Africa, local resentment has been occasionally visible in Latin America as well. Many Latin American manufacturers across the region are increasingly viewing Chinese companies as unfair competitors, and are unhappy with the many informal barriers that prevent their products from entering the Chinese market. The 'loan-for-oil' deals in Venezuela have also led to political repression and economic mismanagement, while in Ecuador, Chinese companies' control over 90 per cent of total oil production has been raising eyebrows, as is relatively easier visa requirements for Chinese workers in Argentina.[67]

It must be noted, however, that notwithstanding occasional resentments, much of the region is appreciative of China's phenomenal economic progress. This gets vindicated through a 2014 Pew Global Research Survey that points to the overall favourable perception of China in Latin America. China's transformation from an impoverished nation to a major economic power is inspirational for several low-income Latin American countries. China's resilience in the aftermath of the global financial crisis of 2009 has reinforced these perceptions. Chinese financial institutions are becoming more prominent in regional business

---

[65] Ibid., 57.
[66] Ibid., 72.
[67] *Today*, 'China's Pivot to South America', 19.

transactions with the China Export–Import Bank and the Inter-American Development Bank (IDB) working together to develop an effective bilateral investment mechanism. Chinese currency is also becoming a sought-after medium for commercial transactions for the region with Uruguay keen on Latin America introducing Yuan in its trade with China: a sentiment resonated by the IDB as well.[68]

China's proactive role during natural calamities in the region[69] has also helped in striking a deeper chord with its people and leaderships. The association is expected to strengthen further through bilateral institutional efforts at developing agricultural cooperation aimed at greater food security.[70] These initiatives are being complemented by China's establishment of research and development centres for agriculture technology and industrial parks for farm product processing.

## Cultural Engagement

Compared with other regions of the world, China's cultural communication with Latin America appears subdued but is gradually picking up. Therefore, Li Keqiang used his visit to Latin America[71] in 2015 to communicate the importance China attached to bilateral cultural exchanges. Since initiatives like the Chinese Cultural Week in Venezuela[72] and the Chinese Film Festival in Costa Rica are few and far between. Chinese culture, though, has gained familiarity with locals through

---

[68] English.xinhuanet.com, 'China, L. America to Strengthen Economic Ties'.

[69] Assistance such as the 'Harmonious Mission' of medical aid and equipment to Jamaica, donations to Chile during the earthquake in 2010, food aid to Cuba during the hurricanes in 2008, aid to Ecuador to fight dengue are just some of the initiatives. For details, see Universia.net, 'Gobierno chino donará a Universidad de Santiago de Chile' ['Chinese government donated to University of Santiago of Chile'] and *The Oakland Post Online*, 'Chinese Navy on Humanitarian Mission', 134.

[70] During his visit to Chile in 2012, Premier Wen proposed a forum for Chinese and Latin American agriculture ministers a bilateral mechanism for building emergency food reserves and an agricultural cooperation and development special fund. See *China Daily*, 'Wen Urges Enhanced Co-op'.

[71] The Premier visited Brazil, Columbia, Peru and Chile.

[72] The Dialogue, 'Inter-American Dialogue'.

'China Towns' in Chile (*El Distrito de la Chinesca*), Costa Rica (*Barrio Chino*) and Peru (*Barrio Chino de Lima*), while Chinese language newspapers exist in Cuba (the *Kwong Wah Po*) and Venezuela.[73] But notwithstanding its relatively limited scope, China's employment of soft power through cultural exchanges has a distinct characteristic for the region. While there are no turf battles over cultural exchange between China and Latin America, vignettes of the latter culture have made inroads into China. These are being encouraged by China in keeping with the idea of cultural exchanges being a two-way process whereby 'principles of listening to' and 'respecting each other' are appreciated. Indeed, 'cosmopolitan constructivism' appears to be at work in this regard with emphasis on cross-cultural cooperation. Thus, Brazilian film festival was held in Shanghai and Beijing in late 2011, while Argentina's National Institute of Tourism Promotion held the 'South America Road Show in China' in 2011 in different Chinese cities. Quality Mexican cuisine and Columbian salsa lessons are now available widely across China with the National Ballet of Cuba featuring in the Beijing International Festival.

While cultural interactions are relatively limited, China has been more vigorous in expanding PD through high-level state visits. This is evident from the increasing exchanges between governments as well as China's efforts to attract more Latin American students. High-level bilateral visits and exchanges are very much on the rise (Annexure III). The urgency for engagement reflected in these visits can be discerned from the priorities highlighted in the Policy Paper on Latin America (2008) mentioned earlier that emphasized political, economic and cultural cooperation with Latin America including high-level exchanges, exchanges between legislatures and political parties, consultation mechanisms in the political field, cooperation on infrastructure and investment and trade cooperation.[74] Former President Hu Jintao's visit to Brazil, Cuba, Chile and Argentina in 2004 set the stage for increased bilateral high-level visits in the following years that have corresponded with the signing of several bilateral agreements and cooperation

---

[73] Chinatowns in Latin America.
[74] *Xinhua News Agency*, 'China's Policy Paper on Latin America'.

initiatives with most of these on culture, science and technology, economics and trade, investment protection, public administration/consular and tourism.[75] President Xi Jinping's visit to Trinidad and Tobago, Costa Rica and Mexico in June 2013 after assuming office further highlights China's eagerness to engage the region.

Media collaboration, identified important for cooperation in the Policy Paper of 2008 and also reiterated by the former premier Wen Jiabao during his visit to Chile in 2012, has taken off. In 2010, the Chinese media sought the cooperation of the Latin American and Caribbean media for bringing a 'new' China to the region. During the SCIO-sponsored visit to China by the Latin American and Caribbean media executives in 2010, executives of the *China Daily*, *CCTV*, and *CRI* as well as the online news service *News.org*[76] explored possible collaborations with their counterparts. The *Xinhua News Agency* is also collaborating with the Latin American (*Prensa Latina*) News agencies.[77]

The former Premier's emphasis on increasing people-to-people contacts during his visit to Chile in 2012 saw him announcing scholarships for Latin American students over the next five years.[78] The number of Latin American students in China is still quite low, and more scholarships should see more regional students with subjects like the Chinese language, traditional Chinese medicine, international trade and international relations becoming increasingly popular.[79] On the other hand, the number of Chinese students in Latin America is also quite insignificant. China has been targeting selected countries (Brazil, Chile) for more students through higher education exhibitions and MoUs.[80] Beijing is also eager to support a China–Latin America and Caribbean Young Political Leaders' Forum for more people-to-people exchange.[81]

---

[75] Koleski, 'Backgrounder'.
[76] *Jamaica Observer*, 'China Seeking Cooperation with Latin American'.
[77] *Prensa Latina*, 'Xinhua, Prensa Latina News Agencies'.
[78] *China Daily*, 'Wen Urges Enhanced Co-op'.
[79] *China Daily*, 'More Scholarships'.
[80] Study in China, 'Brazilian Government and Chilean Government'.
[81] *China News and Report*, 'Speech by Premier Wen Jiabao at the Economic Commission'.

The Latin American interest in China, while increasing, is relatively small compared with its similar interests elsewhere. Beijing's increasingly active role in the region has necessitated a deeper understanding of China and various aspects of its bilateral ties with the region. The number of China Study Centres in the region is increasing along with China-related programmes (Table 7.4). Initiatives such as teaching *taichi* in schools of Mexico and student exchange programmes between Chile and China (e.g., *Universidad Vina del Mar* of Chile's exchange programme Zhejiang Gong Shang University in Hangzhou)[82] reflect a nascent curiosity that would surely prosper over time. This would also be augmented by CIs like elsewhere in the world with 30 CIs in Latin America (Annexure II).

**Table 7.4**
*Latin American Universities with China Centres and Programmes*

| Country | University | Programme |
| --- | --- | --- |
| Mexico | Universidad Nacional Autonoma de Mexico | China–Mexico Studies Centre |
| Mexico | Instituto Tecnologico de Mexico (ITESM) | Mandarin, courses on doing business in Asia. (Representative offices in Beijing, Shanghai and Guangzhou.) |
| Chile | Universidad Catolica, Escuela Militar, Universidad Bernardo O'Higgins, Universidad del Pacifico, Universidad de Santiago de Chile (USACH) | Mandarin language instruction |
| Chile | Universidad Diego Portales | Asia Pacific Programme |
| Brazil | Universidad de Brasilia | Chinese Programme |

---

[82] Ellis, 'Chinese Soft Power in Latin America', 47.

| Country | University | Programme |
|---|---|---|
| Argentina | The Latin American Faculty of Social Sciences (FLASCO), Universidad del Salvador, Buenos Aires | Chinese Programme, Chinese language Programmes |
| Uruguay | ORT University | Mandarin Programme |
| Venezuela | Universidad Central de Venezuela | Mandarin Programme It also provides ten scholarships for Venezuelans to study in the PRC |
| Ecuador | Escuela Superior Politecnica del Litoral (ESPOL) | Mandarin programme |
| Ecuador | Colegio Ecuatoriano–Chino | Courses on Mandarin and Chinese culture |
| Peru | Universidad de Lima | Centre for Asia-Pacific studies |
| Peru | La Pontificia Universidad Catolica | China-oriented programmes and Mandarin |
| Colombia | Universidad Nacional and Universidad de Los Andes, Bogota | Mandarin |
| Colombia | Universidad EAFIT | Centre for Asia-Pacific studies |
| Colombia | Universidad Sergio Arboleda in Bogota and Corporacion Unificada Nacional | Chinese studies programmes and Mandarin |
| Costa Rica | Centro de Investigacion de Mercados Sostenibles | China-oriented programmes |
| Costa Rica | Universidad de Costa Rica | Mandarin |

*Source:* Compiled from Ellis (2011).

Much of the people-to-people contacts in future would be hastened through new institutional initiatives like the China and Latin America Inter-American Dialogue with experts from the US, Latin America, China and Australia for identifying emerging areas of interest in the evolving bilateral relationship. The presence of the US in the initiative[83] is interesting, perhaps indicating that Latin America is Washington's 'backyard' and the US is eager to monitor Chinese growing presence in the region, particularly China's strategic and economic interests. It is also interesting to note the emerging intellectual efforts in Latin America on the region's ties with China as evident from several experts contributing to *Latin America's Answer to Premier Wen Jiabao's Proposal* examining the proposals made by the Chinese Premier at Chile on developing the region's ties with China.[84]

## CONCLUSION

China's great power ambitions make it imperative for it to engage the West, particularly the US. It has been particularly careful and cautious in taking forward what is probably the most important bilateral strategic relation of modern times. Beijing's nuanced engagement with Washington has been marked by a blend of 'hard' and 'soft' strategies. While the former manifests in aggressive positions adopted from time-to-time on the South China and the East China Sea dispute, the territories being dominated by the US's strategic and military allies, a conciliatory rhetoric as well as diplomatic and cultural engagement is distinct on part of the leadership injecting a new sense of realism for furthering national interest. But despite deeper engagement and greater people-to-people contacts, China's image in the West and the US continues to suffer. This is largely due to undemocratic political systems and institutions and clamping of various personal freedoms. Indeed, oft-used phrases by the

---

[83] The WG first met in September 2011 in Washington, and its last meeting was held in February 2012. See The Dialogue, 'Inter-American Dialogue'.

[84] English.xinhuanet.com, 'LatAm Experts to Study Chinese'.

Chinese leadership like the 'rule of law' have been mostly assumed propaganda for 'using law to rule the people'.[85]

The unabashed display of China's aspiration to be a 'big' player in its own backyard has forced the US to be more involved with the region, including a new commitment to enhance military presence in Asia.[86] Clearly, the extent of strategic involvement deemed necessary by different US administrations over time would be watched carefully by China. More belligerent postures by the US would be a critical test for China's 'soft' modes of engaging the former, which, according to a Pew study appear to be yielding partially positive results.[87] Perceptions about the US in China, though, are becoming less favourable. As Wang Jisi, an influential strategic thinker, figuring on advisory boards of the CPC and the Ministry of Foreign Affairs points out, the US is no longer regarded as 'that awesome, nor is it trustworthy, and its example to the world and admonitions to China should therefore be much discounted'.[88] This might encourage China to pursue its own image-building more actively in the US by relying more on the relatively successful instruments like education and culture.

China–Canada relations are still evolving. China's relatively less intense engagement of Canada could be due to China considering Canada a 'middle power' in the global systemic, and hence not a powerful strategic competitor. The bilateral relationship shows a greater urge to engage on part of Canada similar to that of New Zealand. For Canada, stable ties with China are a foreign policy priority and 'central to the success of a New Multilateralism'. China's cultural interaction appears to be making inroads into Canada, consistent with Beijing's objective of casting a benign impression on the West by 'winning hearts and minds'. Such efforts, however, will need to be balanced against wary perceptions of its remarkable rise.[89]

[85] Xuecun, 'Corrupting the Chinese Language', 6.
[86] Perlez, 'Drawing Spheres of Influence', 3.
[87] Pew Research Centre, 'Ask the Expert'.
[88] Perlez, 'Chinese Leaders See Eclipse', 4.
[89] Potter and Adams, 'Issues in Canada–China Relations'.

China–Latin American relations symbolize cooperation driven largely by economic factors. Many countries in the region have economic and political complementarities with China in terms of having had distinctly socialist pasts and later embarking on market-oriented economic policies. China's economic success has contributed to its positive image in Latin America, consolidated by its capacity to extend aid and play a strong role in the region's business landscape. However, China's economic penetration in many Latin American countries has also given rise to resentment, similar to Africa and South and Southeast Asia, thereby questioning the 'real' objectives of Beijing's soft power diplomacy.

China's engagement of the region is expected to continue given the value of energy resources and for gradually marginalizing Taiwan. However, Chinese investment, mostly in the extractive sectors, sometimes with heavy environmental toll, combined with creation of fewer jobs and less skill development of its people in the region, can generate more local resistance. What is distinct in the Chinese approach to these problems is the awareness and willingness to assuage this discontent through high-level visits and announcements of big ticket infrastructure projects. From a larger perspective, China's increasing presence in the US's backyard has strategic implications when viewed through its support of the Venezuelan President Hugo Chavez's emphasis on military ties with Argentina, Brazil and Peru, the signal intelligence site at Bejucal—south of Havana in Cuba—and the commercial container facility operated by the Chinese firm Hutchinson on Grand Bahama Island, just off the Florida coast. Clearly, China's engagement of Latin America is not entirely 'soft', and traces of the 'hard' are visible.

# 8

# Central Asia, Russia, Mongolia and Middle East: Reshaping Relations on New Priorities

Central Asia, Russia, Mongolia and the Middle East cover a wide geographic expanse, and is an important region for China given its energy resources. Russia and Central Asia also have vast untapped agricultural resources. China's growing demand for food makes the region even more critical for the Chinese leadership, given its importance in terms of food security.[1] Coupled with its strategic geographic location and mineral and food resources, China's engagement of the region has been inspired by domestic compulsions too. Engaging Central Asia, Russia and Mongolia is also in line with the larger objective of ensuring a stable external environment.

The National Peoples' Congress (NPC) announced an 11.5 per cent increase in spending on domestic security at its annual parliament-ary session in March 2012.[2] The increase made spending on internal security higher than defence, making China one of the few countries in the world to do so. As this particular aspect of spending made headlines all over, the government refused to publicize the overall figure in 2014, once again underlining Beijing's sensitivity to global and regional perception. China's focus on internal security has sharpened in recent years after several violent incidents in Xinjiang, dubbed by the Chinese media as 'terrorist attack'.[3] With their roots in the neighbourhood, these attacks have created a major security challenge for the Chinese leadership.

[1] Zhang, 'China Marching West for food'.
[2] Xin and Yao, 'China Cuts Growth Target'.
[3] *Xinhua News Agency*, 'Xinhua Insight'.

Engaging the Muslim community[4] in Central Asia and the Middle East is, therefore, critical for China for ensuring stability in the ethnically fragile Xinjiang (which literally means 'New Frontier'), also the mainland's largest administrative division. The Middle East, though geographically at a distance from Xinjiang, has large Muslim populations while the Central Asian Republics (CARs) and Mongolia has contiguous borders with the province. The May 2009 unrest in Xinjiang and the subsequent Arab reaction to the development have forced a significant Chinese rethinking on policies for its extended Muslim neighbourhood. These concerns and predilections have led to a 'soft' engagement with country-specific distinct facets for the region, while 'hard power' is also visible in determining the quality of the engagement.

## CENTRAL ASIA: SECURITY DRIVES ENGAGEMENT

China's engagement of the five CARs—Kazakhstan, Kyrgyzstan, Tajikistan, Turkmenistan and Uzbekistan—is notable and seize the spotlight, given its outplay in a region traditionally dominated by Russia. Strategically, the region is 'the thickest piece of cake given to the modern Chinese by the heavens'.[5] China's rapid economic growth and industrialization has increased its appetite for new sources of energy. At the same time, with 19 per cent of the world population and only 7 per cent of the world's farmland, achieving food security is also a major challenge for the country.[6] Central Asia becomes vital in both respects. The quest for new energy sources and greater energy security has encouraged greater Chinese investments in oil and gas exploration.[7] Apart from investments in strategic resources, Chinese funds are also focusing on projects

---

[4] Engaging South Asia, given its vast Muslim population, has also been a policy priority for the Chinese leadership, as discussed in Chapter 3.

[5] Wong, 'China Quietly Extends Footprints'.

[6] DuPont, 'China's Insatiable Appetite for Change'.

[7] A pertinent example is the China–Turkmenistan natural gas pipeline opened in December 2009. The longest pipeline in the world, it had delivered 10 billion cubic meters of natural gas to China by the end of May 2011. See Jiao and Haipei, 'China, Turkmenistan Sign'.

augmenting regional connectivity, particularly through Kyrgyzstan to the Caspian Sea region for enabling faster movement of goods and expanding trade between China and Central Asian economies.

As mentioned earlier, the non-traditional security imperatives of energy and food security are backed by traditional security imperatives, particularly internal security, behind China's deep engagement of Central Asia. Ensuring a stable Central Asia is important for China, given the close inter-linkage between stability and prosperity of Northwest China and Central Asia.[8] The intricacy will persist as long as Beijing continues to grapple with the challenge of political and cultural integration of Uighurs in the Xinjiang Uighur Autonomous Region.[9] Xinjiang's borders with Kyrgyzstan, Kazakhstan and Tajikistan make them critical in China's management of internal security issues arising from Uighurs. The greater integration of Xinjiang with Central Asia is likely to positively influence China's security and economic prospects by consolidating control over Xinjiang and expanding strategic influence in the region.[10] The internal security and economic prospects are interconnected in Xinjiang, given its oil deposits and strategic geographical location. China has been purposefully trying to *promote peaceful development* in the region for securing a benign environment for its economic growth. The manifestation of the engagement has been in the resolution of border disputes with Kazakhstan, Kyrgyzstan and Tajikistan.[11] Indeed, in this respect, China's Central Asia policy with overt emphasis on 'cooperation', 'multilateralism', 'integration' and 'regionalism' also highlights its efforts to balance the perceived US threat in the region.[12]

---

[8] McMillan, 'Xinjiang and Central Asia', 96.

[9] Many scholars classify Xinjiang and Central Asia as one whole, rather than classifying the former Soviet Union states as one unit and Xinjiang as a separate entity and a part of the PRC. For details, see McMillan, 'Xinjiang and Central Asia', 95.

[10] Clarke, 'China's Integration of Xinjiang', 89.

[11] China has made considerable concessions in this respect, keeping only 20 per cent and 30 per cent of the disputed territories respectively with Kazakhstan and Kyrgyzstan and dropping most of its claim to the Pamir Mountains for Tajikistan.

[12] Wong, 'China Quietly Extends Footprints', 94.

## Economic Initiatives

As discussed earlier in Chapter 3, WDS has been a key driver of China's engagement with South Asia, particularly Pakistan and Afghanistan. The driver impacts China's strategic perspective of Central Asia as well, given the regional development plan, aiming to develop Xinjiang as an industrial and agricultural base and a trade and energy corridor for the national economy.[13] Regional connectivity becomes an essential prerequisite for the objective encouraging Chinese commitment in regional infrastructure development in a manner similar to that noticed for South Asia. The major initiatives in Xinjiang, as part of the WDS, include the opening of international bus routes between Osh (Kyrgyzstan) and Kashgar (Xinjiang), economic assistance for the highway linking Xinjiang and Lake Issyk-Kul in Kyrgyzstan and an agreement to establish highway links between Xinjiang and Tajikistan.

The ambitious OBOR scheme encompasses Central Asia and would contribute significantly to regional connectivity through creation of new infrastructure capacities. As a precursor to the initiative, in April 1994, the Chinese Premier Li Peng during his visit to Central Asia called for a new 'Silk Road' that envisaged a network of roads and railways through a continental Eurasian 'land bridge' as an alternative to the old sea routes for boosting trade and business.[14] The visit marked the beginning of initiatives towards greater connectivity between China and the region through an agreement on the Sino-Kazakhstan border. Since then, China has been investing in regional train systems linking Central Asia, including a transcontinental rail network connecting Southeast and Central Asia with China. The Urumqi–Central Asia line is planned from the Western city of Urumqi towards Kazakhstan, Uzbekistan and Turkmenistan, connecting through Pakistan, Iran and Turkey onwards to Germany. This particular rail link is an essential component of WDS for facilitating access to energy supplies. Such access will be complemented by the trilateral Uzbek–Kyrgyz–China project, linking Andijan (Uzbekistan), Osh (Kyrgyzstan) and Kashgar (Xinjiang) by a 1,000 km

---

[13] Becquelin, 'Staged Development in Xinjiang', 358–78.
[14] Mackerras, 'Xinjiang and Central Asia since 1990', 135.

rail and highway connection.[15] All these projects will strengthen China's capacity to offer vital non-Russian transport routes to Central Asia for facilitating its interaction with the international market along with an eye to develop its western region, particularly Xinjiang.

Many Chinese companies are operating in Central Asia, underlining China's growing economic presence in the region.[16] As in various other parts of the world, ZTE is prominent in Central Asia too having constructed the telephone exchange in Dushanbe in Tajikistan and contributed to modernization of the Tajik telecom network.[17] Turkmenistan is witnessing a more varied Chinese business presence with several Chinese companies spread out across diverse industries including oil and gas, telecommunications, transport, agriculture, textile, chemical and food industries, healthcare and construction.[18] Business engagements are in parallel to China's interventions on various occasions entailing humanitarian support, such as to Uzbekistan in 2010 for assisting refugees from Kyrgyzstan.[19] Human and social development contributions by China are also visible through the Central Asian Regional Economic Cooperation (CAREC)[20] initiative which aims to reduce poverty, increase social development and manage natural resources of the region.

## Cultural Initiatives

While economic ties are strengthening, cultural communication has also been a major focus. SCO, founded in 2001 by China, Kazakhstan, Kyrgyzstan, Tajikistan, Uzbekistan and Russia, while emerging as a major

---

[15] Peyrouse, 'Economic Aspects of Chinese', 30.

[16] In as early as 2005, there were 744 Chinese enterprises in Kazakhstan, 100 in Uzbekistan and 12 in Kyrgyzstan. See Peyrouse, 'Economic Aspects of Chinese', 18.

[17] Lal, 'Central Asia and Its Asian Neighbours'.

[18] China is developing South Iolotan—the largest gas field in in Turkmenistan. See Bhadrakumar, 'China resets terms of engagement in Central Asia'.

[19] *The Sunday Times*, 'China Sends Humanitarian Aid to Kyrgyz Refugees'.

[20] CAREC is an initiative by 10 countries in the region to facilitate regional cooperation. Economic corridors and trade facilitations are amongst its top priorities for the region.

forum for China's cultural and educational engagement with Central Asia also demonstrates China's attempt at regionalization, similar to that of the ASEAN, discussed in Chapter 4. China's willingness to participate in regional and global arrangements comes through clearly as its objectives of (a) improving its national image, (b) promoting its economic interests, (c) enhancing its national security and (d) most importantly, acquiring 'the power to avoid conflict', thus building trust, decreasing concern, developing collaboration and avoiding hostility,[21] are achieved. SCO is also mentioned as one of the several regional organizations China hopes to work with in implementing the OBOR.

With the SCO's enlargement of focus from primarily economic and military issues, more pronounced diplomatic and people-to-people communications are taking centre stage. Apart from SCO, the China–Central Asia Friendship Association (CCAFA), formed in December 2007, is active in promoting cultural exchanges. Considered a propaganda organization under the CPC it marks 'the beginning of a new development phase in our non-governmental diplomacy with Central Asian nations'.[22] Through the Association, Beijing aims to achieve friendship and common development, initiating a step towards 'non-governmental diplomacy, as an important supplement to official diplomacy' in Central Asia.[23] Though the government's role in CCAFA cannot be ruled out completely, it is still interesting given that China's 'non-government diplomacy', if any, is almost non-existent in other countries. Nonetheless, it is not clear what particular form the diplomacy might assume making it distinct from the official Chinese diplomacy led by state agencies. CCAFA has been spearheading cultural interactions between China and the region through various initiatives. In January 2012, CCAFA, steered by the Chinese People's Association for Friendship with Foreign Countries (CPAFFC),[24] celebrated the 20th anniversary of China's diplomatic ties with the

---

[21] Kavalski, *China and the Global Politics of Regionalization*, 9.
[22] Wong, 'China Quietly Extends Footprints' 94.
[23] Lum et al., 'Comparing Global Influence'.
[24] CPAFFC (*zhong guo ren min dui wai you hao xie hui*), founded in 1954, engages in people-to-people diplomacy. Apart from forging friendship, the association also ensures international cooperation, safeguards world peace and promotes common development. CCAFA works under the rubric of CPAFFC.

region[25] by organizing a high-level reception.[26] Such initiatives and other cultural interactions organized by the CCAFA are arguably 'non-threatening' postures—an aspect of its engagement of the region that China is keen on emphasizing for not conveying inappropriate signals to major powers active in the region such as the US and Russia.

Education is shaping as an important avenue for fostering people-to-people contacts. SCO is facilitating educational exchanges. At the 2007 SCO meet, former President Hu called for bolstering scientific, cultural, educational, sports and healthcare exchanges, and cooperation between China and Central Asia. China is currently offering annual college scholarships to SCO member countries and regularly invites college and high-school students from the SCO members for short-term exchange programmes.[27] Though the scale of educational engagement is much smaller than that between China and the Southeast and South Asia, China would be keen on upping the same. The fast-growing interest in learning Mandarin among the young in Kazakhstan, Kyrgyzstan and Tajikistan can lead to more regional students travelling to China. In the meantime, the presence of CIs in the region (Annexure II) also demonstrates its evolving bigger role in spreading Chinese culture and proliferation of Mandarin in the region.[28]

## RUSSIA: OLD FRIEND, NEW TIES

China and Russia are the largest neighbours of each other with profound influence on each other's security, internal stability, development and foreign policy. The China–Russia relationship is significantly predicated by bilateral energy cooperation. As discussed variously earlier in this book, China's soaring demand for energy, which partly shapes its external engagement policy towards countries in Africa and Latin America, is a critical element influencing Beijing–Moscow ties as well. Russia is a

---

[25] China had established diplomatic relations with the CARs in January 1992.
[26] Ministry of Foreign Affairs of the People's Republic of China, 'Dai Bingguo Attends the Reception'.
[27] Ibid.
[28] *Hanban News*, 'Confucius Institute at Tajik National University, Tajikistan'.

major source of oil and natural gas for China, and both are cooperating on developing nuclear power energy. Apart from energy cooperation, the major driver directing Beijing's engagement in the region is linked to its future grand designs of which the OBOR is an integral component, and Russia is a vital player in securing success of the connectivity plan.

The disintegration of the Soviet Union in 1991 paved the way for China's future economic prosperity by dissipating the Soviet economic clout. In order to avoid the Soviet catastrophe in China,[29] the 1990s witnessed Deng Xiaoping's strong commitment to economic reforms along with new foreign policy initiatives like good neighbourly re-lations. While China has been careful to pick up lessons from the Soviet experience, it has been equally emphatic in engaging Russia for stabilizing its frontiers and fostering friends in the neighbourhood. In more recent times, the Sino-Russian ties have strengthened through their partnering in the BRICS as well as the common ambition of structuring alternate coalitions influencing the global and regional balance of power. Deng's call for 'ending the past, opening up the future' in 1989 laid the found-ation for the current bilateral ties. Both countries signed the 'Treaty of Good-Neighborliness and Friendly Cooperation' in 2001 and resolved their border dispute in 2008, imparting a solid push to their strategic partnership. President Putin's re-election as the Russian President in 2012 has considerably strengthened bilateral ties by assigning greater priority to Russia's ties with China vis-à-vis its ties with Europe and the US.[30] While soft power tools like culture and economics are being employed by China for engaging its big neighbour, the 'non-soft' pragmatic character of bilateral engagement is more pronounced. Russia is a major arms and military technology supplier to China, and Beijing is the largest customer of Moscow's military products. It is important to note though that Russia's competition with other arms suppliers—France, Germany, UK and the US—can influence the strategic architecture of the region. At the same time, future Sino-Russian competition as arms

---

[29] Post 1991, several studies were undertaken by distinguished scholars, such as Lu Nanquan, Jiang Changbin, Li Shanming and others, to examine the reasons for disintegration of the former Soviet Union.
[30] Putin, 'Russia and the Changing World'.

producers cannot be overlooked. Though China's defence developments and improved capabilities are yet to ring alarm bells in Russia; some Russian strategic experts argue that Russia's current military strength cannot counter NATO on its West and China on its East.[31]

Sino-Russian cultural interactions picked up momentum from the late 1990s with China emphasizing the importance of people-to-people communication and cultural exchanges in enhancing the strategic cooperative partnership.[32] The varied scope of the collaboration—education, culture, healthcare, sports, tourism, media and youth—was articulated in a joint press communique of 2011,[33] followed by further expansion of collaborative activities in 2012 (including high-level exchanges, media collaboration, youth cooperation in cultural activities and co-production of films).[34]

The Mandarin language has been an important facilitator in this regard, with learning Mandarin for better understanding of the 'other' culture being a trusted technique since the ancient times.[35] Russian students have been travelling to China to learn Mandarin since the mid-17th century, and the St Petersburg University has been offering Chinese courses since the mid-19th century. While the flow of Russian students to China has greatly expanded, more and more undergraduate and post-graduate students are opting to learn Chinese in Russia.[36] While Russian students appear fascinated by Chinese culture and language and aspire to go to China for pursuing graduate studies, it has more than 40 universities and around 20 middle and primary schools teaching Chinese as the first foreign language. These efforts and other cultural initiatives are

---

[31] Minemura, 'China's Growing Military Presence'.

[32] *News of the Communist Party of China*, 'Cultural Exchanges Vital in Sino-Russian Partnership'.

[33] *Xinhua News Agency*, 'China, Russia to Strengthen Cultural'.

[34] *Xinhua News Agency*, 'China, Russia Issue Joint Communique'.

[35] Anecdotal evidence indicates the Ming Emperor Wan Li (1572–1620) had written a goodwill letter to the Russian Tsar which was left unopened for 50 years since nobody knew the Mandarin language during the time. This points to the realization, on part of both countries, for picking up each other's languages for better understanding and communication. See *Xinhua News Agency*, 'Chinese-Learning Craze Sweeps Russia'.

[36] *Xinhua News Agency*, 'Chinese-Learning Craze Sweeps Russia'.

being augmented by 'ambassador' CIs with 17 CIs (Annexure II) currently functional in Russia. The importance of language in carrying forward bilateral ties is evident from the symbolism conveyed through back-to-back celebrations of the 'Year of Russian Language' in China (2009) and the 'Year of Chinese Language' in 2010[37] for commemorating six decades of bilateral ties.

Along with language, bilateral cultural communication and people-to-people contacts are flourishing through organization of art exhibitions and media visits[38] and tourism. Greater people-to-people contact has led to a rapid increase in tourist flows as well. Tourism would remain a facilitator of people-to-people contacts as is evident from the Russian Deputy PM Vladislav Yuryevich Surkov's comment: 'Russia also welcomes Chinese enterprises to invest in tourism and infrastructure, and at the same time hopes to promote the two countries' high-tech cooperation through tourism'.[39]

As mentioned earlier in the Chapter, with respect to the SCO and Central Asia, the former is being utilized by China with respect to Russia as well for expanding people interfaces through scholarships for higher studies and research. The inevitable emphasis on more dialogue following greater strategic prioritization of the relationship has led to a sharp increase in high-level visits with China vigorously pursuing 'major-nation diplomacy'[40]—a key priority of the current leadership—visible in the case of Russia as well. President Xi visited Russia right after assuming office in March 2013—'a testimony to the great importance China places on its relations with Russia'.[41]

China's 'soft' diplomacy, however, faces challenges in its bilateral domain with respect to Russia on multiple grounds. At a regional level, and on China's home turf of the South China Sea, there are issues like Russia's ambiguous position on Senkaku Islands and the South China

[37] *Xinhua News Agency*, 'The Year of Russian Language'.
[38] Ministry of Culture, PRC, 'Russians Get a Taste of Chinese'.
[39] *People's Daily Online*, 'China and Russia Seek to Expand'.
[40] Zongze, 'Winning the Next Decade'.
[41] *BBC News*, 'Chinese President Xi Jinping in Russia'.

Sea dispute[42] which, undoubtedly, continue to affect Chinese perception. The other meddlesome aspect is Chinese migration, which figures
predominantly in the Russian discourse. For Russia, influx of Chinese
migrants[43] for agricultural purposes has been a constant demographic
worry, given its potential to turn the Russian Far East (RFE) into a
Chinese province. The Chinese perspective on the issue is different. Jiayi
Zhou argues that the influx of Chinese labour is not an outcome of issues
related to China's national food security, higher domestic consumption
demand or diminishing returns from agriculture.[44] On the contrary,
Chinese labour inflow is a response to filling of a genuine labour shortage
in the RFE, apart from contributing positively to the local food security.[45]
The contrasting perspectives reflect the variance and unease of both
countries on a subject that has the potential to grow into a major point
of contention over time. They also demonstrate the complexity of the
relationship that might come in the way of smooth implementation of
the OBOR, where the involvement of Chinese labour is expected to be
significant.

The former colonial power Russia's support is strategically critical for
China in Central Asia—the immediate entrance of China's Silk Road
Economic Belt—where Russia is still seen playing a major role as an
external player. China's growing economic power also influences Russia
and Central Asia's policies towards Beijing. Eager to benefit from the flow
of Chinese capital, which an initiative like the OBOR could bring about
for their economies, Putin has already agreed to reach an agreement with
Xi to coordinate Beijing's OBOR initiative with the Russia-led Eurasian

---

[42] Russia and Vietnam have collaboratively pursued energy exploration in the
South China Sea much to the displeasure of the Chinese.

[43] Repnikova and Balzer, 'Chinese Migration to Russia'.

[44] In 2008, the deputy director of National Development and Reform
Commission (NDRC) Zhang Xiaoqiang stated that China's 'Going Out' policy
'supports qualified enterprises to go to other countries and regions... to launch
oil crop, grain, fruit and vegetable production', but that it is 'absolutely not
promoting Chinese farmers or large-scale corporations to go overseas and
purchase or lease long-term land to grow large amounts of food on which China's
food security will depend'. See Zhou, 'Chinese Agrarian Capitalism'.

[45] Zhou, 'Chinese Agrarian Capitalism'.

Economic Union (EEU)[46] in Central Asia, underpinning the 'stickiness' of China's economic power. Apart from Russia's relevance in the OBOR initiative, its role as a partner in the New Development Bank of the BRICS and the AIIB reaffirms its commitment to China-led regional financial and infrastructure initiatives.

## MONGOLIA: A CRITICAL NEIGHBOUR

Mongolia was integrated into the Qing Dynasty for two centuries before declaring independence and subsequently became a Soviet satellite state in the early 20th century. Diplomatic relations were established between Beijing and Ulan Bator in October 1949. As part of China's periphery diplomacy, Mongolia has also been receiving increasing attention similar to the Oceania, discussed in Chapter 5, with the latter's energy reserves and geostrategic location making it an important regional actor in the Chinese strategic perspective. Furthermore, domestic imperatives have also influenced engagement of Mongolia with the mainland's Inner Mongolia province, comprising more than five million ethnic Mongolians distinct by their culture and language.[47] Uighurs have strong cultural ties with Mongolia, while Xinjiang and Mongolia share common borders, making Mongolia a critical country from the vantage point of internal security and stability. Mongolia's non-recognition of Taiwan and steadfast support to China on the issue increases Mongolia's significance in China's foreign policy, and encourages greater engagement of Beijing with Ulan Bator. It is hardly surprising that bilateral ties have been upgraded to a comprehensive strategic partnership in 2014 and Mongolia's active participation has been sought in the OBOR initiative and Asia–Europe cross-border railway transportation. The growing engagement, however, cannot be oblivious to Moscow and Washington's interests in the country

---

[46] Along with China, Russia and Central Asia are eager to promote EEU as an alternative to the West.

[47] China's RMB currency note also features the Mongolian language as one of the five languages spoken by the non-Han population in China.

as well as Mongolia's own ambitions of expanding global relationships, including India.[48]

Ethnic cultural links make cultural interactions an essential component of Sino-Mongolian engagement. The bilateral Treaty on Friendship and Cooperation signed in 1994 has been instrumental in this regard with bilateral cultural exchanges picking up through regular cultural months (Chinese Cultural Month celebrated in Mongolia in August 2012) and culture weeks (e.g., China's Inner Mongolia Culture Week in Ulan Bator in September 2012) organized jointly. The China–Mongolia Culture Forum has also been instrumental in facilitating bilateral cultural exchanges.[49] The strategic relevance of the Forum can hardly be overlooked with the first such forum, organized by the CI at the National University of Mongolia in 2009, celebrating six decades of bilateral ties and the second session, at the time, of signing the Joint Statement on Strategic Partnership in June 2011.[50] These forums, focusing on bilateral cultural and academic interfaces, have been responsible for increasing cultural and educational awareness about China.[51] The Chinese leadership has also not spared efforts to endear Mongolia, with President Xi Jinping describing his visit to Mongolia in 2014 as 'visiting relatives'. It also underscored the use of high-level state visits by China for communicating its 'good neighbourly' policy and encouraging greater people-to-people communication.

Greater land connectivity will be critical in China's future engagement of Mongolia. Connectivity is a mutual imperative given landlocked Mongolia's lack of access to regional markets and seaports. Russia's sparsely populated East is also not as attractive a market for Mongolian producers as the Chinese mainland, which is reinforcing the importance of connectivity. The latter is equally critical for China for accessing Mongolia's abundant reserves of coal, copper and iron ore. Bilateral economic relations are clearly complementary and explains Mongolia's

---

[48] The Indian PM Narendra Modi's visit to Mongolia in May 2015 did raise eyebrows in Chinese media and policy circles.
[49] *Hanban News*, 'Confucius Institute at National University of Mongolia'.
[50] *Hanban News*, 'The Third China–Mongolia Forum on Language'.
[51] The number of Mongolian teenagers learning and taking up advanced studies in China is the largest in the world.

continuing economic engagement with China, notwithstanding uneasiness over the high dependence on China for trade and investment (China is Mongolia's largest trade partner and topmost investor), coupled with memories of China's imperial legacy. Thus, presence of Chinese businesses, already conspicuous through mining companies like PetroChina Company Limited and China Shenhua Group which is a stakeholder in developing Mongolia's Tavan Tolgoi coal mine, is expected to increase further. Such commercial presence would be complemented by more cooperation in social sectors, particularly healthcare,[52] where joint initiatives like establishment of border-region infectious disease control mechanisms are already visible.

Economic considerations are the primary determinant of Mongolia's policy towards its big neighbour. The OBOR is particularly relevant in this regard. The proposed China–Mongolia–Russia Economic Corridor, a part of the OBOR, could fetch enormous economic gains for a country like Mongolia—landlocked and increasingly dependent on China (and Russia). The strategic consideration was probably instrumental in Mongolia, cancelling the Dalai Lama's visit in 2015. Dalai Lama is popular in Mongolia where a majority of Mongols are Tibetan Buddhists and have visited the country on several occasions earlier despite Chinese reservations. While the Mongolian perception of China may not necessarily be positive due to historical factors, such perception can well be counterbalanced by China's economic pull, a factor noticed on several instances in the earlier chapters, underpinning the role of China's financial clout in creating strategic allies.

Despite many soft power tools in place, anti-Chinese attitudes are also prevalent[53] and get regularly reflected in Mongolia's blogosphere and public discourses.[54] This is partly because there is still reluctance by the government officials to actively dismantle the remnant anti-Chinese sentiment stemming from the negativity that built up during the period of Sino-Soviet tensions when Mongolia was under Soviet influence.[55]

---

[52] *Xinhua News Agency*, 'China to Deepen Health Cooperation with Mongolia'.
[53] *Wei xin shang de zhong guo* (2015)
[54] Han, 'The Trouble with China–Mongolia Relations'.
[55] Ibid.

The desire to reunite with ethnic Mongolian areas of China or 'pan-Mongolism' also adds to the tension.[56] A contemporary scholar Jargalsaikhan working on the issues attributes this Mongol attitude towards the Chinese as part of a 'global anti-Chinese phenomenon' rooted in power imbalances, backlash against Chinese economic activities and conflicts over identity issues.[57] The experience highlights the challenges for China's soft power once again with efforts to instil goodwill in the neighbourhood, not producing desired returns. It is possibly for reversing the outcomes that the Chinese leadership is increasingly beginning to focus on the 'software' of PD as opposed to the 'hardware' by attempting to accommodate China's messages into foreign discourses in a manner that they are understood,[58] as discussed in Chapter 2. This also explains the extent by which the government is sensitive image-building and keen on exploring new ways to make PD more effective. Perhaps, India, which is looking for more strategic space in Northeast Asia, is keen on exploiting the anti-China attitude in Mongolia, explaining partly Indian PM Narendra Modi's visit to the country—the first ever visit by an Indian PM.

## MIDDLE EAST: CALIBRATED ENGAGEMENT

China's historical links with the Middle East have been relatively less, at least, compared with those of India's, which could be due to the geographical distance. Zhang Xiaodong, a Chinese scholar on the region argues, 'for new China, the Middle East was a distant and unfamiliar place. The Chinese government and academia did not care about Middle Eastern affairs'.[59] However, China is clearly eager to make up for its relative lack of interest in the region over time by altering its Middle East

---

[56] The people of Mongolia are fearful of being a part of China, and many believe that after Taiwan is unified with China it will be their turn. They strive for a greater Mongolian nation—seen as a security threat by China—which include Inner Mongolia and Autonomous Prefectures of Bortala and Bayingolin in China, apart from the three republics of the Russian Federation. See Wang, 'Mongolia's Delicate Balancing Act'.

[57] Han, 'The Trouble with China–Mongolia Relations'.

[58] Clingendael, 'China's Public Diplomacy Shifts Focus'.

[59] Zhang, 'China's interests in Middle East', 150.

policy. The contemporary Middle East policy began evolving during Deng Xiaoping's era (1978–87), with the most marked sign of the change reflecting in China's neutral posture during the protracted conflict between Iran and Iraq (1980–88). The policy is being further refined for structuring the new and evolving relationship. The refining, as Zhang notes further, is in line with the overall readjustment in policies of all big powers towards the Middle East brought on by readjustments within the region itself.[60]

Energy has been a vital driver of China's engagement of the Middle East. With China's oil imports set to surge from around one million barrels per day (BPD) to more than 12 million BPD by 2035,[61] it is important for China to diversify sources of energy supply for keeping pace with the domestic pattern of consumption of energy and increasing energy security.[62] Energy security has been instrumental behind the inclusion of the Middle East in China's extended neighbourhood, as have been other compelling factors like stronger economic links with the region, maintaining sub-regional peace and participating in the process of restoring and maintaining regional stability.[63] There is a security dimension as well, with a stable extended neighbourhood expected to help in stabilizing Xinjiang too.

Former Premier Wen's visit in January 2012 to the three major oil producers in the Gulf —Saudi Arabia, Qatar and the UAE—underlined the strategic significance of the Gulf Cooperation Council (GCC) countries for China. His visit was the first trip to Saudi Arabia by a Chinese Premier in two decades and the first ever by any Chinese Premier to the other two states. The visit reinforced China's engagement of the Arab world as part of its 'going out' strategy launched in the 1990s. This marked the beginning of China's constructive engagement with the region, deemed a necessity, given the widely held impression among several Chinese scholars that the Arab world's perception of China is influenced by ideas drawn from the Western media. They argue about a

---

[60] Ibid., 156.
[61] Kemp, 'China's Growing Strategic Stake'.
[62] Feng, 'Non-traditional Security and China'.
[63] Dongxiao, *Building up a Cooperative and Co-progressive New Asia*.

limited awareness of China's 'peaceful development' strategy in the region. The limitation and China's lack of success in communicating an alternative view to the Arab world was highlighted by Qian Xiaoqian, the Vice Minister of the State Council Information Office, at the Forum of China–Arab Cooperation in Media in April 2008:[64]

> There are only a few reports about the development of Chinese–Arab relations, reflecting the positive and significant changes in various sides of people's lives. The news about history, culture and even the travel industries both in China and Arabic countries remains infrequent as well. This does nothing but baffle the sense of understanding between Chinese and Arabs... Since the media are considered an important bridge to enhance understanding, the Chinese and Arabic media should play a significant role and assume a more positive function to take this responsibility.

Notwithstanding PD through high-level visits and greater engagement, improving bilateral ties with the Middle East has been challenging for China, given its ambiguous posturing on several notable developments in the Middle East. China's hesitation in supporting the Arab Spring and the region's democratic aspirations, it's veto (along with Russia) on the UN Security Council (UNSC) resolution urging the Syrian President Bashar al-Asad to step down and the unsympathetic attitude towards economic sanctions on Iran have not endeared China to the Arabs.[65] Syria, in particular, appears to have confused China into taking contra-dictory postures. While the UN veto was anti-Syria, Beijing's effort to block the UNSC and the Arab League to force Syria to halt its military offensive against its own people has also been criticized. Various rational-izations of the obstruction range from China's pursuit of the overarching foreign policy goal of 'non-intervention' to the concern that influence of radical Islamic groups can spread down the old Silk Road to Xinjiang.[66]

---

[64] *China Daily*, 'Promoting Media Ties with the Arab World'.
[65] With the sanctions lifted in 2015, many Western companies are returning to Iran to exploit the rich oil reserves. This might put pressure on the Chinese companies already functioning there, despite sanctions.
[66] Grammaticus, 'China's Stake in the Syrian Stand-off'.

Beyond these explanations, the posture clearly reflects Beijing's intention to refrain from 'keeping a low profile'—a dictum coined by Deng Xiaoping in 1989—in the region.

China's relations with Iran project an interesting dimension of international relations. Greater Chinese activism in the Middle East, while implying China's intentions to become a more significant actor in the regional dynamics, has even drawn some international support, with the US supportive of China's bigger role in Iran. Washington's own national interests encouraged an active role by Beijing in the Iran crisis. With Iran being China's third-biggest source of oil imports supplying more than 5 per cent of its total needs, the Obama administration was confident that China's less purchase of Iranian oil will force Iran to revisit its nuclear policy. While the US did encourage China's intervention in Iran to stall its nuclear program in 2012, Washington has subsequently been uneasy with the gradual thawing of relations between the two.[67] Although the new evolving partnership is dubbed 'limited' between Beijing and Tehran, both Washington and Russia are apprehensive of their enhanced military cooperation.[68] The dynamic exemplifies the limited influence of soft power, from a Chinese perspective, as applied in its relations with the US and Russia. Notwithstanding exhaustive employment of soft power tools with the US and Russia, China's search for positive spinoffs continues, with Russia and US clearly unconvinced about Beijing's 'virtuous' engagement with Tehran. Hard realities of potential military cooperation are clearly major checks on

[67] The signing of a Joint Comprehensive Plan of Action (JCPOA) in July 2015 is being seen by analysts as a new platform that will forge closer relations between China and Iran. Under the deal, Iran is expected to limit its uranium enrichment and make other adjustments to its nuclear program in exchange for the removal of international sanctions with China benefiting the most since Chinese firms will have greater access to the Iranian market, especially in the energy sector. See Princeton University, 'Posing Problems without an Alliance'.

[68] While, on the one hand, Washington fears that more military cooperation between China and Iran would improve Iran's ability to threaten US military forces in the Middle East and in turn pose proliferation risks in the region, on the other hand, Russia is not particularly pleased with Iran's return into China's oil market which will further squeeze its supplies there.

the effectiveness of soft power, probably more so for China, whose soft power often gets labelled 'propagandist' and is variously seen not as honest in declaring its desired intents as it should have.

Notwithstanding the evolving activism, China's Middle East policy is noticeable for its careful effort to not to dislodge the US from the region and is characteristically similar to identical efforts in Central Asia with respect to Russia. According to many scholars, this is evident from China not having any agreements impinging on security (particularly military) with the GCC member countries.[69] As noted by a CSIS report 'although Beijing has often provided sympathy and low-key support to indigenous efforts to foil US foreign policy in the Middle East, it has been markedly reluctant to offer overt or high-level assistance'.[70] However, it is also clear that in both Central Asia and the Middle East, Chinese foreign policy has displayed the preference for collaborating with other major global and regional powers while several soft power tools have been employed to shape perceptions in the region.

Care and caution is also visible in China's employment of 'soft' tools in the Arab world. Cultural initiatives have been prominent through Culture Weeks showcasing Chinese art and heritage (in Dubai and Abu Dhabi in the UAE,[71] and in Iran). Apart from Culture Weeks, international fairs, such as those organized by the China–Arab States Economic and Trade Forum (CASETF) showcasing exotic Chinese art performances (like the *kouxian*—an instrument belonging to the Hui[72] ethnic group)[73] are familiarizing Middle Eastern audiences with the rich and varied Chinese culture while demonstrating their assimilation within the Chinese society. Additional 'syntheses' initiatives include TV channels

---

[69] It must be noted that China does have missile cooperation with GCC countries like Saudi Arabia and Kuwait along with non-GCC countries like Iran.
[70] Alterman and Garver, 'The Vital Triangle', 16.
[71] *CCTV+NewsContent*, 'UAE–China Culture Week'.
[72] Hui, the other dominant Muslim group in China, live in Ningxia, an autonomous region of the PRC in the Northwest part of China. Huis are Arab descendants with their distinct culture and historical backgrounds but better assimilated into the Chinese society unlike the Uighurs.
[73] *Xinhua News Agency*, 'China, UAE Issue Joint Statement'.

airing programmes on traditional ethnic cultures of Ningxia and other Chinese provinces in Arabic and English.[74]

It is perhaps not coincidental that cultural communication is particularly active with countries that are China's biggest sources of energy, such as Iran. China and Iran established a joint committee for cultural and educational cooperation in 2012 with both agreeing on reciprocal establishment of cultural centres.[75] A similar agreement exists with Kuwait, another major source and supplier of energy. The agreement on information and cultural cooperation, signed in 2002 with UAE, has been expanded in scope and content by a joint communique framed in 2012.[76] Oman—another energy and mineral abundant country having ancient relations with China beginning from the Han till the Ming dynasty—is also collaborating actively with China for increasing people-to-people contact.[77]

China's education links with the Middle East are yet to become robust. Though Chinese scholarships are offered to countries like Bahrain as part of an international educational exchange programme, the numbers are still very limited.[78] Professional training and scholarships have also been offered to Iraq.[79] The CSC also organizes the Chinese higher education exhibition in countries like Saudi Arabia to engage the students. China studies initiatives are beginning to come up in the Middle East (like the China Programme at Cairo University). China is gradually emerging as an attractive location for technical training for the Middle East. With the US tightening entry permits post 9/11, Saudi Aramco's annual training trip for managers was held in China in 2007.[80] China is also offering training courses to Egypt. Egypt has otherwise also benefitted

---

[74] It is interesting to note the attention being paid on select cultural syntheses through initiatives like the teaching of 'China-Arab' Calligraphy which is becoming immensely popular with the Arabs.

[75] China.org.cn, 'China, Iran Set Up Committee to Enhance'.

[76] *Xinhua News Agency*, 'China, UAE Issue Joint Statement.

[77] Global Arab Network, 'Muscat: Oman, China Launch Friendship Association'.

[78] *Gulf Daily News*, 'China Scholarship Chance for Five'.

[79] Ministry of Foreign Affairs of the People's Republic of China, 'Bilateral Relations: China–Iraq'.

[80] Alterman and Garver, 'The Vital Triangle', 64.

from China's contribution to the Egypt–China model school, opened in 2008–09, with donations, computers, printers, language labs along with Chinese language curriculum.[81]

China's engagement with Israel has continued despite the latter's proximity to the West, particularly the US. While high-level visits[82] and cultural interface strengthen China–Israel ties, education also contributes to the relationship. During Israeli President Netanyahu's visit to Beijing in May 2013, the two sides signed agreements on education, including agriculture, technology and financing.[83] Further, the first CI in Israel was established in Tel Aviv in 2007, marking a milestone in Sino-Israeli academic interaction. CI's have also been established in Iran, Jordan and Lebanon (Annexure II).

## Economic Initiatives

Beijing's engagement of the Middle East has varied facets with the countries from the region, sharing and demonstrating an affinity with the China. A noted Egyptian writer, Naguib Mahfouz, reflects that China has socio-political and historical circumstances similar to the Middle East and has chosen its own path to progress without being swayed by the West,[84] thereby indicating a common bonding between China and the region. This feeling of a common bonding also pushes the Middle Eastern countries' desire to be a significant force like China. China's economic success, like in Africa, has indeed made an impact on the Middle East with appreciation expressed for its alternative model of high-economic growth and development.[85] In a meeting with the Egyptian Foreign Minister Mohammed Amr in March 2012, the then Vice President Xi Jinping expressed willingness to share China's economic reform and development model with Egypt. He also added that Beijing will also

---

[81] Economic and Commercial Counsellor's Office, 'Chinese Donation for Model School'.
[82] Israeli PM Benjamin Netanyahu visited China in May 2013 at the invitation of China's Foreign Minister Li Keqiang.
[83] Li and Cheng, 'China, Israel Boost Cooperation'.
[84] Mahfouz, 'China for Us'.
[85] Alterman and Garver, 'The Vital Triangle', 82.

encourage its companies to invest there, promote the China–Egypt Suez economic and trade cooperation zone while establishing bilateral cooperation in multiple areas.[86] These sentiments and commitments provide fertile ground for the success of China's revamped Middle East policy, particularly through economic engagement. As noticed for Central Asia, Russia and Mongolia, OBOR assumes criticality in this regard with China's largest trading partners in the region—Saudi Arabia, the UAE, and Iran[87]—becoming important nodes in the proposed Belt.

China has been fairly flourishing business ties with Saudi Arabia and Iran. These include the 'strategic oil partnership'[88] and the benefits obtained by China from the advanced Saudi technology of more efficient exploitation of existing domestic oilfields. These technologies would have otherwise been unavailable to China, given the US regulations on export of dual-use and other strategically sensitive items. China is also availing Saudi expertise in increasing capacity to process heavy crude—petroleum with sulphur content greater than 1 per cent—from the Middle East.[89] Former President Hu's visit to Saudi Arabia in 2009, apart from promoting an 'in-depth development of China–Saudi Arabia strategic friendly relations',[90] initiated collaboration in infrastructure too (investments in infrastructure-building in rail, sea ports, electricity and telecommunications). On the other hand, China and Iran's shared history of 2000 years create a conducive background for commercial engagement in modern times, reflecting in large presence of Chinese firms in building dams, steel production, energy, sea-port and airport.[91] A Chinese fibre optic firm is building the country's broadband network, while the Chery Automobile Company is manufacturing micro passenger cars in the northern town of Babol.[92] The 500 years of Western domination and

[86] *People's Daily Online*, 'Chinese Vice President Vows Closer Ties'.
[87] Chang, 'The Middle East in China's Silk Road'. (2015)
[88] Manning, 'The Asian Energy Predicament', 81.
[89] Pham, 'China's Interests in the Middle East', 3.
[90] *China Daily*, 'Chinese President arrives in Riyadh at Start'.
[91] Kemp, 'China's Growing Strategic Stake', 75.
[92] Pham, 'China's Interests in the Middle East', 4.

the resultant experiences seem to have connected both nations that now 'desire to reclaim status and influence on the world stage'.[93]

Despite ambiguity in posturing on strategic issues mentioned earlier, China's economic ties with Syria continue to be strong with the CNPC and Sinopec helping to revive output under rehabilitation contracts for small mature oil fields in Syria. China's 'no strings' attached aid policy is a boon for Syria, facing massive protests as part of the Arab Spring and a civil war. China is active in infrastructure-building in Oman as well. China Gas has a major presence in Oman and manages the city's gas pipeline infrastructure, gas distribution, operation of oil stations and development of oil- and gas-related technologies.[94]

The Muslim connect between Xinjiang and the Middle East is also responsible for Beijing's overtures into infrastructure in the region. In a first-of-its-kind bilateral agreement, the China Railway Construction Corporation was mandated to build a high-speed monorail, linking holy cities of Mecca and Medina by 2013.[95] In addition, a new rail line from Tehran to the Khosravi town on the border with Iraq passing through Arak, Hamedan and Kermanshah is also being developed. The line is expected to link Iran with Iraq and also Syria as part of a Middle-Eastern corridor for facilitating movement of pilgrims to the holy cities of Najaf and Karbala in Iraq.[96]

## CONCLUSION

Beijing's engagement of the vast Asian region comprising Central Asia, Russia, Mongolia and the Middle East is driven by firm national interest of internal security, neighbourhood stability, access to scarce resources and economic growth. Future engagement would continue to be driven by these imperatives, and China is likely to keep up the engagement momentum through the OBOR project and cultural initiatives. Other views occupying increasingly greater space in the strategic discourse

---

[93] Calabrese, *China and Iran*, 3.
[94] Kemp, 'China's Growing Strategic Stake', 86.
[95] Moore, 'China to Build $2bn Railway'.
[96] Ibid.

suggest China utilizing Central Asia for elevating its stature as a rising power and also for testing its new brand of foreign policy.[97] The domain of the argument extends to China's overall soft engagement of Asia for developing a benign image, where large parts of the Asian continent are assumed as testing ground. Like elsewhere in Asia though, the results appear mixed with China's engagement of Central Asia winning plaudits and raising eyebrows at the same time, including concerns over expansion of intelligence networks in the region and surreptitious sponsoring of migration from the mainland with reports of many Chinese settling in Kazakhstan.[98] Adding strength to these views are the 'non-soft' components of the engagement, such as massive military aid and technology equipment support to Kazakhstan.[99]

Sino-Russian relations would remain among the most significant bilateral relations of the modern times. Notwithstanding greater cultural exchanges, people-to-people contact and bonhomie in plurilateral forums like BRICS and the SCO, Russia remains uneasy over China's expanding influence in its turf. Both China and Russia are aware of each other's large needs for energy and the criticality of their obtaining access to energy resources in Central Asia and the competition thereof, which might spark off as a result. There is also resentment in Russia over migration from the Northeast China as pointed out by Alexander Shaikin: 'Chinese are now invading Russia with suitcases'.[100] Mongolia, on the other hand, appears to be balancing both Russia and China through its 'Third Neighbour' Policy—a Western coinage—of building closer ties with the other partners (including India).

As far as its strategy towards the Arab world is concerned, Beijing is treading carefully after weighing all the complexities. This is evident from no Politburo Standing Committee member of the CPC having visited Israel in recent years, and only two CPC leaders having been to Iran. But the latest developments in Iran post withdrawal of nuclear sanctions and the beginning of a new trajectory of bilateral relationship

[97]   Clarke and Wei, 'China's "Look West" Policy', 3.
[98]   Yin and Li, 'Assessing China's Influence in Central Asia'.
[99]   Lengauer, 'China's Foreign Aid Policy', 55.
[100]  Norling, 'China and Russia', 41.

might alter the larger profile of China's relations with the Middle East and adjoining regions down the line. Despite this development, China looks keen on avoiding a confrontationist posture in the region on matters particularly sensitive to the strategic interests of the US. In the process, it also hopes to project itself as a *responsible power*. Notwithstanding the refrain and emphasis on regional cooperation and engagement through soft means, China has not diluted its arms cooperation with either Russia or the Middle East. Arms, evidently, will also determine the course and pattern of China's engagement of the region, as much as its other priorities will.

# PART III

# Indian Soft Power, China–India Engagement and Comparative Dimensions

# 9

# Indian Soft Power: Strategies and Approach

> India has the deepest philosophy still expressed in a vibrant religion, a huge body of literature, amazing art, dance, music, sculpture, architecture, delicious cuisine and yet Indians are in denial mode and wake up only when foreigners treasure India.
>
> —Maria Wirth[1]

Maria Wirth's sentiments resonate widely within and outside India. There is little disagreement on the imperative of shaking off the 'denial mode' and replacing it by the 'acceptance' of what India was and still is. Doing so, though, necessitates a greater appreciation of cultural heritage and sharing the same with the world in an informed and constructive fashion.

Narendra Modi's election as the PM of India in May 2014 is likely to implant a firm cultural drift in India's foreign policy. His efforts to reinvigorate the Indian economy have earned plaudits. At the same time, his conscious attempt to positively transform India's global image through meaningful communication of culture have been widely noted. Modi has brought energy, clarity and focus in India's external engagement with emphasis on soft power. His global outreach has been characterized by spirited extolling of India's cultural magnificence aiming to establish 'India's rightful place in the world'.[2]

The Bharatiya Janata Party (BJP) manifesto for the general election of 2014 mentioned the importance of 'creating a web of allies to mutually

---

[1] Tharoor, *Pax Indica*, 290.
[2] *Asia Unbound*, 'The Indian Elections'.

further our interests'.[3] Modi's foreign policy has spared no pains to engage with his outreach and travels encompassing neighbours, the big powers, as well as the middle and small powers. While some argue that no major change in the direction of foreign policy is still discernible,[4] the dynamism and energy in external engagement is inescapable. At the same time, however, India's foreign policy, particularly the thrust on highlighting the virtues of a civilizational state in articulating soft power, can be a somewhat risky approach to adopt, given that aggressive emphasis on culture and civilization might give birth to fears of cultural colonization among the recipients, particularly in the neighbourhood. It is still too early to say whether it is indeed so. But there is little doubt about Indian foreign policy beginning to articulate soft power through state communication in a more forceful fashion than anytime in the past.

The new robust diplomacy fits well into the larger 'Asian Century' narrative. The 21st century, often dubbed the 'Asian Century', is witnessing major shifts in the international order, following the rise of China and India. With no peaceful mechanism available for the 'rising' powers to gain acceptance in the international hierarchy since the end of the 19th century,[5] the struggle by the 'emerging powers' in their quest to figure at the big table is inevitable. China's global aspirations are backed by large capacities, particularly economic, enabling deployment of soft power instruments on a similar scale. India's size, civilizational history and economic potential endow it with similar aspirations. But India's rise draws attention to perceived status inconsistency between its role ambition and ascribed status,[6] leading to doubts over whether India has developed capacities that could match the status of a global power. Multiple domestic problems impede its rise as a major global player,[7] as does its ineffective communication with the rest of the world. Incoherent

---

[3] Ibid.

[4] Firstpost.com, 'Just Speeches Won't Cut It'.

[5] Holsti, *Peace and War*, 339.

[6] India aspires to play a role commensurate to its stature as a great and ancient civilization and potential (economic and military). But there is a disjoint between its aspiration and what it has achieved. For details, see Nayar and Paul, *India in the World Order*, 9.

[7] Guha, 'Will India Become A Superpower?'

'coercive diplomacy' with neighbours like Pakistan for example, manifesting in periodic mobilization of large troops followed by their recall without realization of tangible strategic outcomes, have adversely influenced global and regional perceptions about India.[8]

While the academic debate over the qualitative aspects of India's rise would continue, India's foreign policy is becoming more *pragmatic* by focusing on economic and strategic interests. Consequently, its soft power efforts are also maturing. While the focus on soft power has been gradually increasing over time, BJP has been emphatic in prioritizing its use by mentioning so in its last election manifesto. India's strategic horizon has expanded into the greater Asian neighbourhood through the LEP.[9] The same is being aimed to be deepened through the 'Act East' policy[10] showing New Delhi's eagerness to play a bigger role in regional and global affairs. This has also led India to partner big powers like the US, given the strategic upside attached to such partnerships. The approach has called for a robust foreign policy with a matching soft engagement strategy. The latter has been less pronounced in scale in the past than similar Chinese strategies but more nuanced in specific thrusts and greater involvement of non-state actors. The approach is likely to undergo some fundamental changes under PM Modi, as the chapter will outline.

Involvement of non-state actors or 'unofficial diplomacy' has been conspicuous in India's foreign policy. Joseph Montville has defined this 'unofficial diplomacy' as a 'Track Two diplomacy' in which non-state actors seek to improve international communication. The Indian government's preference for 'unofficial diplomacy' has made it the hallmark of Indian diplomacy, given its less propagandist flavour. Historian, Akira

---

[8] Mitra, *Politics in India*, 265–66.

[9] Initiated in 1991, the policy represents India's efforts to cultivate economic and strategic ties with its Southeast Asian neighbours. Interestingly, during Li Keqiang's visit to New Delhi in 2013, the Chinese Premier linked India's LEP with China's WDS whereby China has been attempting to develop its western provinces, notably Xinjiang and Yunnan. For details, see *The Times of India*, 'China is Not a Threat to India'.

[10] 'Act East' strategy was first mentioned by Narendra Modi in November 2014 at the ASEAN India Summit, Myanmar.

Iriye, not only calls for recognition of this particular variety of diplomacy in international relations but also hails it as an important contribution to intercultural communication.[11] While not relegating non-state actors to the background, the Modi government appears to be reinvigorating state-driven soft power efforts.

## HISTORICAL EVOLUTION AND RELIGIOUS INFLUENCE

The clay seals of Vainya Gupta, Budha Gupta and Kumara Gupta discovered at Nalanda are the best testimony to the prominence of the Nalanda University during the 4th to 7th century AD as a citadel of learning, dominated by liberal cultural traditions inherited from the Gupta age. Nalanda exemplifies ancient India's prowess in higher education and learning and its employment of education for communicating with the rest of the world. Similar to ancient Chinese texts, Indian history provides a peek into ancient India's cultural traditions and practice of diplomacy, including communication strategies for conducting international relations. Although waging war[12] is never decried in ancient texts like the Mahabharata,[13] noted scholars of the time like Kautilya and Kamandak have referred to 'soft' diplomacy, including the practice of peace (*sandhi*) for achieving progress. In fact, the role of the *doot* (ambassador) in conducting interstate relationship has been emphasized time and again by these scholars. According to Indian historian Hiralal Chattterjee,[14]

Diplomacy as an institution had been in existence since the days of Vedas and we have also plenty of instances in the Ramayana and the Mahabharata to show that diplomatic work (*Dautya*) formed a normal feature of interstate relations. Hanuman and Angad

[11] Iriye, *Cultural Internationalism and World Order*.
[12] Warfare within the subcontinent was more the norm to gain power, wealth and establish/destroy empires, but India has hardly been an expansionist power. See Tanham, 'Indian Strategic Thought'.
[13] The Chola and the Pandyan Empire to a lesser extent were also expansionists in nature.
[14] Kumar, 'Relevance of Ancient Indian Diplomatic Styles'.

in Ramayana, Shri Krishna and Sanjay in Mahabharata, all did
diplomatic works of some kind at different time.

Both *Manu Smriti*[15] and *Arthashastra*[16] also mention the doot's other
important functions like forging alliances and engaging with the art of
communication—two major aspects of the modern soft power strategy.
The doot's participation in public relations through high-level banquets
and public functions were aimed at advancing the interest of the state.
Interestingly, according to Kamandak, a doot should possess a positive
demeanour[17] focusing on the propagation of the glory and influence of
his king in another kingdom[18] rather than by using force. The articulation
fits well into the modern narrative on soft power where a state aims
to achieve similar objectives by employing softer diplomatic tools.
Kamandak also advises the king to win confidence of his allies on
which the state's interest and success depend.[19] Kaultilya, furthermore,
recommends conciliation (*sama*) and gift (*dana*) as key instruments of
diplomacy and foreign policy. During mediaeval India too, there was
ample evidence of religious and interfaith harmony during Mughal
emperors like Babur and Jalaluddin Mohammad Akbar. While Babur's
empire was a sophisticated civilization based on religious toleration,
Akbar was noted for implementing not only an inclusive approach
towards non-Muslims but also for ushering in an era of religious tolerance
based on the Sufi concept of *sulh-e-kul* (peace to all). These examples are
evidences of the ancient Indian state's practice of peaceful strategies for
pursuing peace and harmony in interstate relations and are indications of
the historical existence of soft power in Indian statecraft.

---

[15] It is one of the most studied ancient legal texts in Sanskrit and is variously
dated to be from 2nd century BCE to 3rd century CE.
[16] *Arthashastra* is an ancient treatise on statecraft written by Kautilya, also
identified as Vishnugupta and Chanakya, the teacher and guardian of Emperor
Chandragupta Maurya. It was composed, expanded and redacted between 2nd
century BCE and 3rd century CE.
[17] Kamandak believed that the *doot* should be soft spoken while engaging in
sweet talk.
[18] Kumar, 'Relevance of Ancient Indian Diplomatic Styles'.
[19] Ibid.

Notwithstanding the historical familiarity with application of soft power, India's accommodation of the latter in its strategic culture[20] for furthering national interests is debatable. Understanding India's 'strategic culture' becomes critical in this regard. Western scholars, particularly influential experts like George Tanham, allude to India's ability (or inability) to think 'strategically' and attribute the same to its history and culture. While drawing attention to the importance of Indian culture in shaping its subsequent history,[21] Tanham holds the same cultural notions responsible for constraining the Indian mind to plan.[22] However, the role of culture in shaping India's approach to international relations is undeniable with the notions of peace, universalism, tolerance, internationalism and coexistence, underscoring India's approach to international relations since the ancient times. As early as in 1893, Swami Vivekananda carried the message of tolerance and the harmonizing elements of Hinduism to the Western audience, while introducing yoga for the first time at the Parliament of the World's Religions. A few years later in 1897, the temper of peace was again revisited by Shri C. Sankaran Nair, President of the Congress, when he stated that 'Our true policy is a peaceful policy.... With such capacity for internal development as our country possesses, with such a crying need to carry out the reforms absolutely necessary for our well-being, we want a period of prolonged peace'.[23] While the role and historical tradition of culture in India's external engagement is undisputed, whether culture has found its way in

---

[20] According to Alastair Iain Johnston, 'strategic culture is an integrated set of symbols that acts to establish pervasive and longstanding grand strategic preferences by formulating concepts of the role and efficacy of force in interstate political affairs, and by clothing these conceptions with such an aura of factuality that the strategic preferences seem uniquely realistic and efficacious'. See Johnston, *Cultural Realism*, 109–44.

[21] 'The assumed superiority of Indian culture became a continuing thread running through Indian history, enabling India to accommodate powerful foreign forces that were far more purposeful in the exercise of military power'. See Tanham, 'Indian Strategic Thought'.

[22] According to Tanham, 'man's control over his life is thus limited in Hindu eyes, and he cannot forecast or plan with any confidence'. See Tanham, 'Indian Strategic Thought'.

[23] Rao, 'Nehru and Non-Alignment'.

India's foreign policy as an instrument for securing national interests, like in the case of China, is difficult to establish, largely because such accommodation would reflect the existence of a well-developed strategic culture in India, which, as Tanham argues, might be missing in the first place.

The modern historical tradition of soft power in external outreach and global vision for India is also largely attributable to Rabindranath Tagore, who was 'persistently nonsectarian', and whose writings had the effect of resonating Indian culture in many parts of the world.[24] A champion of cross-cultural education, freedom of the mind, rational criticism and cultural openness, Tagore—a true internationalist—feared that a rejection of the West in favour of an indigenous Indian tradition was not only limiting in itself but could also turn into hostility towards other major cultural influences like Christianity, Judaism, Zoroastrianism and Islam, all of which had significant presence in India.[25] Like Swami Vivekananda, Tagore's emphasis on education was aimed at securing the future of the country and its people. Tagore's creation, *Visva Bharati*, also reflects his vision of making the seat of learning a 'meeting place of ideas, where alumni could rub their minds off visiting scholars and intellectuals' while nurturing aspirations of being 'an intellectual and spiritual guesthouse of India' to cultures of all countries.[26] For Tagore, India was not a territorial but an 'ideational' expression, capturing its cultural diversity and its history a 'mixture of ideas' and an 'interpenetration of opposites'. The idea of India, subsequently expressed eloquently by Nehru in 1947, was much in conformity with Tagore.[27] More contemporary history of the previous century highlights the unique recourse to ahimsa (nonviolence) and its prolonged struggle for winning independence under Mahatma Gandhi,[28] which, again, count among the significant influences shaping modern India's soft power capital.

---

[24] Sen, *The Argumentative Indian*, 90.

[25] Ibid., 108.

[26] Vijapurkar, 'Tagore's Visva-Bharati Dream'.

[27] Dasgupta and Ray, 'Rabindranath Tagore and His Contemporary Relevance'.

[28] Mahatma Gandhi and his doctrine not only has had a world wide appeal but has influenced many great minds like Martin Luther King, Nelson Mandela, Aung Sung Suu Kyi and many others. A Filipino writer had observed, 'that

Nehru significantly shaped India's post-independence foreign policy and approach to international relations. Peace and harmony were prominent in India's vision of non-alignment.[29] Nehru's pursuit of multilateralism and peaceful coexistence underscored India's aspirations for peace and harmony while trying to secure global stability in an era of sharp ideological and military polarization. These tenets, along with Nehru's admiration for the 'other Asian civilization', were the hallmarks of his foreign policy vision.[30] Another important facet of Nehru's vision was his understanding of culture in line with the imperatives of his time. According to Jahanbegloo, an Iranian academic, Nehru's vision of culture was intricately linked to global peace[31] with strong advocation of coexistence and tolerance. Indeed, the emphasis on tolerance notwithstanding disagreement and the willingness to engage in dialogue with other cultures[32] for ensuring peace are the key tenets that continue to define India's approach to international relations. Over time, cooperation based on mutual respect, civilized behaviour in international relations and negation of war and imperialism have been clearly articulated in India's global vision and external engagement. These resonate the fundamentals on which Vivekananda and Tagore wanted the 'idea of India' to be based. The emphasis and articulation of these have, perhaps more implicitly than otherwise, led to convictions like winning over those who may be suspicious or understanding others 'just as we expect them to understand us'[33] as strategies of intercultural communication, and thereby

---

whereas the past one hundred years were dominated by Karl Marx and the armed revolutionary, the next hundred years would be shaped by Gandhi and the unarmed satyagrahi, the votary of Truth'.

[29] The Non-aligned Movement (NAM) was founded in 1961 in Belgrade by India's first PM Jawaharlal Nehru, Indonesia's first President, Sukarno, Egypt's second President Gamal Abdel Nasser, Ghana's first President Kwame Nkrumah and Yugoslavia's President Josip Broz Tito. NAM was a declaration by the five leaders not to align or be against any major power block of that time while pursuing national independence.

[30] Tharoor, *Pax Indica*, 131.

[31] Jahanbegloo, 'Nehru and Dialogue of Cultures'.

[32] Ancient India has had a long tradition of dialogues particularly advocated by Buddhism.

[33] Jahanbegloo, 'Nehru and Dialogue of Cultures'.

instilling soft power as a fundamental character of India's world vision and external engagement.

Growing contemporary interest on India's soft power has made prominent strategic scholars to revisit the notion of India's strategic culture, which, while not as distinct as its Western or Chinese counterparts in conveying soft power,[34] could still do so peripherally. Nehru's writings on international affairs and views on international issues have heavily contributed to the discourse on Indian strategic thinking. Both Nehruvian and neoliberal constructs partly explain India's diplomatic strategy and help to place soft power within the larger paradigm of Indian strategic thinking. Both these approaches view force either as a 'regrettable last resort' or of 'declining utility', and therefore best avoided[35]: the basic fundamentals of Constructivism which emphasizes 'ideas' and culture as discussed earlier in Chapter 1. While Nehruvianism calls for interstate negotiations and enhanced contacts between governments and peoples, neoliberals emphasize economic power more than military power,[36] thereby drawing attention to the basic aspects of soft power. Apart from Nehruvians and neoliberals, there were still others who denounced force in all forms and instead claimed India's world leadership based on moral and spiritual values post-independence,[37] and who further exemplify the presence of the idea of soft power within India's foreign policy leaders. Having lived through colonialism and partition, the latter were keen to avoid mention of force and digging up traumas, a concern easily understandable.

As India matured as a power and dealt with new challenges and experiences, new imperatives began influencing its external engagement policy. Greater economic integration and domestic economic reforms since the early 1990s led to India's aspiration of playing a bigger global and regional role. A supportive external environment was critical for facilitating the aspiration. Emphasis on soft power becomes critical in the quest for a supportive environment that would contribute to benign perceptions. For India, the 'China' factor has also assisted in consolidating

---

[34] Bajpai, 'Indian Strategic Culture'.
[35] Ibid.
[36] Ibid.
[37] Tanham, 'Indian Strategic Thought'.

a benign perception. Given the international anxiety over China's rise, India is seen as a country *complementing rather than challenging* the established strategic cultural and normative regional order.[38] India has also been keen to be the land of the better story,[39] allowing its foreign policy to evolve in line with its national agenda of transforming 'India's economy and society while promoting Indian values of pluralism, democracy and secularism. This requires the government to work for a *supportive external environment that is peaceful, thus permitting us to concentrate on our domestic tasks* (emphasis added)'.[40]

The will to cultivate a 'supportive external environment' by engaging the neighbourhood and countries beyond has been in sharp focus during the last couple of years. BJP government's focus has been on 'fast-track diplomacy'.[41] Supported by a low profiled External Affairs Ministry headed by Sushma Swaraj, the government has maximized opportunities of reaching out to countries in an effort to bolster ties and improve India's image. The External Affairs Minister's skilful yet quiet way of handling the Yemen crisis in early 2015, discussed later, has won India appreciation and improved its image as a constructive global actor. Yet the effort to reach out to neighbours has also received a setback on account of the Madhesi[42] crisis, once again discussed later.

### Benign Neighbourhood and Distant Partners

A benign neighbourhood is a source of several advantages—economic, political, security. Developing close relations with neighbours through economic, security and political cooperation combined with commitment to shared liberal values—democratic principles in case of India—is what India ideally aspires to achieve through its neighbourhood policy. For

---

[38] Lee and Cheong, 'Unrealised potential', 3.

[39] Tharoor, 'Indian Strategic Power'.

[40] Bhasin, *India's Foreign Relations—2009 Documents*, 59.

[41] *Wikinews.org*, 'Foreign Policy of Narendra Modi'.

[42] The Madhesis—ethnically, linguistically and culturally close to the people of Indian states of Bihar and Uttar Pradesh—are demanding the revision of the state boundaries in a manner that Tharu community in South-western Nepal and the Madhesis in the south east of the country get separate states.

India, however, the neighbourhood has been a source of concern and anxiety. The anxiety is substantiated by lack of uniform positive perceptions about India across South Asia: 'Globally, India is being seen as a rising economic power but not in the region where economic development has become hostage to security issues'.[43] Security issues and border management tensions have been persisting in India's interfaces with its South Asian neighbours. Notwithstanding being the largest country in the region, New Delhi's leadership of South Asia has been fraught with challenges with neighbours unhappy over its dominance.[44] While L. Kadirgamar has rightly used the analogy of a wheel to depict centrality of India in regional affairs,[45] India's 'centrality' in South Asian affairs has often caused neighbouring country leaderships to deploy 'blame India' as a default political strategy for influencing perceptions of domestic constituencies.

Despite being looked at with 'suspicion', and the 'blame India' rhetoric, the focus on engaging the neighbourhood has been visible in the Indian foreign policy since independence, highlighting India's efforts at 'soft' engagement for mutual coexistence. The strategy of integrating princely states demonstrated the approach. Nehru viewed the neighbouring kingdoms of Nepal, Sikkim and Bhutan[46] 'as part of India's security perimeter and calculus of frontier defence—thus avoiding forcible accession while binding them into stronger economic interdependence with the Republic'.[47] To further engage these countries and encourage them to consolidate into India's structural core, Nehru made various economic and political concessions such as increasing subsidies for these kingdoms, expanding economic and technical assistance[48] and offering territorial concessions (Bhutan) while fully recognizing sovereignty and territorial integrity (Bhutan and Nepal). Nehru invited the representatives of Nepal and Bhutan to participate at the First Asian Relations Conference held in Delhi in early 1947 for facilitating their global

---

[43] Malone, *Does the Elephant Dance*, 58.
[44] Ibid.
[45] Bhasin, 'India's Role in South Asia'.
[46] Nepal was treated as an independent country, Sikkim as a full protectorate of India and Bhutan enjoyed a status in between.
[47] Dutt, 'India and the Himalayan States', 71–81.
[48] Mohan, 'Beyond Non-Alignment', 7.

interactions.[49] Along with South Asia, cooperation was also sought with Myanmar and Indonesia on the East and the Imperial Government of Iran and the Royal Government of Afghanistan on the West with treaties of peace and friendship being signed with the latter in 1950.[50]

In subsequent years, particularly after the end of the Cold War and advent of globalization, India's regional engagement policy became more expansive and extended to Southeast Asia in an active fashion. The LEP and the Gujral Doctrine[51] became the major drivers in shaping India's relations with its neighbours. The 'Nonalignment 2.0', a document prepared by strategic experts in 2012, while calling for greater engagement of South Asia, pointed out the region's criticality in India's foreign policy: 'India's ability to command respect is considerably diminished by the resistance it meets in the region. South Asia also places fetters on India's global ambitions...'.[52] Modi's efforts to engage South Asian neighbours through various bilateral initiatives and emerging engagement with Southeast Asia through an action-oriented 'Act East' strategy is ample evidence of India's latest efforts to cultivate a benign neighbourhood through the principle of 'neighbourhood first'. Scholars like Bhabani Sen Gupta interestingly hold size (of India) critical for not only understanding foreign policy dynamics in the neighbourhood but also an important factor that would enable them to accept each other:

> The Indian elephant cannot transform itself into a mouse. If South Asia is to get itself out of the crippling binds of conflicts and cleavages, the six will have to accept the bigness of the seventh. And the seventh, that is India, will have to prove to the six that big can indeed be beautiful.[53]

---

[49] Ibid., 7.

[50] Ibid.,12.

[51] I.K. Gujral, the 13th PM of India (April 1997 to March 1998), enunciated the Gujral Doctrine to direct foreign relations with India's immediate neighbours. It was an attempt to forge closer ties with neighbours based on non-reciprocity, non-interference in each other's internal matters, no South Asian country should allow their territory to be used against the interest of any other neighbour, respect for each other's territorial integrity and sovereignty and peaceful negotiations for solving mutual problems.

[52] Khilnani et al., 'Nonalignment 2.0'.

[53] Sen Gupta, 'The Big Brother Syndrome', 122.

Evidently, India's regional policy has been changing constantly depending on the evolving dominant national interests and priorities. The often-pragmatic tone in foreign policy while shifting course has been most apparent in South Asia. India's recent policy of conscious 'non-intervention' in domestic affairs of South Asian countries has been accompanied by a reorientation in its foreign policy posture in view of the new dynamics, unfolding at the regional and global levels. While refraining from intervening in Sri Lanka's internal matters despite allegations of human rights violations against Tamils in early 2013,[54] India attended the Commonwealth Heads of Government Meeting (CHOGM) Summit despite strong protests at home.[55] Subsequently, the Modi government has been proactive in peaceful resolution of old contentious issues with neighbours. This is evident from the signing of the India–Bangladesh Land Border Agreement (LBA) after almost four decades in June 2015, involving the exchange of 162 adversely held enclaves. Apart from its immediate neighbourhood, New Delhi's focus has been on cultivating its Southeast Asian neighbours as well with engagement with bordering countries like Myanmar having increased substantively.[56] Both the Modi government and its predecessor have been engaging Myanmar for economic and political objectives, apart from other Southeast Asian countries like Malaysia and Indonesia, given their strategic geographical locations.

Besides the overlapping economic zones in the Bay of Bengal, four of India's north-eastern states—Arunachal Pradesh, Nagaland, Manipur and Mizoram—share international borders with Myanmar. Growing Chinese presence in Myanmar has also pushed India to avoid marginalization of the country by toning down overt support for the democratic forces. Myanmar's geographic location—the only country in the region

---

[54] *Deccan Chronicle*, 'Accountability Must for Rights Violations in Sri Lanka'.

[55] India was officially present at the forum but the absence of Manmohan Singh, argued many, was an indication that the leadership had bowed to domestic pressure at home. Also, with the impending election, Congress government's decision can also be explained by domestic political concerns as well.

[56] Modi had announced India's 'Act East' policy at the ASEAN summit in 2014 in Myanmar. This was symbolic communicating the government's earnestness in boosting ties not only with Myanmar but with the entire region.

which shares land and sea borders with India—serves as a gateway to the Southeast Asia. Similarly, Malaysia situated at the head of the Straits of Malacca, offers the shortest transit by sea between the Persian Gulf and the Asian economies—noticeably China, Japan, South Korea and the Pacific Rim.[57] Besides, it is also a link between the Indian Ocean, the South China Sea and the Pacific Ocean. On the other hand, Indonesia, the world's largest archipelagic state, owns three of the four Southeast Asian straits through which 38 per cent of world's sea-borne trade passes.[58] While India's 'Act East' policy proposes substantive action-oriented engagement with Southeast Asia and the Asia-Pacific, there are certain implications of the robust neighbourhood policy that India needs to take note of. Faultiness have begun emerging in engagement of parts of South Asia. The Modi government's handling of internal ethnic distur-bances in Nepal has been perceived as 'interference'[59] denting India's sympathetic image in the country while raising questions over its cre-dentials as a secular nation. As an opinion in 'Kathmandu Post' argued, 'The blockade shows Indian displeasure at Nepal not being declared a Hindu state'.[60] The alleged failure of Indian agencies to ensure fuel, food and medicine supplies during the Madhesi unrest and economic block-ade caused substantive hardships in the land-locked Nepali economy, which is critically dependent on India for essential supplies. Nepal's sub-sequent strong engagement with China for fuel and material supplies points to clear hedging on part of Kathmandu. On the South China Sea as well, India has begun taking a far more assertive posture, including issuing a Joint Statement with Japan for the first time calling on countries

---

[57] Roche, 'India, With an Eye on ASEAN'.

[58] Sharma, 'Why Indonesia is Important'.

[59] The *Indian Express* in September 2015 reported that New Delhi wanted Kathmandu to carry out 'seven amendments' to its Constitution to ensure that it is acceptable to the Madhesis and Janjatis. This demand by India was perceived as 'interference' and rightly so by Nepal.

[60] The protest by the agitating community in the Terai region (they blocked traffic in 2015) bordering India paralysed services leading to shortage of essential commodities and fuel which were crippling normal activities, production, tourism and the overall economy. This was perceived in Nepal as India's support of the Madhesis. Wagle, 'Project Hindutva'.

to 'avoid unilateral actions' that could lead to tension in the region.[61] Such proclivity by India, while being welcomed by several constituencies in the region as a necessary 'balancer' to Chinese aggressiveness, can also draw India into the complex web of strategic dynamics between China, the US, Japan and the Southeast Asian countries with long-term implications.

While benign neighbourhood conditions are vital for India's economic growth and strategic expansion, like China, it needs access to new markets, cutting-edge technology, fresh investments and critical resources like energy for reaping economic and strategic benefits. The Indian diaspora can be the most instrumental in this regard by helping India build better ties with institutions and authorities in the countries of their residences such as the US, Canada, Australia, Europe and even Southeast Asia. Other than providing powerful constituencies of support abroad through effective lobbying (during the Indo-US nuclear deal),[62] overseas Indians are valuable resources given their large inward remittances to India and strong political support for BJP.[63] The diaspora has been a firm focus for Modi and his government with Modi's visits overseas often including specific interfaces with the diaspora as high points such as his addresses in New York, Sydney and Shanghai. According to scholars like Ashutosh Varshney, unlike the previous leaders, Modi has focused on blood ties while engaging the overseas Indians and in doing so he has also 'extended the idea of nationhood beyond the constitutional parameters'.[64] However, as pointed out by Devesh Kumar, the same

---

[61] Roy, 'First Time in a Joint Statement'.

[62] According to professor Devesh Kapur who has worked extensively on the Indian diaspora, 'in the case of Indian Americans in the US, the triple combination of economic success in the country of residence, their temporal proximity, and their close links with Indian elites, gives them the *ability, willingness, and access to mechanisms* to influence policies in the countries of origin and settlement'. For details, see Kapur, 'Eclipsed Moon to a Rising Star', 192.

[63] According to the World Bank estimates in 2014, India continues to be the leading nation in remittances. For details, see *The Indian Express*, 'India Tops in Remittances'. Further, BJP's political support from the Overseas Indians also came about through the high octane social media campaign by BJP, coupled with regular online interactions with its overseas members and Modi's charisma.

[64] Varshney, 'Modi's Idea of India'.

diaspora can also bring in 'uncertainty' and 'unpleasant surprises' along with 'greater challenges' to Indian foreign policy.[65]

There are also signs of India increasingly moving ahead of 'non-alignment' by modifying its policies towards the major powers. Abdicating its earlier call for a multi-polar world, India became 'natural allies' with the US from 'estranged democracies'.[66] For an energy-starved country like India, the US–India Nuclear Cooperation Approval and Non-proliferation Enhancement Act, 2008, was necessary not only to end its nuclear isolation for decades but to enable nuclear trade as well. However, the implementation of the nuclear deal remains uncertain since the doubts on sharing of nuclear liability is yet to be removed to the extent that the suppliers can start the process of actually building the plants. The government position has been that it will not amend its liability law—the primary hurdle in beginning commercial operations under the Indo-US Civil Nuclear Agreement—six years after it was inked.[67] While on the one hand the nuclear deal with the US is yet not a 'done deal', Modi has successfully ensured supply of uranium from Australia and Canada for India's nuclear reactors and assurance of technical cooperation from France in construction of six nuclear reactors.[68] In all these countries, and Japan (another potential nuclear energy partner for India), China, Germany and Korea, Modi has also made a strong pitch among the overseas Indians and the investor communities for financial and technological commitments in his signature initiative 'Make in India' for converting India into a global manufacturing hub.[69]

---

[65] As pointed out by Devesh Kumar, 'beached diasporas' in India's neighbourhood (from Guyana to Fiji to Malaysia), is most likely to pose challenges for India. For details, see Kumar and Kumar, *In the National Interest*.

[66] David Malone calls it 'selective partnership' based on specific shared interests in some areas and quid pro quo arrangements in others. See Malone, *Does the Elephant Dance*, 237.

[67] Malik, 'India–US Nuclear Agreement'.

[68] Arevas, a French power firm, signed a pre-engineering agreement (PEA) with Nuclear Power Corporation of India (NPCIL) to set up two evolutional pressurized reactors (EPR) at the Jaitapur Nuclear Power Project in Maharashtra in April 2015.

[69] The 'Make in India' initiative launched by PM Modi in September 2014 not only aims to transform India into a global manufacturing hub but is designed to

The role of geography cannot be ignored in shaping perceptions. This comes increasingly to focus in the case of South Asia. While image make-over is a soft power objective, the will to share common resources like water with neighbours also helps in communicating 'benign' signals characteristic of a major power. The role of the Indian states becomes critical in this regard. Though the Indian Constitution gives limited or no role to subnational units (states and Union Territories) in foreign policy-making, Indian states with links to neighbouring countries, either through common borders and natural resources or cultural characteristics[70] have begun influencing its external engagement. The collapse of a deal in 2011 with Dhaka, when Mamata Banerjee, the chief minister of West Bengal, refused to share the water of the Teesta River with Bangladesh, cast a shadow on India–Bangladesh relations.[71] The Modi government has been pragmatic to realize the interconnection of geography and foreign relations in this regard and has shown willing-ness to take state leaders on board despite political differences. Modi's consultations with Banerjee paved the way for the signing of the historic LBA between India and Bangladesh, and is example of government's eagerness to involve states in foreign policy-making and soft-power applications.[72] The signing fetched significant positive reactions for the Modi government with even the main opposition Party of Bangladesh,

---

urge foreign and domestic companies to invest in India. The effort is also to create jobs while skilling its young population in 25 sectors, including pharmaceuticals, automobiles, tourism and hospitality and so on.

[70] Gujarat has links with Africa, West Asia, China and Japan, Odisha with Indonesia, Goa with Portugal, Pondicherry with France, Tamil Nadu with Sri Lanka, Singapore and Malaysia and Bihar with Buddhist countries. For details, see Rediff News, 'How Modi Will Change India's Foreign Policy'.

[71] The effort of the Central government to involve the State governments in neighbourhood policies is not new but rather has been dependent on the leadership. At the advice of the then External Affairs Minister, I.K. Gujral, the Bangladesh Foreign Secretary sought the help and assistance of the Chief Minister of West Bengal to find a permanent solution to the problem of sharing of the Ganga water sometime around August 1996. Consequently, on 12 December 1996, India and Bangladesh entered into a treaty on the sharing of the Ganga water with the late Chief Minister of West Bengal Jyoti Basu playing a crucial role.

[72] Rediff News, 'How Modi Will Change India's Foreign Policy'.

Bangladesh National Party (BNP), a traditional critic of India, hailing it as a 'new milestone in the long-standing relationship between the two countries'.[73] More such examples of reaching out to state leaders cutting across party lines for ensuring a conducive domestic environment should enable efficient conduct of neighbourhood diplomacy.

As a key strategic entity in Asia with distinct economic and military capabilities, India offers good pay-offs to major global and regional players as partners. However these pay-offs coexist with negative impressions, particularly on the Indian states' ability to provide good governance and other domestic issues. Communicating the right message to the rest of the world becomes critical in this regard. Initiatives such as the high-level visits are being aimed to convey the positive changes taking place in India and the opportunities it presents to investors and businesses.[74]

It is important to note though that pursuit of enabling environment for economic, political and strategic goals does not mean lack of a 'firm hand' in matters of national interest, particularly security. The government in India hardly seems shy in this respect. This is evident from its tough postures with respect to Pakistan, the covert military operation in Myanmar for tackling insurgents in June 2015 and conveying its unhappiness over conduct of border negotiations to China.[75] The Modi government marks a distinct departure from its predecessor in this regard, as much as it does in greater emphasis on soft power deployment. Engagement with China is one of the most relevant examples of the manifestation of both these characteristics.

---

[73] *The Hindu*, 'BNP Hails LBA Ratification by Parliament'.

[74] Narendra Modi used his state visit to Germany in 2015 to unleash 'Make in India' lion at the world's biggest industrial trade fair in Hanover to project India as a strong and attractive destination for investment and doing business.

[75] During his visit to China in May 2015, Modi was not only unhesitant in calling the Sino-India relationship 'complex' but even urged Beijing to think strategically and 'reconsider its approach' on various issues of bilateral interests. While putting economic issues on the table, Modi even pointed out that the bilateral economic relationship was not sustainable in future if Indian industries were not allowed better access into the Chinese market.

## SOFT POWER INITIATIVES

India's engagement with the rest of the world has been characterized by 'moderation' and 'restraint'. A new trend appears to be emerging in this regard with foreign policy becoming increasingly commensurate with India's aspirational status in the world order: 'the long-sustained image of India as a leader of the oppressed and marginalized nations has disappeared on account of its new-found role in the emerging global order'.[76] The possibility of India occupying a seat at the high table with major global powers including the US, Europe, Russia, China and Japan[77] has partly influenced India's quest to become a 'normal' state, thus partly renouncing Nehru's moral high ground in foreign policies,[78] which were deemed necessary for a newly independent country for managing external relations post its colonial past. With realpolitik beginning to influence India's foreign policy, the Indian leadership soon began reorienting its external engagement strategy in the new global context. The determination to engage with the Indian diaspora, aligning with major powers like the US without risking special ties with Russia for advancing national interests, and effort to create a strategic environment conducive to greater integration with the world economy were aimed at widening its global strategic space. These were also essential for greater application of national soft power while communicating that non-alignment,[79] though 'chipped away at its core',[80] continued to remain planted in New Delhi's foreign policy.

Unfortunately, many of India's recent initiatives, with the noticeable exception of the high-profile visits by PM Modi, have been relatively low profile and less discussed. Some of the major initiatives include setting

---

[76] Seethi and Vijayan, 'Political Economy of India's Third World Policy', 47.
[77] Mohan, 'Beyond Non-Alignment', 45.
[78] Malone, *Does the Elephant Dance*.
[79] P.V. Narasimha Rao in an article indicated that the policy of non-alignment 'in essence meant keeping an independence of policy… keeping our options open…and judging each issue on its merit' rather than 'being neutral or staying equidistant from the two super powers'. For details see Rao, 'Nehru and Non-Alignment'.
[80] Mohan, 'Beyond Non-Alignment', 47.

up of the PD Division in the Ministry of External Affairs, establishing the Indian Council for Cultural Relations (ICCR) 'chairs' abroad, participating in infrastructure-building in several countries and extending LoC[81] and humanitarian assistance to countries in need. A few of these initiatives are similar to those by China and are aimed at achieving strategic and economic benefits. The official initiatives, however, need to be looked at in conjunction with non-state efforts, which, while not being motivated strategically, nonetheless contribute significantly to India's global appeal and enlarge its soft power capital. The prominent role of non-state actors in building India's soft power is distinct from the almost exclusive state-driven measures in China, as discussed later in the Chapter.

### State-driven Initiatives

With India 'crossing the Rubicon'[82] through its transition from a largely idealistic foreign policy to a more pragmatic one based on contemporary realism, institutions are contributing more to development, conduct and articulation of India's foreign policy. Harnessing soft power for effective international engagement has also become more distinct enabling creation of what Nye refers to as 'long-lasting relationships'. These have consequently led India to revisit its virtuous civilizational traits, particularly culture, for positively engaging the world. Contextualizing India's foreign relations in modern times, Shashi Tharoor argues, 'Today's India truly enjoys soft power, and that may well be the most valuable way in which it can offer leadership to the twenty-first-century world'.[83] This could be due to the assimilative capacity of the Indian culture in adapting features of other cultures making it diverse and intrinsically 'cosmopolitan' and capable of integrating more seamlessly into the culture of a globally integrated world.

---

[81] An LoC is a financing mechanism through which Exim Bank extends support for export of projects, equipment, goods and services from India. Exim Bank extends LoCs on its own and also at the behest and with the support of Government of India.

[82] Mohan, 'India's Regional Security Cooperation'.

[83] The author attended the Lee Kwan Yew Public Lecture by Shashi Tharoor on 10 September 2012 in Singapore.

While high-level visits were not uncommon and infrequent during previous Indian leaderships, it has gained traction and visibility during the Modi government. These visits (Annexure IV) are evolving as important soft power tools for establishing greater understanding with foreign partners and furthering India's economic and strategic interests. The visits are also underscoring a more active foreign policy by India and the conspicuous use of culture in this regard, such as through gifting of the Bhagavad Gita by PM Modi to President Obama and the Japanese Emperor and presenting a stole to the South Korean President inscribed with Nobel laureate Tagore's poem.[84] Modi's gifting of replicas of a stone casket of Buddhist relics to President Xi Jinping also indicate the use of Buddhist culture to connect to China through the ancient thread of Buddhism.

The neighbourhoods—South Asia and the broader Asia-Pacific including Southeast, Northeast Asia and the Indian Ocean region—have been major focuses of Modi's high-level visits. Beginning from his maiden state visit to Bhutan after assuming office in May 2014, Modi rounded off the first year by visiting China, Mongolia and South Korea in May 2015. In between, he travelled to Nepal and Sri Lanka (South Asia), Japan (Northeast Asia), Mauritius and Seychelles (IOR). All the countries visited bring specific strategic value for India ranging from energy (Bhutan, Mongolia and the five Central Asian countries),[85] investments in infrastructure and 'Make in India' (China, Korea and Japan), engaging the diaspora and addressing domestic ethnic concerns (Seychelles, Mauritius, Sri Lanka), emphasizing empathy and commitment to countries sharing borders with China (Nepal, Bhutan, Mongolia) and initiating more defence collaboration and enhancing economic ties (Russia).

The focus on South Asia in India's more active contemporary foreign policy underpinning 'neighbourhood first' was evident from the invitation to the heads of states of all South Asian countries to attend

---

[84] The text from the poem, written especially for Korea, was published in the Korean Daily, *Dong-A Ilbo,* in 1929.
[85] Kazakhstan is a significant oil producer, while other countries are estimated to have large reserves of natural gas.

Modi's swearing-in ceremony. His visits further reinforced this focus. The criticality of India being a more constructive and active participant in Southeast and Northeast Asian regional affairs in the light of its aspirations to be noted as a global power has been implicit in Modi's travels to the countries in the region, as have been the urge to pitch India firmly in the strategic architecture of the IOR. The engagement with other major Anglo-Saxon powers such as Australia, Canada, US, France and Germany have been given a new impetus by Modi's high-profile visits to these countries right in his first year in office. The strategic thrusts on engaging the diaspora, accessing nuclear energy and cultivating investments for India's long-term economic growth were prominent aspects of his visits to all these nations as well.

As mentioned earlier, more extensive deployment of soft power through deeper and meaningful engagement of neighbours and partners is being accompanied by clearer and firmer postures on security and stability. In this respect, India is probably becoming more assertive and is not hesitating from combining soft power with a more non-compromising attitude. This was clearly articulated by Kiren Rijju, Minister of State for Home, in January 2015 when he remarked: "We are a natural soft power. We don't need to be hawkish (vis-à-vis neighbourhood). We should not tinker with our international image of being a soft power' while emphasizing that 'our apparatus does not need to be soft'.[86] This is interesting, and indicates the government's choice for smart power in foreign policy in an approach similar to that of the Chinese leadership. While conveying soft power regionally and globally, 'hard power' communication is also being assured through defence manufacturing initiatives under 'Make in India', and opening up defence production to foreign investment.[87] In terms of precipitate action, the biggest manifestation of a more non-comprising attitude is visible in nowhere other than the neighbourhood itself. India called off the foreign secretary talks with Pakistan in Islamabad in August 2014, after the Pakistan High Commission in India invited the Hurriyat leaders for consultations, thus halting the dialogue process initiated by PM Modi.

[86] Tiwary, 'Kiren Rijju'.
[87] *Globalsecurity.org*, 'Military Budget'.

## Cultural Initiatives

In what might resemble another interesting parallel with the Chinese foreign policy, culture has been employed as an important tool of soft power. Apart from its communication during high-level visits, India's Ministry of Culture has been taking several initiatives with the aim to 'preserve, promote and disseminate all forms of art and culture' while creating cultural awareness from the grass-roots to the international exchange level. India has cultural agreements with 120 countries apart from 'live' cultural relations[88] with 70 countries.[89] Among developing countries, Africa tops the list, followed by South America and Southeast Asia (Table 9.1). Three are from South Asia (Bangladesh, Maldives and Sri Lanka)[90] with the rest from Europe, the Middle East and other parts of Asia including China.[91] The growth in formal cultural exchanges has picked up in more recent years though the earliest cultural relations were established with Qatar in 1985, followed by Maldives and Kyrgyzstan 7 years later in 1992.[92] India's steady economic integration with the rest of the world after 1991 has increased its external cultural interface with the global community.[93]

The ICCR has been the key agency in formulating and implementing policies on India's external cultural relations. Since the 1980s, it has been instrumental in organizing Indian festivals abroad. The ICCR's 'Outgoing Visitors Programme' facilitates exchange of scholars, intellectuals, artists and academics. Over the years, ICCR has enlarged its global footprint through an elaborate network of cultural centres in various countries for showcasing Indian culture (Table 9.2).

---

[88] 'Live' Cultural relations imply the active ones. The rest are either 'under formulation' or 'pending MEA'.
[89] *Ministry of Culture, Government of India.*
[90] Perhaps, a deliberate policy by the Indian government not to impose Indian culture upon its smaller neighbours.
[91] *Ministry of Culture, Government of India.*
[92] Ibid.
[93] New Delhi has old formal bilateral cultural agreements with 120 countries. The earliest is with Turkey in 1951 and the most recent with Congo in 2009. See *Ministry of Culture, Government of India.*

**Table 9.1**

*India's 'Live' Cultural Exchange Programmes (CEPs)*

| Region | Countries |
| --- | --- |
| Africa | Botswana |
| | Djibouti |
| | Egypt |
| | Ethiopia |
| | Ghana |
| | Kenya |
| | Mauritius |
| | Senegal |
| | Seychelles |
| | South Africa |
| | Sudan |
| | Tunisia |
| | Uganda |
| South America | Brazil |
| | Chile |
| | Colombia |
| | Cuba |
| | Ecuador |
| | Guyana |
| | Mexico |
| | Suriname |
| Southeast Asia | Indonesia |
| | Laos |
| | Malaysia |
| | Myanmar |
| | Singapore |
| | Vietnam |

*Source:* Ministry of Culture, Government of India, available at: http://www.indiaculture.nic.
in/ (accessed on 3 July 2015).

**Table 9.2**
*ICCR Cultural Centres in South Asia, Southeast Asia, Africa and South America*

| | |
|---|---|
| South Asia | Kabul (Afghanistan), Dhaka (Bangladesh), Thimpu (Bhutan), Kathmandu (Nepal), Colombo (Sri Lanka), Maldives (Henveiru) |
| Southeast Asia | Jakarta, Bali (Indonesia), Kuala Lumpur (Malaysia), Bangkok (Thailand), Myanmar (Yangon) |
| Africa | Cairo (Egypt), Durban, Johannesburg (South Africa), Tanzania (Dar es Salaam), Mauritius (Port Louis) |
| South America | Sao Paulo (Brazil), Mexico City (Mexico) |

*Source:* ICCR, available at: http://www.iccrindia.net/georgetown.html (accessed on 3 July 2015).

The ICCR's cultural export initiatives have been further strengthened and diversified through its efforts to integrate Indian Studies and scholars more deeply with global education institutions by establishing 'chairs'. These 'chairs' have been endowed in different foreign universities in culture and social sciences. At present, there are 108 'chairs' in various universities with 9 in South Asia, 11 in Southeast Asia, 7 in China and several others in other parts of Asia, Europe and the US.[94]

The ICCR has also been instituting Tagore 'chairs' in different countries. These chairs are distinct in the distinguished and eminent scholarly excellence they embody in their occupants. The institutionalization of these chairs can hardly avoid comparison with similar efforts by China to brand Confucius through the CIs and CCs notwithstanding Tagore being far more contemporary (7 May 1861 to 7 August 1941) than Confucius (5th century BCE). Again, in contrast to the greater conspicuousness of Confucius in China's state-driven cultural engagement policies, ICCR's use of Tagore has been much low profile. Even the historical landmark of Tagore's 150th birth anniversary in 2011 was confined to establishment of Tagore Chairs in a few universities, including one in Bangladesh, which could have been deliberate given the resonance

---

[94] ICCR, 'List of ICCR's "Chairs" Abroad'.

of Tagore in both Bengals.[95] With CIs courting controversies as propagandist arms of the Chinese government, India has probably been cautious to avoid similar repercussions from its institutional initiatives by the government.

Apart from the ICCR, the Sahitya Akademi has been an active state actor in cultural engagement. Literature has emerged as an integral part of cultural communication and engagement as visible from efforts by the Sahitya Akademi in promoting Indian literature abroad.[96] These efforts have led to translation and interpretation of contemporary literature in different Indian languages into many foreign languages. The Sahitya Akademi has also actively cooperated with the UNESCO, Paris, in implementing the UNESCO's major project of Mutual Appreciation of Eastern and Western cultural values.[97]

An interesting point of comparison with respect to China in the domain of cultural communication is the use of language. No Indian language, not even Hindi, has attracted as much global attention and inclination to learn as Mandarin has. The rush across the world to learn Mandarin might be a result of the 'awe' surrounding China, which is evidently much less for India till now. For outsiders, India's multilingual character, as opposed to a homogeneous linguistic character for China, often makes choice of a particular Indian language for obtaining greater familiarity, a rather vexing problem, given the difficulty of judging its representativeness. The latter is a problem for Indian agencies also given that emphasis on greater spread of a particular language overseas might lead to negative reactions at home. Nonetheless, ICCR has made limited attempts in this regard like familiarizing overseas scholars about Indian culture through Hindi knowledge competitions. These competitions were held in Europe in 2010, apart from a 3-day Hindi festival in Kathmandu and a 5-day Hindi seminar/workshop in Tashkent the same year.[98] While many might expect these efforts to increase under the Modi

---

[95] Rabindranath Tagore, born in undivided Bengal in 1861, is also a cultural icon in Bangladesh. His song 'Amar Sonar Bangla' is the national anthem of Bangladesh, while 'Jana Gana Mana' is the Indian national anthem.
[96] Embassy of India, 'Tradition of Indian Writing'.
[97] *Sahitya Akademi*, 'Cooperation with UNESCO'.
[98] ICCR, 'Annual Report 2010–11'.

government, given the BJP's 'Hindutva' reputation, it will depend much on the government's willingness to do so notwithstanding adverse criticism. Difficulties surrounding a greater state push to indigenous Indian languages overseas have resulted in greater application of English. India has always had the advantage of connecting easier to the English-speaking world due to its proficiency in English. The advantage has also been strategically used by establishing English language training facilities in Southeast Asia—Cambodia, Laos, Myanmar and Vietnam.[99]

## Buddhism

As the noted scholar Nayan Chanda mentions, Buddhist missionaries not only helped in developing global consciousness but also built connections for expanding trade and a profound intermixing of culture that lent a 'commonality to an Asian identity'.[100] Historical texts and archaeological evidence vindicates this thesis. The Mauryan emperor, Asoka, had introduced Buddhism in Thailand sometime around the middle of the 3rd century BCE, underscoring the long religious and cultural relationship between India and Thailand. While Buddhism connected India to other Southeast Asian countries like Indonesia, Singapore, Myanmar and Cambodia and South Asian countries like Sri Lanka and Nepal historically, many were subsequently instrumental in the transmission of Buddhism further to China for most part of the first millennium. India has been keen to employ these Buddhist cultural links to revive old associations with South, Southeast Asia and China for realizing the vision of an 'Asian century'—a theme emphasized by Modi in his visits to China and Mongolia in May 2015.

Buddhism is being employed by New Delhi in charting contemporary relations with its neighbours. Besides setting up an international Buddhist Museum in Kandy, Sri Lanka,[101] the most prominent example of India's active participation in a multi-country initiative, drawing inspiration from Buddhist principles, is the building and restoration of the Nalanda University—a vision illustrated by the former Indian President A.P.J. Abdul Kalam. The pan-Asian character of the project is visible from the

---

[99]  Bijoy, 'India: Transiting to a Global Donor'.
[100] Chanda, *Bound Together*, 183.
[101] Tharoor, *Pax Indica*, 106.

support it has received from the EAS members.[102] Japan, South Korea, Singapore and China are key partners in the project, with China already having established the Xuan Zang Memorial Hall in the University.[103]

Buddhism continues to remain a theme that encourages constructive engagement by Indian state actors[104] and creative outputs from India's non-state ambassadors of soft power (filmmakers like Benoy Behl and Romesh Sharma have explored religious links between India and its neighbours in their movies).[105] Apart from Buddhism, India's secularism and religious 'charm' has far-flung global influence as well. India's secularism,[106] distinct from the Western notion from an Indian perspective and heterodoxy which manifest uniquely in religious tolerance, diversity and spirituality, has also aroused international interest in India. The interest is evident in many countries, including China, as revealed by the author's various interviews in the country. While Indian secularism continues to be admired worldwide, India's *Bhakti yoga*[107] and *Karma yoga*[108] also have a huge following all over the world.

---

[102] The East Asian Summit includes all 10 member countries from the ASEAN and Australia, China, India, Japan, South Korea and New Zealand. Also includes US and Russia now.

[103] The University began its first academic session in September 2014 with 15 students. However, the 'autonomy' of the University has been a major concern with Chancellor George Yeo—a politician from Singapore and one of the important players involved in reviving the University—resigning over the issue in 2016.

[104] ICCR organizes regular conferences and seminars on Buddhism, such as the 'International Buddhist Conference' (2010–11), for tracing the roots of Buddhism in India and its connections with Southeast Asia. See ICCR, 'International Buddhist Conference in Kandy'.

[105] *The Hindu*, 'Delhi's Date with Buddhism'.

[106] Indian secularism emphasizes 'neutrality' between different religions as opposed to 'prohibition' advocated by many Western countries like France. For details, see Sen, *The Argumentative Indian*, 20.

[107] The best example is the huge following that the International Society for Krishna Consciousness (ISKCON) has all over the world. Founded in the US in 1966 to introduce the teachings of Sri Krishna to the English-speaking world, its centres worldwide spreads *Bhakti yoga* which is a spiritual path of devotion espoused in Hindu philosophy to surrender to god.

[108] Another voluntary organization with a significant global presence and inspired by the ideal of *Karma yoga* (taught in Bhagawad Gita espousing discipline

There is, however, the underlying risk of playing the 'religious card' even in a subtle fashion as religion does tend to evoke passions and sentiments that could defeat the larger strategic objective of influencing perceptions 'softly'. India's recent frequent invocation of religion on various occasions for connecting to global audiences[109] can have adverse implications for the perception of a country that has always underplayed religion, including Buddhism, in its strategic outreach. Overt use of religion in diplomacy can be detrimental at a time when various incidents within India are increasingly making the international community take note of religious intolerance within the country. The US President's statement in May 2015, 'Mahatma Gandhi would have been shocked at the acts of intolerance in the country famed for its diversity' at the annual National Prayer Breakfast meeting where US Presidents frequently perorate on religious and human rights, is a case in point. Religious aggression in diplomacy can damage the identity of India that Tagore, Vivekananda and Nehru so painstakingly created. Indeed, in the context of today's India, whether positing religion within the broader context of soft power will deliver positive results is indeed arguable.

## Public Diplomacy

India set up a PD Division in the Ministry of External Affairs in 2006 with an exhaustive mandate for promoting informed discourse on India's foreign policy.[110] The activities included building partnerships with major domestic and international universities, think tanks for organizing seminars and conferences on global issues of India's concern, besides hosting foreign delegations for enabling broad-based exposure to India.[111] In many respects, this was a nuanced effort to connect to

---

of action as a means of surrendering oneself to god) is the Ramakrishna Mission, founded by Swami Vivekananda in 1897.

[109] Modi's address at the concluding session of the international interfaith symposium—attended by delegates invited from Sri Lanka, Nepal and Japan—on the sidelines of Simhastha Kumbh in Ujjain, Madhya Pradesh in May 2016, was projected as part of his cultural diplomacy with religion as its centerpiece.

[110] Indian Public Diplomacy. Available at: http://www.indiandiplomacy.in/About Us.aspx (accessed on 13 September 2012).

[111] Ibid.

influential opinion leaders, thought-makers and institutions in foreign countries for greater engagement and also for building traction on India's perspectives in global and regional affairs. The role of India's PD has matured over time. In 2009, the then Foreign Secretary Nirupama Rao mentioned that India had 'reset' its PD[112] for connecting both domestic and foreign constituencies. This was in line with Shashi Tharoor's argument for developing a 'coherent public diplomacy strategy' combining institutional efforts like those of ICCR with that of the Ministry of External Affairs.[113]

The extensive use of the social media (Facebook, Twitter and YouTube) for PD has been particularly noticeable. In what is increasingly emerging as the key medium for communication, particularly under the Modi government, PD's use of social media has been distinct. The use of social media, often referred to in popular media as 'twitter diplomacy' has assumed extensive proportions given its championing by PM Modi.[114] In a rather novel example of twitter diplomacy, Modi opened an account on Sina Weibo a few days before his visit to China in May 2015 and was greeted by enthusiastic response from a large number of followers. He had resorted to twitter greetings before his visit to Japan as well. The social media-driven PD has clearly been far more engaging and exhaustive than traditional means in communicating India to the international community.

Engaging overseas Indians is an important aspect of India's PD. Historically, efforts to engage the former for influencing overseas public opinion have been underway even before India attained its independence in 1947. The nationalist leader from the Indian National Congress, N.S. Hardikar, in 1922, suggested delegation of propaganda work to overseas Indians and training them in publicity work for conditioning global public opinion.[115] An overseas Department was set up in 1929

---

[112] *Business Standard*, 'Kishan S. Rana: Re-setting India's Public Diplomacy'.

[113] USC Centre on Public Diplomacy, 'Communicating the Idea of India'.

[114] His Chinese counterpart, on the other hand, prefers writing op-eds in leading newspapers before his foreign visits. Just a day before he visited New Delhi on 18 September 2014, his article 'Towards an Asian Century of prosperity' was published in *The Hindu*.

[115] Guha, 'How the Congress Lost the Diaspora'.

under Nehru as an extension of anti-imperialist struggle in other parts of the British Empire.[116] In more contemporary times, it is the BJP, not the Congress, which has consistently and aggressively engaged the diaspora with a purpose.[117] The 'Overseas Friends', a foreign affairs cell of BJP, located in various countries in the world, is tasked to create a favourable global perception of India along with disseminating news overseas about India. There is little doubt over the significant role that the 'Overseas Friends' would play in India's PD during the Modi era by supplementing state efforts.

Though smaller in size than China, the Indian diaspora is being increasingly visualized as a strategic asset, and is in this respect similar to the impression of its Chinese counterpart. Larger roles in mainstream political activities in their adopted countries with democratic traditions like the US, the UK, Canada and Australia and their economic clouts have made the community an imperative in India's foreign policy. While the engagement of the diaspora has picked up over the years, it has escalated under PM Modi. The wealthy segments of the overseas Indian and the Persons of Indian Origin (PIOs), many of whom identify with BJP's 'Hindutva' ideology, are sources of large remittances to India and also potential contributors of funds and other resources to ambitious programmes like 'Make in India'. The effort to 'make the diaspora an integral part of our development journey' was adequately manifested during Modi's visits to the US, Canada, Australia and Fiji. While PD was being targeted at overseas Indians, the success of the PD would be in making the latter its ambassadors—a mission that BJP and Modi are taking forward aggressively.

It will also be interesting to note the extent by which the Modi government's engagement of the diaspora differs from the historical principles followed by India in doing so. The difference from China is also distinct in this regard. While China's state policies for engaging its diaspora encompassed almost all groups of ethnic Chinese overseas, India's greater focus was on relatively more affluent post-independence migrants with less pronounced state efforts to directly influence overseas

---

[116] Kapur, *Diaspora Development and Democracy*, 189.
[117] Ibid.

communities.[118] China's emphasis on 'common blood' and attempt to create a long-distance nationalism by more overt influence of its overseas communities were in contrast with the Indian strategy identified with the 'territory'. The latter encourages assimilation of migrants in their respective host counties, stemming from the historical Nehruvian nationalistic principles of 'Indianness' being a territorial concept.[119] Nehru's encouragement of overseas Indians to integrate deeper into the social and political mainstreams of their countries of domicile was driven by the overarching economic role of the state and limited room for private capital and India's overseas mercantile communities. The approach was also consistent with India's policy of non-intervention in domestic affairs of foreign states for winning 'non-aligned' friends in Asia and Africa—continents with largest presence of ethnic Indians.

The economic rationale of greater foreign participation in a gradually liberalizing Indian economy brought more proactivism in the 'hands off' policy since the 1990s when engaging the diaspora became a part of an evolving state policy. BJP's strategic focus on the diaspora is evident from the establishment of the high-level committee during PM Vajpayee's tenure in 2000. Since then, the diaspora has advanced in foreign policy priorities as a 'response to the emerging contours and compulsions of the international geopolitical economy'.[120] The annual Pravasi Bharatiya Diwas (PBD) was institutionalized at the same time for providing a platform to the overseas Indian community to gather and interact.

The PBD has institutionalized awards (Pravasi Bharatiya Samman) for distinguished overseas Indians—the first being conferred on Samy Velu, the leader of Malaysian Indian Congress in 2003—underlining efforts to engage countries with strong Indian diaspora. Strategic and economic considerations can hardly be overlooked in later awards to distinguished recipients from Africa (e.g., South Africa, Zimbabwe, Kenya and Tanzania), Canada, the US, the UK, Southeast Asia, China and the Caribbean. Other noticeable initiatives for connecting to the diaspora include establishing the Overseas Indian Facilitation Centre, giving

---

[118] London School of Economics, 'The Diaspora as an Economic Asset'.
[119] Ibid.
[120] Sebastian, 'The Power of Diaspora'.

multiple-entry permits to PIOs, creating PM's Global Advisory Council of PIOs and the proposed India Development Foundation, announced during the sixth PBD in January 2008, for assisting overseas Indians to contribute to education, health and rural development in India,[121] and final and the most important, the Ministry of Overseas Indian Affairs (MOIA) for implementing policies for the overseas Indians. More programmes have been launched (e.g., 'Know India Programme' of the MOIA targeting the young diaspora to promote their awareness about India and setting up of the PIO/NRI university)[122] to strengthen the depth and quality of engaging the overseas Indians.

Two major initiatives should connect the diaspora even deeper with India. The first of these, taken up by the Manmohan Singh government and carried forward by the Modi government, is the diaspora participating in domestic elections. It is in the context of the diaspora, many scholars argue, that one encounters 'continuity' rather than change from the previous government and is seen 'not as a policy that will radically set a new course for India'.[123] PM Singh had announced at the PBD 2012 that the government had issued notification for registration of overseas voters under the Representation of People Act, 1950. The necessary amendments in the law in early 2015 enabled overseas Indians to cast votes through electronic ballots or through their nominees residing in India during the assembly polls in Delhi in February 2015, thus helping the diaspora to identify with the functioning of the Indian government.

Another important initiative for increasing the linkages of the diaspora with India is enabling them easier travel through long-term visas and entry permits. The Manmohan Singh government had liberalized visas for easier travel from Pakistan and Bangladesh for specific purposes (e.g., tourism, business and medical treatment). The process is not only being continued under the Modi government but is gaining a lot of momentum as well. The government's efforts to engage the diaspora deeper has led to specific announcements of liberal travel measures and lifelong visas

---

[121] The PM's inaugural speech at the sixth PBD (2008)
[122] Byron, 'University for PIOs'.
[123] Hall, 'Is a "Modi Doctrine" Emerging'.

for overseas Indians announced by Modi during his visit to New York in September 2014. Combined with efforts to make overseas Indians stronger participators in India's political process and allowing them easier access to India, Modi's PD is not only aimed at making the diaspora 'happy' partners in building India's global goodwill but also in investing in India's economic and social growth and consolidate their political commitment to the BJP. In fact, their cultivation during the recent times establish the diaspora as probably the most effective mechanism of India's soft power which has arguably been 'less the export of its culture and more the export of its people'.[124]

## Education

Examples discussed in earlier chapters underscore the significance of education in enhancing soft power and the advances China have made in this regard. While India would be resource constrained to match China in scale in strategic forays such as development assistance and infrastructure-building, it can visualize education as an effective means for creating strategic goodwill in the neighbourhood and beyond. This stems from the overall objective of gradually internationalizing higher education. The Economic Survey (2010–11) stressed the need to develop India as an education hub, while the Planning Commission of India argued that the widespread use of English and cheaper living costs can help India in becoming a global hub for higher education through effective partnerships.[125] However, a row over teaching foreign languages in Indian schools after Modi took over the reins of the government might dampen India's soft power image in this regard. Efforts to capitalize soft power through education also need to counter India's current image of being a 'laggard' among major Asian countries with only 9 Indian universities figuring among Asia's top 100 compared with 21 from China.[126] Internationalization of higher education in India is clearly lagging behind China with no foreign universities having opened campuses in the country. Though collaborations and partnerships with

---

[124] Kapur, *Diaspora Development and Democracy*, 188.
[125] *Business Standard*, 'Making India a Global Education Hub'.
[126] The World University Rankings, 'Asia University Rankings 2015'.

foreign universities are increasing, India is a fair distance from being recognized a global education hub in the same league as other Asian countries like Singapore, Japan and now China.

An important initiative contributing to India's reputation as a regional centre for higher education is the establishment of the South Asian University (SAU). Though, a combined initiative of the SAARC members, India has funded almost 80 per cent of the University which has its campus in Delhi.[127] The SAU has been running successfully based on a steady inflow of students from other parts of South Asia as well as a faculty having representation from other South Asian countries. The SAU has been an important vehicle of India's soft power in the SAARC. The Nalanda University, mentioned earlier, can also grow into an equally significant source of goodwill.

India has been running a fairly extensive programme of awarding scholarships to foreign students for studying in India. The ICCR also offers scholarships to students from South Asia, Southeast Asia, Africa and Middle East countries under various schemes.[128] There are also scholarships for the diaspora such as those of Fiji.[129] Parallel scholarships under the Technical Cooperation Scheme of the Colombo Plan are awarded to students from South and Southeast Asia, Iran, South Korea and PNG.[130] Reciprocal scholarship schemes for South America (Brazil, Chile, Costa Rica, Nicaragua, Panama, Paraguay and Peru) largely focus on the study of art and culture. Education exchanges feature in specific bilateral engagements such as with Kuwait and Oman.[131] India has emerged as a particularly popular education destination for students

[127] South Asian University (SAU).

[128] ICCR has announced ICCR Silver Jubilee Scholarship of 64 slots for Nepalese students while 900 slots under the Africa Scholarship Scheme (2015–16). There are General Cultural Scholarship Scheme as well targeting Asian, African and Latin American countries for pursuing research in Indian Universities. For details, see ICCR, 'General Cultural Scholarship Scheme'.

[129] Ministry of External Affairs, 'India–Fiji Relations'.

[130] Government of India Scholarships. Available at: http://www.jamiahamdard. edu/govschol.asp#sss (accessed on 20 September 2012).

[131] Pradhan, 'Accelerating India's "Look West Policy" in the Gulf'.

from the UAE, given the low costs and less stringent visa restrictions.[132] These positives, however, coexist with the rising spate of attacks on African students in various parts of India underscoring latent racial sentiments that exist deep within the fabric of a country that has been a staunch opponent of apartheid and racial discrimination.[133] Though the Indian government has responded to the attacks reassuring African students of safety and swift action and even offered to 'sensitize' the Indian people, many suggest that 'the effort here is to manage the image, rather than the symptom'.[134] This is again an example of the challenge that Indian soft power has to face in conveying an 'honest' face to its recipients. Like Chinese soft power in Africa, which is increasingly getting criticized for creating conditions for cementing China's financial clout over financially deficient and conflict-ridden African countries, Indian soft power might start getting hit by these racist incidents, notwithstanding grant of larger scholarships.

As attempts to showcase India as an education hub continues, it is not yet clear whether education will become a focus area for connecting closer with Southeast Asia[135] and the larger Asia-Pacific under the Modi Government's 'Act East' strategy. Expanding the scope of the existing Indian Technical and Economic Cooperation (ITEC) initiatives can be useful in this regard. Launched in September 1964 as a part of South–South Cooperation, the ITEC aims to share India's innovative forms of technical cooperation with developing countries.[136] The regional engagement aspect is an important implicit objective of the programme. Indonesia, for example, is a major recipient of ITEC. India's ties with Indonesia go back to their cooperation during the Non-Aligned Movement in 1955. Historical ties apart, Indonesia's demographic characteristic of being the largest Muslim nation, as well as its

---

[132] Alafrangi, 'Study Abroad or Not'.
[133] African diplomats decided to boycott the Africa Day organized by the Indian government in May 2016 to protest 'racism' and 'Afrophobia' against African students.
[134] Sukumar, 'Blacklivesmatter'.
[135] The lack of students from Southeast Asia is still noticeable.
[136] Technical Cooperation Division. Available at: http://itec.mea.gov.in/ (accessed on 14 September 2012).

geo-strategic importance in the IOR, makes it a vital strategic entity. The ITEC also has sizeable slots for Fiji and Sudan, reflecting India's intentions for closer engagement with countries with traditional historical links. More engagements under the ITEC include those with Asia, the Pacific, Africa, Latin America, the Caribbean and East and Central Europe, in addition to bilateral capacity-building efforts as well in countries like Myanmar.[137]

## NON-STATE, PRIVATE INITIATIVES

A careful study of India's history and the later experiences and developments reveals that its soft power strategy is markedly distinct from China. Unlike China's deliberate revival of Confucian values in its efforts of society-building and the combined effort of the Chinese political leadership and academics in articulating soft power engagement through cultural initiatives and PD, as discussed earlier in Chapter 2, India has had a less-pronounced soft power strategy until recently. India's geostrategic position in Asia—'so situated as to be the meeting point of Western and Northern, and Eastern and Southeastern Asia'[138]—its colonial history and a difficult neighbourhood have impacted its external engagement and soft power strategy. The influence has been compounded by unique domestic challenges like religious pluralism and multilingual, multi-ethnic features leading to the 'creation of a pan-Indian identity on the foundations of the past'.[139] Consequently, India's non-state actors, both individuals and private industry, have been much greater emissaries of its soft power than state agencies. Kathryn Sikkink calls for their recognition as 'legitimate political spaces' and argues, 'their power to influence and perhaps democratize the structure of world politics' is

---

[137] Such initiatives include the India–Myanmar Industrial Training Centre, the Myanmar–India Centre for English Language, the Myanmar–India Entrepreneurship Development Centre and the India–Myanmar Centre for Enhancement of IT Skills. See Embassy of India, 'Major Indian Projects in Myanmar'.
[138] *Selected Works of Jawaharlal Nehru*. Available at: http://www.claudearpi.net/maintenance/uploaded_pics/SW02.pdf (accessed on 30 November 2012).
[139] Verma, *Being Indian*, 193.

'through their increasing influence within existing international institutions and their capacity to use this influence to leverage changes in
individual nation states'.[140]

Bollywood—India's major movie industry producing films in Hindi—
has a huge following across the world. Hindi movies are often dubbed in
local languages for viewing by foreign audiences. These movies have cast
their spell on China with *My Name Is Khan* and *3 Idiots* being among the
most downloaded on the *Youku*.[141] Dubbed Hindi movies are shown at
least once a week by the CCTV. A dubbed version of the *3 Idiots* was
commercially released in the mainland in 2011, the same year, when a
Bollywood troupe toured China for collaborating with the Beijing Film
Academy on hosting a Film Festival in major Chinese cities.[142] While
China is one of the relatively later entrants in the Bollywood fan club, the
impact of Indian cinema has spread deep and wide beyond the Indian
diaspora to the local people in Africa and several other parts of the world.

Apart from commercial success, critical acclaim of several mainstream
Indian movies (e.g., *Lagaan*, *Black*, *Taare Zameen Par* and *Lunchbox*) has
fetched them intellectual recognition. Such distinction, earlier, was
achieved only by 'non-mainstream' films made by celebrated filmmakers
like Satyajit Ray, recipient of the Academy award (Oscar) for lifetime
achievement. The transition of mainstream Indian cinema to greater
produce of 'global' movies and deeper connection with international
audiences began from 'crossover' films (*Monsoon Wedding*, *Mitr: My
Friend*, *The Namesake*, *Bend it Like Beckham*) usually made by non-
resident Indian filmmakers and often focusing on Indian families and
characters based overseas. These have been successful 'bridges' between
the diaspora and the local audiences in a mutual process of rediscovery.

The brand of crossover films and the larger global pull of Indian
movies have inspired their production in Hollywood with the *Slumdog
Millionaire* and *The Hundred-Foot Journey* being prominent examples. The
*Slumdog Millionaire* was also responsible for the soaring popularity of
Indian music following its composer A.R. Rahman's musical receipt

---

[140] Einbinder, 'Cultural Diplomacy Harmonizing', 48.
[141] Youku is a leading video-sharing website in China.
[142] *Ministry of External Affairs*, 'India–China Bilateral Relations'.

of the Oscar and Grammy awards. A regular performer in Hollywood, Rahman's music has been frequently sampled by other renowned musicians, such as Singapore's Kelly Poon, Uzbekistan's Iroda Dilroz, the French rap group La Caution, the American artist Ciara and the German band Lowenherz. The large global impact of Hindi film music and Bollywood in general is evident from the regular hosting of Indian movie and music award functions (including television awards) in different parts of the world. Indeed, these shows are hardly held in India anymore, given the enthusiasm of not only the Indian diaspora but also global audiences for Indian movies.

Along with movies, Indian television has also been a great vehicle for exporting India's popular appeal. Indian television entertainment has penetrated deep within South Asia, Southeast Asia, Australia, New Zealand and many Pacific Island countries. China has agreed to free airwaves and telecast programmes produced by India's leading television group, Zee TV.[143] Like Hindi movies, quite a few Indian television soap operas[144] have been dubbed in Mandarin for local audiences. Television channels like Zee TV are also engaging in unconventional engagements and peace-building processes through musical programmes such as *Chote Ustaad*, which featured eminent Indian and Pakistani singers as mentors for young singers from India and Pakistan. Indeed, the popularity of Hindi soap operas has been as much as to compel local TV stations to defy the Afghan government's ban on telecast in 2008.[145]

Apart from Indian cinema, food, cricket and Ayurveda have also linked India deeply with the rest of the world. Indian cuisine is as popular as the Chinese cuisine, particularly in the West, with more than 10,000 Indian restaurants in the US alone. The Indian food industry in Britain accounts for two-thirds of all eating-outs.[146] It is interesting that Indian cuisine has been able to establish itself as a higher end 'fine dining' option in several countries in the West, where most of the Chinese cuisine is seen figuring among affordable 'budget' choices. Indian cuisine

---

[143] INCHINCLOSER, 'Now Catch Your Favourite Zee TV'.
[144] Two soap operas are *Koshish: Ek Asha* and *Sindoor Tere Naam ka*.
[145] Tang and Faiez, 'TV Stations defy Afghan Government Ban'.
[146] Debroy, 'India's Soft Power and Cultural Influence', 114.

has also become part of the mainstream Hollywood productions like *The Hundred-Foot Journey*. The global appeal of curry is as much as that of cricket, if not more.

Cricket has probably been the strongest binding element of South Asia and has time and again allowed Indian and Pakistani heads of states to attempt to normalize relations through 'sports diplomacy'. The commercial success of the Indian Premier League (IPL) has made India the spearhead of what is now the most globalized edition of cricket tournaments across the world. India has also encouraged more nations to play cricket in a bid to strengthen its clout in global cricket. Cricket has also been one of the unlikely mediums for increasing people-to-people contact with China. Mamatha Maben, the former captain of the Indian Women's Cricket team, coached the Chinese women's cricket team ahead of the 2010 Asian Games. Finally Ayurveda—the traditional Hindu medication—has become heavily popular in the US, Europe and Australia. Indeed, Ayurveda has begun achieving as much recognition as traditional Chinese medicine, given its practice over centuries, application of medicinal herbs and focus on healing in close connection to nature. Combined with Yoga, Ayurveda is a powerful alternative therapeutic vision in the modern world, particularly for the West and there is little wonder in its greater global interest.

Three other categories of non-state actors have positively influenced India's soft power. These are the media, Indian authors and Indian industry associations. Occasionally derided for its negative projection of India, Indian print and television media has acquired the global reputation of symbolizing one of the most vibrant and critical media industries of the world, as trenchant and determined in its criticism as its more illustrious counterparts from the West. Media has also been aiding people-to-people contacts through innovative initiatives like the *Aman ki Asha* (Hope for Peace), a collaborative effort of *The Times of India* with the Jang Group from Pakistan. *Maitree Bandhan* (A Bond of Friendship) with *Prothom Alo* (The First Light)—Bangladesh's leading newspaper—was another similar initiative by the *Times of India*. Similar constructive people-to-people initiatives are noted for literary organizations such as the Foundation of SAARC Writers and Literature (FOSWAL) active in facilitating greater interaction between India and its neighbours. Indian literature, much like cricket, food, music and movies, resonates widely in its neighbourhood and the rest of the world.

While vernacular Indian literature (Hindi, Bengali, Urdu, Punjabi and Tamil) has wide readership in different parts of South Asia, Indian authors writing in English are firmly entrenched in modern global literature with wide following in the English-speaking world. Global prominence and recognition of Indian authors writing in English—V.S. Naipaul, Salman Rushdie, Vikram Seth, Amitav Ghosh, Arundhati Roy and Jhumpa Lahiri to name only a few—reflects the natural ability of several Indians to express creatively in English. While demonstrating India's 'accommodation' of the 'other', it also indicates the high degree of comfort of India and Indians have with English (more than 100 million English speakers[147]) —a Western language—unlike China, which while not being averse to picking up functional English, has been wary of Western cultural onslaught.[148]

Finally, India's old and large business and industry chambers such as the Federation of Indian Chamber of Commerce and Industry (FICCI) and the Confederation of Indian Industry (CII) have also been active in people-to-people contacts particularly with neighbours like Pakistan and China. Utilizing the opportunities provided by India's growing business links with the rest of the world for more meaningful strategic interfaces, these chambers have been actively pursuing 'Track II' diplomatic dialogues with several countries like Japan, Singapore and even the US.[149]

## ECONOMIC INITIATIVES

India's economic initiatives for engaging neighbours have been particularly prominent in South Asia. These are gradually becoming larger in Southeast Asia, and beyond the Asian region, in Africa. Urge to access strategic resources has been an important driver of these initiatives

---

[147] *The Washington Times*, 'Linguistically Speaking—English becomes India's "Numero Uno" language'.

[148] *AsiaNews.it*, 'Hu Jintao's Cultural War'.

[149] Yardley, 'Diplomacy in India Rides', 1.

along with the imperative of balancing China's proliferating strategic depth. The current Indian policy for economic engagement in the neighbourhood and elsewhere in the world is a combination of enhancing regional connectivity, offering aid for infrastructure-building, extending credit lines and humanitarian assistance.

Better regional connectivity is an important ambition for India, as much as it is for China, given the strategic advantages of such connectivity in facilitating regional trade and accessing untapped resources and markets. Contributing to expansion of infrastructure capacities is critical in this regard. India's involvement in various infrastructure projects in the region is manifestations of its long-term economic and strategic interests. The Modi government is keen on widening and deepening the initiatives of its predecessors in this regard. It is ready to proceed on greater connectivity even through smaller sub-regional templates like BBIN— Bangladesh, Bhutan, India and Nepal. India is willing to establish a regional cooperation framework with its northern and eastern neighbours in South Asia, which appears feasible and rational, given that problems and issues characterizing Western South Asia (Pakistan and Afghanistan) are not necessarily those that resonate with countries in the region's North and East. The signing of the BBIN Motor Vehicles Agreement in June 2015 for facilitating easier movement of vehicles between the groups shows its eagerness to move forward.[150] For India, this provides the much-needed infrastructural backup to movement of goods and people from its land-locked Northeast. Apart from the BBIN, several transport agreements and framework arrangements were also reached during Modi's visit to Dhaka for securing transit rights to enable an effective 'Act East' policy. The effort is to seek connection through road, rail, rivers, sea, transmission lines, petroleum pipelines and digital links that would link Northeast India to Southeast Asia through Bangladesh.

The salience of connectivity in foreign policy once again was highlighted during Modi's visit to Iran in May 2016. The signing of the 'historic' Chabahar port agreement during his visit, having the potential of becoming India's gateway to Afghanistan, Central Asia and Europe, carries several messages for the world and specific neighbours. While the

---

[150] *Dhaka Tribune*, 'BBIN Motor Vehicle Agreement Signed'.

project does not only underscore India's commitment to its economic development through cooperation, its attempt to chart big projects in line with its status but, perhaps, also communicates India's strategy to isolate Pakistan; thus, underlining its 'hard' posture and ability to manoeuvre. In a similar fashion, India's latest initiative highlighting the construction of the Salma dam in Afghanistan is also probably an indication of the depth and seriousness in India–Afghanistan ties and the fact that such ties do convey distinct signals to Pakistan.

The BBIN framework is another example of India's involvement with other multi-country initiatives in its neighbourhood for accelerating connectivity and achieving greater economic integration. The importance of such frameworks for augmenting economic activity and facilitating people-to-people communication can hardly be overstated. The BCIM Corridor is another typical example. Comprising Bangladesh, China, India and Myanmar, the BCIM is yet another initiative for connecting India's Northeast to its geographically contiguous neighbours through a network of roads, railways, waterways and airways. The bus service connecting Kolkata and Agartala through Dhaka—a major diplomatic achievement by Modi—is an important step in expanding mobility between India and Bangladesh, and a strong signal of India's attempts to cooperation with and connects to neighbours. However, the progress of BCIM is significantly contingent on India and China agreeing to let the corridor pass through areas that are mutually disputed, particularly in India's north-eastern state of Arunachal Pradesh bordering China. China's intention of accommodating the BCIM within the OBOR is also a distinct source of discomfort for India. Indeed, the BCIM is an example of the problems that regional connectivity initiatives involving India might face as the OBOR picks up, given that most of the countries India is planning to get connected to are also those that China is aiming to integrate with through the OBOR. Till now, India has been non-committal to the OBOR, given that it considers the project less of a plan to expand regional connectivity capacities but more of a design to specifically serve China's own national interests: 'A [Chinese] national initiative devised with national interest, it is not incumbent on others to buy it'.[151] However, it

---

[151] India's Foreign Secretary, Jaishankar at the IISS Lecture in Singapore in 2015.

might help in various respects if India shakes off its indecision towards the OBOR and takes a more objective view of the project in terms of the economic benefits that can offer to Indian business and industry.

The Modi government's ambitions on connectivity go beyond the immediate neighbourhood through plans to resuscitate ancient ties for reviving the Indian part of the Spice Road,[152] connecting India to more than 30 countries in Europe and Asia. The project is expected to result in the revival of cultural, historical and archaeological exchanges while boosting tourism across Southern India, particularly Kerala. A similarly ambitious plan is project Mausam[153] for re-establishing India's ties with its ancient trade partners stretching from East Africa, along the Arabian Peninsula, parts of Southern Iran to South Asia and further to Southeast Asia and thus reviving the 'Indian Ocean world'. Project Mausam is seen by many as a counter proposal to China's Maritime Silk Road Initiative (MSRI) initiative. While both the initiatives are geared towards building communication and deepening cooperation with the other countries, there is a growing fear and mistrust of each other. However, in keeping with the current fervour at enhanced cooperation, China has called for

---

[152] As early as the 3rd century BCE, fishermen, sailors and merchants travelled the waters of the Indian Ocean linking the world's earliest civilization from Africa to East Asia. They exchanged gems, metals, medicines and the most important of them all, spices. The Dutch, the French, the Portuguese and the English sailed to the Coromandel coast of Southern India in search of these valued condiments, essential for preservation and flavouring of food which led the coastline to be called the Spice Coast. An initiative of the State Government of Kerala and with the support of the Indian government, the effort is to revive the two millennia Spice Route.

[153] According to the Indira Gandhi National Centre for the Arts website, Mausam is a project under the Ministry of Culture and the Archaeological Society of India. The etymology of the word Mausam signifies the importance of the season to seafarers. This intertwining of natural phenomena such as monsoon winds and the ways in which these were harnessed historically to create cultural networks form the building blocks of Project Mausam. The endeavour of the Project is to position itself at two levels. At the macro level, it aims to reconnect and re-establish communications between countries of the Indian Ocean, which would lead to an enhanced understanding of cultural values and concerns; while at the micro level, the focus is on understanding national cultures in their regional maritime milieu.

linking India's Mausam and Spice Road with its OBOR.[154] As mentioned earlier, India, till now, is non-committal to the OBOR. At the same time, it is yet to flesh out the details of Mausam, though it has begun engaging countries in the Indian Ocean in right earnest (e.g., Sri Lanka, Mauritius and Seychelles), in what is probably a ploy to offset the growing Chinese attention on what it considers as its own backyard.

While again being smaller in scale than China's, India's efforts to contribute to new infrastructure capacities in the neighbourhood are not negligible. Afghanistan has been a particular focus in this regard with some of the major Indian projects being the construction of the new parliament building,[155] a highway linking Zaranj from the Iranian border to Delaram in the northeast, establishing telecommunication facilities in 11 provincial capitals and repairing of a mosque in Mazar-e-Sharif.[156] Similar efforts in Sri Lanka include renovating the Palaly Airport and rehabilitating the Kankesanthurai Harbour.[157] Modi, during his visit to Sri Lanka in early 2015, also commissioned a number of development and rebuilding projects, including a railway track in Talaimannar. Road and rail development have also been India's areas of involvement in Bhutan.[158]

Non-state actors like the Indian industry is also active in infrastructure capacity-building in the neighbourhood and is complementing state efforts; a pertinent example is the GMR Infrastructure's involvement in building the Male International Airport in Maldives. Physical infrastructure capacities are also being created through the LoCs[159] extended by India's Exim Bank to the neighbourhood, most noticeably Bangladesh and Sri Lanka for railway infrastructure. PM Modi announced a concessional LoC to Nepal along with the 'HIT' (H: Highways, I: I-ways

[154] *Yahoo!news*, 'Cooperation Best Way Forward for Beijing',
[155] Ganguly, 'India's Role in Afghanistan', 4.
[156] Tom, 'India Outdoes US Aid Efforts'.
[157] High Commission of India, Colombo. Available at: http://www.hcicolombo. org/index.php?option=com_pages&id=24 (accessed on 24 September 2012).
[158] Price, 'Diversity in Donorship'.
[159] LoCs are in addition to India's development assistance to various least-developed South Asian countries, such as Afghanistan, Bhutan and Nepal, through grants, aid and loans.

and T: Transways) formula during his visit in August 2014, marking India's extensive commitment to infrastructure-building and connectivity in land-locked Nepal.

India has been aiming to complement the focus on connectivity manifesting through physical infrastructure capacity-building with its larger economic interests of securing access to energy supplies. Bangladesh has been an important partner in this regard. The new transmission line between India and Bangladesh—South Asia's first-ever high-voltage direct current interconnection—is a major initiative in augmenting regional electricity supplies through efficient trading of electricity across geographies and growth of a regional energy market.[160] India's initiative in providing a market-based efficient solution to energy shortages in the region should earn it strategic goodwill across the border while addressing some of the electricity deficit at home. The two countries entered into a Power Purchase Agreement in 2010 to enable Dhaka to import subsidized power while the NTPC and the BPDB are collaborating to establish a thermal power plant in Khulna.[161] Access to energy resources have motivated India's involvement in Afghanistan (hydroelectric project at the Salma Dam in Herat) and Sri Lanka (bilateral interconnection of electricity grids and a thermal power plant in Sampur)[162] with matching efforts by Indian industry in Maldives (Suzlon Energy's wind energy project).[163]

India's involvement in creation of infrastructure capacities has been relatively lower in Southeast Asia (Annexure I) compared with South Asia. Apart from the BCIM again, which will be a major cross-regional connectivity initiative, involving India and Myanmar from Southeast Asia, India has been a part of cross-regional initiatives like the Bay of Bengal Initiative for Multi-Sectoral Technical and Economic Cooperation (BIMSTEC) and Mekong–Ganga Cooperation (MGC) that focus on regional transport connectivity. The proposed networks include the

---

[160] Asian Development Bank, 'India Electricity Flows to Bangladesh'.

[161] Bhatia, 'Deepening India–Maldives Relations'.

[162] High Commission of India. Available at: http://www.hcicolombo.org/index.php?option=com_pages&id=24 (accessed on 24 September 2012).

[163] Muni, 'Stabilizing the Neighbourhood', 7.

East-West Corridor project and the Trans-Asian Highway, along with a proposal to build a rail link from Hanoi (Vietnam) to New Delhi (India) which will pass through Myanmar, Laos, Thailand and Cambodia. The link will integrate India's Northeast with the Mekong delta and Southern China and can be of significant strategic value for India.[164]

Myanmar has been a particular focus for India in Southeast Asia as far as infrastructure capacities are concerned given its strategic assets of untapped energy resources and the contiguous border with India's Northeast. Key infrastructure projects in Myanmar with Indian involvement include hydroelectric development in Chindwin River valley[165] and the multimodal transport project, including construction and upgradation of the Rhi-Tiddim road.[166] Apart from multi-country initiatives like the BCIM mentioned earlier, India's efforts to augment physical connectivity between the Northeast and Myanmar could also include an 'economic corridor' between Tripura and Myanmar.[167] India has begun implementing projects in Laos (a modern IT laboratory, an entrepreneurial development centre and a V-sat network in 18 provinces) too.[168]

From a wider regional perspective, Southeast Asia is an interesting example of the complementary efforts between India's state and non-state actors in expanding economic engagement. Major Indian public sector companies (e.g., ONGC Videsh Ltd., Hindustan Machine Tools, Engineers India Limited, Bharat Heavy Electricals Ltd, IRCON International Ltd and Indian Oil Corporation Ltd) have been present in the region for several years. The IRCON, for example, has been developing railways in Malaysia since 1988 and has completed and commissioned 11 major projects.[169] The ONGC's exploration activities in the region have been varied though exploration efforts in Vietnam in the disputed territory of the South China Sea have also created some strategic discomfort for India.

---

[164] Palit, 'India's Economic Engagement with Southeast Asia', 5.
[165] Embassy of India, 'Major Indian projects in Myanmar'.
[166] Ibid.
[167] *The Diplomat*, 'Narendra Modi's Northeast India Outreach'.
[168] *The Peninsula*, 'Natwar Inaugurates'.
[169] High Commission of India, Kuala Lumpur. Available at: http://www.indian highcommission.com.my/ec.php (accessed on 25 September 2012).

Indian businesses[170] have extensive presences in Indonesia. Specific infra-structure-building projects include the Adani Group's rail and port projects in South Sumatra.[171] Singapore, one of the most important financial hubs in the region, has more than 5,000 registered Indian companies including prominent investments like the Singapore Mercantile Exchange (SMX), a wholly owned subsidiary of Financial Technologies (India) Limited, providing trading technology solutions.

India's neighbourhood is vulnerable to natural calamities and cata-strophic incidents arising from various natural disasters. While India's coastal and mountainous populations are often affected by these incidents, the effects are noticeably severe in various parts of South Asia. Ironically, these disasters in the neighbourhood and the role played by India in supporting the affected countries contribute to its benign perception and strategic goodwill. Indeed, India is widely expected to play a constructive role in natural-disaster management given its large size, greater resources and expertise.

India has been responding to various incidents by providing humanitarian aid and allied support. Beginning from the Tsunami in the Indian Ocean in 2004 that severely affected Sri Lanka and Maldives,[172] India has provided aid and supported rehabilitation in the aftermath of the floods in Pakistan in 2010, the earthquake in Northeast Myanmar in 2011 and the earthquake in Afghanistan in 2012. More recently, it played a significant role in supporting Nepal after it was struck by a disastrous earthquake in April 2015.[173] Soon after assumption of office by PM Modi,

---

[170] Like Aditya Birla Group, Adani, Essar, Jindal Steel, Bajaj, TVS, Spice Group and Godrej.

[171] Embassy of India, 'India-Indonesia Relations'.

[172] India provided rapid disaster assistance using the air force, army and navy to Sri Lanka and Maldives. It was also among the first to provide relief supplies to Indonesia. India figured among the four major donors supporting Tsunami relief along with the US, Australia and Japan.

[173] Apart from food supplies, 300 personnel, four aircrafts, a mobile hospital, India, at the request of the Nepal Government, also ran special trains to border areas to help people return home if they wanted. In fact, Nepal thanked the Indian government calling India's extension of assistance as 'extending a 'blank cheque'. For details, see *The Economist*, 'Earthquake: India's Response Was Like Extending Blank Cheque'.

**Table 9.3**
*Indian Investments in Africa*

| Company | Location | Sector |
| --- | --- | --- |
| ONGC | Libya, Nigeria | Oil exploration |
| ONGC | Sudan | Hydrocarbon |
| ONGC | Côte d'Ivoire | Offshore drilling |
| Vedanta Resources | Zambia | Copper mining |
| ONGC/OVL | Egypt, Libya, Ivory Coast, Gabon | Oil |
| Essar Group | Madagascar | Oil and gas exploration |
| IOC | Kenya, Tanzania, Mozambique | Oil exploration |

*Source:* Compiled from Bijoy (2010) and African Development Bank Group (2011).

India also spearheaded efforts to rescue people of various nationalities trapped in Yemen in Africa. The global media and the international community were much appreciative of India's proactive role in the evacuation and action as a responsible maritime power.

India's efforts to connect to countries by becoming stakeholders in their economic development have extended beyond its neighbourhood to Africa and Latin America as well. India has some major investments in Africa (Table 9.3) by state-owned enterprises like the ONGC and IOC, complemented by private industries (Vedanta and Essar). Concentrating in mining and exploration, these investments display 'resource-seeking' characteristics (Annexure I). Apart from developing local industrial infrastructure and generating employment in host countries, these investments augment Africa–India trade, which has gained considerable momentum from India's extension of duty-free tariffs to exports from 49 LDCs, announced in April 2008,[174] and benefitting 33 African countries.[175]

---

[174] In 2014, in order to expand trade with Africa further, India amended its Duty Free Tariff Preference (DFTP) scheme to cover around 98 per cent of the tariff lines.
[175] The African Development Bank Group, 'India's Economic Engagement with Africa'.

Africa is as much a priority in engagement for India, as it is for China, given its immense strategic value. India's engagement of the continent is becoming extensive and varied over the years. The India–Africa Summit of 2008—identical to the third FOCAC in Beijing in November 2006, which produced China's Africa Policy of 2006 and the Beijing Action Plan (2007–09)—provided the framework for stronger bilateral ties. Compared with China, India's strategic advantages in engaging Africa include the presence of a large diaspora (estimated at 8 per cent of global Indian diaspora) which, inter alia, motivated PM Modi's visits to Mauritius and Seychelles. India also enjoys the advantage of long historical exchanges with African countries and benefits from the enormous resonance of 'Mahatma Gandhi' among Africans even today. Finally, though Chinese state-owned enterprises have aggressively invested in African energy resources as discussed earlier in Chapter 6, Indian industry has had a longer and more broad-based presence including in critical sectors like healthcare (Table 9.4) enabling it to earn strategic goodwill.

The second India–Africa Summit in Addis Ababa in 2011 announced that 'Africa is determined to partner in India's economic resurgence as India is committed to be a close partner in Africa's renaissance'.[176] At the summit, India pledged development support for new institutions and training programmes. One of India's major initiatives in augmenting digital connectivity in the region is the collaborative project with the African Union (AU) for the pan-African e-network connecting AU members through satellite and fibre optic network, and equipped to support e-governance, e-commerce, infotainment, resource mapping, meteorological and other services.[177] Several African students have registered with Indian universities for tele-education courses under the project that also facilitates tele-medical consultations and tele-lectures.[178] Other major initiatives in Africa, involving both the state and non-state actors, include the India–Africa Project Partnership Conclave of the CII and the EXIM Bank, supported by the Indian government.

---

[176] Ibid.
[177] *African Union*, 'Pan-African e-Network (PAeN)'.
[178] Ibid.

**Table 9.4**

*Major Indian Companies and their Initiatives in Africa*

| Company | Initiative | Location |
|---------|-----------|----------|
| Ranbaxy | Providing essential affordable generic drugs | Distribution network covering 44 countries in the continent. Two facilities in Nigeria, one in South Africa and an upcoming one in Morocco. Also opened a manufacturing facility—its second—in West of Johannesburg in 2010. |
| Ajanta Pharma | 'Good Health for Fellow Africans'; Comprehensive anti-malarial therapies through educational and awareness programmes. Provides effective anti-retroviral and fixed dose combination (FDC) therapies for AIDS. | 16 countries in West and Central Africa |
| CIPLA (collaboration with Ugandan Quality Chemicals Industries Ltd) | US$ 32 billion plant t in Kampala for producing anti-retroviral and anti-malarial drugs and is the largest supplier of anti-malarial drugs to Africa. | Uganda |
| TCS | IT | South Africa |
| Kalpataru Power Transmission Ltd | 400 kv transmission line | Kenya |

*(Table 9.4 Continued)*

*(Table 9.4 Continued)*

| Company | Initiative | Location |
| --- | --- | --- |
| Airtel | (a) 3G network in covering 36 states<br>(b) 'Sauti ya Mkulima' (Swahili for voice of the farmer)—for providing around 250,000 small farmers with reliable agricultural information via their mobile phones. | (a) Nigeria<br>(b) Kenya |

*Source:* (a) Ajanta Pharma Ltd, available at: http://www.ajantamauritius.com/about_us. html (accessed on 7 July 2015); (b) In-Pharm, available at: http://www.in-pharmatechnologist.com/Ingredients/Ranbaxy-stakes-claim-on-African-drugs-production-market-with-new-Moroccan-plant (accessed on 7 July 2015) and (c) 'Bharti Airtel and GSMA Join Hands to Empower 250, 000 Kenyan Farmers, available at: http://www.techmtaa.com/2012/09/05/bharti-airtel-and-gsma-join-hands-to-empower-250000-kenyan-farmers/ (accessed on 7 July 2015).

Sun Hongbo, a scholar at the Chinese Academy of Social Sciences (CASS), describes India's engagement with Latin America as *xiao bu zi* (small steps), arguing that Latin American countries might actually prefer the 'smaller and calculated' approach to China's more aggressive engagement.[179] India's engagement of Latin America has indeed been gradual with a prominent focus on expansion of business ties. Non-state actors like the Indian industry have been the conspicuous face of engagement since the launch of the Focus:[180] Latin America and the Caribbean programme in 1997. Indian industry presence is increasing in Latin American markets through bilateral Preferential Trade Agreements (PTAs) with Argentina, Brazil, Uruguay, Paraguay and Chile. IT and IT-enabled services have seen the largest Indian business presence followed

[179] China and Latin America, 'India's Approach to Oil Acquisition'.
[180] Focus is a Latin America and the Caribbean (LAC) programme in 1997. It is a trade promotion programme launched by India's Ministry of Commerce and Industry.

by pharmaceuticals, agriculture and energy and mining (Table 9.5). Indian businesses have generated local employment with locals working for Indian companies, out of which more than half are in IT, business process outsourcing and knowledge process outsourcing.[181] The region's energy and mineral resources are increasingly beginning to attract Indian investors, similar to their Chinese counterparts, with several cooperative oil exploration projects coming up in the region, mostly in Brazil and Colombia.

While India's economic engagement has been gaining a lot of traction as a soft power tool, another sector in focus has been tourism. Given the Modi government's simultaneous attention on building India's economy and global image, the tourism sector is being given an increasing push through the 'Make in India' campaign. The third largest foreign exchange earner for the country, tourism can generate employment while boosting India's soft power by conveying Indian values and culture. Several measures are being undertaken (online visas, expansion of visa outsourcing services to complement earlier initiatives such as *Atithi Devo Bhava* and Incredible!ndia) to make travelling convenient and attract more tourists into India. Modi has also availed his foreign trips to announce visas for tourists.[182]

Given the heightened media coverage and anecdotal evidences and experiences of medical tourists helping to build a country's soft power image, granting of visas is also being linked to India's emergence as a medical tourism destination.[183] Pushed simultaneously with tourism under Modi's 'Make in India' initiative, the government released a fresh category of visa—the medical visa (M visa) for encouraging medical tourism as another priority area. In addition, to generate goodwill for India especially in African countries, hospitals (like Apollo) are also

---

[181] Heine, 'The Other BRIC in Latin America'.

[182] Modi announced visa on arrival to Sri Lankan tourists, Fijians, Australians, Americans and several others while announcing extension of electronic tourist visas to Chinese nationals.

[183] According to a KPMG report, released in 2014, India was placed among the top three medical tourism destinations in Asia (Thailand and Singapore being the other two) given the low cost of treatment, quality healthcare infrastructure and availability of highly-skilled doctors.

**Table 9.5**
*Indian Companies in LAC*

| Sector | Company | Country |
|---|---|---|
| IT | Satyam | Brazil |
| | TCS | Uruguay and Mexico |
| | Infosys | Brazil and Mexico |
| | HCL | Argentina and Brazil |
| | Polaris | Chile |
| | WIPRO | Brazil |
| | ICICI | Argentina |
| | APTECH | Brazil, Mexico, El Salvador and Peru |
| Pharmaceuticals | Dr. Reddy's Laboratories | Mexico |
| | Bilcare, Pune | Brazil |
| | Torrent | Brazil |
| | Glenmark | Brazil and Argentina |
| | Cellofarm | Brazil |
| Agro-business | Bajaj Hindustan | Brazil |
| Energy | OVL | Brazil, and Colombia |
| | Bharat Petro Resources (BPR) | Brazil (oil exploration) |
| | Reliance | Colombia, Peru (oil exploration) |
| | Suzlon | Brazil (wind energy) |
| | Essar Group | Brazil |
| | Indo-Borax Ltd | Argentina |

*Source:* Collated from different sources, including 'India, LAC countries can together become a formidable global economic force', *Ministry of External Affairs*, Government of India, 18 August 2014, available at: http://mea.gov.in/in-focus-article.htm? 23937/India+LAC+countries+can+together+become+a+formidable+global+economic+force (accessed on 8 July 2015).

planning an Africa expansion, aiming to buy hospitals in Botswana, Tanzania and Nigeria while a hospital is being planned in Dar es Salam to serve patients from East and West Africa.[184]

## CONCLUSION

There is little doubt on India's rich endowment of captive soft power stemming from ancient history, civilization, assimilative and cosmopolitan culture, democratic institutions and religious plurality. Unlike China, it does not suffer from adverse impressions characterising it overtly assertive. Nonetheless, benign 'non-aggressive' impressions on India coexist with negative impressions on the ability of the Indian state to effectively govern and deliver a decent quality of life to its people. On the other hand, India is also largely perceived 'hands off' and passive in several regional and global spheres. Given such impressions, a dynamic foreign policy is expected to face continuing challenges, as does India's efforts to accommodate an equally pronounced role of soft power in the robust policy.

The Modi government appears keen on correcting adverse impressions about India through more vigorous employment of its soft power. This is evident from the efforts invested in organizing *Yoga* demonstrations globally on 21 June 2015 after successfully persuading the UN to declare the day as 'World Yoga Day'. Other than culture and heritage, PM Modi's high profile visits to various countries and his passionate engagement of the world leaders and the Indian diaspora point to the forceful emphasis on utilization of India's soft power capital. Greater role of the state in pushing soft power might result in it being 'propagandist', as is often the case with China. On the other hand, complacency, arising from the belief that India does not need to strategize its soft power at all, given the general benign global impression it has, can also be counterproductive. The challenge for India's foreign policy is to work out the optimal role for state initiatives in spearheading national power, so much so that state efforts do not produce wrong impressions, and do not in any way distort the strategic gains flowing from non-state actors.

---

[184] *AfricanBusiness*, 'Pharmaceuticals: India's Generics Flow into Africa'.

The application of soft power, eventually, is meant to achieve core strategic national objectives. For India, some of the obvious ones include creating and maintaining a benign external environment, particularly in the neighbourhood, for facilitating peaceful conditions enabling economic growth and advancing its ambitions of being a major regional power, if not global, by pushing through its agenda in major regional and global forums. It aims to do all these by maintaining an independent foreign policy. As far as conditions in the neighbourhood are concerned, circumstances have partly improved, particularly with respect to Bangladesh, Bhutan and Afghanistan. But if that is attributed to robust PD of the Modi government (CD, high-level visits, scholarships, development assistance), the same has not made much of an impact in improving ties with Pakistan and Nepal. These mixed results point to the complicated circumstances in India's neighbourhood and the futility of employing a standard foreign policy, or soft power package, to achieve solutions.

Beyond the neighbourhood, India's robust PD and other 'soft' initiatives have probably succeeded in pulling off important nuclear partnerships such as with Australia and Canada, and have also helped in opening new partnerships with Iran. At the same time, however, criticism continues to prevail in the global media, where, notwithstanding the escalating bonhomie between India and the US—largely facilitated by the personal chemistry between President Obama and PM Modi—criticism of India's inability of control religious intolerance and corruption, remain rampant, as does persistent disapproval of its social development record and poor business conditions. Overt emphasis on culture or virtues of a civilizational state in such a context can probably be counterproductive, necessitating a more nuanced approach to application of soft power.

# 10

# China–India: Searching Solutions Through Engagement

The 'return of Asia' thesis[1] appears distinctly plausible given the increasing Sino-Indian cooperation on various issues. In a globalized and interconnected world, cooperation supersedes confrontation as a necessary choice and has motivated both China and India to deeper engagements with neighbours. From the Chinese perspective, apart from the overarching 'good neighbourly policy', the WDS is a major driver for engaging India, as much as it is for engaging the rest of South Asia (Chapter 3) and Central Asia (Chapter 8) mentioned earlier. Greater engagement of India is also prompted by the latter's rising importance in global and regional affairs.

Greater pragmatism is an increasingly visible aspect of Sino-Indian engagement in recent years. Despite the growing amenability between New Delhi and Washington, China seems agreeable to viewing Indian foreign policy as 'independent'—evident from the *Xinhua's* reporting on the issue during the US Secretary of State, Hillary Clinton's visit to India in 2012, urging India to purchase less Iranian oil. The Chinese media, during the occasion, preferred to take a realist stand and reported, 'US have been asking India to cut its oil imports from Iran. India gets 9 per cent of its oil from Iran and despite pressure from the US, *India has*

---

[1] According to Kishore Mahbubani, a notable academic and former Singaporean diplomat, with three of the world's largest economies being Asian countries (China, India and Japan), the region is returning to the centre stage it had occupied for eighteen centuries before the rise of the West. After two centuries of witnessing surging Western commerce, thought and power, the countries in Asia will rewrite history once again and set a new international order.

*decided to stand firm* (emphasis added)'.[2] In another instance, India's joining the trilateral meeting (with Russia and China) in Moscow in April 2016 was hailed by the Chinese media as sending a 'strong message to the international community' about China and India's preference for engaging in intense cooperation with each other despite roadblocks.[3] India, by way of its participation in the meet, reflected the growing 'multi-alignment' character of its foreign policy, emphasizing New Delhi's intention of taking important foreign policy decisions and engaging major and regional powers in specific discrete fashion, not as part of a pre-decided stereotype. The bonhomie between President Obama and PM Modi, while not going unnoticed in the Chinese media and the strategic community, has drawn more opinions criticizing the US for continuing to 'prop' up India for counterbalancing the strategic dynamics in the South China Sea.[4] It appears that China is prepared to comprehensively engage India as an independent regional actor for ensuring New Delhi keeps distance from strategic coalitions precipitated by extra-regional actors while[5] maintaining *status quo* in the region.

The new phase of Sino-Indian engagement is being eagerly watched by the rest of the world, particularly Western strategists and commentators whose response to the Asian renaissance and the rise of China and India is often sceptical with emphasis on the competitive aspect of the relationship. The overwhelming presence of such views in the popular and academic discourse tends to mask the efforts of both countries for engaging each other for improving communication and ensuring peaceful

---

[2] English.xinhuanet.com, 'Hillary Clinton's India Visit'.
[3] With South China Sea figuring for the first time in the Indo-US Joint Statement in 2014, there are reasons for the Chinese media to perceive India 'as rival to China and believed to be backing the US to internationalize the South China Sea issue'. For details see Wang, 'Tripartite Push for Regional Peace', 14.
[4] According to Ma Jun, a researcher at the Indian studies at the Academy of Military Science of the PLA, India is seen as a country 'not picking sides' and preferring to cooperate with Beijing for economic development. See *China Daily*, 'US, India Stir S. China Sea debate'.
[5] During President Xi Jinping's state visit to India in 2014, he stated that 'when China and India join hands for cooperation, it will benefit not only the two countries but also the entire Asia and the world at large'. See *Xinhua News Agency*, 'China, India Should be Partners for Peace'.

coexistence. While the two countries have been resorting to soft engagement with the rest of the world, such engagement is not exclusive of each
other and has been rising in recent years. With the former Indian PM
Singh asserting the world to be big enough for both countries to grow,
and the former Chinese Premier Wen emphasizing enough areas for
mutual cooperation,[6] partnership building has become a dedicated
initiative on both sides. The spirit has been retained by the current
leaderships with President Xi and PM Modi reiterating the enormous
importance of the Sino-Indian collaboration, 'we have a lot in common
and we can do a lot together'.[7]

China and India have had strategic and foreign policy priorities for
each other for quite some time now. Indeed, notwithstanding tensions
over an unresolved border, differences have never snowballed into
cross-border conflicts. Enabling mechanisms, like establishing a hotline connection between heads of states and another between the two
Army headquarters for use during crises, further minimizes possibility
of conflicts.[8] The maturity shown by both countries in de-escalating
tensions was evident from the quick dissipation of the flare-up in Ladakh
in April 2013[9] when a telephone conversation between India's National
Security Advisor and his counterpart in Beijing helped in resolving the
three-week long impasse.[10] Confrontation was similarly avoided during
President Xi's visit to India in September 2014, when there were reports
of alleged incursion by the Chinese troops.[11]

---

[6] *The Day After*, 'Enough Space for India, China'.

[7] *DNA*, 'Full text of PM Narendra Modi's Speech at the India–China Business
Forum'.

[8] The joint statement signed during PM Modi's visit to China in 2015 worked
on closer military ties including exchange visits of naval ships and holding of
PASSEX (Passing Exercise) and SAR (Search and Rescue) exercises, apart from
expanding the exchanges between the border commanders and establishing
border personnel meeting points at all sectors of the India–China border areas.

[9] According to media reports, China had repeatedly asked the Indian Army to
stop construction of bunkers in Fukche and Chumar areas of Ladakh.
Subsequently, there was a territorial standoff with Chinese military in eastern
Ladakh in April 2013. See Singh, 'Infra Build-up along China Border'.

[10] Singh, 'Infra Build-up along China Border'.

[11] *China Daily Mail*, 'Chinese Army Incursion into India's Territory'.

Both the countries are developing nations (*fa zhan zhong guo jia*) with similar challenges (climate change, access to energy resources and skilling large populations), creating fertile ground for collaboration on multiple fronts. Like China, realization of India's global and regional aspirations requires a peaceful and stable environment, as discussed in the last chapter. This chapter analyses the changing Chinese perception of India and the growing pattern of *constructive engagement* between the two through application of various soft power tools by both the countries.

## INDIA: THE CHINESE PERCEPTION

While both, China and India, are keen to develop their relationship and cooperate for fulfilling national objectives, including vindicating the Asian resurgence, China's contradictory views of India influences its perspective of its neighbour. India's ethnic and religious heterodoxy confuse China with its robust and chaotic democracy adding further to the confusion.

China's foreign policy categorizes priorities in four major fundamentals: relationship with neighbours (*lin guo wei jiao*), great powers (*da guo wei jiao*), the developing world (*fa zhan zhong guo jiao*) and multilateralism (*duo bian wei jiao*). Professor Ma Jia Li, a close follower of Sino-India relations for decades, argues that the categorization makes India a priority for China as it satisfies conditions of being a neighbour, a great power in the making, a major developing country and an advocate of multilateralism.[12] Nonetheless, India is not as high a priority for China as the US or Japan. Scholarly opinions justify this on different grounds. Susan Shirk feels this might be due to China's 'underlying confidence, verging on arrogance, about Chinese capabilities and its low opinion of Indian capabilities'.[13] On the other hand, Lan Jian Xue points out, 'for

---

[12] The author interviewed Professor Ma Jia Li, the author of *Rising India* published in 2010 by Shan Dong Da Xue Chu Ban She (Shandong University Publication) in August 2012 during her field visit to Beijing.
[13] Shirk, 'One-sided Rivalry', 94.

most Chinese, India hasn't appeared on "their screen of big powers".[14] Pei Minxin describes how 'ignorance, stereotyping, and latent hostility characterize the views of India held by a large segment of Chinese society'.[15] He points to a 'strategic competition between India and China more likely in the future' offset by 'the combination of under-appreciation of India's achievement and exaggeration of India's role as a geopolitical rival'.[16] On the whole, Chinese perceptions about India do reflect oddities with India being visualized mostly in parts (*zhi li po sui*) rather than in whole.[17] Indeed, despite being a neighbour, India, for many Chinese, is often more distant than the US.

A survey of Chinese perceptions of the BRICS countries conducted in 2009 by a Beijing-based consultancy group revealed the Chinese viewed India as the 'weakest' among the BRICS with its business and education opportunities perceived below non-BRICS countries like the US, Europe and South Korea.[18] It is difficult to say whether these perceptions have changed after a new government assumed office in India in May 2014. Given the increasing flow of Chinese investments in India and the interest in the 'Make in India' initiative, they might indeed have changed, at least, partially.[19] But positive impressions might not have spilled over to other areas, particularly polity and society. Author's various interviews and meetings reveal that Indian democracy is perceived weaker than Western democracy with the former considered synonymous with poverty, chaos and corruption. Interestingly, these disparaging impressions coexist with consensus on the absence of the possibility of an armed conflict between the two countries; however, most of those interviewed agree on the difficulty of resolving the disputes on the border and Tibet. There is a broad agreement among the academics, media and

---

[14] Randol, 'How to Approach the Elephant', 301.
[15] Tharoor, *Pax Indica*, 150.
[16] Minxin, 'Dangerous Misperceptions'.
[17] Zuo et al., Dragon Dance with Elephant, 322.
[18] Drury, 'Chinese think India'.
[19] Though China has been noticing India's economic rise, China's defence white paper (2015) does not mention India, signalling that India's relevance to China is still considered low. See *China Daily Mail*, 'Full Text: White Paper on Military Strategy'.

strategic experts on the scope of both countries working together, notwithstanding outstanding issues, particularly for strengthening economic relations which are being considered important given the Chinese recognition of India's economic progress.[20]

The framework for the contemporary understanding and engagement of India evolved from a study conducted by the Chinese leadership's 'Foreign Affairs Cell' involving inputs from Chinese experts on South Asia.[21] The study was motivated by the realization that China needed to respond to India's gradual rise by taking measures for maintaining its strategic leverage (in terms of territory and memberships of the exclusive Permanent Five and Nuclear Five clubs); diplomatic advantages (special relationships, membership of regional and international organisations) and economic lead over India.[22] The result has been an adoption or continuation of policies for maintaining the strategic leverage (active Chinese economic and strategic role in South Asia) as well as deeper bilateral engagement with India.

Several Chinese academics are contributing substantively to deeper engagement with India through their objective assessments. Their role is critical, given the relatively limited knowledge about India in China. The work 'Dragon dance with Elephant' (*long xiang gong wu*)[23] is an important contribution from noted Chinese scholars on India in this regard and discusses the need for pronounced engagement of India by articulating the cultural and religious aspects of the Sino-Indian relationship as well as perceptions of each other's rise. The authors urge revision in the Chinese outlook towards India from the prevalent notion of India 'chasing China' (*yin du zai zhui gan zhong guo*) that characterizes the bilateral dynamics as inherently competitive. The authors further argue

---

[20] 'India's National Conditions Blue Book' (2011–12) released by China in May 2013 discusses India's economic progress and potential. The first of its kind, jointly issued by the Yunnan University and the Social Sciences Academic Press, the report recognizes India's economic potential while discussing other problem areas including gender, urbanization and even national security. See *Yunnan Daily Press*, 'Yunnan University in Charge of Publishing'.

[21] Malik, 'India's Response to China's Rise', 183.

[22] Ibid.

[23] Zuo et al., Dragon Dance with Elephant, 321–31.

that China has much to learn from India's success in developing a modern and sophisticated financial sector as well as the distinction achieved by its IITs. Ma Jia Li's *Rising Elephant: Pay Attention to India (Jue qi Zhong de ju Xiang: Guan Zhu Yin Du)* traces India's growing economic prowess along with its military modernization and security aspects, and analyses India's relations with major powers and developing countries. Another prominent academic Shen Dingli, while discussing the relationship, assigns higher priority to 'peaceful coexistence' than 'national sovereignty' as a determinant of bilateral ties.[24]

Distinguished Chinese academics like Ji Xianlin have also been supportive of closer bilateral ties. An Indologist and the first Chinese to be awarded Padma Bhushan (2008), he had secretly translated the Ramayana during the Cultural Revolution.[25] He was not only one of the earliest advocates of closer Sino-India ties, but he also believed that greater bilateral cultural exchanges have enriched China's culture and emphasized cultural interactions and acculturation: 'The reason our Chinese culture has been able to remain consistent and rich throughout its 5,000 years of history is closely linked to translation. Translations from other cultures have helped infuse new blood into our culture'.[26] Cultural engagement is also emphasized by Tan Chung, the doyen of Chinese cultural studies in India, as a binding force in strengthening Sino-Indian relations. Awarded the Padma Bhushan in 2010, he regards the advent of Indian Buddhism into China a 'dream story' and like Ji argues about Sino-Indian cultural fusion significantly transforming Chinese culture.[27] The cultural aspect of the relationship is analysed in his *Tagore and China*, which illustrates Tagore's love, passion and empathy for Chinese culture and civilization. Tan Chung's other work, *Rise of the Asian Giants: Dragon–Elephant Tango*, also focusses on shared and divergent experiences of modernization and economic reform while analysing the ramifications thereof, in each country's role in global affairs.

---

[24] Dingli, 'Building China-India Reconciliation'.
[25] Wikinews.org, 'Ji Xianlin'.
[26] Ibid.
[27] Tan Chung, Historical Chindian Paradigm, 196.

India's great power ambitions have often been rationalized by Chinese scholars such as Yuan by reference to Nehru. According to Yuan, 'India, constituted as she is, cannot play a secondary part in the world. She will either count for a great deal or not count at all'.[28] The Indo-US civil nuclear deal is perceived by China as an important step by India towards the goal and also for balancing China in the region.[29] China has, however, been pragmatic in suppressing its discomfort over the Indo-US nuclear deal with the former Premier indicating that China was 'forth-coming and supportive' of international civil nuclear energy cooperation with India.[30] There appears to be a clear realization on part of the Chinese establishment of India's determination to seek external collaboration for building domestic nuclear capacities in its national interest. There was, therefore, no major official response on PM Modi's visit to Mongolia, a country considered the backyard of China, and with whom India is keen on establishing nuclear cooperation.

## ECONOMIC ENGAGEMENT

India had figured in the Chinese Admiral Zheng He's expeditions when his fleet crossed the Indian Ocean several centuries ago. On his way to India in 410 CE, Zheng erected a tablet in Sri Lanka written in Chinese, Persian and Tamil, *calling on the Hindu deities to bless a world of free trade*.[31] Close economic engagement with India has been ongoing and was an aspiration of the Ming dynasty too. The current robust Sino-Indian economic engagement resonate the ancient vision.[32] Both the Chinese and Indian leaderships have been cognizant of the growing economic engagement and are keen on expanding its depth and scope.

High level visits by heads of states from the two countries are increasingly dominated by the business and economic agenda. This

---

[28] Yuan, 'The Dragon and the Elephant', 126.

[29] Malik, 'India's Response to China's Rise', 184.

[30] *The Indian Express*, 'N-deal: China is Supportive'.

[31] Tharoor, *Pax Indica*, 133.

[32] In 2011, bilateral trade reached a record US$ 74 billion with China becoming India's largest trading partner.

first became evident from the large delegation of around 400 delegates representing more than 250 Chinese firms including top-notch companies that accompanied the former Premier Wen during his visit to India in 2010. Since then, large business entourages have become conspicuous parts of official visits, as noticed during Premier Li Keqiang and President Xi Jinping's visits to India in 2013 and 2014 respectively. Indeed, business appears to have taken precedence over resolution of the border dispute as indicated by reports during PM Modi's visit to China in May 2015.[33]

From an Indian perspective, this visit was noteworthy with three Indian state Chief Ministers (Maharashtra, Gujarat and Karnataka) accompanying Modi, reflecting the role that Indian states have begun playing in deepening economic engagement with Chinese provinces as well as the larger role that they are beginning to acquire in India's overall external engagement. From a Chinese perspective, greater engagement with some Indian states also serves long-term strategic benefits.[34] Greater sub-national engagement between China and India would contribute to flourishing of overall economic ties that have contributed significantly to a more positive Sino-Indian relationship. Confidence building measures (CBMs) like the annual bilateral strategic economic dialogue (SED) institutionalized by the two countries focusing on collaboration in infrastructure development, energy efficiency and water conservation are important steps in this regard. These are significant strategic initiatives, particularly when noted in the context that apart from the US, India is the only country with whom China has an SED, highlighting the significance it attaches to the economic relationship.[35]

---

[33] *The Times of India*, 'China Keen on Indian Business'.

[34] China is keen on investing in the electronics industry in Tamil Nadu under its commitment to 'Make in India'. As one of India's major states on its east coast with close proximity to the Indian Ocean, Tamil Nadu with its ethnic Tamil population influences Indian foreign policy towards Sri Lanka. The geostrategic importance of Tamil Nadu makes it an important spot for greater Chinese 'strategic' commercial presence. Similarly, investment interests in mining projects in Rajasthan—one of India's bordering states with Pakistan—is also understandable.

[35] Palit, 'Wen in India'.

Trade has been the biggest driver of bilateral economic engagement. During the last decade, China became India's largest merchandise trade partner, while India also became one of China's top-10 trade partners. However, the unbalanced pattern of bilateral trade has been a cause of concern for India for several years. A Trade Negotiations Committee established during PM Modi's visit to China is expected to suggest solutions improving access of major Indian exports, like pharmaceuticals, in the Chinese market. India has also been trying to attract greater Chinese capital in domestic industries such as in 'Make in India' industries. Chinese business presence in India has indeed been increasing over time despite security concerns of the Indian establishment. Indian telecom has been one of the biggest beneficiaries in this respect notwithstanding security issues. India's mobile revolution has been fed by a steady supply of imported equipment from China.[36] Indeed, rapid expansion of domestic telecom service networks in India was significantly enabled by Chinese imports, bridging the gap in supply of telecom equipment produced by a limited-scale, low-capacity indigenous equipment manufacturing industry.[37] Chinese companies—Huawei Technologies and ZTE—were initially barred from bidding for the state-owned BSNL's supply of mobile phone lines due to security concerns. Over time, they have become providers of crucial technology for facilitating broadband wireless services.[38]

Electricity production is another area where there are substantive collaborations between Indian and Chinese businesses with the scope of the collaborations including both conventional coal-based thermal power as well as renewable energy (wind and solar power).[39] Growing

---

[36] Palit, 'China-India Strategic Economic Dialogue'.

[37] Ibid.

[38] *China Daily*, 'Chinese Lend a Hand in India 4G', 3.

[39] Reliance Power is collaborating with China Datang—one of the largest state-owned power producers in mainland China—for developing and operating power projects in India, including the 4,000 MW ultra-mega power project at Sasan in Madhya Pradesh. The Power Construction Corporation of China is collaborating with the Infrastructure Leasing & Financial Services Limited in building a thermal power complex. China's third largest wind-turbine manufacturer, China Ming Yang Wind Power Group, also has an agreement with

Chinese business presence in India is augmenting people-to-people contact as is visible from Chinese technicians teaching their Indian counterparts specialized welding skills at the Chandankyari steel plant in Jharkhand while picking up Hindi and local habits like chewing *paan*.[40]

Indian business presence in China has been dominated by IT and IT-enabled businesses.[41] TCS has been able to achieve 'strategic' breakthroughs by providing core banking solutions to Chinese banks and developing trading systems for Shanghai's Foreign Exchange Centre.[42] China is growing into a major research and development centre for innovative solutions for Indian IT firms as is evident from facilities established by Infosys and Wipro.[43] NIIT and Aptech have become distinguished brands in providing IT training and skills to the local populations in China. Other notable Indian industrial presence in China includes the Mahindra & Mahindra in automobiles and Suzlon in production of renewable energy. The State Bank of India has been steadily expanding operations in China, while the Industrial and Commercial Bank of China (ICBC) is doing so in India.

Bilateral economic engagement is also facilitating other initiatives such as China's plans to develop new infrastructure for improving the flow of Indian pilgrims to Tibet. Apart from creating new infrastructure capacities in the Kailash and Mansarovar areas, China is expected to relax visas and permit controls for allowing visitors to Mansarovar in order to extend their journeys to other areas in Tibet, like Lhasa.[44] Business-to-business synergies are again proving significant in

---

the Reliance Power for entering India's green energy market. Finally, China's Suntech Power is collaborating with India's Sunborne Energy for building solar panels.

[40] Palit, 'China Crucial to India's Mobile Revolution', 16.

[41] Some of the noted examples are Infosys, Tata Consultancy Services (TCS), Wipro, Aptech and the NIIT.

[42] *China Daily*, 'India's Tata Consultancy to Triple Investment in China'.

[43] Wipro also has manufacturing operations for its consumer care and lighting group at Dongguan, Guangdong province and an infrastructure group in Changzhou, Jiangsu province. Both have generated sizeable local employment. For details see *Shanghai Daily*, 'Both Nations Benefit from High-tech Partnership', B5.

[44] *The Sunday Times*, 'China Builds Infrastructure for Mansarovar Pilgrims'.

infrastructure-building with the Hyderabad-based Ramky Infrastructure and Jiangshu Provincial Transportation Engineering Group collaborating for building the Srinagar–Banihal road project in Jammu and Kashmir.[45]

Sino-Indian collaboration in the regional infrastructure space is increasingly expanding beyond the bilateral domain in third countries, as Chinese Vice-Foreign Minister Fu Ying has indicated: 'The need for connectivity can be better met if China, India and South Asian countries work together and avail themselves of the good opportunity offered by the strong growth in the region'.[46] Both countries are working with Bangladesh and Myanmar for rebuilding Myanmar's historic 'Stilwell Road' connecting Kunming and Arunachal Pradesh, which can reduce transportation costs between China and India by 30 per cent and boost trade between India's Northeast and China.[47] The two countries might take their collaboration to a higher level if India becomes an active participant in China's OBOR. As discussed in the earlier chapter, India's non-committal approach to the OBOR is beginning to emerge as a constraint in the progress of regional connectivity initiatives like the BCIM. Indeed, as argued earlier again, while being a project largely owned by China and advancing its national interests, the OBOR can still produce opportunities for Indian industries by creating new and upgrading existing regional infrastructure capacities. These capacities can certainly enable India to obtain greater access in regional markets, particularly in South Asia, Southeast Asia and of course, China. Complete dissociation with the OBOR might result in loss of certain vital economic opportunities and is a factor that needs to be thought through hard. Further, in the larger context of expanding economic opportunities, it is also important to revisit the visa policy between China and India. Though India now allows tourists from China to apply for visas online, scrutiny and scanning remain, impacting the volume of Chinese tourist inflows into the country. Globally, Chinese tourists are among the largest visitors in all parts of the world and would be a boon for India's tourism industry if visas are issued quicker and hassle free.

---

[45] *INCHINCLOSER*, 'India–China up Bilateral Co-operation'.
[46] *The Hindu*, 'Eyeing Connectivity to South Asia'.
[47] *INCHINCLOSER*, 'China, India, Myanmar Construct the Stilwell Road'.

## CULTURAL INITIATIVES

Cultural interactions and PD are relatively less discussed in the larger India–China bilateral context compared to economic engagement. However, bilateral cultural interaction has been increasing rapidly with almost all official policy pronouncements (including the Joint Statement of 2015, issued during Modi's visit to China) mentioning such initiatives and the importance of people-to-people communication in defining the discourse on bilateral ties.

### Public Diplomacy and State Visits

PD through high-level state visits has become a major conduit for augmenting people-to-people communication with both leaderships trying to exploit the potentials of such visits. These visits provide opportunities for announcing policy initiatives that are major CBMs. For example, the announcement of e-visas for Chinese tourists visiting India was a key CBM during Modi's state visit to China in 2015. E-visas would not only increase inflow of Chinese tourists to India and boost tourism revenue, but they would also correct impressions about India being reluctant to allow easy access to Chinese visitors due to mistrust. The increasing number of mutual high-level visits in recent years has allowed the leaderships to communicate effective messages to their audiences across the border such as Premier Li's statement during his visit to New Delhi in 2013: 'We should see each other's development as major opportunities for ourselves and we have far more common interests than differences…'.[48]

These visits have occasionally been successful CBMs themselves, such as Premier Li's 'off the protocol' visit[49] a month after the Ladakh impasse

---

[48] *The Times of India*, 'China is Not a Threat to India'.
[49] Though China and India have developed high-level visits as one of the preferred tools for engaging each other at the highest level, it needs to be pointed out that opinions in India interpreted the visit as an attempt by the new Chinese leadership to prod India to sign the bilateral BDCA providing China greater strategic leverage along the Line of Actual Control (LAC). See Jacob, 'The friendly Chinaman'.

in May 2013, underlining the willingness to ease tensions. The follow-up visit by PM Singh to Beijing in October 2013—the first instance of consecutive visits by Premiers of the two countries in the same year since 1954[50]—and the Border Defence Cooperation Agreement (BDCA) signed during the visit and hailed by the Chinese state media as a 'landmark legal document' emphasize the key role that the state visits have been playing in building trust and 'deepening practical cooperation across the board'.[51]

Viewed from the official Indian perspective, state visits have been considered significant for strengthening bilateral ties by both the Congress and BJP. While Rajiv Gandhi's visit in December 1988 revived frozen ties,[52] the BJP government in 1998 employed high-level visits for expanding economic and cultural exchanges marking a 'watershed in the revival of the process of normalization of relations with China'.[53] State visits gained more traction with PM Vajpayee's visit to China in 2003 and the signing of the first comprehensive document on developing bilateral relations at the highest level.[54] This was followed by the establishment of a strategic and cooperative partnership for peace and prosperity in the Joint Statement of 2005 issued during former President Hu's visit to India. The statement emphasized enhanced people-to-people communication with specific mention of 'cultural festivals' for increasing mutual awareness.

Chinese Premier Wen's visit to India in 2010, while focusing primarily on economic engagement, did not overlook people-to-people exchanges. Interacting with the Indian media, Hu Zheng Yue, China's

---

[50] In 1954, China's first Premier Zhou Enlai and India's first PM Jawaharlal Nehru had visited India and China respectively.

[51] Krishnan, 'China Highlights Outcome'.

[52] Former Indian PM Rajiv Gandhi's views on the India–China relationship are worth recalling. In a speech at the Tsinghua University he had stated, 'what must not be forgotten in a listing of differences is a listing of commonality in our world outlook. There has been significant parallelism in the views expressed by India and China on a wide range of issues relating to world security, the international political order, the new international economic order, global concerns in regard to environment and space'.

[53] Dixit, *India's Foreign Policy and Its Neighbours*, 95.

[54] Ministry of External Affairs, 'India–China Bilateral Relations'.

Assistant Foreign Minister, mentioned that China hoped to 'enhance mutual understanding to gain more popular support for our relations to maintain positive cooperation for peace'.[55] Premier Wen added new vigour and warmth to people-to-people interaction through his novel outreach with students of one of the Indian schools—the Tagore International School in New Delhi. Underscoring the high esteem for Rabindranath Tagore in China, the Premier was able to touch a chord with young Indian minds as he elaborated on Chinese cultural heritage as well.[56]

The youth have indeed emerged significant in the vision of both leaderships for enhancing people-to-people communication with high focus on reciprocal visits of youth delegations.[57] The current Indian leadership, which appears keen on consolidating the engagement with China, also has its focus on connecting with the youth and the new generations. This was evident from PM Modi's outreach with the local Chinese through the popular *Weibo*—similar to Twitter and Facebook and widely used by the Chinese youth—even before he set foot in China. The emphasis on connecting with the youth was also evident in PM Modi's decision to speak at the Tsinghua University during his visit primarily for shaping young perceptions on India: 'you will feel the change in India. And, you can see it in our growth rate. It has now increased to 7.5 %, and we are encouraged by international experts speak in one voice of higher growth rates'[58] indicating his government's position on turning India's economy.

High-level visits are also being utilised for the strategic purpose of delivering specific messages. PM Modi underpinned India's foreign policy activism during his visit to China while asking the Chinese leadership to 'reconsider its approach on some of the issues that hold us back from realizing full potential of our relationship'.[59] He was referring inter alia to the large imbalance in bilateral trade—an irksome issue for

[55] *DNA*, 'Wen Jiabao's Visit to India'.
[56] *Rediff News*, 'Grandpa Wen'.
[57] Ministry of External Affairs, 'India–China Bilateral Relations'.
[58] *The Times of India*, 'Read Full text: PM Modi's speech at Tsinghua University, Beijing' (2015).
[59] *IndustryWeek*, 'India's Modi Tells China to "reconsider" Approach'.

India, on which, despite Indian concerns expressed time and again, China has hardly been proactive. Modi's candid approach came through the discussion when he stated that 'in the long-term, the partnership was not sustainable if Indian industry didn't get better access to the Chinese market'.[60] Earlier, during her visit to China in February 2015 for attending a trilateral meeting between China, India and Russia, the Indian External Affairs Minister had conveyed India's interest in all three countries coming down firmly on terrorism. This was notwithstanding China's close ties with Pakistan. It is becoming increasingly clear that the Modi government would not be hesitant to utilize high level state visits as occasions for pursuing the 'soft' strategy of PD along with occasional emphasis on 'hard' national interests.

## PEOPLE-TO-PEOPLE COMMUNICATION: NON-STATE ACTORS AND BUDDHIST TRADITIONS COMPLEMENT STATE ACTORS

Culture figures prominently in several Sino-Indian initiatives for augmenting people-to-people contacts. India has been trying to utilise the charm of Bollywood in this regard. Indian films are extremely popular in China like they are elsewhere.[61] The Shanghai International Film Festival held in June 2013, screened 18 Indian films ranging from early-Bollywood productions (*Raja Harishchandra*) to recent movies (*Jolly LLB*) that were received well by the Chinese audience. Along with films, the Indian television has also been connecting with the Chinese audience as is visible from the sub-titled telecast of *Satyamev Jayate*—an Indian television show presented by leading Bollywood actor Amir Khan and dealing with social issues—in China. The significance of enhancing cultural communication is underlined by the 'zhong guo gong gong wai jiao yan jue bao gao' (China's Public Foreign Relations Research Report)

---

[60] Madan, 'Modi's Trip to China'.

[61] The evergreen 1950s Raj Kapoor starrer *Awaara* has apparently been viewed around 40,000 times on Weibo while the more recent movie *Wake up Sid* has also been watched an almost equal number of time.

that takes note of various ongoing efforts as necessary for facilitating deeper interaction between the two countries.[62]

A prominent example of the joint initiatives by two countries in this regard is the effort to employ Rabindranath Tagore, or Zhu Zhendan (*thunder of the Oriental dawn*)[63] as a 21st century icon promoting Sino-Indian intercultural communication. Given the great respect and admiration for Tagore in China, there is probably no better figure that can be highlighted as a common cultural emblem by both countries. Tagore's spiritualism continues to echo in China with an enormous amount of his various writings having been translated into Chinese from Bengali.[64] Tagore's 150th birth anniversary was widely celebrated in China in 2011. Marking the occasion, several Chinese publishing houses (the Jiangsu Wenyi, Communication University of China and Tourism Education) published collected works of Chinese scholars and poets like late Zheng Zhenduo and Bingxin on Tagore for the last 100 years. While Chinese institutions staged Tagore's plays in Chinese, the Indian Embassy in China complemented the celebrations by collaborating with leading Chinese institutions for holding seminars, exhibitions and movie screenings on Tagore.[65]

Along with Tagore, Gandhi—another Indian, widely respected and regarded in China—is also emerging as a common point for greater people-to-people interface, as is evident from the establishment of a Centre on Gandhian Studies in Fudan University during PM Modi's visit to China. This latest centre is an addition to an earlier centre for Indian Studies, established in the Peking University in 2003, and various 'chairs' on Indian studies set up in Shenzhen, Jinan, Fudan and the Yunnan Universities.[66]

*Yoga* is also being widely employed to acquaint the Chinese with the ancient Indian culture. With India's popularity in China increasing through proliferation of *yoga* teaching, several private *yoga* centres have

---

[62] 'China's Public Foreign Relations Research Report'.
[63] Chinese scholar Liang Qichao had presented Tagore with the Chinese name when the latter visited China in April 1924.
[64] *Hindustan Times*, 'Tagore's Novels, Plays Translated'.
[65] *Embassy of India*, 'Joint Communique of the Republic of India'.
[66] Ministry of External Affairs, 'India–China Bilateral Relations'.

come up across China. Apart from Beijing, there are *yoga* studios in Ningbo, the port city in Zhejiang province close to Shanghai where both local and international faculty from the city's Nottingham University campus and others gather for lessons. Many new *yoga* schools are coming up in Beijing and elsewhere in China and large-scale events (the India–China *Yoga* Summit at Guangzhou in 2011)[67] are contributing to the spread of *yoga*. The latest push by India on *yoga* was through the celebration of the World Yoga Day on 21 June, an occasion that was marked enthusiastically in China.[68]

Buddhism was, and continues to remain, a shared philosophy reverberating across vast sections of both countries. As alluded in the earlier chapter, Nayan Chanda's drawing of attention to the 'critical role that religious preachers and Buddhism played in reaching out and connecting with various communities' finds resonance in India's engagement with China as well. Chinese scholar Tan Yun-Shan has aptly commented that 'Buddhism was born in India, enriched in China, and then scattered over the world'.[69] Therefore, it is hardly surprising that Buddhism is being regarded a facilitator of contemporary cultural interaction between India and China. Former Indian President Pratibha Patil inaugurated an Indian style Buddhist Temple in Luoyang in Central China—one of the four great ancient capitals[70]—in May 2010, and dedicated it as a gift from India to China.[71] Discussions and discourses going on in both countries on the role of Buddhism in defining Asia and its centrality in Asian history[72] have been engaging both Chinese and Indian scholars. OBOR—a major strategic-economic initiative of the Chinese government for regional connectivity—draws its geographical vision from the ancient path taken by Buddhist pilgrims for travelling across Asia.

---

[67] Iyenger, 'China–India yoga summit'.
[68] *Shanghai Daily*, 'First World Yoga Day Celebrated in Shanghai'.
[69] Chanda, *Bound Together*, 183.
[70] The phrase, four great ancient capitals of China (*Zhong Guo si da gu du*) refers to Beijing, Nanjing, Luoyang and Chang'an (Xian).
[71] Ministry of External Affairs, 'India–China Bilateral Relations'.
[72] *The Hindu Business Line*, 'India, China to Hold Cultural Summit'.

The spirit of Buddhism has also been conspicuous in the interfaces between President Xi and PM Modi. During Xi's visit to Gujarat in 2014, Modi highlighted the importance of Gujarat in Buddhist links connecting India and China by mentioning Hiuen Tsang's visit to the Valabhi University in Gujarat in 629 AD. Hiuen Tsang was further responsible for Xi inviting Modi to Xi'an in May 2015 as this was where Hiuen Tsang spent his last years after returning from India. Indeed, Buddhism and the shared heritage was responsible for the Chinese authorities deviating from protocol by welcoming Modi at Xi'an—an exceptional departure from the established norm of receiving heads of states at the national capital of Beijing only. Future Sino-Indian engagement, no doubt, will continue to rely on Buddhism as a key driver, particularly the great tradition of cultural and social accommodation displayed by Hiuen Tsang and many other Chinese pilgrims, who, as China scholar John Kieschnick notes, were 'more open to the habits, customs, foods and furniture of India than, for instance, the Chinese literati, for whom Chineseness was much more a central part of their identity'.[73]

China's involvement in the revival of the ancient Buddhist university of Nalanda[74] is another example of the common Buddhist chord connecting not only India and China but several other Asian countries like Japan, Korea and Singapore as well. China is keen on exploiting the strategic capital of Buddhism in strengthening multi-country cooperation as is evident from the Chinese Foreign Minister's suggestion to partner India and Sri Lanka to develop tourist routes based on the shared 'abundant Buddhist resources'.[75] Buddhism clearly will be a focal point in facilitating strategic cooperation both bilaterally between India and China, as well as in regional initiatives involving both.

---

[73] Kieschnick, *The impact of Buddhism*, 262.
[74] On 28 March 2006 the 11th President of India, A.P.J. Abdul Kalam proposed the idea while addressing the Joint Session of the Bihar Vidhan Mandal for revival of Nalanda University.
[75] *China Daily*, 'Sri Lanka Affirms Sino Ties', 9.

## The Role of the Media

Media has played a key role in the Sino-Indian relationship in influencing perceptions. Scholars and academics studying the relationship agree on the rather harsh posture of media in this regard, manifesting mostly through opinions and commentaries exaggerating threat perceptions and security concerns about each other. Reporting on each other too often lacks objectivity and tends to be cynical. Much of this is due to a lack of informed opinion about each other. From the Chinese media's perspective, India is also a relatively lower priority, well behind the attention and space devoted to coverage of the US, Europe, Japan as well as the Arab world. Furthermore, there is precise little knowledge in China and India about the various complexities of each other (multiple languages and the constitutional division of administrative authority between the Centre and states in India; and the variation in cultural characteristics and habits across provinces in China).[76] Matters have worsened due to the absence of adequate on-ground correspondents from China and India based in India and China respectively, and reliance on third party news agencies, usually Western media sources, for reporting on each other.[77]

However, it is encouraging to note that both the Indian and Chinese media are trying to adopt increasingly pragmatic and objective postures in their depiction of each other. The growth of social media has been important in this regard as it has enabled state actors to expand communication and outreach with foreign audiences (the Indian Embassy in China's account on the popular Chinese micro blogging site, *Sina Weibo*, has many followers).[78] Greater interface between Chinese and Indian media is also being encouraged by both the leaderships.[79]

[76] The author's interview with a journalist from the CCTV China.
[77] Chinese media has greater presence in India than Indian media in China. *Xinhua*, the *People's Daily* and the *CCTV* all have representatives in India. The *China Daily* and the *CCTV* also have some Indian staffers. *The Hindu* is the only mainstream Indian paper with the longest history of a correspondent in China.
[78] Ministry of External Affairs, 'India–China Bilateral Relations'.
[79] The China–India Joint Statement of 2015 aims to institutionalize the 'High Level Media Forum' and has tasked the Ministry of External Affairs and the SCIO to convene it annually and alternately in India and China.

Awareness about lack of understanding between the two countries has led to efforts by Indian dailies like the *Financial Express* to bring out regular columns on China.

Apart from shaping perceptions, outreach by the media has the potential to achieve strategic ambitions as well. The Chinese media's efforts in this regard are becoming noticeable compared with almost lack of similar efforts by Indian media. The CRI currently broadcasts programmes in four Indian languages—Hindi, Bengali, Urdu and Tamil. It has recently entered into an MOU with Bharathiar University in Coimbatore for establishing a CC for facilitating cultural interactions and business between China and the state of Tamil Nadu.[80] Preparations are underway for building more on-air CCs in India[81] for spreading Chinese language and facilitating a better understanding of the neighbour.[82] The efforts are strategically significant given that China has not been successful in opening CIs in India for showcasing Chinese culture and heritage the way it has in several other countries.

## Education

There is little doubt about the growing urge to learn Mandarin in India which has increased rapidly as it has been in other parts of the world. Mandarin-learning centres have come up in several Indian cities along with Chinese Studies programmes in leading Indian universities and institutes (Table 10.1). In the last few years, demand for Mandarin courses has expanded manifold with more than 300 students enrolling at various colleges affiliated to University of Delhi, up from a mere 30–40

---

[80] China's ambition to project a strong naval force in the Indian Ocean partly necessitates its engagement policy towards Tamil Nadu.

[81] Confucius Institute at CRI. Available at: http://english.cri.cn/7046/2009/12/10/167s534682.htm (accessed on 18 January 2010).

[82] Economics and language popularity goes hand in hand. This thesis once again has been proved in the Gujarat case. Gujarat's excellent infrastructure and connectivity provides a great alternative to Chinese companies looking at reducing cost with an easy access to Gulf and the European markets. Gujarat's economic value is responsible for the growing popularity of its language in China. See *INCHINCLOSER*, 'The Chinese are Learning Gujarati', and *The Diplomat*, 'Chinese Companies Eyeing Gujarat for Investments'.

**Table 10.1**
*China Study Centres in India*

| State/University | Programme |
| --- | --- |
| West Bengal, Visva Bharati, Shantiniketan | The first Sinological Institute (1927) in India and was established by the Buddhist scholar, Tan Yun Shan, a contemporary of Chiang Kai Shek and Mao Tse Tung, upon being invited by Tagore. |
| New Delhi, Jawaharlal Nehru University (JNU) | Centre for East Asian Studies |
| New Delhi | Institute of Chinese Studies |
| New Delhi, Rajiv Gandhi Institute for Contemporary Studies (RGICS) | China Studies |
| New Delhi, Delhi University | East Asian Studies |
| Chennai | Chennai Centre of Chinese Studies |
| IIT-Madras, Chennai | China Study Centre |

*Source:* Compiled from various sources.

less than a decade ago.[83] The interest is primarily driven by China's expanding economy and the opportunities it offers. Given the salience of Indo-China engagement and economic relations, efforts of the private sector and business in expanding Mandarin-learning opportunities need to be complemented by greater similar initiatives from public sector higher education institutions. Such efforts can similarly pave ways for greater interface between graduate students from Chinese and Indian universities, which, till now, is much limited than its potential. Much of the deficit in this important aspect of engagement, notwithstanding the interest of many Indians, particularly the youth, to be a part of the Chinese economic growth story, continues to be hampered by security concerns. Though CBMs have been in place, as the chapter discusses, a serious trust deficit still exists between the two neighbours which

---

[83] Jetley, 'Why Indians Have No Choice'.

necessitates an effective change of people's mentality towards the big neighbour. Learning languages in an attempt to know the neighbour has not been one-sided with many Chinese, also showing an interest to pick up Indian languages.[84]

Education has been effectively employed to make each other's presence felt in both the countries. An important contribution by India in China has been in IT education with the NIIT Global establishing several IT training and software literacy franchises in China and running training courses in collaboration with a large number of Chinese universities. Infosys China Education Centre in Jiaxing, Zhejiang province is the first foreign residential education centre of Infosys and has trained more than 1,000 school and college students in IT.[85] Scholarships and education exchanges are important in enhancing people-to-people contacts and alleviating 'trust deficit'. The Huawei Maitree Scholarship Programme enabling Indian students to move to China for undergraduate and postgraduate studies is an excellent example[86] as are the Indian government's annual scholarships to Chinese students for higher studies in India.[87] The Sino-India Joint Communique of 2010 was significant by its emphasis on expanding education exchanges and establishing the India–China Outstanding College Students Exchange Programme through consultations[88] while deciding on an interschool communication mechanism for language teaching between Chinese and Indian schools.[89] School-level initiatives, though nascent, are also gradually picking up.[90] Following the Joint Communique of 2010, both countries are working on finalizing an agreement on mutual

---

[84] Apart from Sanskrit, Hindi and Bengali have long traditions of being taught in China. The Beijing University has begun teaching Gujarati in collaboration with the Gujarat University.

[85] Infosys, 'Infosys China Education'.

[86] Scholarship-positions.com, '2011 Huawei Maitree Scholarship'.

[87] Embassy of India, 'Academic Studies'.

[88] *Embassy of India*, 'Joint Communique of the Republic of India'.

[89] An agreement between the CI Headquarter and India's CBSE has led to introduction of Mandarin as a foreign language in 11,000 CBSE affiliated schools from Class 6. For details, see *Rediff News*, 'Grandpa Wen'.

[90] Delhi's Tagore International School has an MOU with Shanghai's Jinyuan Senior High School for teaching students through video conferencing.

recognition of degrees and diplomas.[91] This has particularly become important with more and more Indian students travelling to China for studying medicine, engineering and management.[92]

Education is expected to remain a major avenue for greater Sino-Indian engagement. In fact, according to Chinese Ministry reports in April 2016, the countries along the belt and road, including India,[93] have grown as sources of international students in China.[94] As of now, it is more of a one-way traffic with much greater number of Indian students moving to China for higher studies. Management and business education in China have become top draws for Indian students followed by the high global ranks achieved by Chinese institutions—School of Management, Fudan University; School of Economics and Management, Tsinghua University; Guanghua School of Management and Peking University. Greater movement of Indian students to Chinese university campuses has been important in building people-to-people contact and alleviating 'trust deficit'. More collaborative efforts by education institutes (Renmin–Jindal India China Centre on Negotiations for research on Asian law and business) along with initiatives focusing on business synergies—the annual China–India Cooperation Forum organized by the CEIBS—are clearly going to make a difference in altering mutual perceptions.

## CONCLUSION

India's rising priority for China is evident from its figuring in the new 'major-nation diplomacy' of the new Chinese leadership. Notwithstanding persistence of bilateral differences and disputes, robust economic ties

---

[91] *Embassy of India,* 'Joint Communique of the Republic of India'.

[92] In 2010, there were more than 8,000 Indian students pursuing medical studies in China, motivated by good facilities, competitive fees and reduced chances of good medical study in India due to intense competition for limited seats.

[93] As of early 2016 India still has reservations joining the China-led OBOR, though many have been suggesting that the initiative might prove beneficial for India.

[94] India is still not a part of the initiative. See *China Daily,* 'International Student Numbers on the Rise', 12.

and enhanced people-to-people contact through historical linkages like Buddhism and new connections created by state and non-state actor initiatives in culture and education are establishing the foundation for even wider and deeper bilateral engagement. Both countries have also begun looking at each other's strategic ambitions and national interests more objectively. The imperative of building trust between Asia's two major powers for enabling their respective rises should continue in as uncomplicated fashion as possible.

Positive and constructive engagement between China and India indeed necessitates deployment of soft power. Leaderships of both countries appear convinced by the virtues of soft power in this regard, particularly in connecting with the youth for augmenting greater contacts, meaningful communication and more benign national perceptions. The younger generations in India are displaying a more open and receptive attitude towards China as is evident from the rising number of Indian students in China as well as a steady increase in inflows of tourists. The younger Chinese, while evidently curious to know more about India, are searching for more contemporary positives. The fact that India's problems and limitations get covered far more extensively than its positives in both international and domestic media does not help in building benign perceptions, particularly in China, where information about India, as such, is limited. Most Chinese identify Indian democracy with corruption, poverty and apathy: many distinguish between Indian and Western democracies in this regard with far more positive impression of the latter. While many Chinese academics and experts recognize India's virtues in a holistic manner and accept its rise, particularly economic progress and military capacities, most of the Chinese youth still comprehend these as limited to Buddhism and Bollywood, occasionally punctuated by IT. Indian soft power has a considerable distance to travel in this regard in China. The challenge of connecting to the youth can be overcome by a more judicious and unconventional approach to expanding people-to-people communication as discussed variously in this Chapter. Beginning from greater emphasis on expanding the learning of Mandarin at graduate education level and encouraging greater interface between students of both countries, taking India to China through mediums particularly appealing to the youth—films, music, *yoga*, food— and packaging the same for drawing the young Chinese to India should make considerable difference to growth of mutual perceptions among the young India and China over time.

While the work on building trust should proceed unimpeded, it is perhaps important to take stock of the current engagement policies and examine whether they can be refashioned for making both countries more attractive to each other's core constituencies. The Chinese interest in contemporary India, for example, has increased manifold due to the Chinese fascination for Bollywood—films and music—as well as Indian accomplishments in *yoga* and IT. With joint film productions already being planned, there is no reason why more Indian film festivals, including regional films, should not be showcased in China, and why similar festivals held in India should not have segments devoted to modern Chinese cinema for attracting both the audiences. India's success in institutionalizing the World Yoga Day has been enthusiastically responded in China and offers India a great opportunity for building 'out-of-the-box' packages like *Yoga* demonstrations in chosen centres across the country for attracting Chinese and global tourists. These nuanced applications are expected to add more teeth to India's greater soft power outreach and achieve good results in people-to-people communications.

For India, engaging China is no longer a choice but a 'necessity'. China's overarching influence in the neighbourhood and in regional and global affairs leaves it with little choice other than constructive engagement for facilitating its own rise. Notwithstanding the shrill rhetoric in India's strategic community and the media about the China threat and attendant security concerns, India's benefits are far more in *pragmatic collaboration*. The Indian leadership has accepted this reality, as much as its Chinese counterpart has. Again, from the vantage point of the latter, while not being the topmost priority, as the largest and most populous neighbour with enormous economic potential and concomitant strategic capacities, India can no more be ignored by China; China's pragmatism has ensured that it does not. Time will reveal whether the sense of pragmatic collaboration and the emphasis on constructive engagement through greater use of soft power creates more benign impressions on both sides by denting the trust deficit.

# 11

# China's Soft Power: Strategic Outcomes and Structural Comparison with India

The paradigm of soft power in modern world is being shaped by China's exhaustive employment of the same. Given the historical sanctity of 'winning hearts and minds' in Beijing's external relations, its recourse to soft power for constructive engagement in modern times is natural. China has imparted the typical 'Chinese' flavour to soft power by making the latter comprehensive by combining cultural initiatives and PD with economic engagement, buoyed by efforts to build 'people-to-people' contacts through education and an active role of its media agencies. The ultimate objective of such a variegated strategy has been to secure a benign image for minimizing threat perceptions on its phenomenal rise.

Active deployment of soft power has not led to dilution of Chinese hard power. Indeed, China has been employing both in what might be interpreted as an effective demonstration of 'smart power'. Beijing's approach to international affairs in this regard resonate Gallarotti's observation: 'powerful states should seek to "optimize" their utilization of hard and soft power resources to maximize their influence and avoid undermining their positions by an over-reliance on either approach'.[1] The current Chinese leadership under President Xi Jinping has been emphatic in conveying the 'hard' posture: 'no foreign country should expect us to make a deal on our core interests and hope we will swallow the bitter pill…'.[2] However, at the very same forum—the Collective Study Session of the Politburo of the CPC in 2013—the concepts

---

[1] Gallarotti, *Cosmopolitan Power in International Relations*, 68–69.
[2] *Shanghai Daily*, 'Xi Vows No Compromises over China's Sovereignty'.

of 'peaceful development' and 'developing together' were highlighted vigorously. Another interesting display of smart power was at the celebrations for marking the 70th anniversary of the World War II in Beijing in September 2015, where an enormous display of China's military might was accompanied by Xi's decision to cut troops, as mentioned earlier. The 'peaceful' aspect of the latter announcement, however, did not go down as entirely convincing.[3] These conflicting imperatives will continue to generate paradoxes and controversies about China, and consistency should not be expected.

China is keen on assessing the strategic dividends of its soft power. This is evident from its conduct of China's National Image Global Survey in 2014 for examining its overall image. The survey points to its increasing recognition by the global community as a major power in the countries surveyed (the US, the UK, Australia, Japan, South Africa, India, Russia, Brazil and China).[4] Even the Washington-based Pew Research Centre in a survey conducted in September 2015 found that President Xi Jinping fared better in handling international issues compared to his counterparts Japanese Prime Minister Shinzo Abe and Indian Prime Minister Narendra Modi.[5] China would be keen on maintaining the 'reputation'.

As the earlier chapters have variously reiterated, benign image matters to China for securing global ambitions. The latter can hardly be fulfilled unless China's economic progress continues unabated and its producers obtain access to new markets and strategic resources. Moreover, domestic priorities necessitate the importance of making its economic development more egalitarian and geographically balanced by creating economic opportunities for all of its regions and provinces, particularly backward Western provinces like Xinjiang. Barring a benign image and positive outlook of China's regional policies by neighbours and extra-regional

---

[3] Che-Po Chan at Lingnan University, Hong Kong argues, 'they know that if they have to win any war, it must be a high-tech war', making the troop cut an effort at military reforms to keep pace with developments in modern military preparedness. See *International New York Times*, 'Xi of China Announces Military Cuts at Parade', 1, 4.

[4] *People's Daily Online*, 'China's Global Image on the Upswing'.

[5] *Pew Research Centre Publications*, 'How Asia-Pacific Publics See Each Other and Their National Leaders'.

powers, generous development assistance and commitment to infra-structure-building might not translate into wholesome strategic benefits. These engagements need to be coupled with a benign image for fulfilling China's long-term strategic goals.

It is, therefore, likely that major initiatives like the AIIB and OBOR for expanding connectivity and regional infrastructure would be combined with efforts for enhancing people-to-people communication. The latter would aim at minimizing adverse perceptions about China and the Chinese. While it is still early to decisively conclude on China's success in this regard, China's unique approach in combining the 'traditional' and the 'modern' for connecting to people remains a fascinating source of academic curiosity. As a rising power, China is notable for vigorous deployment of ancient culture and traditions (such as calligraphy, painting, martial arts and gifting pandas) for fascinating overseas audiences, along with equal emphasis on its contemporary evolution as a regional hub for higher education. Indeed, both cultural initiatives and education linkages have been remarkable in connecting China deeper with the rest of the world at a time when the world has been visibly impressed by its economic achievements and interested in knowing more about the Middle Kingdom. As a symbol of the socio-economic progress achieved by modern China reflected in the high rankings achieved by many of its universities,[6] education has emerged as a remarkable 'modern' element complementing the rich cultural heritage of the mainland.

Are the efforts paying off, and is China securing its much cherished 'benign' image? Opinion surveys like those mentioned earlier, as well as scattered impressions reflected in the earlier chapters, might not reveal the true picture, given that positive perceptions do coexist with nega-tive ones. As earlier chapters discovered, adverse impressions range from discomfort over high cost of Chinese development assistance and indebtedness to China, Chinese businesses displacing local jobs and livelihoods (in Southeast Asia, Africa, Latin America), Chinese investments being primarily resource-seeking with scant attention on

---

[6] According to *The Times Higher Education* (World University Rankings 2015), Tsinghua University (ranks 26) and Peking University (ranks 32) are amongst the top 100 global universities.

host country benefits (again seen in many African and Latin American countries), CIs being largely instruments of state propaganda (in Malaysia, Vietnam, US) to mistrust over the sincerity of China's claims of peaceful development and harmonious coexistence. The latter, again, draws steam from China's overt exercise of 'smart power' where the 'hard' necessarily accompanies the 'soft'.

Chinese 'neo-nationalism', manifesting through manifold aggressive intentions in the neighbourhood over territorial claims, such as in the South China Sea, is clearly an anti-thesis to notions of peaceful development and regional harmony. Such actions contradict the emphasis on peaceful development and harmonious coexistence with neighbours, as does China's unabated military modernization.[7] The latter can hardly avoid notions of aggressive posturing in a neighbourhood wary of China's rapid rise. Even restricting the PLA to homeland security, deterrence and reassurance—none of which has involved direct use of the armed forces to coerce other countries since the end of the Cold War as argued by Lampton[8]—has done little to assuage fears about the Chinese threat in the neighbourhood and beyond. Initiatives such as the OBOR rationalized on the virtuous and appealing ground of regional connectivity and mutual development can also not avoid impressions pointing to China's territorial ambitions. Indeed, as is natural for any great power, China is keen on making a lasting impact on the international order. The OBOR does contribute to fulfilment of the desire by proposing restructuring of relations across Asia to secure China's future as a great power.[9]

China is conscious of the limitations of its soft power and might refine its use through specific calibrations. Inviting hordes of foreign journalists for witnessing the leadership transition ceremony during the 18th People's Congress in November 2012 and allowing facilities for interpretation and other help is one such example. So are the Chinese media's efforts through its overseas arms to project an alternate 'Chinese' perspective on domestic issues as well as regional and global matters. It has also been encouraging

---

[7] China's military budget is the second largest in the world and is steadily increasing.
[8] Lampton, 'The Faces of Chinese Power'.
[9] Arase, 'China's Two Silk Roads', 28.

scholarship on the CPC for facilitating a better understanding of China. But there are issue-based difficulties in this regard. While selling the China story at a time when the West is suffering economic decline is easier, such efforts face increasing challenges in a world where explosive growth of social media has cramped room for control and censorship, throwing more light on several domestic issues that could be strategically embarrassing for China. Indeed, China's internal developments remain a major focus of the world, particularly the Western media, which is evident from the extensive coverages received by several incidents in recent times (blind activist Chen Guangcheng, its clamping down on activists and civil rights lawyers, and the stock market bloodbath in 2015). Beyond mainstream Western media, copious reflections on these incidents have surfaced on social blogging and networking sites. It is hardly easy for the Chinese media to counter these impressions with convincing 'alternate' perspectives. Such impressions also cannot be changed by inviting foreign journalists to momentous domestic events. This is probably where China's soft power is coming up against hurdles created by its own systems and structures forcing it to cope with the contradiction between China's projected benign image outside vis-à-vis the controls and restrictions it continues to maintain inside.

Ultimately, perhaps, the effectiveness of soft power can hardly be dissociated from the sincerity and genuineness with which it portrays a country, notwithstanding the grey impressions about the host country that it might convey on occasions. This is where the evaluation of the success of China's soft power acquires a piquant qualitative dimension. Many might argue that China has been able to secure its key strategic objective of winning allies in the neighbourhood and in many other parts of the world through vigorous exercise of various arms of its soft power: economic assistance, CD, high-level visits, education support and humanitarian assistance. Economic assistance has perhaps been the most instrumental among all these aspects in gaining allies for China. But does political and geostrategic support for major initiatives such as the OBOR and the AIIB, expanding a territorial agenda in the South China Sea, or containing many countries from diplomatically recognizing Taiwan, necessarily imply a 'benign' perception of China among all constituencies in supporting countries? Is China earning strategic support primarily because it provides, albeit partially, an alternative to the current unipolar world order, where countries are happy to hedge? Is China's support also a result of the gaps it can fill in supplying responses to many urgent requirements—public goods funding, education and disaster management support? If it is indeed so, then more than 'soft', it is probably 'smart' power, as argued earlier, that is earning China strategic capital. The benign image on top of all this could have come had the world been well and truly 'charmed' by China, where the impact of its CD would have had to be phenomenal. While Chinese CD has indeed helped in arousing curiosity and interest, whether its aggressive flavour, often amounting to propaganda, has rather been damaging to the goal of a benign image is worth pondering. This is precisely where the genuineness of soft power, or CD, in showing China in its true colours becomes significant.

## SOFT POWER OF CHINA AND INDIA: A COMPARATIVE EXPOSE[10]

China and India are engaging each other more for seizing the spillovers from constructive engagement. Business and economics are sustaining the engagement, while people-to-people contacts show distinct improvement. Domestic constituencies in both remain uncomfortable with each other, partly due to unresolved issues, as well as the discomfort associated with strategic elevations and ambitions of each other. Pragmatic leaderships, however, appear determined to stay on course and boost engagement. It is here, however, that perspectives on engagement must note the fundamental: India is yet to figure as high in China's priorities, as China does in India's. India's greater economic success and strategic significance will ensure its higher prioritization with China. Such efforts are already visible through initiatives like the bilateral SED. As of now, the relative figuring in each other's priorities reflects the dynamics of the current global order where China's greater strategic importance enables

---

[10] A detailed paper on this aspect was coauthored by the author in a separate commissioned paper earlier. For details, see Palit, 'Strategic Influence of Soft Power'.

it to *command* priority in engagement from other countries, big powers and small nations alike.

India, despite being compared incessantly with China, is yet to command a similar global pull. Some experts argue that India's soft power remains weaker than China's, given its lower socio-economic achievements.[11] Matters are not helped by India's poor track record on corruption and economic governance. Indeed, Xi Jinping's massive anti-corruption drive is yet to be matched on a similar scale by India. Thus, negativities continue to influence perceptions on India and China as much as they do in the rest of the world. Constructive bilateral engagement, while removing information gaps and limiting trust deficit, cannot ensure radical revamp of perceptions. The effectiveness of India's soft power with respect to the rest of the world, including China, is visibly constrained in this regard. On the other hand, India too, like many in the rest of the world, harbours doubts over China's 'benign'ness, given the other 'hard' posturing of the Chinese state to the extent that India still has not been able to take a position on OBOR[12] which might have several advantages for India. Evidently, states themselves, through their specific features and failings, are probably the biggest impediments to virtuous outcomes of both China and India's soft powers from global and bilateral domains.

While influence of specific state characteristics on effectiveness of soft power is observed for both countries, some structural features of their respective soft powers are distinct. The first of these are *scale* and *pace*. Whether it is cultural initiatives or economic engagement, China is engaging the rest of the world on a much bigger scale and faster pace than India. China is involved in a lot more infrastructure projects across the world and is also ahead in the sheer volume of cultural initiatives. One of the key determinants of China's higher scale and pace is the ability of the Chinese state to mobilize greater resources for its soft power engagement compared with India, reflecting the difference in financial capacities

---

[11] Blarel, 'India: The Next Superpower?'

[12] The Indian side appears unclear about the objectives behind OBOR with border issues remaining with China and its encirclement still dominating the Indian narrative.

between the two countries and the ability to spend on soft engagement. The sheer scale of China's initiatives dwarfs those of India's. Chinese efforts also show greater *focus* and *intensity*, particularly those of the *Hanban*, in strengthening the CIs. However, the Modi government's active pursuit of soft power has resulted in initiatives that underscore new scales and energy, a primary example being the celebration of the World Yoga Day on 21 June. While not emulating Chinese initiatives in size, the 'visibility' quotient of India's soft power is likely to become larger over time.

The difference in scale, pace and intensity between soft power strategies of China and India are also attributable to the *degree of involvement of the state* in exercising soft power. India has been happy to allow its *non-state actors* to be more proactive in advancing its soft power. It is relatively recently that people-to-people communication through high-level visits and state agencies like the ICCR have begun playing a more noticeable role in increasing cultural and educational interfaces with the world. India's state-driven PD efforts have been comparatively low profile. Such an approach—conspicuous in greater encouragement of non-state actors and a somewhat 'hands-off' attitude by the state—has avoided India's engagement from being labelled propagandist. But it also symbolizes the absence of a well-articulated and thought-out strategy for deploying soft power in the larger domain of India's foreign policy. China's entirely state-driven soft power efforts are in this respect a complete contrast, as is the repeated emphasis on its strategic importance by the Chinese leadership and articulation of the same in various policy pronouncements. But again, the Modi government's emphasis on soft power is likely to see the Indian state, including Indian provinces, become much more proactive in PD.

It is, of course, hardly surprising that India and China's respective approaches to soft power are conditioned by greater (or lesser) presence and *diktat* of the state, given their different *political systems and practices*. India's democracy has traditionally allowed far greater political freedom to its citizens. Its adoption of parliamentary democracy after independence allowing exercise of universal adult franchise was a major gamble. As the world's largest democracy, India has brought credibility to the global projection of democratic ideals, particularly through the multilingual, multi-ethnic and multi-religious character that such a democracy has accommodated.[13] However, as pointed out by Elizabeth Hanson, whereas the image of India as a poor country is sharp and clear, its image as a democratic country is more blurred[14] vindicating the adverse impressions produced by the Indian state's inability to improve the living conditions of its vast majorities notwithstanding established democratic foundations.

D.W. Kearn Jr rightly points out that 'democratic systems allow for major swings in ideology, with varying degrees' often sending 'mixed signals to foreign observers', given the exceedingly difficult time they encounter with the domestic opposition which often affects implementing a coherent agenda.[15] The inability to enforce policies, or the delay involved in doing so, is in sharp contrast to China which is known for its strong state machinery and quick delivering capacity. The impression has reinforced under Xi Jinping. On the other hand, for India, the lack of governance influencing delivery of public goods is often a result of faulty ad hoc policies lacking long-term vision. Coupled with this is the reluctance of the state authorities 'to place obligations on people…then excused and, indeed, idealized…. The abstention from compulsion has thus permitted to masquerade as part of the modernization ideals'.[16] To an extent, India's long-term soft power strategy, or the absence of it till now, is a result of this larger policy inertia, though the trend appears to be changing. On the other hand, democracy has allowed non-state actors to flourish notwithstanding the policy inertia. India's global soft power campaign is marked by the spell cast by its music, movies, food, writing and authors, along with much less noticeable presence of government agencies, in contrast to the overarching presence of the latter for China. An overt role of the state in brandishing national image does have its downsides as was evident during the London 2012 Summer Olympics, where excessive thrust on performance and the race for securing medals led to the Chinese athletes suffering from serious injuries. Questions were raised about the state's aggressive thrust on sporting glory and whether international esteem was actually worth in a country, which still suffers from poverty and where tax payers finance its entire sporting community.

---

[13] Kumar and Kumar, *In the National Interest*, 46.
[14] Hanson, 'India Wants to be Your Friend', 4.
[15] Kearn, 'The Hard Truths about Soft Power', 78.
[16] Myrdal, *Asian Drama*, 66–67.

The greater involvement of state actors in exercise of soft power and external engagement can often project soft power in a 'packaged' fashion, which, while otherwise attractive, might only be so on the surface. Indeed, state-driven packaged production of soft power has the risk of being labelled propagandist—an issue that has become a serious problem with China's soft power. Non-state actors are intrinsically less susceptible, if not at all, to such propagandist projections. India needs to be cautious in using its state actors too actively in spreading soft power, as such actions might start getting criticized in a similar fashion like China. Although India's alert media and civil society are always in a position to provide the alternative perspective, a large and ambitious programme of state-driven soft power would perhaps be best projected in as nuanced and subtle fashion as possible to depict its true and honest character.

An important point of difference between the engagement efforts of the two countries pertains to *education*. This is where China is expected to enjoy a distinct lead over similar efforts by India in the foreseeable future, given its active 'internationalization' of higher education. China has not only been encouraging foreign students through generous scholarships but has also been upgrading domestic education capacities to international levels by allowing more foreign faculty in local universities, encouraging international partnerships and allowing reputed foreign education service providers to open campuses in the mainland. The New York University, the University of Nottingham and the University of Liverpool are key examples. At the same time, Chinese higher education institutions such as the Peking University, Tsinghua University, Fudan University and Shanghai Jiao Tong University, along with collaborative ventures such as the CEIBS, are rapidly marching upward in global education rankings. These have contributed to China's growing image as a major Asian hub for higher education. Education is a powerful aspect of national soft power with almost all major powers of the world not only having reputed education systems but also deriving positive national perceptions from the latter. India appears to be falling way behind China in this regard, particularly in its failure to internationalize. In a sense, India has more advantages than China in developing as an education hub because of proficiency in English and long interfaces with Western education institutions. But unfortunately, the priorities of India's education system are neither to attract overseas students nor foreign faculty. As a result, the advantages are hardly being utilized in a manner that can enable India to spring into the league of major education providers in the world.

While India's vibrant free press can hardly be expected to act as a strategic vehicle for providing alternate perceptions like its Chinese counterpart, the two *media* are distinct in their global outreach reflected in on-ground presence in overseas locations. The CCTV and *China Daily* have firm footprints in almost all parts of the world. India's Zee Television, Star and Sony are still mostly localized in the Asia-Pacific. Moreover, Chinese media, particularly the audiovisual segment, offers a balanced mix of entertainment and current affairs, whereas the Indian content is largely entertainment. No Indian newspaper has yet stepped overseas unlike *China Daily*, and the number of foreign correspondents of Indian newspapers is also distinctly limited compared with their Chinese counterparts. While more financial resources and dedicated state focus explain the greater overseas presence of the Chinese media compared with much less of it for the Indian media, such presence over time is probably important even for shaping domestic perceptions in an objective manner. More Indian correspondents in China and South Asia, for example, would help in adding greater objectivity to reporting on these countries and regions, which, often, gets biased due to reliance on reports by Western agencies.

Despite several differences with neighbours in Northeast and Southeast Asia, China has not refrained from investing in infrastructure-building in these countries, nor has it tightened the flow of cultural engagement and greater people-to-people contacts. The other countries have also responded due to a variety of factors, including the necessity of engaging with an overarching China (such necessity might include awe and 'fear' for the smaller countries as well) and benefiting from its economic growth and expansion. India, which was hesitant to engage in such realpolitik, is increasingly showing signs of welcome pragmatism in this regard, particularly in South Asia, and also with respect to China. This is necessary since India's tradition of strategic restraint, while imparting it a 'non-aggressive' flavour, has also probably not 'forced' the neighbourhood into greater reciprocal engagement out of necessity (or fear), as in the case of China.

As both China and India continue to engage the rest of the world, and each other, through their different soft power strategies for achieving largely identical objectives, they need to ensure that their strategies remain dynamic and in sync with the habits and customs of the world and its people. Both countries have been showing encouraging signs in this respect by using social media as means for greater communication. At the same time, they must also realize that the biggest tests for their soft powers are in their regions and also between themselves. The challenge of engaging Asia, particularly neighbours, is entirely different from engaging the West in a world where global strategic priorities are increasingly concentrating in different parts of Asia, and the presence of non-state actors in the region is rising rapidly.

Crafting diplomacy and engagement in an Asia becoming more and more strategically complex is not easy. As rising powers and Asian countries, China and India realize this more than anyone else. The common challenge for both is to reduce the anxieties prevailing in many parts of their neighbourhoods and the rest of the world about their simultaneous strategic ascent. The possibility of strategic competition in this respect cannot be ruled out, as India's more 'assertive' engagement policies focus on similar themes and turfs as China's. While on smaller scales and unclear scopes till now, initiatives like Mausam probably represent India's counter-response to grand regional connectivity plans of China. Similarly, efforts to engage the Pacific Islands[17] could also be seen as India's attempt to expand its sphere of strategic influence to uncharted territories. It is important though to ensure that potential competition in expanding sphere of strategic influence through more aggressive exercise of soft power does not lead to greater flashpoints in regional affairs. An even bigger challenge in this regard is to reduce anxieties between each other. Soft power strategies in both countries will have to grapple and adjust to emerging realities, situations and circumstances for overcoming these significant challenges.

---

[17] India hosted the second Forum for India-Pacific Islands Cooperation in Jaipur, India in August 2015. It is the first regional summit hosted by the Indian Prime Minister Narendra Modi, thus underlining the importance attached to developing closer ties with the Pacific Island counties.

# *Annexures*

## ANNEXURE I: RECIPIENTS OF CHINESE AND INDIAN DEVELOPMENT ASSISTANCE

| Region | China | India |
|---|---|---|
| Africa | Angola, Congo, Gabon, Ethiopia, Equatorial Guinea, Mozambique, Kenya, Liberia, Madagascar, Niger, Nigeria, Rwanda, Sierra Leone, Sudan, Uganda, Zambia | Angola, Cameroon, Chad, Congo, Ethiopia, Gambia, Ghana, Kenya, Lesotho, Madagascar, Mali, Mauritius, Mozambique, Niger, Rwanda, Seychelles, Sierra Leone, Sudan, Suriname, Tanzania, Zambia |
| Latin America & Caribbean | Bolivia, Brazil, Chile, Columbia, Costa Rica, Cuba, Grenada, Peru, Venezuela, Uruguay | Columbia, Ecuador, Guyana, Honduras, Jamaica, Peru, Venezuela |
| Southeast Asia | Indonesia, Myanmar, Cambodia, Laos, Philippines, Thailand, Vietnam | Cambodia, Myanmar, Laos, Vietnam |
| South Asia | Afghanistan, Bangladesh, Nepal, Pakistan, Sri Lanka | Afghanistan, Bangladesh, Bhutan, Nepal, Pakistan, Sri Lanka |

*Source:* Palit (2011).
*Note:* The above list of countries is not entirely exhaustive.

## ANNEXURE II: LOCATION OF CONFUCIUS INSTITUTES (CIs) WORLDWIDE

| Region | Country | Number | Total |
|---|---|---|---|
| North America | USA | 71 | 80 |
| | Canada | 9 | |
| South America | Mexico | 5 | 32 |
| | Peru | 4 | |
| | Colombia | 3 | |
| | Cuba | 1 | |
| | Chile | 2 | |
| | West Indies | 1 | |
| | Jamaica | 1 | |
| | Brazil | 7 | |
| | Argentina | 2 | |
| | Costa Rica | 1 | |
| | Ecuador | 1 | |
| | Bahamas | 1 | |
| | Bolivia | 1 | |
| | Guyana | 1 | |
| | Trinidad & Tobago | 1 | |
| Europe | Ireland | 2 | 108 |
| | Austria | 2 | |
| | Belarus | 1 | |
| | Bulgaria | 1 | |
| | Belgium | 3 | |
| | Iceland | 1 | |
| | Poland | 4 | |
| | Denmark | 2 | |
| | Germany | 11 | |

| Region | Country | Number | Total |
|--------|---------|--------|-------|
| | Russia | 17 | |
| | France | 14 | |
| | Finland | 1 | |
| | Netherlands | 1 | |
| | Czech Republic | 1 | |
| | Romania | 2 | |
| | Norway | 1 | |
| | Portugal | 2 | |
| | Sweden | 1 | |
| | Serbia | 1 | |
| | Slovakia | 2 | |
| | Ukraine | 3 | |
| | Spain | 4 | |
| | Greece | 1 | |
| | Hungary | 1 | |
| | Italy | 10 | |
| | UK | 14 | |
| | Malta | 1 | |
| | Moldova | 1 | |
| | Slovenia | 1 | |
| | Estonia | 1 | |
| | Lithuania | 1 | |
| Africa | Egypt | 2 | 22 |
| | Botswana | 1 | |
| | Zimbabwe | 1 | |
| | Cameroon | 1 | |
| | Kenya | 2 | |
| | Liberia | 1 | |
| | Rwanda | 1 | |
| | Madagascar | 1 | |

*(Annexure II Continued)*

(*Annexure II Continued*)

| Region | Country | Number | Total |
|--------|---------|--------|-------|
| | South Africa | 4 | |
| | Nigeria | 2 | |
| | Sudan | 1 | |
| | Morocco | 1 | |
| | Togo | 1 | |
| | Benin | 1 | |
| | Ethiopia | 1 | |
| | Zambia | 1 | |
| *Asia* | Afghanistan | 1 | 83 |
| | Armenia | 1 | |
| | Bangladesh | 1 | |
| | Pakistan | 1 | |
| | Philippines | 3 | |
| | Korea | 17 | |
| | Kazakhstan | 2 | |
| | Kyrgyzstan | 2 | |
| | Lebanon | 1 | |
| | Malaysia | 2 | |
| | Mongolia | 1 | |
| | Nepal | 1 | |
| | Japan | 13 | |
| | Sri Lanka | 1 | |
| | Thailand | 12 | |
| | Uzbekistan | 1 | |
| | Tajikistan | 1 | |
| | Singapore | 1 | |
| | Iran | 1 | |
| | India | 2 | |
| | Indonesia | 7 | |
| | Israel | 1 | |

| Region | Country | Number | Total |
|--------|---------|--------|-------|
|  | Jordan | 1 |  |
|  | Hong Kong | 1 |  |
|  | Cambodia | 1 |  |
|  | Laos | 1 |  |
|  | Azerbaijan | 1 |  |
|  | Georgia | 1 |  |
|  | Turkey | 2 |  |
|  | UAE | 2 |  |
| Oceania | Australia | 9 | 12 |
|  | New Zealand | 3 |  |

*Source:* Confucius Institute/Classroom, available at: http://english.hanban.org/node_10971. htm (accessed on 29 August 2013).

**ANNEXURE III: PRESIDENT XI JINPING'S GLOBAL VISITS**

| Year | Date | Event |
|---|---|---|
| 2013 | March 22–30 | President Xi Jinping visited Russia, Tanzania, South Africa and the Republic of Congo and attended the BRICS leaders' meeting in Durban, South Africa. A total of 72 cooperative agreements were signed with the four countries. |
| 2013 | May 31–June 8 | Xi visited Trinidad and Tobago, Costa Rica and Mexico and held the first summit with US President Barack Obama in California. A total of 24 cooperative agreements were signed with the three countries. |
| 2013 | September 3–13 | Xi elaborated on the concept of the New Silk Road Economic Belt project for the first time while visiting Central Asia. He also attended the 8th G20 leaders' summit in St. Petersburg, Russia and the 13th Shanghai Cooperation Organization leaders' meeting in Bishkek, Kyrgyzstan. |
| 2013 | October 2–8 | Xi visited Indonesia and Malaysia and proposed to establish an Asian infrastructure investment bank while attending the 21st APEC leaders' meeting in Bali, Indonesia. |
| 2014 | February 6–8 | Xi attended the opening ceremony of the 22nd Winter Olympic Games in Sochi, Russia. |
| 2014 | March 22–April 1 | Xi visited Western Europe and attended the 3rd Nuclear Security Summit in The Hague, Netherlands. China signed over 120 cooperative agreements with the Netherlands, France, Germany and Belgium. |
| 2014 | July 3–4 | Xi paid a state visit to the ROK and the two countries released a statement including more than 90 cooperative items, covering 23 fields. |
| 2014 | July 15–23 | Xi attended the 6th BRICS leaders' meeting and visited Brazil, Argentina, Venezuela and Cuba. A total of 142 cooperative documents were signed with the four countries. |
| 2014 | August 21–22 | A total of 26 cooperative agreements were signed when Xi paid a state visit to Mongolia. |
| 2014 | September 11–19 | Xi attended the 14th Meeting of the Council of Heads of States of the SCO in Dushanbe, Tajikistan and paid state visits to Tajikistan, Maldives, Sri Lanka and India. A total of 48 cooperative documents were signed. |
| 2014 | November 15–23 | Xi attended the 9th G20 leaders' summit in Brisbane, Australia, and paid state visits to Australia, New Zealand and Fiji. Over 79 agreements were signed with the three countries. |
| 2015 | April 20–21 | Xi visits Pakistan and signs 51 projects as part of the China-Pakistan Economic Corridor. |

Source: *China Daily* (16–22 January 2015).

| 2015 | |
|---|---|
| April | July |
| Pakistan | Russia |

## ANNEXURE IV: PRIME MINISTER NARENDRA MODI'S GLOBAL VISITS 2014–15

| 2014 | | | | | |
|---|---|---|---|---|---|
| June | July | August | August–September | September | November |
| Bhutan | Brazil to attend the BRICS Summit | Nepal | Japan | US to attend General Debate of the UN General Assembly | Myanmar to attend the East Asia Summit, Australia to attend the G20 Summit, Fiji, Nepal to attend the SAARC Summit |

*Source:* 'List of Prime Ministerial trips made by Narendra Modi,' available at: http://en.wikipedia.org/wiki/List_of_Prime_Ministerial_trips_made_by_Narendra_Modi (accessed on 20 March 2015).

| 2015 | | | | |
|---|---|---|---|---|
| March | April | May | June | July |
| Seychelles, Mauritius, Sri Lanka, Singapore | France, Germany, Canada | China, Mongolia, South Korea | Bangladesh | Central Asia |

*Source:* 'List of Prime Ministerial trips made by Narendra Modi,' available at: http://en.wikipedia.org/wiki/List_of_Prime_Ministerial_trips_made_by_Narendra_Modi (accessed on 20 March 2015).

# Bibliography

'Hu Jintao: Deepen Reform of Cultural Institutions and Strengthen China's Cultural Soft Power'. 23 July 2010. Available at: http://www.chinanews. com.cn/gn/2010/07-23/2422727.shtml (accessed on 5 December 2010).

'Maldives and China Sign Memorandum of Understanding on Sports Cooperation'. 26 May 2008. Available at: http://www.maldiveshigh commission.org/archive/?s=10&grupa=2&id=314&new=ok (accessed on 10 January 2017).

'Pakistan Welcomes More Chinese Telecom Investment'. 18 February 2009. Available at: https://www.chinatechnews.com/2009/02/18/8855-pakistan-welcomes-more-chinese-telecom-investment (accessed on 10 January 2017).

'Sino-American Relations'. Available at: http://en.wikipedia.org/wiki/Sino-American_relations (accessed on 19 July 2012).

'Sino-European Forum Pang Diwo'. Available at: http://observatoriosinoeuropeo. blogspot.com/ (accessed on 11 May 2012).

'Ti sheng ruan shi li: jie du zhong yang zheng zhi ju di shi san ci ji ti xue xi' (Enhance China's Soft Power: Interpreting the Thirteenth Group Study Session of the Politburo of the Central Committee and 'Zhong guo xu yao ruan shi li' [China needs Soft Power]. Available at: http://dangxiao.jmu.edu.cn/show. asp?id=1156 (accessed on 3 December 2010).

'Zhong guo he ping jue qi wenti yan jiu zong shu' [Summary of Research Problems with China's 'Peaceful Rise']. Available at: http://www.docin.com/p-465 743.html (accessed on 13 May 2009).

Ziyang, Zhao Prisoner of the State: The Secret Journal of Premier Zhao Ziyang. New York: Simon & Schuster, 2009.

ABC Radio Australia. 'China an Example to Others on Pacific Aid and Business'. 17 May 2013. Available at: http://www.radioaustralia.net.au/international/ radio/program/pacific-beat/china-an-example-to-others-on-pacific-aid-and-business/1131878 (accessed on 26 July 2013).

Across the Himalayan Gap. Prime Minister Rajiv Gandhi at Qinghua University. 21 December 1988. Available at: http://ignca.nic.in/ks_41005.htm (accessed on 16 November 2012).

African Union. 'Pan African e-Network (PAeN) for Tele-medicine and Tele-education'. Available at: http://pages.au.int/infosoc/pages/pan-african-e-network-paen-tele-medicine-and-tele-education (accessed on 7 July 2015).

African Business. 'Pharmaceuticals: India's Generics Flow into Africa'. 19 January 2012. Available at: http://africanbusinessmagazine.com/special-reports/ pharmaceuticals-indias-generics-flow-into-africa/ (accessed on 7 July 2015).

*Africa practice Report.* 'The Impact of the Chinese Presence in Africa'. 2007. Available at: http://www.davidandassociates.co.uk/davidandblog/newwork/ China_in_Africa_5.pdf (accessed on 11 April 2012).

Ahrari, M. Ehsan. *The Great Powers Versus Hegemon.* UK: Palgrave Macmillan, 2011.

Alafrangi, Manal. 'Study Abroad or Not: That is the Question'. *Gulfnews.com.* 27 September 2005. Available at: http://gulfnews.com/news/gulf/uae/general/ study-abroad-or-not-that-is-the-question-1.302192 (accessed on 8 July 2015).

Alterman, B. Jon, and Garver, W. John. 'The Vital Triangle: China, the United States and the Middle East'. *CSIS Report* 30, no. 2 (2008). Available at: http://csis.org/files/media/csis/pubs/080624-alterman-vitaltriangle.pdf (accessed on 12 March 2012).

Arase, David. 'China's Two Silk Roads Initiative What It Means for Southeast Asia'. In *Southeast Asian Affairs,* edited by Daljit Singh. Singapore: ISEAS Publishing, 2015.

Armstrong, Patrick, Shiro. 'The Politics of Japan–China Trade and the Role of the World Trade System'. 24 July 2012. Available at: https://editorialexpress. com/cgi-bin/conference/download.cgi?db_name=ACE10&paper_id=81 (accessed on 30 April 2015).

*Asahi Shimbun.* 'China, Russia Developing Infrastructure in N. Korean Port City'. 7 September 2011. Available at: http://ajw.asahi.com/article/asia/korean_ peninsula/AJ201109079495 (accessed on 31 January 2012).

*Asia Unbound.* 'The Indian Elections—What the BJP Has to Say About Foreign Policy'. 7 April 2014. Available at: http://blogs.cfr.org/asia/2014/04/07/ the-indian-elections-what-the-bjp-has-to-say-about-foreign-policy/ (accessed on 19 May 2015).

*Asian Correspondent.com.* 'Wen Says China Might Contribute to Europe Fund'. 3 February 2012. Available at: http://asiancorrespondent.com/75174/ wen-says-china-might-contribute-to-europe-fund/ (accessed on 15 May 2012).

Asian Development Bank. 'India Electricity Flows to Bangladesh in First South Asian HVDC Cross-border Link'. 4 October 2013. Available at: http:// www.adb.org/news/india-electricity-flows-bangladesh-first-south-asian-hvdc-cross-border-link (accessed on 7 June 2015).

*AsiaNews.it.* 'Hu Jintao's Cultural War Against the West (and Christianity). 1 February 2012. Available at: http://www.asianews.it/news-en/Hu-Jintao% E2%80%99s-cultural-war-against-the-West-(and-Christianity)-23588. html (accessed on 8 July 2015).

*Asiaone.* 'Taiwan, China Leaders to Hold Surprise Meeting in Singapore'. 4 November 2015. Available at: http://news.asiaone.com/news/singapore/ taiwan-china-leaders-hold-surprise-meeting-singapore (accessed on 21 May 2016).

*At0086*. 'Twelve Kinds of Chinese Scholarships Available to International Students'. 2010. Available at: http://news.at0086.com/China-Universities/Win-a-Scholarship-Know-it-first.html (accessed on 9 June 2016).

Bajpai, P. Kanti. 'Indian Strategic Culture'. In *India's Foreign Policy: A Reader*, edited by P. Kanti Bajpai and V. Harsh Pant. New Delhi: Oxford University Press, 2013.

Baldwin, A. David. *Economic Statecraft*. UK: Princeton University Press, 1985.

Bank of Indonesia. 'Trade and Investment News'. 5 September 2005. Available at: http://www.bi.go.id/web/en/Publikasi/Investor+Relation+Unit/Highlight+News/Trade+and+Investment+News+5+Sept+05.htm (accessed on 7 February 2012).

*BBC News*. 'Chinese President Xi Jinping in Russia for First Foreign Tour'. 22 March 2013. Available at: http://www.bbc.co.uk/news/world-asia-china-21873944 (accessed on 12 July 2013).

Becquelin, Nicolas. 'Staged Development in Xinjiang'. *The China Quarterly* 178 (June 2004): 358–78.

Beibei, Ji. 'Public Diplomacy Gains Ground'. *Global Times*. 15 September 2010. Available at: http://www.globaltimes.cn/content/661523.shtml (accessed on 9 January 2017).

*Beijing Daily*. 'Chen Guangcheng—A Tool Used by American Politicians to Discredit China'. 5 May 2012. Available at: http://www.chinaaid.org/2012/05/beijing-daily-chen-guangchenga-tool.html (accessed on 20 March 2013).

Benavides, Marissa. 'When Soft Power is too Soft: Confucius Institutes' Nebulous Role in China's Soft Power Initiative'. 2012 August. Available at: http://yris.yira.org/essays/644 (accessed on 28 January 2014).

Bhadrakumar, M.K. 'China Resets Terms of Engagement in Central Asia: Energy and Great Power Conflict'. *The Asia Pacific Journal* 52, no. 2 (28 December 2009). Available at: http://apjjf.org/-M-K-Bhadrakumar/3277/article.html (accessed on 9 January 2017).

Bhasin, Madhavi. 'India's Role in South Asia—Perceived Hegemony or Reluctant Leadership?' Available at: http://www.globalindiafoundation.org/Madhavi Bhasin.pdf (accessed on 16 January 2014).

Bhatia, Rajiv. 'Deepening India–Maldives Relations'. 31 August 2011. Available at: http://www.thehindu.com/opinion/lead/article2415585.ece?home page=true (accessed on 8 July 2015).

Bijoy, C.R. 'India: Transiting to a Global Donor'. 2010. Available at: http://www.realityofaid.org/wp-content/uploads/2013/02/ROA-SSDC-Special (accessed on 8 July 2015).

Binder, Andrea and Conrad, Bjorn. 'China's Potential Role in Humanitarian Assistance'. Humanitarian Policy Paper Series 209. 2009. Available at: http://www.gppi.net/fileadmin/gppi/Binder_Conrad_2009_CHN_in_Hum_Assis.pdf (accessed on 23 August 2012).

Binhua, Chen and Yong, Zhang. 'Hu Jinatao he Lian Zhan zai Beijing Juxing Jengshi Huitan' [Hu Jintao and Lien Zhan hold formal meeting in Beijing]. *Xinhua News Agency*. 29 April 2005. Available at: http://news.xinhuanet.com/tai_gang_ao/2005-04/29/content_2897082.htm (accessed on 2 April 2012).

Blarel, Nicolas. 'India: The Next Superpower? India's Soft Power: From Potential to Reality'. *LSE Research Online Report*. 2012 May. Available at: http://eprints.lse.ac.uk/43445/1/India_India%27s%20soft%20power%28lsero%29.pdf (accessed on 18 September 2012).

*Bloomberg*. 'Ecuador Seeking up to $1.4 Billion from China, Minister Says'. 8 July 2013. Available at: http://www.bloomberg.com/news/2013-07-08/ecuador-seeking-up-to-1-4-billion-from-china-minister-says.html (accessed on 28 July 2013).

Boehler, Patrick. 'China's Gateway to Burma Booming'. 31 January 2012. Available at: http://www2.irrawaddy.org/article.php?art_id=22950 (accessed on 21 May 2012).

*Borneo Bulletin*. 'Brunei, China Extend Cultural Ties Through Art Exhibition'. 27 April 2012. Available at: http://www.brudirect.com/index.php/Local-News/brunei-china-extend-cultural-ties-through-art-exhibition.html (accessed on 29 August 2012).

Bound, K., R. Briggs, J. Holden and S. Jones. *Cultural Diplomacy*. London: Demos, 2007.

Brady, Anne-Marie. 'China's Foreign Propaganda Machine'. 26 October 2015. Available at: https://www.wilsoncenter.org/article/chinas-foreign-propaganda-machine (accessed on 22 February 2016).

Brant, Philippa. 'The Geopolitics of Chinese Aid'. 4 March 2015. Available at: https://www.foreignaffairs.com/articles/china/2015-03-04/geopolitics-chinese-aid (accessed on 30 April 2015).

Bristow, Michael. 'China White Paper Highlights US Military "Competition"'. *BBC News*. 31 March 2011. Available at: http://www.bbc.co.uk/news/world-asia-pacific-12917338 (accessed on 9 September 2011).

Brodsgaard, Erik, Kjeld. 'China Studies in Europe'. In *China–EU Relations*, edited by David Shambaug, Eberhard Sandschneider, Zhou Hong. New York: Routledge, 2008.

Brown, Peter. 'Australian Influence in the South Pacific'. 2012. Available at: http://www.defence.gov.au/adc/docs/Publications2012/07_Brown%20SAP%20Final%20PDF.pdf (accessed on 1 February 2014).

Browne, Andrew. 'A Kinder, Gentler Regional Hegemon?' *The World Street Journal*. 7 January 2015.

Bullbeck, Pip. 'Sky News Australia, China's CCTV Ink Live News Agreement'. 18 August 2011. Available at: http://www.hollywoodreporter.com/news/sky-news-australia-chinas-cctv-224884 (accessed on 29 May 2012).

*Business Standard*. 'Kishan S. Rana: Re-setting India's Public Diplomacy'. 16 January 2011a. Available at: http://www.business-standard.com/india/

news/kishan-s-rana-re-setting-indias-public-diplomacy/421889/ (accessed on 7 July 2015).

*Business Standard.* 'Making India a Global Education Hub'. 26 February 2011b. Available at: http://www.business-standard.com/india/news/making-indiaglobal-education-hub/426592/ (accessed on 8 July 2015).

Byron, Rejaul Karim. 'University for PIOs in Bangalore by 2012'. 19 August 2008. Available at: http://www.business-standard.com/india/news/university-for-pios-in-bangalore-by-2012/331819/ (accessed on 8 July 2015).

Byun, See-Won. 'Sino-South Korea Ties Warming?' *The Diplomat.* 2 September 2011. Available at: http://the-diplomat.com/new-leaders-forum/2011/09/02/sino-south-korea-ties-warming/ (accessed on 25 January 2012).

Calabrese, John. *China and Iran: Mismatched Partners.* Washington, D.C.: Jamestown Foundation, 2006.

*CCTV.com.* 'China Helps Build First Children's Hospital in Trinidad & Tobago'. 2 June 2013. Available at: http://english.cntv.cn/program/newshour/20130602/102253.shtml (accessed on 24 July 2013).

*CCTV+NewsContent.* UAE–China Culture Week. 10 March 2012. Available at: http://newscontent.cctv.com/news.jsp?fileId=134561 (accessed on 14 March 2012).

Chacko, Priya. *The Indian Foreign Policy.* New York: Routledge, 2012.

Chanda, Nayan. *Bound Together: How Traders, Preachers, Adventurers, and Warriors Shape Globalization.* New Haven, CT: Yale University Press, 2007.

Chang, Jennifer Wei-I. 'The Middle East in China's Silk Road Visions: Business as Usual?' 14 April 2015. Available at: http://www.mei.edu/content/map/middle-east-china%E2%80%99s-silk-road-visions-business-usual (accessed on 14 May 2015).

*Channelnewsasia.com.* 'Chinese Firms Buy into Europe'. 19 February 2012. Available at: http://www.channelnewsasia.com/stories/afp_asiapacific_business/view/1183907/1/.html (accessed on 9 May 2012).

Chen, Zhimin and Pan, Zhongqi. 'China in Its Neighbourhood: A Middle Kingdom' Not Necessarily at the Centre of Power'. *The International Spectator: Italian Journal of International Affairs* 46, no. 4 (2011). Available at: http://www.tandfonline.com/doi/pdf/10.1080/03932729.2011.6280 98 (accessed on 5 September 2012).

Cheng Guangjin,Yanrong, Zhao. 'China to Strengthen Ties with Uganda'. 4 July 2013. Available at: http://www.cdeclips.com/en/world/fullstory.html?id=79290 (accessed on 4 July 2013).

Cheng, Tun-jen, Jacques deLisle and Deborah Brown. *China under Hu Jintao: Opportunities, Dangers, and Dilemmas.* Singapore: World Scientific Publishing, 2006.

Chenxi, Wang and Wei Jianhua. 2012. 'China–Africa friendship enhanced by diverse, growing cooperation'. 29 January 2012. Available at: http://news.xinhuanet.com/english/indepth/2012-01/29/c_131381009.htm (accessed on 3 April 2012).

Cheru, Fantu and Cyril Obi. *The Rise of China and India in Africa*. New York: Zed Books, 2010.

Chey, Jocelyn. 'From Rosny to the Great Wall: Cultural Relations and Public Diplomacy'. In *Re-orienting Australia-China Relations: 1972 to the Present*, edited by Nicholas Thomas. UK: Ashgate Publishing Company, 2004.

Chia, J. 2008. Buddhism in Singapore-China Relations: Venerable Hong Choon and his visits, 1982–90. The China Quarterly. pp. 864–883. Available at http://www.academia.edu/344604/Buddhism_in_Singapore-China_Relations_Venerable_Hong_Choon_and_his_Visits_1982-1990 (accessed on 9 January 2017).

*China and Latin America*. 'India's Approach to Oil Acquisition in Latin America: A Chinese Perspective'. 9 December 2011. Available at: http://www.chinaandlatinamerica.com/2011/12/indias-approach-to-oil-acquisition-in.html (accessed on 30 September 2012).

*China Copyright and Media*. 'China's Foreign Propaganda Chief Outlines External Communication Priorities'. 10 October 2013. Available at: https://chinacopyrightandmedia.wordpress.com/2013/10/10/chinas-foreign-propaganda-chief-outlines-external-communication-priorities/ (accessed on 31 March 2015).

*China Copyright and Media*. 'Communique of the 3rd Plenum of the 18th Party Congress'. 12 November 2013. Available at: http://chinacopyrightandmedia.wordpress.com/2013/11/12/communique-of-the-3rd-plenum-of-the-18th-party-congress/ (accessed on 26 November 2013

*China Daily Mail*. 'Chinese Army Incursion into India's Territory'. 20 September 2014. Available at: http://chinadailymail.com/2014/09/20/chinese-army-incursion-into-indias-territory/ (accessed on 19 July 2015).

———. 'Full Text: White Paper on Military Strategy'. 26 May 2015. Available at: http://www.chinadaily.com.cn/china/2015-05/26/content_20820628.htm (accessed on 23 May 2016).

*China Daily*. 'China to Boost Public Diplomacy, Exchanges'. 1 January 2013. Available at: http://www.chinadaily.com.cn/cndy/2013-01/01/content_16073723.htm (accessed on 17 April 2013).

———. 'International Student Numbers on the Rise'. 29 April–5 May 2016.

———. 'Former Ambassador Shares His Views on Sino-Japan Relations'. 31 March 2015. Available at: http://www.chinadaily.com.cn/china/2015-03/31/content_19958311.htm (accessed on 21 September 2015).

———. 'China Urges Sri Lanka Secure Further Chinese Investment'. 13 March 2015. Available at: http://www.chinadaily.com.cn/china/2015-03/13/content_19807432_2.htm (accessed on 9 April 2015).

———. 'Returning with a Fresh Perspective'. 4–10 September 2015.

———. 'US, India Stir S. China Sea Debate'. 6 August 2014. Available at: http://usa.chinadaily.com.cn/china/2014-10/06/content_18698961.htm (accessed on 19 July 2015).

*China Daily.* 'Sri Lanka Affirms Sino Ties'. 2015.

———. 'School's in for First Overseas Campus'. 17 June 2013.

———. 'Chinese Lend a Hand in India 4G'. 20–26 July 2012.

———. 'Australia Maps Out Its Asia "Pivot"'. 29 October 2012.

———. 'Band of Brothers Sets Tone'. 30 October 2012.

———. 'Silk Route Builds Bridge'. 23 March 2012. Available at: http://china
dailyapac.com/article/silk-route-builds-bridge (accessed on 19 October
2012).

———. 'Wen Urges Enhanced Co-op with Latin America'. 28 June 2012.
Available at: http://usa.chinadaily.com.cn/china/2012-06/28/content_
15527561.htm (accessed on 22 August 2012).

———. 'Xinhua, MCIL Jointly Launch News Portal in Malaysia'. 30 August
2012. Available at: http://www.chinadaily.com.cn/xinhua/2012-08-30/
content_6872731.html (accessed on 16 October 2012).

———. 'Shopping for Power: Chinese Investors Seal Energy Deals in South and
Southeast Asia as Diversification Strategy'. 10–16 August 2012.

———. 'Advance Sino-US Partnership'. 9 March 2012. Available at: http://
www.chinadaily.com.cn/opinion/2012-03/09/content_14793843.htm
(accessed on 24 July 2012).

———. 'India's Tata Consultancy to Triple Investment in China'. 8 October
2011. Available at: http://www.chinadaily.com.cn/business/2011-10/08/
content_13846105.htm (accessed on 16 November 2012).

———. 'Mainland, Taiwan Cultural Exchanges Promoted'. 7 September 2010.
Available at: http://www.chinadaily.com.cn/china/2010-09/07/content_
11264981.htm (accessed on 31 January 2012).

———. 'Chinese President Arrives in Riyadh at Start of "Trip of Friendship,
Cooperation"'. 10 February 2009. Available at: http://news.xinhuanet.
com/english/2009-02/10/content_10796711.htm (accessed on 10 March
2012).

———. 'China, ASEAN Sign Agreement on Investment'. 16 August 2009.
Available at: http://www.chinadaily.com.cn/china/2009-08/16/content_
8575056.htm (accessed on 7 March 2012).

*China News.* 'Consultative Committee of the Ministry of Foreign Affairs is
Revealed Publicly for the First Time'. 30 September 2016. Available at:
http://www.chinanews.com/gn/2010/09-30/2567185.shtml (accessed on
2 August 2012).

*China News and Report.* Speech by Premier Wen Jiabao at the Economic
Commission for Latin America and the Caribbean of the United Nations.
26 June 2012. Available at: http://english.cri.cn/mmsource/images/2012/
08/01/eng120801.pdf (accessed on 22 August 2012).

*China US Focus.* Agreement between US and China for Cooperation in Educational
Exchanges. 2006. Available at: http://www.chinausfocus.com/library/
government-resources/bilateral-resources/bilateral-agreement/people-to-

people-exchange/implementing-accord-for-cultural-exchange-for-the-period-2007-2009-under-the-cultural-agreement-between-the-us-and-china-june-11-2007/ (accessed on 26 July 2012).

*China.org.cn.* 'Top 30 Confucius Institutes in 2011'. 7 May 2012. Available at: http://www.china.org.cn/top10/2012-05/07/content_25252751_3.htm (accessed on 30 August 2012).

———. 'Samoa Re-affirms One China Policy'. 10 May 2005. Available at: http://china.org.cn/english/international/128189.htm (accessed on 9 June 2016).

———. 'Experience China to Promote Mutual Understanding Between China and Australia'. 8 April 2011. Available at: http://www.china.org.cn/learning_chinese/news/2011-04/08/content_22314514.htm (accessed on 9 June 2016).

———. 'Xi Seeks New Outlook on Foreign Affairs'. 30 November 2014. Available at: http://www.china.org.cn/china/2014-11/30/content_34188844.htm (accessed on 6 April 2015).

———. 'China–US Economic Relations: Accords and Discords'. 27 February 2012. Available at: http://www.china.org.cn/opinion/2012-02/27/content_24744473_3.htm (accessed on 18 October 2012).

———. 'Hu, Obama Meet on Sidelines of G20 Summit'. 20 June 2012. Available at: http://www.china.org.cn/world/2012-06/20/content_25691858.htm (accessed on 18 July 2012).

———.'China, Iran Set up Committee to Enhance Cultural Exchanges'. 16 February 2012. Available at: http://www.china.org.cn/world/2012-02/16/content_24655897.htm (accessed on 14 March 2012).

———. 'China's Path of Peaceful Development Is a Choice Necessitated by History'. 6 September 2011. Available at: http://www.china.org.cn/government/whitepaper/2011-09/06/content_23362786.htm (accessed on 11 August 2012).

———. 'China's Foreign Policies for Pursuing Peaceful Development'. 6 September 2011. Available at: http://www.china.org.cn/government/white paper/2011-09/06/content_23362744.htm (accessed on 11 August 2012).

———. 'South Korea–China Cultural Exchange'. 28 May 2010. Available at: http://www.china.org.cn/video/2010-05/28/content_20135162.htm (accessed on 31 January 2012).

*Chinaculture.org.* (*zhong guo wen hua wang*). 'Chinese Cultural Centre in Bangkok, Thailand to Attend and Mr Wu Bangguo Laid the Foundation Stone'. 15 October 2010. Available at: http://www.cccweb.org/en/jjwhzx/4895.shtml (accessed on 18 May 2012).

Chinese Culture and Education Centre. Available at: http://www.ccecbridge.org/school.html (accessed on 28 July 2013).

Chinh, Van, Nguyen. 'Confucius Institutes in the Mekong Region'. 2014 December. *Issues & Studies*. Available at: http://viet-studies.info/kinhte/ ConfuciusInstitutes_December2014.pdf (accessed on 19 May 2016).

Chuan-Hsiu, Shih. 'China Aid Linked to Taiwan Issue-cable'. 1 May 2011. Available at: http://www.taipeitimes.com/News/taiwan/archives/2011/05/ 01/2003502135 (accessed on 7 February 2012).

Chunshan, Mu. 'China and Middle East'. *The Diplomat*. 9 November 2010. Available at: http://the-diplomat.com/china-power/2010/11/09/china-and-the-middle-east/ (accessed on 10 March 2012).

Clarke, Michael. 'China's Integration of Xinjiang with Central Asia: Securing a "Silk Road" to Great Power Status?' *China and Eurasia Forum Quarterly* 6, no. 2 (2008).

Clarke, Ryan and Shan Wei. 'China's "Look West" Policy Towards Central Asia'. *EAI Background Brief* No. 638. 1 July 2011.

*Clingendael*. 'China's Public Diplomacy Shifts Focus from Building Hardware'. 2013 October. Available at: http://www.clingendael.nl/publication/china %E2%80%99s-public-diplomacy-shifts-focus-building-hardware-improving-software?lang=nl (accessed on 5 May 2016).

Clinton, Hillary. 'America's Pacific Century'. *Foreign Policy*. 22 July 2012. Available at: http://www.foreignpolicy.com/articles/2011/10/11/americas_ pacific_century?page=full (accessed on 23 July 2012).

Clover, Charles and Lucy Hornby. 'China's Great Game: Road to a New Empire'. *Today*. 14 October 2015.

*Confucius Analects*. Book XVI. Available at: http://www.indiana.edu/~p374/ Analects_of_Confucius_(Eno-2015).pdf (accessed on 9 January 2017).

Confucius Institute at Ritsumeikan. Available at: http://www.chinese.cn/conference 11/article/2011-12/12/content_394522.htm (accessed on 28 January 2012.

Congressional Research Service (CRS) Library of Congress. 'China's Foreign Policy and "Soft Power" in South America, Asia, and Africa'. April 2008. Available at: http://www.gpo.gov/fdsys/pkg/CPRT-110SPRT41927/pdf/ CPRT-110SPRT41927.pdf (accessed on 11 October 2012).

Corben, R. 'Laos Looks to Balance China's Growing Economic Influence'. *VOA News*. 23 April 2015. Available at: http://www.voanews.com/content/laos-looks-to-balance-china-growing-economic-influence/2731417.html (accessed on 17 May 2016).

*CPC Encyclopedia*. 'Full Text of Hu Jintao's Report at the 17th Party Congress'. Available at: http://www.cpcchina.org/2010-09/07/content_13901643_6. htm (accessed on 5 September 2012).

*CRIEnglish.com*. 'Chinese Audiences Has a Favour of North America Movies'. 26 April 2012. Available at: http://english.cri.cn/7146/2012/04/26/2702s 695626.htm (accessed on 24 July 2012).

———. 'Mandarin-speaking Canadians Population Jumps 50 Per Cent'. 25 October 2012. Available at: http://english.cri.cn/6966/2012/10/25/2701s 728960.ht (accessed on 7 May 2015).

*Daily Star.* 'Analysis: "Pakistan is Our Israel"'. 19 September 2011. Available at: http://www.dailytimes.com.pk/default.asp?page=2011%5C09% 5C19%5Cstory_19-9-2011_pg3_2 (accessed on 9 September 2012).

Dasgupta, Uma and Anandarup Ray. 'Rabindranath Tagore and His Contemporary Relevance'. 2009. *Parabaas.com.* Available at: http://www.parabaas.com/ rabindranath/articles/pContemporaryTagore.html (accessed on 12 May 2016).

*Dawn.* 'Free Trade Zone in Gwadar'. 2 February 2015. Available at: http://www. dawn.com/news/1160849 (accessed on 11 August 2015).

Debroy, Bibek. 'India's Soft Power and Cultural Influence'. In *Challenges of Economic Growth, Inequality and Conflict in South Asia*, edited by Tan Tai Yong. Singapore: World Scientific, 2010.

*Deccan Chronicle.* 'Accountability Must for Rights Violations in Sri Lanka: India'. 27 February 2013. Available at: http://www.deccanchronicle.com/130227/ news-current-affairs/article/accountability-must-rights-violations-sri-lanka-india (accessed on 8 July 2013).

Deng, Yong. 'The New Hard Realities: "Soft Power" and China in Transition'. In *Soft Power: China's Emerging Strategy in International Politics* edited by Mingjiang Li. Maryland: Lexington Books, 2009.

DeSilvia-Ranasinghe, Sergei. 'Why the Indian Ocean Matters'. *The Diplomat.* 2 March 2011. Available at: http://thediplomat.com/2011/03/02/why-the-indian-ocean-matters/2/ (accessed on 6 September 2012).

*Dhaka Tribune.* 'BBIN Motor Vehicle Agreement Signed'. 16 June 2015. Available at: http://www.dhakatribune.com/bangladesh/2015/jun/16/bbin-motor-vehicle-agreement-signed (accessed on 6 July 2015).

Dhanapala, Jayantha and John Gooneratne. 'Sri Lanka: China as a Model of Growth and Modernisation'. In *A Resurgent China: South Asian Perspectives* edited by S.D. Muni and Tan Tai Yong. New Delhi: Routledge, 2012.

Ding, Sheng. *The Dragon's Hidden Wings: How China Rises with Its Soft Power.* UK: Lexington Books, 2008.

Dingli, Shen. 'Building China–India Reconciliation'. *Asian Perspective* 34, no. 4 (2010). Available at: http://www.asianperspective.org/articles/v34n4-g. pdf (accessed on 15 October 2012).

Dixit, J.N. *India's Foreign Policy and Its Neighbours.* New Delhi: Mehra Offset Press, 2001.

*DNA.* 'Wen Jiabao's Visit to India Aims to Build Mutual Trust: China'. 13 December 2010. Available at: http://www.dnaindia.com/world/report_ wen-jiabao-s-visit-to-india-aims-to-build-mutual-trust-china_1480655 (accessed on 3 October 2012).

———. 'Full Text of PM Narendra Modi's Speech at the India–China Business Forum'.16 May 2015. Available at: http://www.dnaindia.com/money/ report-full-text-of-pm-narendra-modi-s-speech-at-the-india-china-business-forum-2086368 (accessed on 23 May 2016).

Dobuzinskis, Alex. 'More U.S. Students Learning Chinese as School Language Programs Expand'. 21 April 2011. Available at: http://www.huffingtonpost. com/2011/04/21/more-us-students-learning_n_852093.html (accessed on 24 July 2012).

Dollar, David. 'China's Rise as a Regional and a Global Power: The AIIB and the "One Belt, One Road"'. 2015, Summer. Available at: http://www.brookings. edu/research/papers/2015/07/china-regional-global-power-dollar (accessed on 17 May 2016).

Dongxiao, Cheng. *Building up a Cooperative and Co-Progressive New Asia: China's Asia Strategy Towards 2020*. Shanghai: Shanghai Institute of International Studies, 2008.

Dover, Bruce. 'The Image of China in Australia: A Conversation with Bruce Dover'. *Global Media Journal* 8, no. 2 (2014). Available at: http://www.hca. uws.edu.au/gmjau/?p=841 (accessed on 16 April 2015).

Drury, Joe. 'Chinese Think India "Not Advanced" According to Survey'. 18 May 2010. Available at: http://www.2point6billion.com/news/2010/05/18/ chinese-think-india-%E2%80%98not-advanced%E2%80%99-according-to-survey-5700.html (accessed on 24 August 2011).

DuPont. 'China's Insatiable Appetite for Change'. White Paper. 2013 June. Available at: http://www.dupont.com/content/dam/assets/corporate-functions/our-approach/global-challenges/food/articles/documents/DuPont-Strategy-For-Food-Security-In-China-2.pdf (accessed on 5 February 2014).

Dutt, Srikant. 'India and the Himalayan States'. *Asian Affairs* 67, no. 1 (1980).

Economic and Commercial Counsellor's Office of the Embassy of the People's Republic of China in the Arab Republic of Egypt. 'Chinese Donation for Model School'. 17 October 2011. Available at: http://eg2.mofcom.gov.cn/ aarticle/bilateralvisits/201110/20111007784388.html (accessed on 6 March 2012).

Einbinder, Mary. 'Cultural Diplomacy Harmonizing International Relations Through Music'. *Master of Arts Thesis*. 2013 May. Available at: http:// www.culturaldiplomacy.org/pdf/case-studies/Cultural_Diplomacy_ Harmonizing_International_Relations_through_Music_-_Mary_Einbinder. pdf (accessed on 14 January 2014).

Ellis, R. Evan. 'Chinese Soft Power in Latin America'. *NDU Press*. 2011. Available at: http://www.ndu.edu/press/lib/images/jfq-60/JFQ60_85-91_Ellis.pdf (accessed on 21 August 2012).

Embassy of India. 'Academic Studies'. Available at: http://www.indianembassy. org.cn/DynamicContent.aspx?MenuId=47&SubMenuId=0 (accessed on 4 October 2012).

———. 'India–Indonesia Relations'. 2013 June. Available at: http://www. indianembassyjakarta.com/index.php/2013-05-20-10-02-04 (accessed on 28 July 2013).

Embassy of India. 'Major Indian Projects in Myanmar'. 2016 Available at: http://
www.indiaembassyyangon.net/index.php?option=com_content&view=
article&id=54&Itemid=137&lang=en (accessed on 8 June 2016).
————. 'A Talk on "Tradition of Indian Writings and Literature in India"'. 10 May
2011. Available at: http://www.indianembassy.org.cn/NewsDetails.aspx?
NewsId=199&NAID=1 (accessed on 28 November 2012).
————. 'Embrace a Better Tomorrow for China–Canada Educational
Cooperation'. 19 October 2011. Available at: http://ca.china-embassy.org/
eng/zjgx_1/jyjl/t868977.htm (accessed on 28 August 2012).
————. 'Joint Communique of the Republic of India and the People's Republic of
China'. 16 December 2010. Available at: http://www.indianembassy.org.cn/
NewsDetails.aspx?NewsId=162&NAID=1 (accessed on 4 October 2012).
Embassy of the People's Republic of China in Australia. 'Chinese, Vietnamese
New Agencies Hold Photo Exhibition to Mark 60 Years of Diplomatic
Relations'. 15 January 2010. Available at: http://au.china-embassy.org/eng/
zggk/wh/t651664.htm (accessed on 23 January 2012).
Embassy of the People's Republic of China in the Islamic Republic of Pakistan.
'PM Gilani Concludes Successful Visit to China'. 17 October 2009.
Available at: http://pk.chineseembassy.org/eng/zbgx/t620978.htm
(accessed on 2 February 2010).
Embassy of the People's Republic of China in the United States of America.
'China–US Relations'. 1 July 2012. Available at: http://www.china-embassy.
org/eng/zmgxs/ocusr/ (accessed on 24 July 2012).
*Energy Daily.* 'China Investing in South Korean Power Grid'. 25 July 2011.
Available at: Available at: http://www.energy-daily.com/reports/China_
investing_in_South_Korean_power_grid_999.html (accessed on 9 June
2016).
*English.chinamil.com.cn.* 'China–Myanmar Religious Exchange Enters New Phase
of Friendly Cooperation'. 23 February 2012. Available at: http://eng.
chinamil.com.cn/news-channels/2012-02/23/content_4798660.htm
(accessed on 16 October 2012).
*English.xinhuanet.com.* 'China, L. America to Strengthen Economic Ties, Explore
Further Cooperation'. 20 March 2012. Available at: http://news.xinhuanet.
com/english/china/2012-03/20/c_131478040.htm (accessed on 24
August 2012).
————. 'Chinese Premier Expresses Sympathy with Thai Flood Victims,
Announces More Aid'. 29 October 2011. Available at: http://news.xin
huanet.com/english2010/china/2011-10/29/c_122213429.htm (accessed
on 6 June 2016).
————. 'Hillary Clinton's India Visit Focuses on Iran'. 10 May 2012. Available at:
http://news.xinhuanet.com/english/video/2012-05/10/c_131579986.htm
(accessed on 25 August).

*English.xinhuanet.com.* 'LatAm Experts to Study Chinese Premier's Proposals for China–LatAm Cooperation in New Book'. 8 August 2012. Available at: http://news.xinhuanet.com/english/china/2012-08/08/c_131769324.htm (accessed on 23 August 2012).

*EU-China News.* 'European Culture in Constant Evolution'. 2011 April. Available at: http://newsletter.eu-in-china.com/newsletters/201104/014_en.html (accessed on 27 October 2012).

European Union Committee. 'Stars and Dragons: The EU and China'. Volume I: Report. 23 March 2009. Available at: http://www.publications.parliament. uk/pa/ld200910/ldselect/ldeucom/76/76i.pdf (accessed on 24 April 2012).

Feng, Xiao Yu. 'Non-traditional Security and China'. In *Transformation of Foreign Affairs and International Relations in China 1978–2008*, edited by Wang Yizhou. Beijing: Social Sciences Academic Press, 2008.

*Firstpost.com.* 'Just Speeches Won't Cut It: Modi Needs to Follow Up on China's $20 bn Investment Plan to India'. 12 May 2015. Available at: http://www. firstpost.com/world/just-speeches-wont-cut-it-modi-needs-to-follow-up-on-chinas-20-bn-investment-pledge-to-india-2236680.html (accessed on 2 July 2015).

*Flyingzone.* 'Chinese Letters in Japan, Korea, and Vietnam: Past, Present, and Future'. Available at: http://www.allempires.com/article/index.php?q=chinese_letters (accessed on 20 June 2013).

Foreign and Commonwealth Office. 'One China? Beijing and Its Diaspora: Opportunities, Responsibilities and Challenges'. Available at: https://www.gov.uk/government/uploads/system/uploads/attachment_data/file/384752/One_China_III.pdf (accessed on 7 May 2015).

Forum on China–Africa Cooperation. 'Chinese Medicine in East Africa'. 2 March 2012. Available at: http://www.focac.org/eng/zfgx/rwjl/t910390.htm (accessed on 4 April 2012).

———. 'China's Medical Aid Benefits 48 African Countries'. 22 February 2012. Available at: http://www.focac.org/eng/zxxx/t907457.htm (accessed on 7 April 2012).

———. 'Chinese Cultural Group Thrills Audience in Nairobi'. 9 September 2011. Available at: http://www.focac.org/eng/zfgx/rwjl/t857719.htm (accessed on 4 April 2012).

———. 'First Africa–China Young Leaders Forum Concluded, Declaration Reached'. 23 May 2011. Available at: http://www.focac.org/eng/zfgx/rwjl/t824873.htm (accessed on 4 April 2012).

———. 'China–Africa Media Cooperation: A Joint Force for Truth'. 25 April 2011. Available at: http://www.focac.org/eng/zfgx/rwjl/t817720.htm (accessed on 6 April 2012).

Forum on China–Africa Cooperation. 'Chinese Embassy in Morocco Briefing Media on 4th Session of 11th NPC'. 7 April 2011. Available at: http://www.focac.org/eng/zfgx/rwjl/t813150.htm (accessed on 6 April 2012).

————. 'China Forms Research Alliance to Upgrade China–Africa Medical Cooperation'. 12 February 2011. Available at: http://www.focac.org/eng/zfgx/rwjl/t794186.htm (accessed on 6 April 2012).

————. 'China's Aid to Africa: Enters Institutionalized New Stage'. 6 December 2011. Available at: http://www.focac.org/eng/xsjl/xzzs/t907005.htm (accessed on 18 April 2012).

Foster, Vivien, William Butterfield, Chuan Chen and Nataliya Pushak. 'Building Bridges: China's Growing Role as Infrastructure Financer for Sub-Sahara Africa'. *Executive Summary*. 2008. Available at: http://siteresources.world bank.org/INTAFRICA/Resources/BB_Final_Exec_summary_English_ July08_Wo-Embg.pdf (accessed on 17 April 2012).

Fox, Jonathan and Shmuel Sandler. *Bringing Religion into International into International Relations*. New York: Palgrave Macmillan, 2004.

French, W. Howard. 'Another Chinese Export is all the Rage: China's Language'. *New York Times*. 11 January 2006. Available at: http://www.nytimes. com/2006/01/11/international/asia/11china.html?pagewanted&_r=0 (accessed on 9 June 2016).

Fuller, Thomas. 'Myanmar Backs Down, Suspending Dam Project'. 30 September 2011. Available at: http://www.nytimes.com/2011/10/01/world/asia/ myanmar-suspends-construction-of-controversial-dam.html?adxnnl= 1&adxnnlx=1353413000-xAPCgPVO7UNARzVDgMteng (accessed on 20 November 2012).

Gagliardone, Iginio, Maria Repnikova and Nicole Stremlau. 'China in Africa: A New Approach to Media Development?' *Economic and Social Research Council*. Available at: http://global.asc.upenn.edu/fileLibrary/PDFs/china inafrica.pdf (accessed on 9 June 2016).

Gallarotti, G.M. 'Soft Power: What It Is, Why It's Important, and the Conditions for Its Effective Use'. *Journal of Political Power* 4, no. 1 (30 March 2011): 25–47.

————. *Cosmopolitan Power in International Relations: A Synthesis of Realism, Neoliberalism and Constructivism*. Cambridge: Cambridge University Press, 2010.

Ganguly, Sumit. 'India's Role in Afghanistan'. *CIDOB*. 2012 January. Available at: http://www.google.com.sg/url?sa=t&rct=j&q=&esrc=s&source=web& cd=1&ved=0CCcQFjAA&url=http%3A%2F%2Fwww.cidob.org%2Fes% 2Fcontent%2Fdownload%2F35196%2F567874%2Ffile%2FOK_SUMIT %2BGANGULY.pdf&ei=htA3U5eCI9HKrAeNlIHwBg&usg=AFQjCNEYc VsfU4IxAdCTF6BzuIj0ydrLOA&bvm=bv.63808443,d.bmk (accessed on 30 March 2014).

Ganguly, Sumit. *India's Foreign Policy: Retrospect and Prospect*. New Delhi: Oxford University Press, 2010.

Gettleman, Jeffrey. 'As Ivory Fuels African Wars, Elephants Vanish'. *International Herald Tribune*. 5 September 2012. Available at: https://www.questia.com/newspaper/1P2-36290852/as-ivory-fuels-african-wars-elephants-vanish (accessed on 9 January 2017).

*Global Arab Network*. 'Muscat: Oman, China Launch Friendship Association'. 8 November 2010. Available at: http://www.english.globalarabnetwork.com/201011087981/Oman-Politics/muscat-oman-china-launch-friendship-association.html (accessed on 14 March 2012).

*Global Development*. 'China Commits Billions in Aid and to Africa as Part of Charm Offensive: Interactive'. 29 April 2013. Available at: http://www.guardian.co.uk/global-development/interactive/2013/apr/29/china-commits-billions-aid-africa-interactive (accessed on 20 June 2013).

*Global Times*. 'Xi Meets with Honorary KMT Chairman Wu'. 14 June 2013. Available at: http://www.globaltimes.cn/content/788735.shtml#.UdAYkF-wrIU (accessed on 30 June 2013).

————. 'More Cultural Exchanges Will Enhance Nepal–China Relations'. 5 August 2012. Available at: http://www.globaltimes.cn/content/725162.shtml (accessed on 3 September).

————. 'China Gets Sea of Japan Trade Access'. 10 March 2010. Available at: http://china.globaltimes.cn/diplomacy/2010-03/511351_2.html (accessed on 31 January 2012).

*Globalsecurity.org*. 'Military Budget'. 4 March 2015. Available at: http://www.globalsecurity.org/military/world/india/budget.htm (accessed on 28 May 2015).

Goh, Evelyn. 'The Modes of China's Influence: Cases from Southeast Asia'. *Asian Survey* 54, no. 5 (2014, September/October): 825–48.

*Gov.cn*. 'China, Latin American and Caribbean States Troika Launch Regular Foreign Ministers' Dialogue. 9 August 2012. Available at: http://www.gov.cn/misc/2012-08/09/content_2201462.htm (accessed on 22 August 2012).

Government of India Scholarships. Available at: http://www.jamiahamdard.edu/govschol.asp#sss (accessed on 20 September 2012).

Grammaticus, Damian. 'China's Stake in the Syrian Stand-off'. 24 February 2012. Available at: http://www.bbc.co.uk/news/world-asia-china-17158889 (accessed on 4 April 2012).

Grant, Jeremy, Ben Bland and Gwen Robinson. 'South China Sea Issue Divides ASEAN'. *FT.com*. 16 July 2012. Available at: http://www.ft.com/intl/cms/s/0/3d45667c-cf29-11e1-bfd9-00144feabdc0.html#axzz4An4RH7QJ (accessed on 6 June 2016).

Gries, Hays Price. 'The Koguryo Controversy: National·Identity, and Sino-Korean Relations Today'. *East Asia* 22, no. 4 (2005, Winter). Available at: http://www.ou.edu/uschina/gries/articles/texts/Gries2005KoguryoEAIQ.pdf (accessed on 18 March 2013).

Guha, Ramachandra. 'Will India Become a Superpower?' 2012 March. Available at: http://www2.lse.ac.uk/IDEAS/publications/reports/pdf/SR010/guha. pdf (accessed on 13 September 2012).

————. 'How the Congress Lost the Diaspora'. 28 September 2014. Available at: http://www.hindustantimes.com/ramachandraguha/how-the-congress-lost-the-diaspora/article1-1269211.aspx (accessed on 27 May 2015).

*Gulf Daily News*. 'China Scholarship Chance for Five'. 8 January 2012. Available at: http://www.gulf-daily-news.com/NewsDetails.aspx?storyid=321148 (accessed on 8 March 2012).

Gupta, Sourabh. 'China–India Ties: Lessons from a Himalayan Standoff'. 19 May 2013. Available at: http://www.eastasiaforum.org/2013/05/19/china-india-ties-lessons-from-a-himalayan-standoff/ (accessed on 29 July 2013).

Haiyan, Jiang. 'Hong yang zhong hua minzu de you xiu wen hua yu zeng qiang wo guo de ruan shi li' (Promoting the Outstanding Culture of the Chinese Nation and Strengthening China's Soft Power). *Journal of the Party School of the Central Committee of the CCP* 11, no. 1 2007): 107–112.

Hall, Ian. 'Is a "Modi Doctrine" Emerging in Indian Foreign Policy?' *Australian Journal of International Affairs*. 2015. Available at: http://www.tandfonline. com/doi/abs/10.1080/10357718.2014.1000263#.VgUScU0cT4g (accessed on 25 September 2015).

Hall, Todd and Keren Yarhi-Milo. 'The Personal Touch: Leaders' Impressions, Costly Signalling and Assessments of Sincerity in International Affairs'. *International Sudies Quarterly* 56, no. 3 (2012) 560–73.

Han, Bochen. 'The Trouble with China–Mongolia Relations'. *The Diplomat*. 18 November 2015. Available at: http://thediplomat.com/2015/11/the-trouble-with-china-mongolia-relations/ (accessed on 5 May 2016).

*Hanban News*. 'The Third China–Mongolia Forum on Language, Philosophy and Social Science Kick-started'. 11 May 2012. Available at: http://english. hanban.org/article/2012-05/11/content_434447.htm (accessed on 4 June 2012).

————. 'Confucius Institute at Tajik National University, Tajikistan'. 12 December 2011. Available at: http://www.chinese.cn/conference11/article/ 2011-12/12/content_394535.htm (accessed on 17 February 2012).

————. 'Confucius Institute at National University of Mongolia Hosts the China–Mongolia Culture Forum'. 28 June 2011. Available at: http://english. hanban.org/article/2011-06/28/content_274583.htm (accessed on 9 January 2017).

Hanson, Elizabeth. 'India Wants to Be Your Friend: India and the "New Public Diplomacy"'. Paper presented at the Annual Meeting of the International Studies Association, San Diego, California. 3 April 2012.

Hanson, Fergus. 'Chinese Aid in Fiji: Behind the Hype'. 4 February 2010. Available at: http://www.lowyinterpreter.org/post/2010/02/04/Chinese-aid-in-Fiji-Behind-the-hype.aspx (accessed on 18 January 2012).

Harding, Brian. 'The Role of the Chinese Diaspora in Sino-Indonesian Relations'. 1 August 2008. Available at: http://www.jamestown.org/single/?tx_ttnews %5Btt_news%5D=5099 (accessed on 2 May 2016).

Heine, Jorge and R. Viswanathan. 'The Other BRIC in Latin America: India'. 2011 Spring. Available at: http://www.americasquarterly.org/node/2422 (accessed on 11 November 2012).

High Commission of India, Colombo, Sri Lanka. Available at: http://www. hcicolombo.org/index.php?option=com_pages&id=24 (accessed on 24 September 2012).

———. Kuala Lumpur. Available at: http://www.indianhighcommission.com. my/ec.php (accessed on 25 September 2012).

*Hindustan Times.* 'Tagore's Novels, Plays Translated into 16 Million Chinese Characters'. 5 May 2016. Available at: http://www.hindustantimes.com/ world/tagore-s-novels-plays-translated-into-16-million-chinese-characters/ story-NYOJS2vbn9NrIUe8wv2fXO.html (accessed on 9 January 2017).

Ho Jae, Chung. 'The "Rise" of China and Its Impact on South Korea'. *EAI Background Brief* No. 200, East Asia Institute, National University of Singapore. 26 July 2004.

Ho, Benjamin and Sun, Oh Ei. 'Beijing's Renewed Resolve: Treading the Path of Peaceful Development'. *RSIS Commentaries.* 25 February 2013. Available at: https://www.rsis.edu.sg/wp-content/uploads/2014/07/CO13036.pdf (accessed on 9 January 2017).

Ho, Chi-Ping. 'Australia "Biting the Hand" of China'. 4 July 2013. Available at: http://www.cdeclips.com/en/hongkong/fullstory.html?id=79296 (accessed on 4 July 2013).

Holden, John. 'Cultural Diplomacy'. 26 November 2011. Available at: http://www. gov.je/SiteCollectionDocuments/Leisure%20and%20entertainment/R%20 CulturalDiplomacyTalk%2020111126.pdf (accessed on 31 March 2015).

Holsti, J. Kalevi. *Peace and War: Armed Conflict and International Order.* Cambridge: Cambridge University Press, 1991.

Hong, Junhao. 'Mao Zedong's Cultural Theory and China's Three Mass-culture Debates: A Tentative Study of Culture, Society and Politics'. *Intercultural Communication Studies.* 1994. Available at: http://web.uri.edu/iaics/files/ 05-Junhao-Hong.pdf (accessed on 29 April 2016).

Hong, Zhao. 'Sino-African Relations: Going Beyond Energy Resources'. *EAI Background Brief* No. 435, East Asia Institute, National University of Singapore. 5 March 2009.

Hongmei, Li. 'China, Japan Endeavor to Seek Win-Win Relationship'. 2011. Available at: http://news.xinhuanet.com/english/indepth/2011-12/26/c_ 131327834.htm (accessed on 25 January 2012).

Hongyi Lai and Yiyi Lu. *China's Soft Power and International Relations.* New York: Routledge, 2012.

Hongyi, Lai. 'China's Soft Power: New Developments and Challenges'. *EAI Background Brief* No. 660. 22 September 2011.

Hongyi, Lai. 'China's Cultural Diplomacy: Going for Soft Power'. *East Asia Institute Background Brief* No. 308. 2006 October.

Hooghe, d'Ingrid. 'The Rise of China's Public Diplomacy'. *Netherlands Institute of International Relations*. 2007. Available at: http://www.clingendael.nl/publications/2007/20070700_cdsp_paper_hooghe.pdf (accessed on 27 September 2010).

————. *China's Public Diplomacy*. Netherlands: Koninklijke, 2015.

Hsiao, Michael H.H., and Yang, Alan. 'Ins and Outs of China Courtship'. *Asia Times Online*. 4 December 2008. Available at: http://www.atimes.com/atimes/Southeast_Asia/JL04Ae03.html (accessed on 11 June 2010).

Hu, Shaohua. 'Revisiting Chinese Pacifism'. *Asian Affairs: An American Review* 32, no. 4 (2006).

Hua, Hong Men. '*Zhong Guo ruan shi li ping gu bao gao*' (China's Soft Power Evaluation Report). China: Guo Ji Guan Cha (International Observe), 2007.

Huang, Jing and Xiaoting Li. *Inseparable Separation: The Making of China's Taiwan Policy*. Singapore: World Scientific, 2010.

Huning, Wang. '*Zuo wei guo jia shi li de wen hua: Ruan quan li*' [Culture Regarded as National Power: Soft Power]. *Journal of Fudan University* 3 (1993): 23–28.

*INCHINCLOSER*. 'Now Catch Your Favourite Zee TV Serials in China'. 15 April 2012. Available at: http://inchincloser.com/2012/04/15/now-catch-your-favourite-zee-tv-serials-in-china/ (accessed on 21 September 2012).

————. 'The Chinese Are Learning Gujarati'. 31 July 2012. Available at: http://inchincloser.com/2012/07/31/the-chinese-are-learning-gujarati/ (accessed on 8 October 2012).

————. 'China up Bilateral Co-operation; Sign Two Deals'. 22 February 2011. Available at: http://inchincloser.com/2011/02/22/india-china-up-bilateral-co-operation-sign-two-deals/ (accessed on 8 October 2012).

————. 'China, India, Myanmar Construct the Stilwell Road to Boost Regional Trade'. 14 January 2011. Available at: http://inchincloser.com/2011/01/14/china-india-myanmar-construct-the-stilwell-road-to-boost-regional-trade/ (accessed on 8 October 2012).

Bhasin, Singh, Avtar (ed). *India's Foreign Relations—2009 Documents*. 'Address by Foreign Secretary Shiv Shankar Menon at the Bureau of Parliamentary Studies and Training on 'India's Foreign Policy: opportunities and Challenges'. 21 July. New Delhi: Geetika Publishers, 2010.

Indian Council for Cultural Relations (ICCR). 'List of ICCR's "Chairs" Abroad'. Available at: http://www.iccrindia.net/chairslist.html (accessed on 3 July 2015).

————. 'General Cultural Scholarship Scheme'. Available at: http://www.iccrindia.net/gereralscheme.html (accessed on 6 July 2015).

————. 'International Buddhist Conference in Kandy, Sri Lanka'. 20–21 March 2011. Available at: http://www.iccrindia.net/majorevents.html (accessed on 12 November 2012).

Indian Council for Cultural Relations (ICCR). 2010–11. *Annual Report*. Available at: http://www.iccrindia.net/iccr-annualreport-2010-11/ICCR%20Annual %20Report%202010-2011.pdf (accessed on 29 November 2012).

Indian Public Diplomacy, Ministry of External Affairs, Government of India. Available at: http://www.indiandiplomacy.in/AboutUs.aspx (accessed on 13 September 2012).

*IndustryWeek*. 'India's Modi Tells China to "Reconsider" Approach'. 15 May 2015. Available at: http://www.industryweek.com/global-economy/indias-modi-tells-china-reconsider-approach (accessed on 2 June 2015).

*Infolanka.Asia*. 'China's Silicon Sea Route via Thailand Boon to Hambantota, but Threat to Singapore—China and Kra Canal'. 14 September. 2008. Available at: http://infolanka.asia/opinion/sri-lanka/chinas-silicon-sea-route-via-thailand-boon-to-hambantota-but-threat-to-singapore/impact-on-sri-lanka (accessed on 19 June 2013).

Information Office of the State Council of the People's Republic of China. 'Freedom of Religious Freedom in China'. 1997 October. Available at: http://chineseculture.about.com/library/china/whitepaper/blsreligion.htm (accessed on 1 December 2011).

*Infosys*. 'Infosys China Education & Research Head Conferred the Title of "Honorary citizen" of Nanhu District by Jiaxing Government'. Available at: https://www.infosys.com/newsroom/press-releases/Pages/honorary-citizen-jiaxing.aspx (accessed on 9 January 2017).

Inter-American Dialogue. Available at: http://www.thedialogue.org/page.cfm? pageID=117#Working (accessed on 23 August 2012).

————. 'Gobierno chino donará a Universidad de Santiago de Chile $800 millones en equipamiento docente' [Chinese government donated to University of Santiago of Chile]. 14 November 2011. Available at: http://noticias. universia.cl/vida-universitaria/noticia/2011/11/14/888320/gobierno-chino-donara-universidad-santiago-chile-800-millones-equipamiento-docente. html (accessed on 23 August 2012).

*International Market News*. 'Australian Food Goes Asian'. 5 July 2001. Available at: http://info.hktdc.com/imn/01070501/food03.htm (accessed on 21 January 2012).

*International New York Times*. 'Xi of China Announces Military Cuts at Parade'. 4 September 2015.

*Introduction Export Education*. Available at: http://cnx.org/content/m14289/latest/ China.pdf (accessed on 28 January 2012).

Iriye, Akira. *Cultural Internationalism and World Order*. Baltimore, MD: John Hopkins University Press, 1997.

*Iyenger Yoga*. 'China–India Yoga Summit'. Available at: http://iyengar-yoga. hu/188/ (accessed on 29 July 2013).

Jackson, Robert H., and Georg Sorensen. *Introduction to International Relations: Theories and Approaches*. New York: Oxford University Press, 2007.

Jacob, Jayanth. 'The Friendly Chinaman'. 24 May 2013. Available at: http://www.
    hindustantimes.com/India-news/NewDelhi/The-friendly-Chinaman/
    Article1-1065084.aspx (accessed on 18 June 2013).
Jacques, Martin. *When China Rules the World: The End of the Western World and the
    Birth of the New Global Order*. New Delhi: Penguin, 2009.
Jahanbegloo, Ramin. 'Nehru and Dialogue of Cultures'. 17 November 2012.
    Available at: http://jahanbegloo.com/content/nehru-and-dialogue-cultures
    (accessed on 8 June 2016).
*Jamaica Observer*. 'China Seeking Cooperation with Latin American, Caribbean
    Media'. 6 July 2010. Available at: http://www.jamaicaobserver.com/news/
    China-seeking-cooperation-with-Latin-American--Caribbean-media_
    7775429 (accessed on 23 August 2012).
Jetley, Neerja Pawha. 'Why Indians Have no Choice But to Learn Chinese'. *CNBC*.
    23 May 2013. Available at: http://www.cnbc.com/id/ (accessed on 9 May
    2016).
Jin, Wu. 'China's Public Diplomacy at Crossroads'. *China.org.cn*. 5 March 2012.
    Available at: http://www.china.org.cn/china/NPC_CPPCC_2012/2012-
    03/05/content_24811109.htm (accessed on 2 August 2012).
Jiwei, Lou. 'China Can Help West Build Economic Growth'. 27 November 2011.
    Available at: http://www.ft.com/cms/s/0/e3c5aacc-18ed-11e1-92d8-001
    44feabdc0.html#axzz1svhzWTJ9 (accessed on 24 April 2012).
Johnson, Christopher K., Ernest Z. Bower, Victor D. Cha, Michael J. Green and
    Goodman, Matthew P. 'Decoding China's Emerging "Great Power"
    Strategy'. *China File*. 2014 June. Available at: https://www.chinafile.com/
    library/reports/decoding-chinas-emerging-great-power-strategy-asia
    (accessed on 13 April 2016).
Johnson, Ian and Jackie Calmes. 'US Making Presence Felt in Beijing's Backyard'.
    *The International Herald Tribune*. 16 November 2011.
Johnston, Alastair Iain. *Cultural Realism: Strategic Culture and Grand Strategy in
    Chinese History*. Princeton, NJ: Princeton University Press, 1996.
Jones, Dan. 'London to Beijing....By Rail?' *EU Infrastructure*. 17 March 2010.
    Available at: http://www.euinfrastructure.com/news/china-europe-rail-
    link/ (accessed on 11 May 2012).
Ka-ho YU. 'Japan Challenging China's Rare Earth Hegemony'. *Journal of Energy
    Security*, 21 November 2012. Available at: http://www.ensec.org/index.php?
    option=com_content&id=391:challenging-chinas-rare-earth-monopoly-a-
    japanese-perspective&catid=130:issue-content&Itemid=405 (accessed on
    15 September 2015).
Kang, Hyungseok. 'Reframing Cultural Diplomacy: International Cultural
    Politics of Soft Power and the Creative Economy'. 2013. Available at:
    http://www.scribd.com/doc/205757571/Reframing-Cultural-Diplomacy-
    International-Cultural-Politics-of-Soft-Power-and-the-Creative-Economy-
    Hyungseok-Kang#scribd (accessed on 15 June 2015).

Kapur, Ashok. 'Eclipsed Moon to a Rising Star'. In *Security Beyond Survival*. New Delhi: SAGE Publications, 2004.

Kapur, Devesh. *Diaspora Development and Democracy*. Princeton, NJ: Princeton University Press, 2010.

Kavalski, Emilian. *China and the Global Politics of Regionalization*. Ashgate Publishing Company, 2009.

Keaney, A. Brian. 'The Realism of Hans Morgenthau'. 2006. Available at: http://scholarcommons.usf.edu/cgi/viewcontent.cgi?article=3579&context=etd (accessed on 22 October 2012).

Kearn, D.W., Jr. 'The Hard Truths about Soft Power'. *Journal of Political Power* 4, no. 1 (30 March 2011): 65–85.

Kember, James, and Paul Clark. *China and New Zealand: A Thriving Relationship Thirty Years on*. Auckland: New Zealand Asia Institute, 2003.

Kemp, John. 'China's Growing Strategic Stake in the Middle East: Kemp'. *Reuters*. 2 March 2012. Available at: http://www.reuters.com/article/2012/03/02/column-china-middle-east-oil-idUSL5E8E229T20120302 (accessed on 6 March 2012).

Khilnani, Sunil et al. 'Nonalignment 2.0: A Foreign and Strategic Policy for India in the Twenty First Century'. 2012. Available at: http://www.cprindia.org/sites/default/files/NonAlignment%202.0_1.pdf (accessed on 2 March 2013).

Khoo, Nicholas, Michael L.R. Smith and David Shambaugh. 'Correspondence'. *International Security* 30, no. 1 (2005).

Kieschnick, John. *The Impact of Buddhism on Chinese Material Culture*. Princeton, NJ: Princeton University Press, 2003.

Klingner, Bruce. 'China Shock for South Korea'. 11 September 2004. Available at: http://www.atimes.com/atimes/Korea/FI11Dg03.html (accessed on 29 November 2011).

Koike, Yuriko. 'China's Softly, Softly Approach'. *Today*. 1 February 2012.

Koleski, Katherine. 'Backgrounder: China in Latin America'. 27 May 2011. Available at: http://www.uscc.gov/Backgrounder_China_in_Latin_America.pdf (accessed on 21 August 2012).

Krishnan, Anant. 'China Highlights Outcome of Manmohan's Visit'. *The Hindu*. 26 October 2013. Available at: http://www.thehindu.com/todays-paper/tp-international/china-highlights-outcome-of-manmohans-visit/article5274223.ece (accessed on 31 March 2014).

Kumar, Madhurendra. 'Relevance of Ancient Indian Diplomatic Styles in Contemporary Era of Globalization. Available at: http://paperroom.ipsa.org/papers/paper_37301.pdf (accessed on 9 May 2016).

Kumar, Prasanna. 'China Eyes Big in Electronics Investment in Tamil Nadu'. 12 November 2014. Available at: http://www.deccanchronicle.com/141112/nation-current-affairs/article/china-eyes-big-electronics-investment-tamil-nadu (accessed on 8 January 2015).

Kumar, Rajiv and Santosh Kumar. *In the National Interest: A Strategic Foreign Policy for India*. New Delhi: BS Books, 2010.

Kurlantzick, Joshua. *Charm Offensive.* Yale University Press, 2007.

Kurlantzick, Joshua. 'China's Charm: Implications of Chinese Soft Power,' *Carnegie Policy Brief* No. 47. 2006 June. Available at: http://www.car negieendowment.org/files/PB_47_FINAL.pdf (accessed on 7 May 2009).

———. 'China's Charm Offensive in Southeast Asia'. *Current History.* 2006. Available at: http://www.carnegie-mec.org/publications/?fa=18678 (accessed on 21 June 2010).

Lal, Rollie. 'Central Asia and Its Asian Neighbours: Security and Commerce at Crossroads'. *Rand Corporation.* 2006. Available at: http://www.rand.org/pubs/monographs/2006/RAND_MG440.pdf (accessed on 15 February 2012).

Lampton, M. David. 'The Faces of Chinese Power'. *Foreign Affairs* 86, no. 1 (2006). Available at: http://www.comw.org/cmp/fulltext/0701lampton.pdf (accessed on 7 November 2012).

Lawrence, Dune. 'China's "Soft Power" Strategy Threatened by Obama, Slow Growth'. *Bloomberg.* 16 February 2009. Available at: http://www.bloomberg.com/apps/news?pid=newsarchive&sid=aS0aumUfVIyM (accessed on 2 December 2011).

Lebovic, James H. and Elizabeth N. Saunders. 'The Diplomatic Core: How the United States Employs High-level Visits as a Scarce Resource'. 2014 March. Available at: http://home.gwu.edu/~esaunder/ISA2014.Lebovic&Saunders.pdf (accessed on 13 June 2015).

Lee, Donna and David Hudson. 'The Old and New Significance of Political Economy in Diplomacy'. *Review of International Studies* 30 (2004).

Lee, Jung-Nam. 'The ROK's Perception of China's Role: Interviews with the ROK General Public. *Contemporary International Relations* 21, no. 6 (2011 November/December).

Lei, Zhao. '*Zhong guo ruan shi li ti sheng yin ren guan zhu*' [Increase of China's Soft Power Raises Attention]. *Zhong guo dang zheng ganbu lun tan* [Forum of Party and Government officials], 2007.

Lengauer, Sara. 'China's Foreign Aid Policy: Motive and Method'. *Bulletin of the Centre for East-West Cultural and Economic Studies* 9, no. 2 (2011 September–December). Available at: http://www.international-relations.com/CM2011/PRC-Foreign-Aid-2011.pdf (accessed on 13 March 2012).

Li, Changchun. 'Vigorously Promoting the Guiding Thought of the Sixth Plenary Session of the Seventeenth Central Committee of the Communist Party of China'. *Qiushi* (Organ of the Central Committee of the Communist Party of China). 1 January 2012. Available at: http://english.qstheory.cn/leaders/201204/t20120401_149157.htm (accessed on 11 August 2012).

Li, Hak Yin and Zhengxu, Wang. 'Assessing China's Influence in Central Asia: A Dominant Regional Power'. 2009 July. Available at: https://www.nottingham.ac.uk/cpi/documents/briefings/briefing-53-central-asia.pdf (accessed on 9 June 2016).

Li, Huang-chang. 'Problems of Industrialization'. 1967.

Liena, Fei and Xiong Sihao. 'Interview: China's Involvement in Africa's Infrastructure Development Has Fundamental, Transformative Impact: Ethiopian PM'. *China View*. 29 January 2009. Available at: http://news. xinhuanet.com/english/2009-01/29/content_10731854.htm (accessed on 16 April 2012).

Litao, Zhao. 'China's Higher Education as Soft Power'. *East Asia Institute (EAI) Background Brief* No. 659. 22 September 2011.

Liu, Haiming. 'The Chinese Diaspora: Space, Place, Mobility and Identity'. *Journal of Chinese Overseas* 2, no. 1 (2006, May).

Liu, Siwei. 'China Threat in South Asia: A Perspective from China'. *Institute of Peace and Conflict Studies* No. 4695. 16 October 2014. Available at: http://www.ipcs.org/article/india/china-threat-in-south-asia-a-perspective-from-china-4695.html (accessed on 1 April 2015).

London School of Economics Dissertation. 'The Diaspora as an Economic Asset'. 2009. Available at: http://www2.lse.ac.uk/economicHistory/Research/CCPN/publications/Dissertations/DissertationsCCP/72190.pdf (accessed on 19 September 2012).

*Loop*. 'China Boosting Aid to Pacific'. 3 March 2015. Available at: http://www.pngloop.com/2015/03/03/china-boosting-aid-south-pacific/ (accessed on 30 April 2015).

*Los Angeles Times*. 'Wanda of China Set to Buy More U.S. Entertainment Assets'. 4 September 2012. Available at: http://articles.latimes.com/2012/sep/04/business/la-fi-ct-amc-china-20120905 (accessed on 28 July 2013).

Lum, Thomas, Christopher M. Blanchard, Nicolas Cook, Kerry Dumbaugh, et al. 'Comparing Global Influence: China's and US Diplomacy, Foreign Aid, Trade and Investment in the Developing World'. *CRS Report for Congress* RL 34620. 2008. Available at: http://assets.opencrs.com/rpts/RL34620_20080815.pdf (accessed on 26 July 2013).

Lum, Thomas, Hannah Fischer, Julissa Gomez-Granger and Anne Leland. 'China's Foreign Aid Activities in Africa, Latin America and Southeast Asia'. *CRS*. 25 February 2009. Available at: www.accessmylibrary.com/coms2/summary_0286-38209015_ITM (accessed on 16 October 2012).

Lum, Thomas, Wayne M. Morrison and Bruce Vaughn. 'China's "Soft Power" in Southeast Asia'. *CRS report for Congress*. 4 January 2008. Available at: http://www.fas.org/sgp/crs/row/RL34310.pdf (accessed on 6 May 2009).

Lynch, C. Daniel. 'Securitizing Culture in Chinese Foreign Policy Debates: Implications for Interpreting China's Rise'. *Asian Survey* 53, no. 4 (2013 July/August).

Lyon, Rod. 'The Southeast Asian Emphasis in DWP2013'. Defence White Paper. 2013. Available at: http://www.aspistrategist.org.au/the-southeast-asian-emphasis-in-dwp2013/ (accessed on 1 February 2014).

Mackerras, Colin. 'Xinjiang and Central Asia Since 1990: Views from Beijing and Washington'. In *China, Xinjiang and Central Asia*, edited by Colin Mackerras and Michael Clarke. New York: Routledge, 2009.

Madan, Tanvi. 'Modi's Trip to China: 6 Quick Takeaways'. 15 May 2015. Available at: http://www.brookings.edu/research/opinions/2015/05/15-modi-china-takeaways-madan (accessed on 3 June 2015).

Mahfouz, Naguib. 'China for Us'. *Al Ahram Weekly Online*. 31 January–6 February 2002. Available at: http://weekly.ahram.org.eg/2002/571/op6.htm (accessed on 13 March 2012).

*Mail Online*. 'China's Vice President Revisits Youth with a Trip to the Midwest to Meet Farming Family He Stayed with on Exchange Trip'. 15 February 2012. Available at: http://www.dailymail.co.uk/news/article-2101652/Xi-Jinping-Chinas-Vice-President-visits-Midwest-farming-family-stayed-exchange-trip.html (accessed on 17 June 2015).

Malik, Aman. 'India–US Nuclear Agreement: India Clarifies, Says Supplier not Directly Liable in Case of a Mishap'. 2 August 2015. Available at: http://www.ibtimes.com/india-us-nuclear-agreement-india-clarifies-says-supplier-not-directly-liable-case-1809012 (accessed on 16 May 2016).

Malik, J. Mohan. 'India's Response to China's Rise'. In *The Rise of China and International Security: America and Asia Respond*, edited by Kevin J. Cooney and Yoichiro Sato. New York: Routledge, 2009.

Malone, David. *Does the Elephant Dance: Contemporary Indian Foreign Policy*. New York: Oxford University Press, 2011.

Manning, A. Robert. 'The Asian Energy Predicament'. *Survival* 42, no. 3 (2000 Autumn).

*MarineBuzz.com*. 'China Funds Sri Lanka Hambantota Port Development Project'. 2 November 2007. Available at: http://www.marinebuzz.com/2007/11/02/china-funds-sri-lanka-hambantota-port-development-project (accessed on 2 February 2010).

*Matangi Tonga Online*. 'Pacific Islands Parliamentarians Visit China'. 22 May 2013. Available at: http://matangitonga.to/2013/05/22/pacific-islands-parliamentarians-visit-china (accessed on 26 July 2013).

Mathew, C. Joseph. 'China–South Asia Strategic Engagements: Bhutan–China Relations'. *ISAS WP* No. 157. 2012 August. Available at: http://www.isas.nus.edu.sg/Attachments/PublisherAttachment/ISAS_Working_Paper_157_-_Bhutan_-_China_23082012174042.pdf (accessed on 31 August 2012)

Matthews, David. 'Sway: WikiLeaks, Universities and "Soft Power"'. 2 February 2012. Available at: http://www.timeshighereducation.co.uk/story.asp?story code=418884 (accessed on 6 June 2012).

Mbeki, Thabo. 'President Thabo Mbeki: At the Heavenly Gate in Beijing Hope Is Born!'. 13 November 2006. Available at: http://www.chinese-embassy.org.za/eng/zxxx/t279923.htm (accessed on 13 April 2012).

McMillan, Ann. 'Xinjiang and Central Asia: Interdependency-not Integration'. In *China, Xinjiang and Central Asia*, edited by Colin Mackerras and Michael Clarke. New York: Routledge, 2009.

Mead, W.R. 'America's Sticky Power'. *Foreign Policy* 141 (2004 March/April): 46–53.

*Media Network*. 'CRI Expands Its FM Coverage Across Nepal'. 28 October 2010. Available at: http://blogs.rnw.nl/medianetwork/cri-expands-its-fm-coverage-across-nepal (accessed on 5 September 2012).

Mengzi. 'Fallout of Snowden Expose'. *China Daily*. 13 July 2013. Available at: http://www.chinadaily.com.cn/opinion/2013-07/13/content_16770447. htm (accessed on 28 July 2013).

Miller, Manjari Chatterjee. 'Re-collecting Empire: "Victimhood" and the 1962 Sino-Indian War'. In *India's Foreign Policy: A Reader*, edited by Kanti P. Bajpai, Harsh V. Pant. New Delhi: Oxford University Press, 2013.

Minemura, Kenji. 'China's Growing Military Presence Has Russia on Edge'. *The Asahi Shimbun*. 21 February 2012. Available at: http://ajw.asahi.com/ article/asia/china/AJ201202210024 (accessed on 4 April 2012).

Ming'ai, Zhang. 'VP's Visit Warms US Impressions of China'. *China.org.cn*. 25 February 2012. Available at: http://www.china.org.cn/opinion/2012-02/25/content_24723040.htm (accessed on 26 July 2012).

Mingjiang, Li. 'Explaining China's Proactive Engagement in Asia'. In *Living with China: Regional States and China Through Crises and Turning Points* edited by Tang et al. New York: Palgrave Macmillan, 2009.

———. 'Soft Power in Chinese Discourse: Popularity and Prospect'. Rajaratnam School of International Studies (RSIS) Working Paper No. 65. 1 September 2008. Available at: http://www.rsis.edu.sg/publications/WorkingPapers/ WP165.pdf (accessed on 8 May 2009).

Ministry of Culture, Government of India. Available at: http://www.indiaculture. nic.in/ (accessed on 3 July 2015).

Ministry of Culture, PRC. 'Russians Get a Taste of Chinese Culture'. 2007. Available at: http://www.chinaculture.org/gb/en_focus/2007-06/01/ content_98584.htm (accessed on 21 March 2012).

Ministry of Education of the People's Republic of China. 'International Student Enrolments Exceeded 230,000 in 2009'. Available at: http://www.moe. edu.cn/publicfiles/business/htmlfiles/moe/moe_2862/201008/97180. html (accessed on 16 October 2012).

Ministry of External Affairs. 'India–Fiji Relations'. India. Available at: http://mea. gov.in/mystart.php?id=50042459 (accessed on 14 February 2012).

———. India–China Bilateral Relations. 2012 January. Available at: http://me aindia.nic.in/mystart.php?id=50042452 (accessed on 3 October 2012).

Ministry of Foreign Affairs of the People's Republic of China (*zhong hua ren min gong he guo wai jiao bu*). 'Dai Bingguo Attends the Reception on the 20th Anniversary of China's Diplomatic Ties with Five Central Asian

Countries'. 11 January 2012. Available at: http://www.fmprc.gov.cn/eng/zxxx/t895032.htm (accessed on 19 February 2012).

Ministry of Foreign Affairs of the People's Republic of China (*zhong hua ren min gong he guo wai jiao bu*). 'Xi Jinping Attends Welcome Luncheon Hosted by Overseas Chinese in Malaysia, Hoping that Overseas Chinese Will Make New Contributions to Friendly Cooperation between China and Malaysia'. 4 October 2013. Available at: http://www.fmprc.gov.cn/mfa_eng/topics_665678/xjpfwynmlxycx21apec_665682/t1085195.shtml (accessed on 2 May 2016).

———. Bilateral Relations: China–Iraq. 22 August 2010. Available at: http://www.fmprc.gov.cn/eng/wjb/zzjg/xybfs/gjlb/2823/ (accessed on 28 October 2012).

———. 'China and Pakistan'. 23 October 2010. Available at: http://www.mfa.gov.cn/eng/wjb/zzjg/yzs/gjlb/2757/t16110.htm (accessed on 20 January 2010).

———. Remarks of Chinese Vice Foreign Minister Song Tao at the Special Conference on Afghanistan Convened Under the Auspices of the Shanghai Cooperation Organisation. 27 March 2009. Available at: http://www.fmprc.gov.cn/eng/zxxx/t555299.htm (accessed on 8 February 2010).

———. 'Declaration of the Beijing Summit of the Forum on China–Africa Cooperation'. 2006. Available at: http://www.fmprc.gov.cn/eng/wjdt/zyjh/t279852.htm (accessed on 31 March 2012).

———. 'China's EU Policy Paper'. 13 October 2003. Available at: http://www.fmprc.gov.cn/eng/wjb/zzjg/xos/dqzzywt/t27708.htm (accessed on 24 April 2012).

———. 'Wen Jiabao Attends the 13th EU–China Summit'. 7 October 2010. Available at: http://www.fmprc.gov.cn/eng/topics/wenjiabaozonglifang wenouyasiguo/t759689.htm (accessed on 27 April 2012).

Ministry of Overseas Indian Affairs. 'The Prime Minister's Inaugural Speech at the sixth PBD'. 2008. Available at: http://www.overseasindian.in/pdf/2008/feb/ParvasiEnglishFeb08forweb.pdf (accessed on 19 September 2012).

Minxin, Pei. 'The Dark Side of China's Rise'. *Foreign Policy* 153 (2006).

———. 'Dangerous Misperceptions: Chinese Views of India's Rise'. 23 May 2011. Available at: https://casi.sas.upenn.edu/iit/pei (accessed on 20 July 2015).

Mission of the People's Republic of China to the European Union. 'China Sticks to Reform, Opening Up Policy: Wen'. 7 December 2005. Available at: http://www.chinamission.be/eng/sbgx/sbjw/t225202.htm (accessed on 3 June 2016).

Mitra, K. Subrata. *Politics in India*. New Delhi: Oxford University Press, 2014.

Mohan, C. Raja. 'Beyond Non-Alignment'. In *India's Foreign Policy: A Reader*. New Delhi: Oxford University Press, 2013.

Mohan, C. Raja. *Crossing the Rubicon: the Shaping of India's Foreign Policy.* New Delhi: Viking, 2003.

———. 'India's Regional Security Cooperation: The Nehru Raj Legacy'. ISAS Working Paper No. 168. 7 March 2013.

Moon, Kyu-toi. 'South Korean Public Opinion Trends and Effects on the ROK–US Alliance'.2011 February. Available at: http://asiafoundation.org/resources/pdfs/MoonPubilcOpinion.pdf (accessed on 26 July 2013).

Moore, Malcolm. 'China to Build $2bn Railway for Iran'. *The Telegraph.* 7 September 2010. Available at: http://www.telegraph.co.uk/finance/china-business/7985812/China-to-build-2bn-railway-for-Iran.html (accessed on 6 March 2012).

Moyo, F. Dambisa. *Winner Take All.* New York: Basic Books, 2012.

Muni, S.D. 'Stabilizing the Neighbourhood: India's Flip-flop Approach to Maldives Crisis'. ISAS Working Paper No. 145. 16 March 2012.

Munter, Cameron. 'Anticipating China's "One-Belt-One Road" in South Asia'. *The Diplomat.* 3 February 2016. Available at: http://thediplomat.com/2016/02/anticipating-chinas-one-belt-one-road-in-south-asia/ (accessed on 19 May 2016).

Myrdal, Gunnar. *Asian Drama: An Enquiry into the Poverty of Nations.* New York: Pantheon, 1968.

Nayar, Baldev Raj and T.V. Paul. *India in the World Order: Searching for Major-power Status.* Cambridge University Press, 2003.

Ness, Van, Peter, 'Japan, the Indispensable Power in Northeast Asia'. *Global Asia.* 2010 January. Available at: http://www.globalasia.org/V4N4_Winter_2010/Peter_Van_Ness.html (accessed on 29 January 2012).

News of the Communist Party of China. Cultural Exchanges Vital in Sino-Russian Partnership: Chinese VP'. 25 March 2010. Available at: http://english.cpc.people.com.cn/66102/6930530.html (accessed on 21 March 2012).

Nolte, Detlef. 'How to Compare Regional Powers: Analytical Concepts and Research Topics'. Review of International Studies. 2010. Available at: http://www.giga-hamburg.de/dl/download.php?d=/content/staff/nolte/publications/how_to_compare_nolte.pdf (accessed on 9 September 2012).

Norbu, Dawa. 'Chinese Strategic Thinking on Tibet and the Himalayan Region'. Strategic Analysis. 1988 July. Available at: http://www.idsa.in/system/files/ChineseStrategicThinking_DawaNorbu.pdf (accessed on 19 July 2013).

Norling, Nicklas. 'China and Russia: Partners with Tension'. *Policy Perspectives* 4, no. 1 (2007).

Nye, Joseph. *The Future of Power.* New York: Public Affairs, 2011.

———. 'In Mideast, the Goal Is "Smart Power"'. *Boston Globe.* 19 August 2006. Available at: http://www.boston.com/news/globe/editorial_opinion/oped/

articles/2006/08/19/in_mideast_the_goal_is_smart_power/ (accessed on 18 February 2013).

Official Website of SCO Summit. 'China to Provide 150-mln-yuan Grant to Afghanistan During 2012'. 2012. Available at: http://www.scosummit2012. org/english/2012-06/08/c_131639621.htm (accessed on 4 September 2012).

Pacific Media Centre. 'PNGs Ramu NiCo Mine: An Environmental Time Bomb'. 8 November 2012. Available at: http://www.pmc.aut.ac.nz/articles/ pngs-ramu-nico-mine-environmental-time-bomb (accessed on 25 April 2015).

Pak, Jennifer. 'Will China's Rise Shape Malaysian Chinese Community'. 30 December 2011. Available at: http://www.bbc.co.uk/news/world-asia-16284388 (accessed on 13 June 2012).

Pakistan–China Institute. 'First Sino-Pakistan University Students' Forum Concluded'. 27 May 2011. Available at: http://nihao-salam.com/news-detail.php?id=Nzg (accessed on 3 September 2012).

Palit, Amitendu. *China–India Economics: Challenges, Competition and Collaboration*. Routledge, 2012.

———. 'China Crucial to India's Mobile Revolution'. Asia Pacific Memo. 11 September 2012. Available at: http://www.asiapacificmemo.ca/china-crucial-to-india-mobile-revolution (accessed on 16 November 2012).

———. 'China–India Strategic Economic Dialogue: Avoiding Unavoidables?' *ISAS Insights* 147. 7 December 2011. Available at: http://www.isas.nus. edu.sg/Attachments/PublisherAttachment/ISAS_Insights_147__-_China-India_Strategic_Economic_Dialogue_07122011165513.pdf (accessed on 7 October 2012).

———. 'Wen in India, Time for business'. *Financial Express*. 15 December 2010. Available at: http://www.financialexpress.com/news/column-wen-in-india-time-for-business/724747/0 (accessed on 3 October 2012).

———. 'India's Economic Engagement with Southeast Asia: Progress and Challenges'. ISAS Working Paper No. 60. 4 June 2009.

Palit, Parama Sinha and Amitendu Palit. 'Strategic Influence of Soft Power: Inferences for India from Chinese Engagement of South and Southeast Asia'. ICRIER Policy Series. No. 3. 2011 August. Available at: http://www. icrier.org/pdf/policy_series_no_3.pdf (accessed on 30 March 2014).

Palit, Parama Sinha. 'China's Cultural Diplomacy: Historical Origin, Modern Methods and Strategic Outcomes'. *China Currents*. 12, no. 2 (13 January 2014). Available at: http://www.chinacenter.net/chinas-cultural-diplomacy-historical-origin (accessed on 28 January 2014).

———. 'Soft Power Through Education: Indian and Chinese Strategies in South and Southeast Asia'. In *China, USA and the World–Theatres of Soft Power*, edited by Naren Chitty, Beijing: Project 211 National Key University, 2015.

Palitiel, Jeremy. 'China's Regionalization Policies: Illiberal Internationalism or Neo-Mencian Benevolence?' In *China and the Global Politics of Regionalization*. Ashgate Publishing Company, 2009.

Pan, Esther. 'South-Korea's Ties with China, Japan and the US: Defining a New Role in a Dangerous Neighbourhood'. *Council of Foreign Relations Backgrounder*. 8 February 2006. Available at: http://www.cfr.org/east-asia/south-koreas-ties-china-japan-us-defining-new-role-dangerous-neighborhood/p9808 (accessed on 31 January 2012).

Pandey, Jhilmil Mukherjee. 'Chinatown Revival at Tiretta Bazar, Tangra'. 3 January 2014. Available at: http://articles.timesofindia.indiatimes.com/2014-01-03/kolkata/45834940_1_tangra-new-chinatown-project (accessed on 22 January 2014).

Pant, Harsh V. Full Text of *Li Keqiang's Speech at Opening Ceremony of Boao Forum*. 3 April 2012. Available at: http://english.peopledaily.com.cn/90883/7777309.html (accessed on 4 April 2012).

*People.cn*. 'China's Public Diplomacy: Let the World Understand a Real China'. 25 July 2011. Available at: http://theory.people.com.cn/GB/49150/49152/15233878.html (accessed on 2 August 2012).

*People's Daily Online*. 'China Donates Mobile Hospital to Ecuador'. 20 July 2013. Available at: http://english.peopledaily.com.cn/90883/8334480.html (accessed on 24 July 2013).

———. 'China's First Public Diplomacy Research Center Established in Beijing'. 27 August 2010. Available at: http://english.peopledaily.com.cn/90001/90776/90883/7120535.html (accessed on 20 September 2010).

———. 'China's Foreign Aid Comes with "No Strings Attached"'. 27 April 2011. Available at: http://en.people.cn/90001/90776/90883/7362863.html (accessed on 3 June 2016).

———. 'Third Plenary Session of the 18th CPC Central Committee Deepening Reform & Upgrading China'.9 November 2013. Available at: http://en.people.cn/102775/208695/ (accessed on 30 March 2015).

———. 'China's Global Image on the Upswing'. 19 March 2015. Available at: http://en.people.cn/n/2015/0319/c90882-8865231.html (accessed on 20 March 2015).

———. 'China Grants 30 mln USD to Sierra Leone for Construction'. 22 February 2013. Available at: http://english.peopledaily.com.cn/90883/8139009.html (accessed on 18 March 2013).

———. 'China Grants 200 mln USD in Loans for New Railway Project in Sri Lanka'. 4 March 2013. Available at: http://english.peopledaily.com.cn/90883/8152884.html (accessed on 15 March 2013).

———. 'China and Russia Seek to Expand Tourism Ties'. 24 March 2012. Available at: http://english.peopledaily.com.cn/90883/7767721.html (accessed on 27 March 2012).

*People's Daily Online.* 'China's "Peace Ark" Hospital Ship to Anchor at Port Victoria in Seychelles'. 26 October 2012. Available at: http://english.peopledaily. com.cn/90001/90776/90785/7178315.html (accessed on 15 March 2013).

———. 'China Reiterates Opposition to Ivory Smuggling'. 6 September 2012. Available at: http://english.peopledaily.com.cn/90883/7938184.html (accessed on 7 September 2012).

———. 'Chinese Vice President Vows Closer Ties with Egypt'. 22 March 2012. Available at: http://english.peopledaily.com.cn/90883/7765427.html (accessed on 22 March 2012).

'China, Thailand to Cement Cooperation on High-speed Railway Construction'. 20 April 2012. Available at: http://english.peopledaily.com.cn/90883/ 7793448.html (accessed on 24 April 2012).

———. 'Chinese Medical Team Renews Free Eye Surgery in Myanmar'. 8 May 2012. Available at: http://english.peopledaily.com.cn/90883/7811268. html (accessed on 13 May 2012).

———. 'China, Japan, Rok Agree to Enhance Cultural Cooperation'. 7 May 2012. Available at: http://english.peopledaily.com.cn/90883/7809105. html (accessed on 13 May 2012).

———. 'Chinese Firms Look More and More to Europe'. 29 March 2012. Available at: http://english.peopledaily.com.cn/90778/7773176.html (accessed on 29 March 2012).

———. 'China Eyes Urbanisation, Energy Cooperation with Europe'. 24 April 2012. Available at: http://english.peopledaily.com.cn/90883/7796634. html (accessed on 24 April 2012).

———. 'Cultural Exchange Plays Important Role in China–Africa Relationship'. 5 November 2009. Available at: http://english.peopledaily.com.cn/90001/ 90782/90873/6804545.html (accessed on 31 March 2012).

People's Government of Guangdong Province, Foreign Affairs Office. *'Guan yu xia fang bu fen dui wai wen hua jiao liu xiang mu shen pi quan xian de tong zhi'* (About providing authority to the provinces to organize cultural activities with other countries). 10 August 2011. Available at: http://www.gdfao. gd.gov.cn/Item.aspx?id=7961 (accessed on 11 July 2013).

Perlez, Jane. 'Drawing Spheres of Influence, Without the US'. *International Herald Tribune.* 6 June 2012.

———. 'Chinese Leaders See Eclipse of US'. *International Herald Tribune.* 3 April 2012.

Pew Research Centre Publications. 'Ask the Expert: Public Opinion about US and China'. 13 February 2012. Available at: http://pewresearch.org/pubs/2194/ china-united-states-relations-xi-jinping-barack-obama-ask-the-expert (accessed on 24 March 2012).

———. 'How Asia-Pacific Publics See Each Other and Their National Leaders'. 2 September 2015. Available at: http://www.pewglobal.org/2015/09/02/ how-asia-pacific-publics-see-each-other-and-their-national-leaders/ (accessed on 17 September 2015).

Pew Research Centre Publications. 'China's Image'. 14 July 2014. Available at: http://www.pewglobal.org/2014/07/14/chapter-2-chinas-image/ (accessed on 8 April 2015).

Peyrouse, Sebastien. 'Economic Aspects of Chinese-Central Asia Rapprochement'. *Silk Road Paper*. 2007 September. Available at: http://www.silkroadstudies. org/resources/pdf/SilkRoadPapers/0709China-Central_Asia.pdf (accessed on 21 September 2015).

Pham, Peter, J. 'China's Interests in the Middle East and North Africa in the Light of Recent Developments in Those Regions'. *Atlantic Council*. 13 April 2011. Available at: http://www.uscc.gov/hearings/2011hearings/written_ testimonies/11_04_13_wrt/11_04_13_pham_testimony.pdf (accessed on 10 March 2012).

Poon, Aries. 'Soft Power Smackdown! Confucius Institute vs Taiwan Academy'. *Wall Street Journal*. Available at: http://blogs.wsj.com/chinarealtime/ 2011/08/12/soft-power-smackdown-confucius-institute-vs-taiwan- academy/ (accessed on 31 January 2012).

Potter, Pitman B. and Thomas Adams. 'Issues in Canada–China Relations'. Canadian International Council. Available at: http://www.opencanada. org/wp-content/uploads/2011/11/CIC-Issues-in-Canada-China- Relations-2011.pdf (accessed on 27 August 2012).

Pradhan, Prasanta Kumar. 'Accelerating India's "Look West Policy" in the Gulf'. IDSA Issue Brief. 3 February 2011. Available at: http://www.idsa.in/ system/files/IB_IndiaLookWestPolicy.pdf (accessed on 8 March 2012).

*Prensa Latina*. 'Xinhua, Prensa Latina News Agencies Strengthen Ties'. 9 August 2012. Available at: http://www.plenglish.com/index.php?option=com_ content&task=view&id=534106&Itemid=1 (accessed on 23 August 2012).

Price, Gareth. 'Diversity in Donorship: The Changing Landscape of Official Humanitarian Aid: India's Official Aid Programme'. Available at: http:// www.odi.org.uk/resources/docs/416.pdf (accessed on 24 September 2012).

Prime Minister of Canada. 'PM Wraps-up Third Official Visit to Canada'. 10 November 2014. Available at: http://pm.gc.ca/eng/news/2014/11/10/ pm-wraps-third-official-visit-china (accessed on 7 May 2015).

Princeton University. 'Posing Problems without an Alliance: China–Iran Relations After the Nuclear Deal'. *China and the World Program*. 12 February 2016. Available at: http://cwp.princeton.edu/news/posing- problems-without-alliance-china-iran-relations-after-nuclear-deal (accessed on 9 May 2016).

Putin, Vladimir. 'Russia and the Changing World'. 27 February 2012. Available at: http://rt.com/politics/official-word/putin-russia-changing-world-263/ (accessed on 20 March 2012).

Ramo, Joshua Cooper. 'Brand China'. 2007 February. Available at: http://fpc.org. uk/fsblob/827.pdf (accessed on 2 November 2012).

Randall, Peerenboom. 'The Fire Breathing Dragon and the Cute, Cuddly Panda: The Implication of China's Rise for Developing Countries, Human Rights, and Geopolitical Stability'. *Chicago Journal of International Law* no. 1 (2006).

Randol, Shaun. 'How to Approach the Elephant: Chinese Perceptions of India in the Twenty-first Century'. In *China's International Relations in Asia*. Vol. I, edited by Li Mingjiang. New York: Routledge, 2010.

Rao, P.V. Narasimha. 'Nehru and Non-alignment'. *Mainstream* 47, no. 24 ( 30 May.2009). Available at: http://www.mainstreamweekly.net/article1399. html (accessed on 10 May 2016).

Raska, Michael. 'Australia's Evolving "Smart Power" Strategy'. *RSIS Commentaries.* 28 May 2013. Available at: https://www.rsis.edu.sg/wp-content/uploads/2014/07/CO13101.pdf (accessed on 9 January 2017).

Rebol, Max. 'Public Perceptions and Reactions: Gauging African Views of China in Africa'. *African Journal of Agricultural Research* 5, no. 25 (2010). Available at: http://www.academicjournals.org/ajar/pdf/pdf%202010/25%20Dec/Rebol.pdf (accessed on 28 March 2012).

*Rediff News.* 'Grandpa Wen' Spends Time with School Kinds'. 16 December 2010. Available at: http://www.rediff.com/news/report/grandpa-wen-spends-time-with-school-kids/20101216.htm (accessed on 3 October 2012).

———. 'How Modi Will Change India's Foreign Policy'. 14 May 2014. Available at: http://www.rediff.com/news/column/ls-election-how-narendra-modi-will-change-indias-foreign-policy/20131014.htm (accessed on 1 June 2015).

Ren, Guixiang. *Haiwai Huaren Huaqiao yu Zhongguo Gaige Kaifang.* (Overseas Chinese and Chinese Overseas in China's Reforms and Opening Up. Beijing: Zhonggong Dangshi Chubanshe-History of Chinese Communist Party Press, 2009.

Repnikova, Maria and Harley Balzer. 'Chinese Migration to Russia: Missed Opportunities'. Kennan Institute. 2009. Available at: https://www.wilsoncenter.org/sites/default/files/No3_ChineseMigtoRussia.pdf (accessed on 6 May 2016).

Roche, Elizabeth. 'India, with an Eye on ASEAN, Looks to Deepen Ties with Malaysia'. *The Mint.* 8 July 2013.

Rong, Zhao Chang. 'Zhong Guo xu yao ruan shi li' (China Needs Soft Power). *Liao Wang Xin Wen Zhou Kan.* 7 June 2004.

Roy, Shubhajit. 'First Time in a Joint Statement: India, Japan Unite on South China Sea'. *The Indian Express.* 13 December 2015. Available at: http://indianexpress.com/article/india/india-news-india/first-time-in-a-joint-statement-india-japan-unite-on-south-china-sea/ (accessed on 8 June 2016).

*Sahitya Akademi.* 'Cooperation with UNESCO'. Available at: http://sahitya-akademi.gov.in/sahitya-akademi/cultural-exchange-programme/cooperation_with_unesco.jsp (accessed on 11 November 2012).

Sahoo, Pravakar and Abhirup Bhunia. 'BCIM Corridor a Game Changer for South Asian Trade'. *East Asia Forum*. 18 July 2014. Available at: http://www.eastasiaforum.org/2014/07/18/bcim-corridor-a-game-changer-for-south-asian-trade/ (accessed on 6 April 2015).

Sahoo, Pravakar. 'India Should Be Part of the New Silk Route'. *Business Line*. 22 December 2015. Available at: http://www.thehindubusinessline.com/opinion/india-should-be-part-of-the-new-silk-route/article8018656.ece (accessed on 16 May 2016).

Sambath, Phou. 'Cambodia–China Relation: Past, Present and Future'. Available at: http://www.ncku.edu.tw/cseas/98CSEAS/report%20SEA/CAM/cam11%20phou%20sambath.pdf (accessed on 9 August 2010).

Schmetzer, Uli. *The Chinese Juggernaut*. Tizuli Publishing, 2011.

*Scholarship-positions.com*. '2011 Huawei-Maitree Scholarship for Applicants of China, India'.2011. Available at: http://scholarship-positions.com/2011-huawei-maitree-scholarship-for-applicants-of-india-china/2011/05/07/ (accessed on 4 October 2012).

Schurmann, Franz and Orville Schell. *Imperial China: The Decline of the Last Dynasty and the Origins of Modern China, the 18th & 19th Centuries*. New York: Vintage.

Sebastian, Eugene. 'The Power of Diaspora'. 16 June 2006. Available at: http://insideasia.typepad.com/ (accessed on 19 September 2012).

Seethi, K.M., Vijayan, P. 'Political Economy of India's Third World Policy'. In *Engaging with the World: Critical Reflections on India's Foreign Policy*. New Delhi: Orient Blackswan, 2009.

Segal, Gerald. 'China and the Disintegration of the Soviet Union'. *Asian Survey* 32, no. 9 (1992 September).

*Selected Works of Jawaharlal Nehru*. 2, no. 2. Available at: http://www.claudearpi.net/maintenance/uploaded_pics/SW02.pdf (accessed on 30 November 2012).

Sen Gupta, Bhabani. 'The Big Brother Syndrome'. *India Today*. 30 April 1984.

Sen, Amartya. The *Argumentative Indian*. England: Penguin Books, 2005.

Seng, Tin, Lim. 'Renewing 35 Years of Malaysia–China Relations: Najib's Visit to China'. *EAI Background Brief* No. 460. 23 June 2009.

Seong, John Lee Cheong. 'Unrealised Potential: India's 'Soft Power' Ambition in South Asia'. *Foreign Policy Analysis*, no. 4 (2010).

Shambaugh, David. 'China Eyes Europe in the World'. In *China–EU Relations*, edited by Shambaugh, David, Sandschneider, Eberhard, Hong, Zhou. New York: Routledge, 2008.

———. 'China Engages Asia: Reshaping the Regional Order'. *International Security* 30, no. 1 (2005 Summer).

*Shanghai Daily*. 'Both Nations Benefit from High-tech Partnership'. 15 August 2012.

*Shanghai Daily.* 'Xi Vows no Compromises Over China's Sovereignty'. 30 January 2013. Available at: http://www.shanghaidaily.com/nation/Xi-vows-no-compromises-over-Chinas-sovereignty/shdaily.shtml (accessed on 7 June 2016).

———. 'First World Yoga Day Celebrated in Shanghai'. 21 June 2015. Available at: http://www.shanghaidaily.com/metro/health-and-science/First-World-Yoga-Day-celebrated-in-Shanghai/shdaily.shtml (accessed on 21 July 2015).

Sharma, Navrekha. 'Why Indonesia Is Important for India'. IDSA issue Brief No. 20 January 2011. Available at: http://www.idsa.in/issuebrief/Why IndonesiaisImportanttoIndia.html (accessed on 25 May 2016).

Shepard, Wade. 'The Story Behind the World's Emptiest International Airport'. *Forbes.* 28 May 2016. Available at: http://www.forbes.com/sites/wadeshepard/2016/05/28/the-story-behind-the-worlds-emptiest-international-airport-sri-lankas-mattala-rajapaksa/#4359e36262fd (accessed on 3 June 2016).

Shirk, Susan. 'One-sided Rivalry: China's Perceptions and Policies Toward India'. In *The India–China Relationship: What the United States Needs to Know*, edited by Frankel, R. Francine, Harding, Harry. New Delhi: Oxford University Press, 2004.

Shivananda, H. 'China's Pipelines in Myanmar'. IDSA Comment. 10 January 2012. Available at: http://www.idsa.in/idsacomments/ChinasPipelines inMyanmar_shivananda_100112 (accessed on 21 May 2012).

Shu-ling Ko. 'Officials Propose Taiwan, China Cultural Exchanges'. *Taipei Times.* 7 September 2010. Available at: http://www.taipeitimes.com/News/front/archives/2010/09/07/2003482290/1 (accessed on 31 January 2012).

Siddiqa, Ayesha. 'Expansion by Stealth: China's Interest, Infrastructure and Investments in Pakistan and Afghanistan'. CIDOB Policy Research Project. January 2012.

*Sina English.* '28 Years on: China, Bhutan Gain Remarkable Headway in Border Talks'. 13 August 2012. Available at: http://english.sina.com/china/p/2012/0812/495879.html (accessed on 31 August 2012).

Singh, Akanksha. 'China to Set Up Two ASEAN Funds to Help Strengthen Trade and Investment'. *Bangkok Post.* 18 August 2009. Available at: http://thailand-business-news.com/asean/4132-china-asean-funds-setting-up-proposed (accessed on 7 March 2012).

Singh, Rahul. 'Infra Build-up Along China Border to Go On'. 11 May 2013. Available at: http://www.hindustantimes.com/India-news/Goa/Infra-build-up-along-China-border-to-go-on/Article1-1058663.aspx (accessed on 29 July 2013).

Sino-American Culture and Arts Foundation (SACAF). 'Mission and Vision'. Available at: http://www.sacaf.org/aboutus.html (accessed on 10 January 2017)

Smith, M. Jeff. 'China's Investments in Sri Lanka'. *Foreign Affairs*. 23 May 2016. Available at: https://www.foreignaffairs.com/articles/china/2016-05-23/chinas-investments-sri-lanka?cid=nlc-fatoday-20160525&sp_mid=51455977&sp_rid=YXllc2hhLndpamF5YWxhdGhAZ21haWwuY29tS0&spMailingID=51455977&spUserID=MTI5NDM1Nzg0MjM0S0&spJobID=923114236&spReportId=OTIzMTE0MjM2S0 (accessed on 3 June 2016).

Smith-Wesley, Terence and Edgar A. Porter. *China in Oceania: Shaping the Pacific?* London: Berghahn Books, 2010.

*Spotlight*. 'China's New Look West Policy to Give Primacy to India'. 9 November 2012. Available at: http://www.spotlightnepal.com/News/Article/-Chinas-new-Look-West-policy-to-give-primacy- (accessed on 11 August 2015).

Srivalo, Piyanart. 'Thailand–China High-speed Rail Talks to Get Cabinet Go-ahead'. 8 September 2010. Available at: http://www.thaivisa.com/forum/topic/396547-thailand-china-high-speed-rail-talks-to-get-cabinet-go-ahead/ (accessed on 17 October 2012).

Starr, Don. 'Chinese Language Education in Europe: The Confucius Institute'. *European Journal of Education* 44, no. 1 (2009).

Stearns, N. Peter. 'The Spread of Chinese Civilization to Japan'. 2000. Available at: http://history-world.org/Chinese%20Civilization%20To%20Japan.htm (accessed on 27 January 2012).

*Study in China*. 'Statistics of International Students in China in 2011'. 29 February 2012. Available at: http://www.csc.edu.cn/laihua/newsdetailen.aspx?cid=122&id=1399 (accessed on 2 February 2014).

———. 'Brazilian Government and Chilean Government Support Students to Study in China'. 13 December 2012. Available at: http://en.csc.edu.cn/laihua/newsdetailen.aspx?cid=68&id=1983 (accessed on 2 February 2014).

Su, Changhe. '*Zhong guo de ruan quan li: yi guo ji zhi du yu zhong guo de guan xi wei li*' (China's Soft Power: An Example in the Relationship Between China and International Institutions). *Guo Ji Guan Cha* (International Observations), 2007.

Su, Xiaohui. '*Cong xin jiu baogao kan mei dui hua renshi bian hua*' (What Changes Does the US See in China). *People's Daily Online*. 10 February 2015. Available at: http://en.people.cn/n/2015/0210/c98649-8848573.html (accessed on 11 February 2015).

Sukma, Rizal. 'Indonesia–China Relations: The Politics of Re-engagement'. *Asian Survey* 49, no. 4 (2009, July/August).

Sukumar, Meghna. 'Blacklivesmatter: India Must Accept Its Racism Problem'. 27 May 2016. Available at: http://www.sify.com/news/blacklivesmatter-india-must-accept-its-racism-problem-news-national-qf1lNbbcdfghf.html (accessed on 29 May 2016).

Suzhou Industrial Park (SIP). 'New Mode of International Cooperation, Opens a New Chapter in Reform and Opening Up'. Available at: http://www.sipac. gov.cn/english/zhuanti/fnotpoc/fnotpoc_nmoic/ (accessed on 19 June 2013).

Tan Chung. 'Historical Chindian Paradigm: Inter-cultural Transfusion and Solidification'. *China Report* 45, no. 3 (2009).

Tang, Alisa and Rahim Faiez. 'TV Stations Defy Afghan Government Ban on Indian Soap Operas'. *USAToday*. 23 April 2008. Available at: http://www. usatoday.com/news/world/2008-04-23-933079557_x.htm (accessed on 29 November 2012).

Tanham, K. George. 'Indian Strategic Thought: An Interpretative Essay'. *RAND*. 1992. Available at: http://www.rand.org/content/dam/rand/pubs/reports/ 2007/R4207.pdf (accessed on 10 May 2016).

Tat, Meng, Chia, Jack. 'Buddhism in Singapore–China Relations: Venerable Hong Choon and His Visits, 1989–90'. Thesis. 2007. Department of History, National University of Singapore (NUS).

Technical Cooperation Division, Ministry of External Affairs, Government of India. Available at: http://itec.mea.gov.in/ (accessed on 14 September 2012).

Teh-Yao, Wu. 'Southeast Asia and China: Asian Neighbours'. NUS Occasional Paper No. 8, NUS, Singapore, 1974 September.

*Thaindian News*. 'Indo-US Ties a Model for Bangladesh and China'. 24 February 2010. Available at: http://www.thaindian.com/newsportal/world-news/indo-us-ties-a-model-for-bangladesh-and-china_100325300.html (accessed on 8 September 2012).

Tharoor, Shashi. *Pax Indica: India and the World of the 21st Century*. New Delhi: Penguin, 2012.

———. 'Indian Strategic Power: 'Soft''. *Global Brief*. 13 May 2009. Available at: http://globalbrief.ca/blog/2009/05/13/soft-is-the-word/ (accessed on 13 September 2012).

Thayer, A. Carlyle. *The Borderlands of Southeast Asia: Geopolitics, Terrorism, and Globalization*. Washington, D.C.: National Defense University Press, 2011.

The African Development Bank Group. 'India's Economic Engagement with Africa'. Africa Economic Brief. Vol. 2, no. 6 (11 May 2011). Available at: http://www.afdb.org/fileadmin/uploads/afdb/Documents/Publications/ India's%20Economic%20Engagement%20with%20Africa.pdf (accessed on 26 September 2012).

*The Day After*. 'Enough Space for India, China: Manmohan to Wen'. 2011. Available at: http://www.dayafterindia.com/detail.php?headline=content &catid=2700 (accessed on 4 October 2012).

*The Diplomat*. 'Narendra Modi's Northeast India Outreach'. 14 December 2014. Available at: http://thediplomat.com/2014/12/narendra-modis-northeast-india-outreach/ (accessed on 6 July 2015).

*The Diplomat.* 'China Set to Expand Influence in Africa on Back of Xi Jinping's Trip'. 31 March 2013. Available at: http://articles.economictimes.indiatimes. com/2013-03-31/news/38163340_1_african-leaders-south-africa-brics (accessed on 10 July 2013).

————. 'Chinese Companies Eyeing Gujarat for Investments'. 16 June 2012. Available at: http://articles.economictimes.indiatimes.com/2012-06-16/ news/32269221_1_chinese-companies-gujarat-excellent-infrastructure-and-connectivity (accessed on 8 February 2014).

*The Economist.* 'Trying to Pull Together: Africans Are Asking Whether China Is Making Their Lunch or Eating It'. 20 April 2011. Available at: http://www. economist.com/node/18586448 (accessed on 3 April 2012).

————. 'The Beijing Consensus Is to Keep Quiet'. 6 May 2010. Available at: http://www.economist.com/node/16059990 (accessed on 20 August 2012).

————. 'Earthquake: India's Response Was like Extending Blank Cheque, Says Nepal'. 28 April 2015. Available at: http://articles.economictimes.india times.com/2015-04-28/news/61616236_1_blank-cheque-relief-work-kathmandu-airport (accessed on 6 July 2015).

*The Global Times Ticker.* 'China and Southeast Asian Nations Expand Study-Abroad Ties'. 22 August 2011. Available at: http://chronicle.com/blogs/ global/china-and-southeast-asian-nations-expand-study-abroad-ties/ 30614 (accessed on 6 June 2012).

*The Guardian.* 'China Daily Launches Europe Issue'. 3 December 2010. Available at: http://www.guardian.co.uk/media/greenslade/2010/dec/03/china-news papers (accessed on 15 May 2012).

*The Hindu Business Line.* 'India, China to Hold Cultural Summit to Boost Ties'. 11 June 2011. Available at: http://www.thehindubusinessline.com/industry-and-economy/article2096102.ece (accessed on 10 October 2012).

*The Hindu.* 'Delhi's Date with Buddhism'. 23 April 2012. Available at: http:// www.thehindu.com/news/cities/Delhi/article3345091.ece (accessed on 20 September 2012).

————. 'BNP Hails LBA Ratification by Parliament'. 8 May 2015. Available at: http://www.thehindu.com/news/international/bangladesh-nationalist-party-hails-lba-ratification-by-indian-parliament/article7184892.ece (accessed on 7 June 2015).

————. 'Eyeing Connectivity to South Asia, China Calls for India's Cooperation'. 17 August 2012. Available at: http://www.thehindu.com/news/international/ article3781166.ece (accessed on 8 October 2012).

*The Indian Express.* 'India Tops in Remittances, Receives $70 Billion: World Bank'. 14 April 2015. Available at: http://www.financialexpress.com/article/ economy/india-tops-in-remittances-receives-us-dollar-70-billion-world-bank/63475/ (accessed on 2 July 2015).

*The Indian Express.* 'N-deal: China Is Supportive, Wen Tells Singh'. 22 November 2007. Available at: http://www.indianexpress.com/news/ndeal-china-is-supportive-wen-jiabao-tells-singh/241912/ (accessed on 4 October 2012).

*The Oakland Post Online.* 'Chinese Navy on Humanitarian Mission to Treat Poor Jamaicans'. 24 November 2011. Available at: http://content.postnews group.com/?p=15081 (accessed on 24 August 2012).

*The Peninsula.* 'Natwar Inaugurates Laos-India IT Centre'. 29 November 2004. Available at: http://archive.thepeninsulaqatar.com/component/content/article/348-indiaarchiverest/47186.html (accessed on 25 September 2012).

*The Sunday Times.* 'China Builds Infrastructure for Mansarovar Pilgrims'. 3 July 2012. Available at: http://articles.timesofindia.indiatimes.com/2012-07-03/china/32522593_1_pilgrims-indian-visitors-s-jaishankar (accessed on 8 October 2012).

———. 'China Sends Humanitarian Aid to Kyrgyz Refugees'. 22 June 2010. Available at: http://articles.timesofindia.indiatimes.com/2010-06-22/china/28296910_1_humanitarian-aid-refugees-coordination-of-humanitarian-affairs (accessed on 12 March 2012).

*The Times of India.* 'China is not a Threat to India, Li Keqiang Says'. 22 May 2013. Available at: http://articles.timesofindia.indiatimes.com/2013-05-22/india/39444361_1_china-and-india-strategic-mutual-trust-china-ties (accessed on 9 July 2013).

———. 'Read Full Text: PM Modi's Speech at Tsinghua University, Beijing'. 15 May 2015. Available at: http://timesofindia.indiatimes.com/india/Read-full-text-PM-Modis-speech-at-Tsinghua-University-Beijing/articleshow/47295807.cms (accessed on 23 May 2016).

———. Full Text: *Joint Statement of India–China Bilateral Talks.* 15 May 2015. Available at: http://timesofindia.indiatimes.com/india/Full-text-Joint-statement-of-India-China-bilateral-talks/articleshow/47293192.cms (accessed on 3 June 2015).

———. 'China Keen on Indian Business, Not Resolving Border Dispute'. 17 October 2013. Available at: http://articles.timesofindia.indiatimes.com/2013-10-17/india/43142871_1_border-dispute-hua-chunying-china-india (accessed on 8 February 2014).

*The Voice of Vietnam.* 'Chinese Youths Join Cultural Exchanges in Vietnam'. 19 September 2010. Available at: http://english.vov.vn/Home/Chinese-youths-join-cultural-exchanges-in-Vietnam/20109/119714.vov (accessed on 20 May 2012).

*The Wall Street Journal.* 'China's Xi Jinping Launches Investment Deal in Pakistan'. 20 April 2015. Available at: http://www.wsj.com/articles/chinas-xi-jinping-set-to-launch-investment-deal-in-pakistan-1429533767 (accessed on 11 August 2015).

*The Washington Times.* Linguistically Speaking—English Becomes India's "Numero Uno" Language'. 23 September 2011. Available at: http://communities.washingtontimes.com/neighborhood/indian-journal-seeking-balance-india/2011/sep/23/linguistically-speaking-english-becomes-indias-num/ (accessed on 8 July 2013).

The White House Office of the Press Secretary Press Release. 'Press Conference with President Obama and President Hu of the People's Republic of China'. 19 January 2011. Available at: http://www.whitehouse.gov/the-press-office/2011/01/19/press-conference-president-obama-and-president-hu-peoples-republic-china (accessed on 23 July 2012).

The World University Rankings. 'Asia University Rankings 2015'. 2015. Available at: https://www.timeshighereducation.co.uk/world-university-rankings/2015/regional-ranking#/ (accessed on 6 June 2015).

Thussu, Daya. *Communicating India's Soft Power.* New York: Palgrave Macmillan, 2013.

Tiwary, Deeptiman. 'Kiren Rijju: Pakistan Obsession Is a North Indian Thing'. 20 January 2015. *The Times of India.* Available at: http://timesofindia.indiatimes.com/india/Kiren-Rijiju-Pakistan-obsession-is-a-north-Indian-thing/articleshow/45947416.cms?utm_source=email (accessed on 20 January 2015).

*Today.* 'Made by China Stamp on S. Asia'. Singapore. 17 February 2010.

———. 'China's Pivot to South America'. 28 May 2015.

Tom, A. Peter. 'India Outdoes US Aid Efforts in Afghanistan'. 9 September 2010. Available at: http://www.globalpost.com/dispatch/afghanistan/100908/india-outdoes-us-aid-efforts-afghanistan (accessed on 24 September 2012).

Tung-Tse, Mao. *Selected Works of Mao Tse-tung.* Vol. 2. London: Lawrence and Wishart, 1954.

United Nations Development Programme (UNDP). 'Enhancing China–ASEAN Economic Integration: Cross Border Economic Cooperation Zones at the China-Vietnam Border (CBEZ)'. Available at: http://www.cn.undp.org/content/china/en/home/operations/projects/poverty_reduction/enhancing-china-asean-economic-integration--cross-border-economi.html (accessed on 10 April 2015).

*USA Today.* 'China: Aid to Burma Should Not Be Politicized.' 5 August 2008. Available at: http://www.usatoday.com/news/world/2008-05-08-china-burma_N.htm (accessed on 7 February 2012).

USC Center on Public Diplomacy. 'Communicating the Idea of India'. 22 September 2011. Available at: http://uscpublicdiplomacy.org/blog/communicating_the_idea_of_india (accessed on 7 July 2015).

Varshney, Ashutosh. 'Modi's Idea of India–1'. 27 January 2016. Available at: http://indianexpress.com/article/opinion/columns/narendra-modi-idea-of-india-republic-day/ (accessed on 27 May 2016).

Venu, M.K. 'Trading a New Route'. 27 May 2012. Available at: http://www.indianexpress.com/news/trading-a-new-route/795973/0 (accessed on 7 November 2012).

Verma. K. Pavan. *Being Indian: The Truth Why the Twenty-First Century Will Be India's*. New Delhi: Viking, 2004.

Vijapurkar, Majesh. 'Tagore's Visva-Bharati Dream Now in Tatters'. 6 September 2012. Available at: http://www.firstpost.com/india/tagores-visva-bharati-dream-now-in-tatters-446453.html (accessed on 13 May 2016).

Vincenti, Daniela. 'EU Lawmakers Reject Granting China the Market Economy Status'. *EurActiv.com*. 13 May 2016. Available at: http://www.euractiv.com/section/trade-society/news/eu-lawmakers-reject-granting-china-the-market-economy-status/ (accessed on 4 June 2016).

Wagle, Achyut. 'Project Hindutva'. 5 January 2016. Available at: http://kathmandupost.ekantipur.com/news/2016-01-05/project-hindutva.html (accessed on 8 June 2016).

Wang Huiyao. 'Attracting Talent Globally for the Future'. *Pakistan Defence*. 14 September 2010. Available at: http://www.defence.pk/forums/chinese-defence/72686-china-national-talent-development-plan-attracting-talent-globally-future.html (accessed on 7 June 2012).

Wang Yi. 'Toward a New Model of Major-country Relations Between China and the United States'. Speech at the Brookings Institution, Washington, D.C. 20 September 2013. Available at: http://www.brookings.edu/~/media/events/2013/9/20-us-china-foreign-minister-wang-yi/wang-yi-english-prepared-remarks.pdf (accessed on 25 June 2015).

Wang, F. 'Preservation, Prosperity and Power'. *Journal of Contemporary China* 14, no. 45 (2005).

Wang, Hui. 'Tripartite Push for Regional Peace'. *China Daily*. 29 April–5 May 2016.

Wang, Peiran. 'Mongolia's Delicate Balancing Act'. *WSI China Security* 5, no. 2 (2009 Spring). Available at: http://www.isn.ethz.ch/Digital-Library/Publications/Detail/?lang=en&id=117005 (accessed on 6 May 2016).

———. 'With Europe Visits, Chinese Leaders Signal Region's Importance'. 25 April 2012. Available at: http://www.wantchinatimes.com/news-subclass-cnt.aspx?id=20120425000040&cid=1501 (accessed on 4 May 2012).

*Wei Xin*. '*Wei shen ma meng gu ren zui tong hen zhong guo*' (Why Mongolians hate China). 18 April 2015. Available at: http://wechatinchina.com/thread-100721-1-1.html (accessed on 5 May 2016).

Wei, He. 'US' 100,000 Strong Initiative Gets Funding Boost'. *China Daily*. 3 July 2012. Available at: http://www.chinadaily.com.cn/cndy/2012-03/07/content_14773680.htm (accessed on 26 July 2012).

Wei, Shan and Weng Cuifen. 'China's New Policy in Xinjiang and Its Challenges'. 2010. Available at: http://www.eai.nus.edu.sg/Vol2No3_ShanWei&WengCuifen.pdf (accessed on 6 September 2012).

Welch, Holmes. *Buddhism under Mao*. Cambridge, MA: Harvard University Press, 1972.

Wen, Jiabao. 'Win-win Cooperation for Common Development'. *Chinese Premier's keynote speech at opening of 1st Ministerial Conference of China-Pacific Island Countries Economic Development and Cooperation Forum*. 5 April 2006. Available at: http://english.gov.cn/2006-04/05/content_245681.htm (accessed on 10 January 2012).

Wendt, Alexander. *Social Theory of International Politics*. Cambridge, MA: Cambridge University Press, 1999.

Wenting, Zhou. 'Accurate Information and Calm Analysis Media's Duty'. *China Daily*. 23 August 2011. Available at: http://www.chinadaily.com.cn/china/beijing_tokyo/2011-08/23/content_13168389.htm (accessed on 22 March 2012).

Weston, Jonathan, Caitlin Campbell and Katherine Koleski. 'China's Foreign Assistance in Review: Implications for the United States'. *US–China Economic and Security Review Commission Staff Research Backgrounder*. 1 September 2011. Available at: http://www.uscc.gov/researchpapers/2011/9_1_%202011_ChinasForeignAssistanceinReview.pdf (accessed on 18 April 2012).

*Wikinews.org*. 'Foreign Policy of Narendra Modi'. Available at: http://en.wikipedia.org/wiki/Foreign_policy_of_Narendra_Modi (accessed on 1 June 2015).

———. 'Humanitarian Response to the 2011 Tohoku Earthquake and Tsunami'. Available at: http://en.wikipedia.org/wiki/Humanitarian_response_to_the_2011_T%C5%8Dhoku_earthquake_and_tsunami (accessed on 29 January 2012).

———. 'Chinatowns in Latin America'. Available at: http://en.wikipedia.org/wiki/Chinatowns_in_Latin_America (accessed on 18 October 2012).

———. 'South Asian University'. Available at: http://en.wikipedia.org/wiki/South_Asian_University (accessed on 24 September 2012).

———. 'ISKCON'. Available at: http://en.wikipedia.org/wiki/International_Society_for_Krishna_Consciousness (accessed on 27 September 2012).

———. 'Ji Xianlin'. Available at: http://en.wikipedia.org/wiki/Ji_Xianlin (accessed on 3 October 2012).

———. 'Agenda-setting Theory'. Available at: http://en.wikipedia.org/wiki/Agenda-setting_theory (accessed on 20 June 2013).

Wirjawan, Gita. 'News Analysis: China: A Catalyst for Infrastructure Development'. *The Jakarta Post*. 5 July 2010. Available at: http://www.thejakartapost.com/news/2010/05/07/news-analysis-china-a-catalyst-infrastructure-development.html (accessed on 31 January 2012).

Wong, Edward. 'China Quietly Extends Footprints into Central Asia'. *New York Times*. 2 January 2011. Available at: http://www.nytimes.com/2011/01/03/world/asia/03china.html?pagewanted=all (accessed on 12 February 2012).

Wong, John and Catherine Siew Keng Chong. 'The Nanning–Singapore Economic Corridor: Its Promises and Problems'. East Asia Institute (EAI) Background Brief No. 587 East Asia Institute, National University of Singapore, 2010.

World Food Programme. 'WFP Lauds Landmark Chinese Aid Shipment for Sri Lankan Tsunami Victims'. 29 June 2005. Available at: https://www.wfp. org/news/news-release/wfp-lauds-landmark-chinese-aid-shipment-sri-lankan-tsunami-victims (accessed on 4 February 2010).

Wu, Jiao and Cui Haipei. 'China, Turkmenistan Sign Key Gas Agreement'. China Daily.com. 24 November 2011. Available at: http://www.chinadaily.com. cn/china/2011-11/24/content_14150679.htm (accessed on 28 May 2012).

Xiang, Yong Shu. 'Xin guo ji zhu yi yu zhong guo ruan shi li wai jiao' (New Country Doctrine Soft Power Foreign Affairs). Guo Ji Guan Cha (International Observe). Vol. 2, 2007.

Xiaokun, Li and Cheng Guangjin. 'China, Israel Boost Cooperation'. 9 May 2013. Available at: http://www.chinadaily.com.cn/cndy/2013-05/09/content_ 16486609.htm (accessed on 5 July 2013).

Xiaokun, Li. 'Neighbours Explore Cooperation'. China Daily. 18–19 August 2012.

———. 'Hu Vows More Aid for Africa'. China Daily. 2 August 2012.

Xiaomin, Zhang and Luo Jianbo. 'China's African Policy and Its Soft Power'. Online Journal of World Affairs. 2009. Available at: http://www.victoria. ac.nz/atp/articles/pdf/JianboXiaomin-2009.pdf (accessed on 13 April 2012).

Xin, Zhou and Kevin Yao. 'China Cuts Growth Target to 8-year Low, to Boost Consumption'. Reuters. 5 March 2012. Available at: http://smallbusiness. yahoo.com/advisor/china-targets-2012-gdp-7-5-percent-premier-000009208.html (accessed on 20 March 2012).

Xinhua News Agency. 'Confucius Institute Builds Bridge Between Bangladesh and China'. 16 December 2009. Available at: http://www.chinese.cn (accessed on 2 January 2009).

Xinhua. 'China Focus: China Continues to Help Quake-stricken Nepal'. 11 May 2015. Available at: http://news.xinhuanet.com/english/2015-05/11/c_134229 786.htm (accessed on 11 August 2015).

———. 'China Focus: China 2015 Defense Budget to Grow 10.1 pct, Lowest in 5 years'. 5 March 2015. Available at: http://news.xinhuanet.com/english/ 2015-03/05/c_134040390.htm (accessed on 19 August 2015).

———. 'Xi: China to Promote Cultural Soft Power'. 1 January 2014. Available at: http://news.xinhuanet.com/english/china/2014-01/01/c_125941955.htm (accessed on 31 March 2015).

———. 'China, India Should Be Partners for Peace, Development: Xi'. 19 September 2014. Available at: http://news.xinhuanet.com/english/china/ 2014-09/19/c_133653930.htm (accessed on 19 June 2015).

*Xinhua.* 'Xinhua Insight: Investigations Reveal Details of Xinjiang Terror Attack'. 6 June 2013. Available at: http://news.xinhuanet.com/english/indepth/ 2013-07/06/c_124966189.htm (accessed on 12 July 2013).

———. 'China's Xi Pledges Peace, Opening-up in First Meeting with FOREIGNERS'. 5 December 2012. Available at: http://news.xinhuanet. com/english/china/2012-12/05/c_132021979.htm (accessed on 4 May 2015).

———. 'China Celebrates 65th Anniversary'. 30 September 2014. Available at: http://news.xinhuanet.com/english/china/2014-09/30/c_133686044.htm (accessed on 4 May 2015).

———. 'Full Text of Resolution on CPC Central Committee Report'. 14 November 2012. Available at: http://news.xinhuanet.com/english/special/ 18cpcnc/2012-11/14/c_131973742.htm (accessed on 25 September 2013).

———. 'The Year of Russian Language Kicks Off in China'. 27 March 2009. Available at: http://news.xinhuanet.com/english/2009-03/27/content_ 11085316.htm (accessed on 21 March 2012).

———. 'Xi Eyes More Enabling Int'l Environment for China's Peaceful Development'. 30 November 2014. Available at: http://news.xinhuanet. com/english/china/2014-11/30/c_133822694_2.htm (accessed on 1 April 2015).

———. China, UAE Issue Joint Statement on Establishing Strategic Partnership'. 17 January 2012. Available at: http://news.xinhuanet.com/english/china/ 2012-01/17/c_122598697.htm (accessed on 14 March 2012).

———. 'China to Deepen Health Cooperation with Mongolia: Minister'. 3 May 2012. Available at: http://news.xinhuanet.com/english/china/2012- 05/03/c_131564765.htm (accessed on 4 June 2012).

———. 'China, Russia Issue Joint Communique on Ties'. 7 December 2012. Available at: http://news.xinhuanet.com/english/china/2012-12/07/c_124 059533.htm (accessed on 29 July 2013).

———. 'China, Russia to Strengthen Cultural and Social Exchanges'. 12 October 2011. Available at: http://news.xinhuanet.com/english2010/china/2011- 10/12/c_131187565.htm (accessed on 21 March 2012).

———. 'Chinese Buddha Sacred Tooth Relic Conveyed to Myanmar for Obeisance'. 6 November 2011. Available at: http://news.xinhuanet.com/ english2010/culture/2011-11/06/c_131231898.htm (accessed on 30 August 2012).

———. 'Cross-strait Cultural Exchange Continues with Chinese Mainland Statue Donated to Taiwan'. 14 December 2011. Available at: http://news. xinhuanet.com/english/china/2011-12/14/c_131306827.htm (accessed on 31 January 2012).

———. 'Full Text: China's Foreign Aid'. 21 April 2011. Available at: http://news. xinhuanet.com/english2010/china/2011-04/21/c_13839683_10.htm (accessed on 18 April 2012).

*Xinhua.* 'Yang Jiechi: Public Diplomacy is Now Born Upon Demand and Timely and Much Can Be Done'. 7 March 2010. Available at: http://news.xinhuanet.com/politics/2010-03/07/content_13115553.htm (accessed on 2 August 2012).

———. 'Chinese-learning Craze Sweeps Russia'. 23 March 2010. Available at: http://news.xinhuanet.com/english2010/indepth/2010-03/23/c_13221481.htm (accessed on 24 March 2012).

———. 'Full Text: China–Africa Economic and Trade Cooperation. 23 December 2010. Available at: http://news.xinhuanet.com/english2010/china/2010-12/23/c_13661470_7.htm (accessed on 18 April 2012).

———. 'Full Text: China's Policy Paper on Latin America and the Caribbean'. 5 November 2008. Available at: http://news.xinhuanet.com/english/2008-11/05/content_10308117.htm (accessed on 21 August 2012).

Xuecun, Murong. 'Corrupting the Chinese Language'. *International New York Times.* 27 May 2015. Available at: http://www.nytimes.com/2015/05/27/opinion/murong-xuecun-corrupting-the-chinese-language.html?_r=0 (accessed on 27 May 2015).

XueJin, Zuo, Pan Guang, Wang DeHua and Zhu Bian. *Long Xiang Gong Wu: dui Zhong Guo he Yindu liang ge fu xing da guo de bi jiao yan ju* (Dragon Dance with Elephant: Research to Compare China and India Revival of Ties). Shanghai: Shanghai Social Science Department Publication, 2006.

*Yahoo!news.* 'Cooperation Best Way Forward for Beijing, Delhi: Chinese Daily'. 27 March 2015. Available at: https://sg.news.yahoo.com/cooperation-best-way-forward-beijing-delhi-chinese-daily-131216565.html (accessed on 16 May 2016).

Yang, Jian. *The Pacific Islands in China's Grand Strategy: Small States, Big Games.* New York: Palgrave Macmillan, 2011.

Yardley, Jim. 'Diplomacy in India Rides on Coattails of Business'. *International Herald Tribune.* 2 April 2012. Available at: https://www.questia.com/newspaper/1P2-36283662/diplomacy-in-india-rides-on-coattails-of-business (accessed on 2 April 2012).

Ying He, Ji, Zhou, Mei Xiang. '*Qian Xi Guo Jia "Ruan quan li" li lun*' ('Primary Analysis of a Country's "Soft Power" Theory'). 1994–2006 China Academic Journal Electronic Publishing House, 2005.

Yongkun, Luo. 'A History of Socio-cultural Cooperation with Southeast Asia'. *China.org.cn.* 4 July 2011. Available at: http://www.china.org.cn/world/experience_china_in_indonesia/2011-07/04/content_22918250.htm (accessed on 29 May 2012).

Yuan, Jing-dong. 'The Dragon and the Elephant: Chinese–Indian Relations in the 21st Century'. In *China' s International Relations in Asia*, edited by Li Mingjiang. Vol. IV. New York: Routledge, 2010.

Yunling, Zhang and Shiping Tang. 'China's Regional Strategy'. In *Power Shift: China and Asia's New Dynamics*, edited by David Shambaugh. Berkeley, CA: University of California Press, 2005.

*Yunnan Daily Press Group*. *'Yun nan da xue ling xian chu ban zhong guo shou bu Yindu "lan pi shu"'* (Yunnan University In Charge of Publishing the First India "Blue Book" in China). 21 May 2013. Available at: http://yndaily.yunnan.cn/html/2013-05/21/content_706442.htm?div=-1 (accessed on 15 July 2013).

Zhang, Feng. 'The Tianxia System: World Order in a Chinese Utopia'. China Heritage Quarterly. 2010 March. Available at: http://www.chinaheritage quarterly.org/tien-hsia.php?searchterm=021_utopia.inc&issue=021 (accessed on 18 May 2016).

Zhang, Honzhou. 'China Marching West for Food'. *RSIS Commentary*. 4 February 2014.

Zhang, Jian. 'China's New Foreign Policy under Xi Jinping: Towards "Peaceful Rise 2.0"?' *Global Change, Peace & Security* 27, no. 1 (2015, 28 January). Available at: http://www.tandfonline.com/doi/abs/10.1080/14781158.2015.993958#.Vs5_IU3ovIU (accessed on 25 February 2016).

Zhang, Xiaodong. 'China's Interests in Middle East: Present and Future'. *Middle East Policy* VI, no. 3 (February 1999): 150–59.

Zhang, Yongjin. 'The "English School" in China: A Travelogue of Ideas and Their Diffusion'. *European Journal of International Relations* 9, no. 1 (2003): 87–114.

Zhao, Tingyang. *Tian xia Ti xi: Shi jie Zhi du Zhe xue Dao lun* (Tian Xia System: An Introduction to a Philosophy About World Order). Nanjing: Jiang su Jiao yu Chu ban she, 2005.

Zheng, Wang. 'Does Beijing Have a Foreign Policy?' *International Herald Tribune*. 20 March 2013. Available at: http://www.nytimes.com/2013/03/19/opinion/does-china-have-a-foreign-policy.html (accessed on 20 March 2013).

Zhiqun, Zhu. *China's New Diplomacy: Rationale, Strategies and Significance*. England: Ashgate Publishing Limited, 2010.

*Zhong guo gong gong wai jiao yan jue bao gao* (China's Public Foreign Relations Research Report, China), 2012.

Zhongqi, Pan and Huang Renwei. 'Zhongguo de diyuan wenhua zhanlue' (China's Geo-Cultural Strategy). *Xiandai Guoji Guanxi*, I, 2008.

Zhou, Jiayi. 'Chinese Agrarian Capitalism in the Russian Far East'. Chiang Mai University. 2015 May. Available at: http://www.iss.nl/fileadmin/ASSETS/iss/Research_and_projects/Research_networks/LDPI/CMCP_34-_Zhou.pdf (accessed on 6 May 2016).

Zongze, Ruan, 'Winning the Next Decade: China's Multi-pivot Diplomacy'. 4 September 2013. Available at: http://www.ciis.org.cn/english/2013-09/04/content_6272955.htm (accessed on 5 February 2014).

Zweig, David, Chung Sui Fung, Donglin Han. 'Redefining the Brain Drain: China's "Diaspora Option"'. 2004 January. Available at: http://www.princeton.edu/cwp/publications/sts13_1-01-David-et-al.pdf (accessed on 24 July 2012).

Zweig, David. 'Learning to Compete: China's Efforts to Encourage a "Reverse Brain Drain"'. 2006. Available at: http://www.cctr.ust.hk/materials/working_papers/LearningtoCompete.pdf (accessed on 21 September 2015).

# Index

# About the Author

**Parama Sinha Palit** is a scholar of international relations, specializing in the study of soft power, cultural and public diplomacy and Chinese and Indian foreign policies. Currently based in Singapore, she is a research associate with the China in Comparative Perspective Network (CCPN) Global—a UK-based global academic society. Parama had earlier worked for the Institute for Defence Studies and Analyses (IDSA) and the United Services Institution (USI), India. She finished her PhD from the Jawaharlal Nehru University (JNU), India, and is currently engaged in research projects pertaining to national image-building and strategic aspects of national soft power strategies. Her works have been published in several academic journals and leading newspapers; furthermore, she has delivered lectures at various universities in the UK, Australia, China, New Zealand and India.